sleeping where I fall

for Kim —

from

Peter Coyote

5/13

PETER COYOTE

sleeping

where I

fall

a chronicle

COUNTERPOINT

BERKELEY

Copyright © 1998 by Peter Coyote

First paperback edition 1999

The author wishes to thank the editors and publishers of *Pequod*, *Steelhead*, and *Zyzzyva*, where portions of this text have appeared in slightly different form.

The author gratefully acknowledges permission to reprint excerpted materials: Pages 17, 36, 59: Excerpt from *The San Francisco Mime Troupe: The First Ten Years* by R. G. Davis (Palo Alto, Calif.: Ramparts Press), copyright © 1975 by R. G. Davis, reprinted courtesy of Ronald G. Davis. Page 59: Excerpt from song lyric "Tangled Up in Blue" reprinted courtesy of Bob Dylan. Page 311: Excerpt from "Next, Please" in *The Less Deceived* by Philip Larkin copyright © 1955. Permission pending from the Marvell Press. Pages 327, 347: Excerpt from *Sonnets to Orpheus* by Rainer Maria Rilke. Copyright 1942 by W. W. Norton & Company, Inc., renewed © 1970 by M. D. Herter Norton. Reprinted by permission of W. W. Norton & Company, Inc.

The author notes: some names of individuals in the text have been changed to protect the guilty.

Library of Congress Cataloging-in-Publication Data
Coyote, Peter.
 Sleeping where I fall : a chronicle / Peter Coyote.
 Includes index.
  1. Coyote, Peter. 2. Hippies—California—San Francisco—Biography.
 3. Subculture—California—San Francisco—History—20th century. 4. San Francisco (Calif.)—Social life and customs. 5. San Francisco (Calif.)—Biography. 6. Communal living—California—San Francisco—History—20th century. I. Title.
F869.S353C69 1998
979.4'61053'092—dc21
[B]   97-47740

ISBN: 978-1-58243-496-4

Book and jacket design by David Bullen
Composition by Wilsted & Taylor Publishing Services
Printed in the United States of America

COUNTERPOINT
1919 Fifth Street
Berkeley, CA 94710

www.counterpointpress.com

Distributed by Publishers Group West

10 9 8 7 6 5 4

To Ruth,

To Morris,

To Ariel and Nick

Incomprehensible gaiety and dread
Attended what we did. Behind, before
Lay all the lovely postures of the dead;
The spirit and the flesh cried out for more.
We . . . together on a darkening day
Took Arms against our own obscurity.

THEODORE ROETHKE, *"Four for Sir John Davies"*

contents

acknowledgments

Several people bear more responsibility for the existence of this book than they may know. Howard Junker, intrepid editor of *Zyzzyva* magazine, solicited a piece for his journal that was published in 1989. Its title serves as the title of this book. Jack Shoemaker, then editor-in-chief of North Point Press, read that piece and urged me to expand it. Following his suggestion, I began writing. When a piece called "Carla's Story," also published in *Zyzzyva* (and incorporated in the present text), won the 1993–94 Pushcart Prize for nonfiction, it offered me sufficient encouragement to complete what had by then become a daunting task.

My literary agents, Joe Spieler and Lisa Ross, have guided my efforts with great patience and delicacy, and Lisa in particular did yeowoman's work in helping me edit the first half of the text. While they may have wished for a simpler book and one easier to sell, they understood and supported my intentions from the beginning.

My old comrade, novelist Terry Bisson, an award-winning and elegant writer, went through the text four times and suggested cuts, shifts of material, and condensing that have given the book its present shape. Not only have Terry and I been best friends for thirty-eight years, but as a fellow communard who adheres to his political principles with courage and tenacity, he has understood as perhaps no one else the essential political intentions of the manuscript. Everyone should have a friend like Terry.

The staff at Counterpoint was enthusiastic and helpful beyond all my expectations. Trish Hoard, Becky Clark, and Jessica Francis Kane were acute, dedicated, and charming in equal measures. Managing editor Carole McCurdy, despite having other authors under her charge, made me feel that there was limitless time for my queries and concerns, even as she ensured, with graceful skill, that I and the project remain on point.

Line editor Nancy Palmer Jones is the most fastidious reader I have ever encountered; her suggestions and questions never failed to make my intended meaning clearer, more graceful, and succinct. She is an author's treasure.

Thanks to Jack Shoemaker, now editor-in-chief of Counterpoint, for his unwavering and selfless support of this project and for assembling such an impeccable team to assist its birth.

Thanks to Stefanie Pleet, my adored life partner and spiritual plumb line, whose meticulous sense of language and clarity of thought have rescued me in these pages and beyond on numerous occasions.

Special thanks to Gary Snyder for taking the time from his own work and daunting schedule to read a seven-hundred-page rough draft and offer clarifying insights and much-needed encouragement. It is he, more than anyone else, who inspired me to document this West Coast cultural history and relate my experiences in the sixties to my forebears of the Beat Generation. Gary has been a constant reference point in my creative and spiritual growth for more than thirty years, and a fine and fast friend.

I hope the reader will find these pages worth this bounty of attention from such sterling people.

preface

During the period covered by this book, I was a member of an anarchic West Coast community that had taken as its collective task the rethinking and re-creation of our national culture. Such intentions were not unique; my generation was struggling openly with problems of racism, grossly inequitable distribution of goods and services, dishonorable foreign policies, and the war in Vietnam. Many people, dissatisfied to the point of despair with the available options of being either a "consumer" or an "employee," were searching for new and more liberating social structures. My peers and I were calling in the nation's markers on promises of social justice, and change was in the air.

These stories focus on a West Coast subset of this critical generation—a group whose original nexus was the San Francisco Mime Troupe, a radical street-theater company, from which several members spun off and evolved into the Diggers. The Diggers, in turn, became the larger Free Family.

This book attempts to describe what the pursuit of absolute freedom felt like, what it taught me, and what it cost. It is neither an apologia for nor a romance of the sixties. Coming to understand the necessity and value of limits should not be construed as either a defense of the status quo or as the contrite repentance of someone who has flapped his wings a few times and decided that flight was impossible.

Every culture has its priests and devils, its intoxications and follies, and the counterculture we created was neither more nor less ethical, diverse, or contradictory than the majority culture. You can't grow tomatoes without shit, they say, and while we may have had much of the latter, we also had plentiful tomatoes. The ideas and moral positions that emerged during this period—the civil rights movement, the peace movement, the ecology movement, feminism, holistic medicine, organic farming, numerous alternative physical and spiritual therapies and disciplines, and perhaps most important, bioregional or watershed political organization—were abetted by agents like the people remembered here: flawed and imperfect people certainly, but genuinely dedicated to creating more enlightened options for themselves and others.

One side of the story should not be sacrificed to the other. We may not approve of the fact that Sigmund Freud was shooting cocaine and writing randy letters during his investigations of the psyche or that the Reverend Martin Luther King Jr. may have enjoyed sex outside of marriage, but these very combinations and conjunctions of aspiration and frailty reveal the complex humanity of such stellar people and allow us to believe that we too, flaws and all, can mature and contribute something of worth.

I apologize to the numerous friends who should have been included or more fully represented in these pages. Such failures are due solely to the thrust of the narrative and the vagaries of memory, which could not always retrieve the appropriate story that included a valued friend. To those who may feel that I have misrepresented them, I can only say that this is how I perceived things: This is my own truth.

Peter Coyote
Mill Valley
March 1997

sleeping

where I

fall

a chronicle

you have to
start somewhere

The *thwack-thwack-thwack* of the choppers hovering over the aerial balloons, angling for clear shots, made it hard to hear the guitars. The pool had been covered with a temporary black and white parquet floor, and rows of white cane chairs were arranged to create an aisle leading to the bridal bower. Resting on alternate chairs, fans of white feathers were available to whisk the grimy Los Angeles heat away from some of the most famous faces in the world. Liveried waiters and waitresses, most of them beautiful enough to be prom kings and queens in their hometowns, served the silver trays of chicken satay, miniature egg rolls, pancetta pizzas, and minced vegetables to the crowd of men and women who, with a simple nod or favor, might change their fortunes forever. Security men with discreet gold buttons in their lapels screened arrivals in a small black tent that featured a prominent sign reading, "NO CAMERAS, NO BULLSHIT."

A suited security guard handed me a white book of advertising photos of -myself taken in Paris for fashion designer and good friend Nino Cerruti, whose clothes I represented for a year. The guard asked me to autograph it as a wedding present for the bride. I was the date of Ellen Sebastian, a sleepy-eyed, dangerously witty director and writer who was an old friend of the bride's and had written many of her performance works. We were issued purple lapel pins giving us highest security clearance and told that the bride was expecting us in her bedroom.

Whoopi Goldberg, at one point or another the highest-paid woman in Hollywood, was marrying Lyle Trachtenberg, a union organizer. The year was 1994. The guests included her old friends from the Blake Street Hawkeyes, a theater company in Berkeley where we met in the seventies, and new friends from the stratosphere of the entertainment world, among them Steven Spielberg, Robin Williams, and Quincy Jones. Ellen and I were ranked somewhere between the sea level of her early days and the rarefied peaks of the present. Where we lived, the air was still breathable and people still had dirt clinging to their shoes.

After visiting with Whoopi as she was being readied to appear, I wandered through the crowd of guests, making small talk, and had a long chat with Steven Spielberg, whom I had not spoken to since he had hired me to perform the role of the compassionate scientist in *E. T.* He had a bit more gray in his beard, as did I, but remained the same generous, present soul who had allowed me, as a neophyte, to criticize and rewrite a central scene in the film and who then, after the film's unprecedented success, sent a "thank-you" check amounting to nearly 50 percent of my original salary.

From the patio where we noshed and talked, I had a superb overview of the party. Scattered around the yard were numerous people from my own past, which had intersected Whoopi's from an unusual angle. David Crosby was standing in front of the band, greeting old friends on their way to the bar as if it were a receiving line. The last time I had seen him was in 1967 at the Grateful Dead's ranch, when I skinned a squirrel he'd just shot and didn't know how to prepare.

Joan Shirle from the Del Arte School of Physical Theater in Blue Lake was there, representing my days with the San Francisco Mime Troupe. Dancers and choreographers John LeFan and Freddie Lum had run Theater Artaud in San Francisco while I was chairman of the California State Arts Council during Jerry Brown's tenure as governor. They now lived in the small logging town of Willits, once a regular rest stop during the many long road trips I made to North Coast communes and friends during the sixties.

LeFan and Lum danced through the crowd with their old pal Bob Ernst, who had been with Whoopi and my date Ellen Sebastian in the Blake Street Hawkeyes when the arts council was giving them their first grants. If this was Whoopi's life, it was also mine.

I knew most of the actors there, though I did manage to confuse Harry Hamlin with Peter Gallagher. Harry's riposte when I apologized with a lame "Of course, what was I thinking" was a quick-witted "You must have been thinking of yourself." The rest—the family, agents, and producers—may have known something about me from the films I'd made; Roman Polanski's *Bitter Moon* and Pedro Almodóvar's *Kika* had played simultaneously that year and garnered me some press. No one there, however—not my old theater comrades, nor my compatriots from the Left, nor the sleek and sexy men and women who were hunting power with such perseverance and polished charm—had the slightest idea of the circuitous route I had taken to join them that day.

People in Hollywood knew I had "done the sixties," but beyond that I was a cipher, living "up north" in Marin County and spending much of my professional career in Europe. I was distanced from them—not through my own judgment, for I respect and value their extraordinary talent and skill—but by indelible experiences and intentions so removed from their reality that even I could barely understand how I had arrived there.

I came to be a guest at this wedding by way of my own meandering search for understanding and wisdom. This book is an attempt to understand how far apart the borders of my life stand to date, and to make comprehensible, as best I can, what rests between them.

1

themes and anticipations

I feel like a word in the breath of a voice.
JOHN BERGER

While still an undergraduate at Grinnell College, I had fallen in love with Jessie Benton, a captivating woman I met one summer on Martha's Vineyard. In 1964, after graduating, I moved to San Francisco to pursue a master's degree in creative writing at San Francisco State College. Jessie was going to move out and join me, bringing her young son Anthony. My life as an adult seemed about to begin.

Jessie was raised in Kansas City, Missouri. Her father, the painter Thomas Hart Benton, was a local hero, a crony of Truman and his smoke-tanned pols. Benton's fluid and colorful murals feature working people in their daily lives. He believed in the importance of detail. A few years before his death, when he was about eighty, I visited him in Kansas City while he was working on an epic canvas of the Teton Mountains. The floor surrounding his easel was littered with notebooks filled with botanically accurate sketches of shrubs and wildflowers collected during an expedition west the previous summer. He was also a flinty character who once removed one of his paintings from a museum and placed it in a bar, claiming that a better class of people would see it there.

Jessie was heir to this cranky sensibility. She was a natural aristocrat, haughty and achingly beautiful, blessed by her Italian mother with dark, tangled hair and a Caravaggio mouth. Her unerring instinct for the first-rate and the precision of her dismissive ridicule invigorated any room she entered, charging the atmosphere and alerting people to impending adventure or disgrace. Her behavior was restless and bold, and her natural incandescence made others pale by comparison. Her gifts were so abundant that her peers (the best and the brightest of Radcliffe and Harvard) seemed to accept as just her uncontested status as reigning queen.

She was pursued by men, many of them rich and powerful, but she dismissed them all with a laugh and, for incomprehensible reasons, chose me, a larval, overeager stripling, as her consort.

Perhaps she fell in love with a passionate letter I wrote her once or the fact that I made a bone-chilling midwinter drive from Iowa to Kansas City just to say hello. It couldn't have been much else. I was tall and stringy, with a wispy mustache barely past requiring judicious touches of eyebrow pencil to be visible. I affected a pipe and was as obstinately opinionated as I am today, but less graceful at insinuating my perspectives into conversation.

I arrived in San Francisco a month before school to make things ready for the arrival of Jessie and Anthony, and rented a small, lusterless apartment on Clayton Street, half a block north of Haight and a few blocks west of Ashbury. The apartment had the charm of a mausoleum, but I was blinded to that by the glamour of being on my own in San Francisco, setting up my first household with a woman and child, and preparing to be a writer. The apartment's only problem, I felt, was that it was not romantically shabby enough. It was, however, practical and adequate, if aesthetically null, a short walk to shops and Laundromat, which I thought would make life easy for Jessie. (Of course it never occurred to me I might do my own laundry; I had a Jewish mother!)

We only know what we know when we know it. The environs that shimmered with possibility for me became a crypt for Jessie. I can now remember her sitting forlornly in that very same Laundromat, among the chewed and coverless women's magazines, wrapping herself in memories as a shield—or perhaps as a shroud—for our relationship. When she gazed absently out the windows, was she comparing the pocky, littered street to the piazzas of Florence, where she'd once lived?

At the time I was completely unaware that she was unhappy and starving for grace. I was writing poems in the mornings and rehearsing afternoons and evenings at the Actors' Workshop, where, to my great delight, I had been cast in the lead of their next play. (The founders of the workshop, Herb Blau and Jules Irving, had just moved—with the best actors—to New York to create Lincoln Center, leaving behind the name, the board, a disappointed audience, and a few loyalists eager to recapture the company's earlier glory. These facts might explain the ease of my admission to this once-august ensemble.) I was happy to be out of undergraduate school, removed from my personal history in the East, and beginning what I expected to be the life of an artist. I imagined myself strolling the crooked backstreets of Paris with Hemingway and Henry Miller; I daydreamed casual conversations with Sartre and Neruda. I was certain that poems were germinating in my synapses and that the patterns of pigeons roosting on a wire could be transcribed as musical masterpieces. I enthused about everything that came into my head, unaware of the assault these juvenile raptures made on Jessie. She tried hard, assembling sumptuous Italian meals, organizing soirees of Kansas City pals, and trying to become interested in our neighbors, a sweet, beaten couple with a chronically unhappy child. For a woman accustomed to being the oracle for the best of the East, her demotion to coffee-klatcher with the depressed in the West must have felt like a terminal downward spiral.

Jessie changed what could be changed and moved us to the third floor of an elegant Victorian house owned by an elderly Italian woman named Mrs. Beltramo that dominated the intersection of Fell Street and Steiner, a block above Fillmore, the main artery of San Francisco's black ghetto. Yet as our living standards rose, other parts of my life took a diametrically different course. My work toward a master's degree in poetry ended. I was spending mind-numbing hours in class deciphering the lectures of Robert Duncan, a poet I had admired as an undergraduate who subsequently became a friend. He bobbed and dashed about the classroom energetically. His magnificent leonine head, topped by an unruly gray mane, featured pronounced wall-eyes brimming with electricity and humor and animating his flat Slavic face. Those eyes were unnerving; since you could not be sure exactly where he was looking, you never knew whether or not one of his impenetrable questions had just been directed at you. Duncan communicated in waves of association, metaphor, and mythic references in several languages. Students on either side of me nodded sage assent, apparently understanding everything he said, while I remained stupefied and progressively disconsolate at my intellectual failings. (Twenty-five years later I told this story to poet Michael McClure, a good friend of mine and Duncan's. Michael smiled wryly and of the nodding students said, "They lied.") I reluctantly decided that my future as a poet was limited. At least I had the theater—or so I thought.

My initial triumph over being cast in the lead of the workshop's first post-Blau/Irving production was dashed by the arrival of the company's new artistic director, John Hancock, an endomorphic Harvard grad with slouching shoulders and ill-fitting clothes. Hancock watched one rehearsal and unceremoniously canceled the production, while I was simultaneously demoted to the status of an apprentice and assistant to an assistant director. I had no idea what acting was about; my experience in college, though serving me well in the rudiments of analyzing a scene into "beats" (emotional moments), had not prepared me at all for the subtle reemphasis of aspects of personality needed to create *character*—the basic building block of drama. I was adrift.

Serving as assistant to a man barely older than myself was humbling when only days earlier I had been a rising star. But there were recompenses for my disgrace. As in the days of Samuel Johnson, "the silk stocking and white bosoms of . . . actresses excite . . . amorous propensities," and occasional love affairs and furtive "green room" couplings during performances softened the wounds to my ego.

In retrospect I can see that there was more to these sexual diversions than Johnson's business-as-usual in the life of actors. Unfaithfulness to Jessie never appeared on my moral radar screen as an issue, nor would sexual fidelity to anyone become either a consideration or a remote possibility for many years. My eagerness for adventure and sensation, my desire to live as I imagined artists and creative people lived, disguised to myself an unsteadiness and an indulgent streak in my character that would not become apparent to me until they had wreaked much more havoc in my personal relationships.

Near the end of 1965, the company was preparing the world premiere of Bertolt Brecht's *Edward the Second*—the story of a mad, murderous, homosexual king who refused to forswear his lover and was dethroned by the populace and imprisoned in the sewers. The lead was played by an obsessively heterosexual actor named Barton Heyman, one of the new players imported by Hancock. I wouldn't go so far as to say that Barton was crazy, but he was definitely not wrapped too tightly. Perhaps one small anecdote will defend this assertion.

In the second act of *Edward the Second*, the king escapes from the sewer and gives a moving soliloquy. Barton decided to heighten his performances by taking LSD during the intermission so that when he emerged from below the street, in rags and smeared with offal, he *was*, in fact, like the king, quite mad. His dedication to Method acting disadvantaged the other actors who, perhaps lacking Barton's dedication or inventiveness, relied for their dialogue on the *script*. No one knew what Barton would say, when he would say it, or at what point he might stop. When he *did* stop finally, it was incumbent on his fellow players to invent logical segues from Barton's last utterance back to the main body of the play. Cast members were not judgmental about Barton's use of drugs. Most people I knew smoked marijuana occasionally, and by 1964 it was ubiquitous. LSD was becoming more prevalent, although I had yet to take my own first trip. What really bothered me about Barton's drug use onstage was how it made him appear brilliant at my expense.

The workshop constructed a revolving stage for the Brecht production, to spin battle scenes offstage and return court scenes onstage. It was a balky, cumbersome behemoth that created innumerable delays in rehearsals, and during one such delay I ambled down the hill from the Marines Memorial Theater to the company's second stage, the Encore Theater, rented to a funky little acting ensemble called the San Francisco Mime Troupe. I was intrigued by the manner in which they had transfigured our tiny lobby, filling it with photos of the company laughing, cavorting, and performing, interspersed with blowups of reviews and news stories chronicling their arrest for performing in the parks without a permit. They had transformed the space from a bleak transition between the street and the theater into an engaging promise of delights to come. Their colorful commedia dell'arte masks and costumes were bold and provocative, their display radiated irreverence, energy, and fun—and two of the women in the photos were extraordinarily attractive. My curiosity was piqued, and once again, a physical attraction to women was unconsciously organizing a major decision in my life. I never once considered that this might be a problem.

I convinced the authorities at the workshop that a comparable photo exhibit would enhance our opening night. They agreed to reimburse my out-of-pocket expenses, and I labored mightily to shoot, develop, print, and mount almost eighty images capturing the labor, frustration, humor, and dedication required to create a major theatrical production. On opening day I hung my enlargements in the barren foyer of the theater, proud of the change they wrought in the sterile environment. It now seemed ready for the event.

The performance was well received, and the postshow gala buzzed with enthusiasm. Canapés disappeared, glasses were filled and emptied with gusto, the roar of conversation swelled the room, gestures were large and emphatic. The reception suggested that the company had recaptured its earlier glory.

The next day passed and the next, and finally several weeks, without a thank-you or any mention of my efforts at all. I had felt stifled and underappreciated since my demotion to apprentice and had hit upon this photo display as an opportunity to express my creativity and distinguish myself in the company again. *Still* no one had noticed. I concluded that the Actors' Workshop and I were not a good match and that since the Mime Troupe had been the inspiration for my photos, perhaps they might be a source for an idea about what to do next. That day I went to see them perform for the very first time.

The Panhandle of Golden Gate Park is a Popsicle stick of green attached to the eastern edge of the park's rectangular main body. It is bordered by two broad, busy, one-way streets that are flanked by faded Victorian houses. I arrived in the Panhandle early, drawn by a canvas banner announcing the coming performance. I watched a group remove and assemble a prefabricated stage from the back of a flatbed truck. Stakes were pounded in to secure the guy wires that anchored the frame of a proscenium; then the stage, constructed of large rectangles on a lattice of two-by-fours, was placed on top of overturned wine-barrel halves. An abstractly painted canvas curtain with a slit in the center formed the back wall.

While construction proceeded, actors dragged costumes and musical instruments from battered trunks. Some changed clothes and applied makeup; others sang, played the recorder or tambourine, joked, and did gymnastics to attract a sizable crowd. Finally, the company warmed up together (unheard of at the workshop) by singing and dancing, generating a palpable energy that flowed among the players and over the stage. During this warm-up, which was a calculated part of the performance, the company members exuded the assurance and bawdy humor of a beggar's opera.

Commedia dell'arte was the sixteenth-century Italian form of street theater—living headlines, Renaissance rap. Masked stock characters such as Pantalone, Arlecchino, and Dottore were recognizable types distinguished by their exaggerated personalities: crankiness, ebullient foolishness, and pomposity. These archetypes had been lovingly researched and resurrected by the troupe to serve radical agit-prop theater. The company spoofed hypocrisy, misuse of power, and official venality with barbed wit, sexual innuendo, and gusto. They were enthralling. The men were physically tuned and athletic, dressed in tattered cloaks and tights. The women's shoulderless bodices exposed tantalizing cleavage they used playfully to befuddle and seduce the male characters, to whom they were clearly superior. Characterizations were as transparent as Punch and Judy, and just as outrageous and wickedly funny. Performances appeared to arise in the moment: if a car horn honked or a voice cried out in the street, it was acknowledged onstage and immediately worked into the show.

At the end of an hour, the troupe leaped off the stage to wild applause and shamelessly exhorted the audience for money. They made ludicrous promises, obscene proposals, scathing observations, and were as entertaining offstage as on, urging the grateful crowd to give more. They became my heroes on the spot, the closest thing to the primal energy and intellectual acuity I had always imagined theater might possess. They articulated issues that I confronted in my own life, and they expressed them in a direct and passionate manner. Ideas and political positions were analyzed and expounded with partisan fervor, great humor, and few subtleties.

As Sandy Archer and Kay Hayward took their deep, sweeping bows, I decided then and there that anything that simultaneously allowed for this kind of free expression and the company of such women was irresistible. I was psychically shanghaied.

Within a few days I had arranged to meet R. G. Davis, founder and organizing genius of the troupe. I dressed in my best "actor's" clothes, a dandyish three-piece houndstooth suit custom-made on the cheap by a drunken Ivy League con man tailor who shipped his measurements off to Hong Kong for assembly. I polished my cumbersome English shoes and pointed them toward the troupe's address on Howard Street, in the city's grimy industrial district.

The company was housed in a raisin-colored two-story brick building. Each end of the large space had been walled off to make an office and a costume and prop room. The rest had been left open for rehearsals. Light entered slantwise through a wall of sooty windows, illuminating the unpainted girders, the tatty cinderblocks, and the well-worn dance floor. Women flowed to and fro in faded sweats and leotards. Men carrying gigantic papier-mâché animal heads referred me to the office door.

I entered a gloomy room with a pitted floor and three stained wooden desks. The windows afforded a view of a tangle of trolley and phone wires. R. G. (Ronnie) Davis rose to meet me. He was a compact, precise man bristling with energy and intelligence. His hair was close-cropped and combed forward like Napoleon's, and he was dressed in some variant of a Mao suit in blue denim. He had a large nose and a wacky, erratic way of moving, as if his body were commenting on his speech like an independent critic. His no-nonsense, total dedication might have been oppressive if it had not been frequently punctured by a manic giggle whenever he found something amusing. What made the greatest impression on me, however, was Sandy Archer, the beauty I'd seen performing in the park. She sat at her desk typing, her large, expressive eyes fixed levelly on her work, lips relaxed and perfectly shaped. High cheekbones stretched the skin on her face so that it was tight as a drum. I had seen that face onstage, radiating light, switching instantly from pure buffoonery to intelligent, sexual power. Young Anne Bancroft was already a movie star, but here was the prototype from which she had been struck, laboring in obscurity, shimmering a few feet away from me. The dedication of such beauty and talent to this impoverished company only increased my interest and curiosity.

Ronnie greeted me cordially, and somehow we began a discussion of Marshall McLuhan, whose writings on media were beginning to attract attention. This was a lucky break for me. I had a mentor at that time, an advertising guru named Howard Gossage whose wife, Sally Kemp, was an actress in the Actor's Workshop. Howard's insight that people would actually read advertising copy if it contained real information had made him wealthy. He had often talked to me about Marshall McLuhan, had introduced him to U.S. audiences, and had even arranged for me to escort one of McLuhan's daughters on several dates.

Fueled by the desire to impress Sandy Archer, I launched into a blitzkrieg of information and opinion—I was swinging. Ronnie poked and probed at my monologue with his combative intellect, clearly delighted to be tossing around ideas with someone as ardent as he was.

I have no idea how long we debated, over the *click-click* of Sandy's typing, but suddenly Ronnie wheeled away and asked her, "Well, Sandy, whaddya think of this guy?"

Sandy never blinked. *Click-click,* she continued while I waited for her verdict.

"Mmmmm," she said finally, without lifting her eyes from the page. "He talks a lot."

Ronnie broke the awkward silence that followed by ushering me out to meet the rest of the troupe, and I followed, suddenly acutely aware of just how large and noisy my shoes were.

First he introduced me to John Robb, one of the group's stars, who was dressed in Pantalone's tattered long red underwear. John was my height, rail-thin, with hickory-tough, Marlboro-man good looks. He took a Pall Mall from behind one ear, broke it in half contemplatively, returned half to his ear, and lit the other as he scoped me up and down. He exhaled luxuriously, then turned to Ronnie: "Pretty fancy for the troupe, isn't he?"

Ronnie mumbled something and asked John to show me around. I stumbled along behind him, now feeling ludicrous and clammy in my thick suit and graceless shoes.

This was not the Royal Shakespeare Company, nor was it any manner of theatrical company I had encountered before. This was the abrasive, cutting voice of the 1960s, edgy heirs of Lenny Bruce and Mort Sahl—a sensibility I was soon to internalize and propagate. On this day I received my first lesson: "How you look is part of it."

The San Francisco Mime Troupe—uncompromising, fearless, rude, truthful, iconoclastic, and unswerving—was shock therapy and a crash course in a new curriculum. It would be the portal through which I would enter my adulthood.

2

the perpetual present

If I had felt underused at the Actors' Workshop, I was running to keep up at the Mime Troupe, leaving Jessie increasingly alone and isolated. Obligatory movement classes, workouts, training in mime, political discussions, playwriting sessions, performing, and of course earning a living (since the troupe paid performers only five dollars a show) dominated every day. I had been back East to visit my father earlier in the year, 1965, and he had "broken my plate," as he put it, telling me it was time to survive on my own. I managed this as a driver for Yellow Cab.

I was learning that mime was not pantomime. Ronnie's teacher, Etienne Decroux, the great Parisian master, came from a very different lineage than Marcel Marceau—to Americans, the quintessential whiteface. Decroux had refined the ability to present the *weight distribution* of ordinary activities through isolating the parts of that activity. His minute examinations of the precise details of movement contributed to the powerful visual images he created onstage.

Pantomime presents the illusion of physical reality to suggest things that are not there: a glass of water, a horse, or a kite at the end of a line. Mime, on the other hand, uses physical reality to suggest *concepts:* a cane becomes a pool cue, a rifle, or a crutch, and rather than disappearing into its function as an indicator, it remains simultaneously what-it-is and what-it-is-supposed-to-be, offering the possibility of commenting on both simultaneously. It is difficult to communicate ideas in pantomime because it is silent, whereas mime, at least our school of it, was very, very verbal.

The Mime Troupe was passionately and collectively political; it was here that I first learned to extrapolate social phenomena, such as poverty, foreign policy, and racism, from their political and economic causes. The troupe's bias was decidedly leftist and anarchic, yet while conservatives might have assumed that we were Communists (or worse) because of our social critiques, the truth was that no party line could have survived the company's ideological mongrelism. Our politics sprang from a passionate dedication to principles that our nation expounded at home and abroad. It was the troupe's expectation that America should live up to her promises and play by her stated rules—and we intended to provoke her until she did.

The intellectual brouhaha was exciting. The diverse demographics of troupe members, perhaps twenty people at the core of a larger, loose community, included dockworkers, college students, socialist organizers, market analysts, musicians, opera singers, vegetarians, drug addicts, ballet dancers, criminals, and bona fide eccentrics. (I am reminded here of Stewart Brand's apt adage about outlaw communities simultaneously attracting the best and worst of people.) In his introduction to Ronnie's book, *The San Francisco Mime Troupe,* journalist Robert Scheer offers an accurate picture of what the troupe felt like in those days:

> It would be difficult to exaggerate the staggering number of hours that went into the ideas and form of new plays. Outsiders were brought in to give talks, reading lists appeared, and endless committees functioned or malfunctioned. To be sure there were wine and spaghetti feeds and the best parties in town and numerous romantic affairs and occasional bouts with drugs and nature. There were also obviously periods of laziness, incompetence, trucks crashed, scripts lost, tempers thrown. In a certain way Mime Troupers, Davis included, didn't take themselves too seriously—they were (and still are) a ribald and genuinely nonpretentious group. You would want to go to a Mime Troupe party. They

were just a lot more fun to be with than most other groups, given to impromptu bands, general spontaneity, and a more diverse and interesting bunch of characters than one expected around the Left.

At the same time, this ragtag beggars' army . . . was more responsible and less high-handed in its political commitment than any group which I encountered around the Bay Area's new Left. I think it was an awareness of this that caused the normally fratricidal Left to be united in its appreciation of the Mime Troupe.

In June of 1966, Jessie and Anthony left to spend the summer at her family's compound on Martha's Vineyard, and I let Karl Rosenberg, a Mime Troupe friend, move into our apartment. His wife, Judy Goldhaft, also a Mime Troupe member, had left him when she fell in love with the troupe's preeminent (after Ronnie) writer-director, Peter Berg. Peter was then, as he is today, a penetrating thinker, hypnotically articulate and animated by a moral outrage expressed in rapid-fire, highly associative dialogue and mad humor of the low-German, slapstick variety. Mercurial, charming, coercive, subliminally menacing, and intellectually uncompromising, he frightened people who did not know him well. For anyone who did, it was easy to understand why Judy fell in love with him.

Judy's husband Karl was Berg's opposite: a wiry visual artist whose habitual costume consisted of a painter's white coveralls and a floppy white cap jammed over his unruly black hair. He was quietly ambitious, politically uninvolved, and drawn to complicated and daunting physical tasks. When I first met him, he was painting large canvases of Judy—sensuous nudes that accentuated her dreamy demeanor and lissome dancer's body. If you knew nothing else about their relationship, you could discern from these paintings that Judy's departure was a serious loss to Karl.

Judy, like me, was a refugee from a privileged background, determined to fulfill her own vision of an authentic life. A skilled dancer and actress, she moved beautifully; beneath her cultured voice and ethereal demeanor lay a steely dedication to principle. She was as avowedly political as Karl was not, and with no fault or blame, their roads simply forked.

She, Karl, and their son Aaron had been living in a shabby little red-and-white-trimmed cabin in the stratospheric heights of San Francisco's Mars or Saturn streets (I forget which). When Karl moved out, Peter moved in. Meanwhile, personal affairs in my life, as in theirs, were being dramatically realigned.

While Jessie summered in Martha's Vineyard with her family, she took LSD for the first time. Her guide for this trip was Mel Lyman, a harmonica-playing astrologer and guru to a community of souls centered in and referred to by the name of their locale at Fort Hill, near Boston. They were a high-powered, energetic group, continually building and rebuilding their communal houses to last for eternity. The community published a locally famous counterculture newspaper, *The Avatar*, and generated wildly bipolar feelings in outsiders. Bruce Chatwin gives a bleak and unflattering portrait of them in his book *What Am I Doing Here*, but other than losing my lover to them and their playing a few mind games when I visited years later, no members ever harmed me. Furthermore, over the years they have maintained their communal family integrity and are now respected as master builders and artisans. They have constructed homes for such luminaries as David Geffen and Steven Spielberg, and their cohesiveness and fidelity to their original intention are, in my opinion, to be regarded as a triumph.

Jessie had a bad trip. Mel spent the night cleaning up her vomit and witnessing her fear and confusion, and she fell in love with him. She called me not long afterward and told me that she'd found "God" and was moving in with him. She asked me to send her stuff.

"Do you mind?" she asked.

"What's to do?" I replied realistically (and somewhat dysfunctionally).

"It wouldn't have worked, you know," she explained.

"If you say so, I guess not."

"Are you sad?" she asked.

"Yeah."

"I'm sorry," she said, "but you know it wouldn't have worked."

What I could not explain to Jessie or even myself at the moment was that what hurt, as much as my insufficiency to her, was the death of my illusion of maturity. I had made a mental pet of the idea that I was embodying the vital life of an artist, with a richly creative, beautiful woman at my side; I had assumed that our united talents would attract the best that the world had to offer. Her decision that the best lay elsewhere had relegated me, in my own mind, to the mediocre.

I packed up her possessions: the wonderful Thomas Hart Benton paintings and sketches in gilded frames; the clothes that had trapped the smells of Vineyard nights; the assorted ceramic containers for hairpins, single earrings, and bangles—all the detritus of a dead relationship. Looking at a suitcase of Anthony's forlorn toys was so heartbreaking that I vowed never to have a child with someone unless I lived with her for the rest of my life. (A vow twice broken, I'm pained to acknowledge.) It was a melancholy task, emptying drawers, folding socks like bandages for the wounded, listening to bare wire hangers susurrating in closets vacuumed of all trace of my family.

Karl helped me construct large wooden crates in which to ship Jessie's things back East, and he and I settled down to bachelor austerities in the sunny, cheerless rooms.

I opened the door to the apartment one afternoon a week later and stopped short in bewilderment. A black plastic toy train about three feet long was fixed to one yellow wall, midway between the floor and the ceiling. An open black umbrella was hanging upside down in the upper right corner where two walls and the ceiling created a pyramid-shaped join. One of Karl's large paintings of Judy with black Hebrew letters was mounted on the opposite wall.

I had two simultaneous experiences of the room. If I *thought* about what I was looking at, it was surreal and unsettling, but if I took it in without judgment, the forms were beautiful. Karl's black objects commanded the eye to hop from shape to shape, transferring loyalties in a restless dance. Only a short time earlier, ornate antique frames had lined the walls, dividing the "art" of Thomas Benton's paintings quite clearly from the "non-art"—the rest of the environment. Karl's assemblage destroyed those easy distinctions and turned the apartment itself into the frame. We were *in* the art! This was more than redecoration or a change of style. It was an alteration of perception that would inform the rest of my life in some manner—my first (non-drug) experience in crossing this perceptual threshold. In fact, this dissolution of the boundaries between art and life would become the dominant subtext of the next fifteen years for me. At the time, however, my appreciation of Karl's sensibilities masked the radical transition I was making: from the assumed stability and order of my family's reality, with its comforting assurances of a predictable future, into the playful possibilities of existing spontaneously in the perpetual present. It was not that the black umbrella and toy train set against a yellow wall signified something profound in themselves; rather, like poet William Carlos Williams's "red wheel barrow glazed with rain water beside the white chickens," they precipitated a profound realignment of my sensibilities.

To contrast these Weltanschauungs even more graphically, I think it might be useful if I pull a loop here from the weave of this narrative and focus on my family, its values, and my parents' expectations for my future. They were unconventional, certainly, and to many of my childhood friends appeared colorful and exotic. Compared to the world I was entering, however, my past seemed to me then to be, in the words of Sheldon Zitner, my most influential college professor, "well rounded and half an inch in diameter."

3

home is hard

When I joined the Mime Troupe, it was not altogether clear to me that I had taken a fork in the road. I had grown up in a political family. During the Mc-Carthy years, my mother's cousin was forced out of the New York City school system for refusing to answer whether he was or ever had been a Communist. My father, a successful investment banker and underwriter, was friendly with Paul Swayze and Leo Huberman, founders of the socialist *Monthly Review*. My mother was active in the National Urban League, working for civil rights in the forties and fifties; she took me to hear Martin Luther King Jr. speak at the Englewood Library long before he became a national figure. Our house buzzed with intellectual challenge and a wide range of accents and dialects. Yet the household also embodied the liberal dichotomy between thought and action that remained invisible to me until I joined the Mime Troupe.

My father, Morris Cohon, was a complicated, driven man. He had attended the Massachusetts Institute of Technology when he was fifteen, gaining admission through his uncanny facility with numbers; he could perform mental computations faster than I can type them into a calculator today. This talent, coupled with boundless curiosity, natural shrewdness, and prodigious, perhaps compulsive work, had produced some real wealth: thriving cattle ranches, a brokerage house on Wall Street, the presidency of the Hudson-Manhattan Railroad, and the chairmanship of an oil company called Phoenix-Campbell. If he bothered to know anything about a subject, he knew everything about it. He pursued knowledge much as Lenin pursued languages. (Lenin would "break the back," as he put it, of a new language by memorizing all the words in the dictionary.)

My father had a broad flat face with high cheekbones and Mongolian folds over his eyes. In fact, according to his mother, he was genetically Mongolian, having been born in Mt. Morris Park, New York, with jet black hair and the typical small blue birthmark on his back common to the Mongolian race. His father, Benjamin "Jack," was an Uzbek or Kazakh. A carnival strongman in his youth, he had developed extraordinary muscles in his back cranking the wheels that powered looms in a weaving mill. As intelligent as he was strong, he invented a gasoline-powered machine gun that did not require brass or gunpowder, and later invented numerous manufacturing techniques to save money and expedite production in a lamp company he created. He was also a fine classical painter who won the Sudan medal for his draftsmanship, who emigrated to America in the latter part of the nineteenth century. Family legend recounts his courtship of my grandmother when she was fourteen. She had five brothers who planned to kill him for what they considered his inappropriate attentions (he was twenty-seven then), but their father, an amateur painter, was so impressed by Jack's talent that he held his sons at bay. On his deathbed the next year, the father agreed to the marriage, and my father was born when my grandmother, Rose, was sixteen.

Jack lived for a while in Greenwich Village as a protégé of American artist Jacques Lipchitz; after they quarreled, he went to work as a sign painter for the United Cigar stores. He worked his way up to vice president and invested shrewdly in real estate, making a fortune, only to lose it in one day during the stock-market crash of 1929. He walked into the house that afternoon, took a shot of Scotch, walked out again, and took a job as a cab driver. In his fifties he founded several lamp factories in Paterson, New Jersey, fighting union organizers toe-to-toe with baseball bats. One of those factories still supports my uncle's side of the family.

Contrasts of art and commerce, collective ideals and personal needs, were only a few of the contradictions merged in my family history. There were other rivers and confluences, some dark and quite dangerous. My father inherited a murderous temper from his father Jack, who once punished his horse for biting him by smashing its forehead with a hammer—killing it. He nearly killed his own son as well. One day, Jack stepped on a rake while doing yard work and smacked himself in the face with the handle. My father, just six at the time, laughed at the slapstick of it, and Jack exploded with rage, chasing him into the house and up two flights of stairs. Morris, fleeing for his life, ran into the attic and slammed the door behind him. Unfortunately, he slammed the door on his father's fingers. When Rose arrived, drawn by the tumult, she discovered the door staved in and her husband stuffing his son through a small round window just beneath the peak of the roof, three stories above the ground. She knocked Jack unconscious with a heavy brass lamp, undoubtedly saving her child's life. When I heard this story as a little boy, what terrified me even more than my identification with my young father was that my grandmother chuckled bemusedly when she recounted it.

Normally, my own father's violence was channeled toward more constructive goals. He was an Olympic-class collegiate wrestler whose competitive hopes were shattered when an opponent snapped his leg during a qualifying match. He loved boxing as well and, in college, worked as a sparring partner for Philadelphia Jack O'Brian. He frequented gymnasiums all his life and enjoyed the rough company of fighters and trainers and the one-on-one competition of handball and wrestling.

Among his friends, Morris was famous for his rages. My mother Ruth tells the story of a drunk who brandished a longshoreman's hook at her on the subway while she was pregnant with me. Morris beat the man so badly that the engineer was forced to stop the train midtunnel and organize passengers to pull him off in order to save the man's life.

If Morris's temper bothered other people, it seemed to give him minimal trouble. His eyes twinkled, his shoulders hunched up, and he dropped into a boxer's crouch when he described a good fight. The memory of a well-thrown punch would make him cackle with pleasure, and he'd often say, "I hit him and his face broke open like a melon." Though he was a great reader and lover of literature, he dismissed Hemingway as a phony because he had fought him at Bothner's Gym one day and found him wanting. As a son who would rather read than hurt people, such stories were disturbing. I was proud of my father's power and fearlessness, but I couldn't understand his delight in inflicting pain. And of course I couldn't help but ponder my own fate if I should anger him.

Childhood with him was peppered with unsettling events. If someone cut his car off in traffic, there was no rest until the offender had been driven off the road. One day, on our way to Long Island to watch the Russian Olympic Wrestling Team (which Morris had helped sponsor on a visit to America), some hapless soul cut him off with the predictable result. But this time, having forced the other man off the highway, Dad got out of the car. The other driver, anticipating what was in store, rolled up his windows and locked his doors. Morris bellowed at him, "Get out of the fucking car!" When the man refused, Dad took out his wallet and began laying bills on the fender, accenting each deposit with "I'll give you *fifty* dollars to get out of the car. I'll give you a *hundred!*" This was so irrational that finally the other driver shrieked through the glass, "*Why* do you want to pay me to get out of my car?" Morris responded candidly, "So I can tear your fucking head off your body."

This pugnaciousness did not diminish with age. One summer when I was about twenty and working as a bartender in Martha's Vineyard, I was visiting my mother one afternoon when we received a call from Morris urgently instructing me to get Sidney Kramer, his lifelong friend and lawyer, and "plenty of cash." He was under arrest at La Guardia Airport. He had been waiting on line to purchase tickets for the shuttle flight to the Vineyard when the clerk closed the ticket window. Dad complained and somebody behind him in line told him to shut up, calling him "an old Jew bastard" in the process. It was an extremely unfortunate thing for that man to do.

Morris, who was then over fifty, beat the man and his friend (both in their late twenties) so badly that they sued *him* for assault. For his court appearance, Morris craftily chose a baggy coat and oversized hat that rested on his ears, diminishing his menace considerably. The victims, both in plaster body casts, towered on either side of him. The judge laughed at the disparity in size and age and threw the case out of court. What did he know?

Morris *was* a Jew and proud of it. In the thirties, he and Jewish friends wielding baseball bats broke up Nazi Bund meetings. His barrel-shaped body was propelled by thin, springy legs and powered by a will that would tolerate no resistance or perceived insult to his dignity. He once obliterated a multimillion-dollar underwriting deal at the signing ceremony, scattering photographers and dignitaries by leaping across the table to throttle his prospective partner for a casually anti-Semitic remark.

Morris's pride had a crippled twin that I suspect every Jew outside Israel is acquainted with to some degree. It is the certain knowledge that on the deepest level, no matter what degree of success and power you may achieve, you will be known first and foremost as a Jew and, consequently, as an outsider. The evidence of this stain on my father's self-esteem was the dedication with which he imitated English baronial life. He acquired lands, hounds, silk Oriental carpets, floor-to-ceiling bookshelves stuffed with books (actually read), and fine Colonial furniture and silver. His addiction to "the best" and his costly impulse to identify himself stylistically with the English aristocracy (long before Ralph Lauren) probably contributed to his early death. The pressure of maintaining such a life without the inherited wealth that made it possible would have pulverized granite.

I was afraid of this man, haunted by images of someone whose face had been "broken open." I imagined a man with brains slipping like cake batter through fingers vainly attempting to suture his wound. When displeased, Morris would growl, a low animal rumble that rose from his belly while he shook his head slowly from side to side. If I was the source of his displeasure, he'd swear that he would send me to reform school, usually threatening to snap something graphically specific like my knees or my thumbs. I understood *reform* as "re-form" and imagined a gruesome factory where children were pulled apart and reassembled into something more pleasing to their parents.

While he would never admit it, even to himself, Morris went to some lengths to ensure that I would remain afraid. Several times a week, to my horror, we would have "wrestling lessons," a semisadistic perversion of today's concept of "quality time." I am sure that in his own mind, Morris felt he was preparing me for the rough world he lived in (and, indeed, helped to create). In reality, however, these lessons demonstrated the potential cost of any challenges to his authority, for he "taught" me by tying me into suffocating knots, my knees jammed under my chin, my back torqued, my neck twisted claustrophobically. He punctuated such lessons with refinements like "Use your wrist bone across his forehead *here*—it hurts like hell, doesn't it?" When I struggled, he twisted harder, until finally I learned to stop resisting and send my mind on excursions until he was finished with me.

I have a son who loves to wrestle, and while it resurrects memories I would rather never confront again, I do wrestle with him because it gives him such obvious delight. I take pains to ensure that he can sometimes triumph over my superior strength and size. I am careful to see that he learns both the limits of his own power and that he can surpass his own expectations and beliefs through perseverance and spirited effort. Confidence *can* be taught if we can arrange for it to be experienced. I can see the fruits of my efforts in my son's fearlessness with me. A man who teaches a son that he can never win—whose own competitiveness or fear is such that he can never allow his child a victory, even in fun—inhabits a world of persistent terror and violence. It took me years to understand this reality of my father's, and, even after understanding it, it took many more years to forgive him these persecutions.

I must also acknowledge my own childhood cowardice, because my younger sister, though exempted from wrestling lessons (and other expectations to the point of neglect sometimes), was psychologically immune to Morris's threats. A torment to me in childhood, she was faster, braver, and smarter, and when Morris rampaged through the house, smashing things, she would stand up to him. Once, enraged by her pluck, he jerked her off her feet by her shirtfront, lifting her face level to his own. She stuck her tiny mug in his and said, "Go ahead, hit me. I'll sue ya!"

Had I done that, the retribution would have been unimaginable, but Morris was first taken aback, then roared at her fierce bantam-hen spirit, and ended by hugging and kissing her extravagantly. I fumed with jealousy, conflicted as to whether I was angrier at being denied such affection or at being exposed as a coward by a younger girl.

When I sought comfort or witness to these injustices from my mother, there was little available, because as far as Morris was concerned she too was in over her head. She urged me to "be an adult" and "understand" my father, tried to make me see how desperate and frightened he was beneath his bellicose surface. Once, when I was particularly distraught (I think it was the afternoon he knocked me unconscious during a boxing lesson), she whispered, "You and I are not like your father, darling. He *has* to win. We are the gentle people. We are the *losers.*" It was a crushing moment.

My mother, Ruth Fidler, was the first member of her family to leave an extended household of aunts and grandmothers, an orthodox Jewish home run by a mother who was a fierce gambler and a sweet, gentle father who had studied to be a rabbi before fleeing the Russian draft. Slim, beautiful, and fascinated with the bustle of Manhattan in the thirties, she worked as a model and as a secretary at the *Daily Mirror.* My father was ten years older than she, and when they met, he seemed to her to be dashingly handsome, already well established in the world, and awesomely competent. By the time she had discovered his failings, she had two young children and a new life far from the nurturing clutter of her family. She believed Morris's threat that if she ever left him, she would never see my sister and me again. I did not understand her dilemmas when I was young; I knew only that I needed a champion and had none. For many years I held her accountable.

The losing I experienced at my father's hands produced feelings so demeaning and debilitating that the idea of inflicting a comparable experience on anyone else by defeating them was inconceivable to me. The only option available to my immature understanding was simply *not to play.* I realized this one particularly bitter day and vowed deeply, the way children sometimes do, *never* to play, never to enter the realm of winning and losing. Of course, I had no inkling of the consequences of such a decision and certainly no awareness that my vows were banishing me from life as it is conventionally understood by most people. It took me years even to discover the existence of that crippling vow and more years after that to vanquish it. Until then, I avoided all competitive sports and the childhood contests of my peers. I refused to learn chess and Go (both of which my father played with chess master Edward Lasker every week). This injunction not to play went so deep that my son, when he was ten, could beat me handily at chess and could never understand the curious way I "go to sleep" and stop thinking at the board.

My pleasures became solitary ones: reading, writing, observing people and animals, and first and foremost, daydreaming. Although the term *drop-out* did not gain currency until the 1960s, my peculiar "not-playing" posture removed me from the world and its binary concerns with high and low status, profit and loss, as effectively as did my later decision to join the counterculture. In fact, the counterculture seemed like the one place where my personal predilection might be, if not totally understood, at least accepted.

When my father died suddenly years later, leaving his financial affairs in ruin and my mother in a perilous situation, I was little help to her, I'm afraid. My feelings of abandonment and rage had become a corrosive wedge between us. It took years and children of my own before I was able to tender her the love and respect she deserved. Still, some events are never entirely reparable. I didn't get my champion when I needed one, and I learned to do without. When the tables had turned and my mother needed a son in her corner, I was not there as I should have been.

She is over eighty now and lives simply in a small apartment with a few good things, memorabilia of a richer time. She has a tiny circle of old friends whom death seems to glean regularly. Today, we are very close and speak often, and I have rediscovered my childhood love for her: her passion, her endurance, her refusal to whimper. Yet I think there is still some trace of a gulf between us, perhaps only a healed scar on the landscape of our relationship. We have healed our relationship again, but that is not the same thing as its never having been wounded. I am certain that her constancy never wavered; I am embarrassed to admit that mine did.

Had Morris been simply a monster, neither she nor I would ever have survived nor, perhaps, would our feelings for him have been complicated by love. But the truth is he could be extraordinarily kind and impulsively, extravagantly generous and thoughtful; he had a keen eye for when people (outside his family) were suffering and took immediate steps to aid them. Sorting papers after his death, my mother discovered that he had quietly helped many people by giving them loans or financing their education. He appeared impervious to status games and afforded people identical measures of respect (or disrespect if they displeased him) regardless of their wealth and social position. He had an uncanny ability to communicate with a catholic variety of people. And I admired his uncompromising fidelity to his own impulses. During my tenure in his household I was not always sure *what* my impulses were, and when I was clear, it was often necessary to stifle them. Such behavior was unthinkable to Morris.

While my family may not have been the standard garden-variety, it was, for all its turmoil and discontents, conventional. We played by the rules of the majority culture, and except for what I thought were our personal eccentricities, we appeared to share the same reality as everyone else. My father went to work every day, labored hard, and enjoyed the rewards he accumulated. While he may have been critical of the government's racist policies or infringements of civil liberties, he did so from the standpoint of a loyal critic and never took it upon himself to radically alter a system that, after all, had been very good to him. I grew up in the shadow of his privileges and beliefs, and it was not until I saw McCarthyism shatter my friends and family and later saw Bull Conner set fire hoses and vicious dogs on black people peacefully demonstrating for their rights that I began to seriously question the validity of our political and economic ground rules.

When I joined the Mime Troupe, these issues began to cohere in my thinking. I was introduced there to an analytical perspective that explained how money was created and privileges protected by the political process. It explained the root causes of environmental degradation and the oppression of workers, which I felt had no place in a decent country. The analysis corresponded to my own perceptions, and was clear, cogent, and easy to translate into theatrical action. Most of all, heated intellectual debate was a vital part of the heady, stimulating atmosphere at the Mime Troupe, and I was excited by that. For the first time I seemed to know clearly and unmistakably what I felt about my world and why, and this expansion of understanding liberated prodigious energy.

Unlike most troupe members, I knew firsthand about the personal costs of inauthenticity and unearned privilege. My father was *not* an English lord but a complicated Sephardic Jew who coveted aristocratic style and confidence with the hunger of a displaced person. This sense of displacement is what enslaved him, I believed. Despite his fidelity to his momentary desires, his imagination of what a life might be had been co-opted and contained, like a fine prizefighter whose struggles enrich his manager. Now I had the opportunity to tell the cautionary tale, with art, ribald humor, youthful vigor, and a sense of play. My life might possibly redeem his and in the process liberate others from the thrall of the dominant culture's prefabricated visions, allowing them to live congruently with their deepest instincts and beliefs.

The Mime Troupe helped me to examine the insufficiencies of liberalism: the generosity toward others that is predicated on first sustaining one's own privilege. Things appeared clear to me and offered hope for constructive change. While a portion of this newfound certainty might be traced to youthful exuberance, I could also see my father clearly for the first time as imprisoned by a received vision, in the same way that most citizens were slotted into preordained roles and relationships. In his quixotic largesse, I saw parallels to the way government doled out favors to disenfranchised and impotent wards. I was developing a political point of view from which to investigate my present and my past, and was determined to honor my own observations and conclusions. I suppose that it never occurred to me that perhaps this determination itself was an inheritance from my father.

4

breaking the glass

The most articulate teacher of this new intellectual perspective was Peter Berg, perhaps the most radical and cranky member of the troupe, and arguably the most brilliant. He had an imposing round head with a face plucked from a Breughel painting: high cheekbones and crooked teeth semipermanently revealed in a death's-head grin. Long, thin blond hair fell across a domed brow, and his eyes, except for their humor, possessed the indignant fury of a raptor. Genghis Khan might have smiled like Berg, and in fact Berg's nickname was "the Hun." He walked into the Mime Troupe office by chance one day, wearing a brown suit, and told them that he was a writer-actor-director and that they should give him a chance. He was ushered into the back room where he met William Grishonka, a former New York actor who had discovered a flair for business and was managing the Mime Troupe's financial affairs. Grishonka gave him a translation of Giordano Bruno's *Il Candelaio* and told him that if he could turn it into a three-act commedia dell'arte piece the troupe could perform, then they would believe he was who he said he was. Peter retreated to his apartment. When he returned with a play, Ronnie Davis liked it and began production.

One day during rehearsal, Ronnie confessed that they were probably *not* going to perform the play but intended to get arrested for attempting to per-

form it without a park permit. Earlier, the troupe had been issued a permit
to perform in the city's parks, but after the park commission had seen one of
the shows, it had been revoked. Marshall Krause, the troupe's lawyer, refused to accept that, claiming censorship. The troupe performed the next
week without a permit. On August 7, 1965, Ronnie substituted himself in
Luis Valdez's role and was arrested for "parking on the grass." Although
they lost the case in court (the court refused to address the constitutional issue), it was such an embarrassment to the city that the troupe simply went
on performing and no one bothered them again.

This experience precipitated Peter's thinking about theater as a vehicle
for radical change and led him to the idea of "guerrilla theater"—a small
mobile company that would perform at rallies and other public events and
instigate a kind of theater that he described as "breaking the glass":

> Theater as breaking the glass . . . the convention of theater [as] sit-
> ting in an audience watching a play was like the convention of
> being a member of society watching television, or cop opera . . .
> the enforcement of society. . . . If you broke the glass people would
> stream through to the other side of the stage and become life-
> actors. That's the whole riff.

The phrase "life-actor" was Peter's contribution, describing a person
who consciously creates the role he or she plays in everyday, offstage life,
a person who marshals skill, imagination, and improvisation in order to
break free from imposed roles and restrictions and, by example, demonstrate a path that will free others. Timothy Leary's edict to "turn on, tune
in, and drop out" was a less-focused but parallel commitment to breaking
the glass.

When actors perform roles onstage, audiences realize unconsciously that
the performance is happening in a protected space but may never consider
the implications of that fact. Such protected space is necessary for art and is
the reason that paintings and stages are framed and sculpture placed on a
pedestal. This is to remind audiences that it is not the reality of their own
world they are viewing but an alternate universe with its own premises and
rules, and the creation of such a parallel reality is often a useful device for
determining characteristics about our own. Despite its utility and necessity,

such a remove may prevent audiences from seeing the correspondence between the artificial reality and their own and, more importantly, from fully
integrating and responding to the implications of the correspondence.

If, however, actors were to leave the stage, and *leave the theater*—performing in the streets and public spaces, offering no clues that these were
performances—people would be unprotected by their ideas of art and notions concerning its place in society. They would have to determine for
themselves what to make of the apparently strange behavior, even if only
to determine whether or not self-defense was necessary. Consequently, they
would be engaged. In fact, if it is the artist's intention to highlight distinctions between being inside and outside of society's dominant values, performing in public is a very appropriate venue.

In the charged social climate of the sixties, many people struggling for
critical social change felt that the lines between what was inside and outside
the values of majority culture needed to be clearly drawn. For those of us
who rejected the specter of armed revolution and what would certainly be
its ghastly consequences, drawing such lines required new forms of creative
expression.

Unfortunately for the Mime Troupe, pursuit of this subject carried Berg
out of the troupe and directly into a loose confederation of friends called the
Diggers. It would have happened anyway eventually. Both Ronnie and Peter
were brilliant, angry, committed guys, and both tended toward autonomous behavior. The troupe was too small for such replication.

The Diggers was an anarchistic experiment dedicated to creating and
clarifying distinctions between society's business-as-usual and our own
imaginings of what-it-might-be, in the most potent way we could devise. It
is a feature of youth, I suppose, to distinguish itself and its values from the
domination of the adults they are soon to become. Each generation attempts to find a style too outré to be co-opted by the majority culture. Over
the years, Beats, hippies, punks, and followers of the "grunge" style have deliberately flouted conventional ideas of taste and propriety to contrast their
group's values from those of the majority. And it was always a matter of only
months before their fashions appeared in the pages of *Harper's Bazaar* and
Vogue and the once-revolutionary distinctions between them and everyone
else began to be fuzzed. The cycle led invariably to long-haired dope smok-
ers doing their thing at the corporate office. (We've all seen what I call the

"bank-teller's haircut": short in the front for the customers, with a tidy little ponytail tucked away behind for after work.) Part of the power and flexibility of our profit-oriented economy is that it can co-opt nearly everything. Everything but *doing things for free.* The Diggers understood that *style* was infinitely co-optable. What could not be co-opted was doing things for free, without money.

In the Diggers, Peter Berg found it possible not only to create events that clarified the line separating inside and outside but also to do so in a manner that changed people from *audience* to *participants.* Peter's term for this transformation was "creating the condition you describe." Of course the first question was "What is the condition you want to describe?" From the Diggers' point of view, it was a society liberated from the carnivorous aspects of capitalism, a culture offering more enlightened possibilities for its members than the roles of *employee* or *victim.*

The Diggers will be prominently featured in this narrative later. What is important at this moment are the questions and intentions that eventually led us off the stage and into the streets.

This Digger vision was soon to claim my allegiance as well—but at the moment I was fascinated with absorbing the rudiments of a new style of acting and other skills particular to a commedia performer.

My first performance for the troupe was as Dottore, a pompous, caped blowhard with a ruffed collar and black half-mask featuring a bulbous nose. The production was a retooled version of Molière's *The Miser,* and though I can no longer remember the political spin we put on it, I have seen excerpts of my performance on an old film and cringe at my substitution of enthusiasm for physical precision.

Performing outdoors demands a certain vocal power and grandness of scale from the actor. You are competing with traffic, dogs, children, drunks, and the myriad distractions of urban life. Posture and gesture must reinforce (or purposely contradict) the intention of dialogue, and to do this effectively, gestures must be precise. To be precise, a movement must have a clear beginning and end, sharply discriminating it from gestures that precede or follow it. Random movements and nervous fidgets must be rigorously eliminated.

Movements of commedia characters begin from *zero,* a technical term for one of several postures that exemplify the fundamental attitudes or attributes of the character. One of Pantalone's zeros, for instance, is modeled on a duck: chest puffed with self-importance, butt thrust back, left hand raised with the index finger pedantically erect, right hand flat on the belly, head cocked with self-satisfaction, knees bent, and feet almost at right angles to each other. Pantalone has other zeros as well, and when the actor is not moving, he returns to one of those postures to present a clear physical ideogram of the character.

Because they are so simplified, movements that originate from zero are powerful. It takes much practice, however, to isolate the body's various parts and edit out all superfluous motion. Try whipping an arm and hand out from the chest and pointing without looking at the hand, as if you were saying, "Never darken my door again!" in a melodrama. Make sure the movement is executed so that the shoulder, arm, hand, and finger finish in a perfectly straight line, parallel to the floor. If the finger dips or rises at the end of the hand, even minimally, the gesture's visual power will be diminished. Such responses must be automatic, something you could do in your sleep, so that you are free to concentrate on stage business and creative impulses that arise during a performance. This is equally true of knowing your lines. Nothing will stifle an impulse or break concentration more rapidly than having to grope for dialogue. Roman Polanski once phrased it aptly: "If you have to think about hitting the brakes in your car, it's already too late."

The Mime Troupe had adapted commedia dell'arte for contemporary purposes, and consequently our relationship to it was more complex than it would have been had we simply been living in the sixteenth century. Ronnie Davis explained it to us in the following way:

> In a highly stylized play, the actor usually has one task—to play the character. In our adaptations we [give] our actors three jobs: play yourself, play the character and play an Italian who was a *commedia* performer. The person [must] act himself while reading the script, simply to understand the situation, the conditions, the motives of the character and the point of the play. This is the simple Stanislavsky technique where action and objectives are discovered without trying to perform the text.

The second layer of refinement or the development of the physical mask requires physical characteristics such as a duck walk for Pantalone; a swinging bravado for the lover; snap, crackle and suspicious looks for Brighella. And accents—French (for lovers), Italian (Dottore and servants), or Jewish and Mexican with their concurrent gestures. The personal attributes of the actor [are] changed or extended to create the mask.

The third level—historical imitation of Italian actors—require[s] some study of *commedia dell'arte* and preparation [to] produce a rich stage characterization. Each modern actor [must] find his/her Italian counterpart. Francesco Andreini played Capitano Spavento (ca. 1600); Guiseppe Biancolelli as Dottore; Isabella Andreini as first lady. . . .

These levels of reality, one concrete (self) and the other two assumed (mask and Italian actor), allowed for constant shifting of characterization and play. When the actor lost the character's believability or failed to make the audience laugh he could change to the Italian role . . . or when a dog walked across the stage, the performer could break character as Italian actor and comment from his own vantage point, or if he was skilled enough he might stay inside the mask (role) and deal with the intrusion as the character. The ad lib (improvisational wisecrack) was the oil of transition.

While we were writing scripts and splitting political hairs about content, we would also dedicate long hours to practicing physical and psychic transitions under the drill-sergeant watchfulness of Ronnie and senior members John Robb, Judy Goldhaft, Jane Lapiner, or Sandy Archer.

It was thrilling, setting up shop in a park under the pungent eucalyptus trees, summoning a crowd, and making them laugh and hoot appreciatively. The archetype of the traveling player is a powerful one, and I felt imbued with it every time we drove our vehicles to a performance site, unloaded our baskets and boxes, and erected the stage. Following the troupe's notorious arrest the previous year, our audiences became fiercely partisan and appreciative. There could be no better balm for the confidence.

As my skills developed, I took pride in my newfound ability to improvise with the best of the company. The split consciousness that both participates in and witnesses an event (which had helped me survive my father's "wrestling lessons") now served me excellently. One part watched, corrected, anticipated, and strategized while the other part performed. Ironically, I felt whole instead of divided, as if I had found a use for a heretofore extra part of myself. I discovered a natural propensity for movement and goofy looniness. Acting was a way to excel at something that existed outside the construct of winning and losing. It demanded much and was unforgiving of failure, but it was great fun—and best of all, my victories caused no one else pain. In fact, the reverse was true. Audiences *want* people to succeed onstage. They get nervous if they see lapses of confidence in a performer. When I recognized this fact, it unleashed large amounts of previously conflicted energy in a very constructive manner.

The unexpected was commonplace at Mime Troupe performances. When church bells drowned out a performance, the entire cast spontaneously began pantomiming speech, pretending that we were screaming at one another and could not be heard. When a noisy drunk clambered onstage in midperformance one day, I embraced him, in character, as if I had mistaken him for a lover. We twirled around the stage together in an infatuated dance, flirting, while the audience roared its appreciation. On the fourth blissful pass, I "accidentally" danced him off the edge of the stage back onto the grass. Whatever pique might have been generated by his dismissal was mitigated by the applause, and he rejoined me onstage for a grand bow while the audience cheered the troupe's adaptability and his good sportsmanship.

It is a heady experience (one from which I have never recovered), doing something you love and believe in and getting paid for it. Bonds of friendship and mutual experience thickened rapidly, and before long, I was a certified member of this quirky family. Changed by hard work, new skills, and new ideas, I was establishing myself among the other actors as a peer. I remember thinking during my first Thanksgiving dinner with my new family, "This is as good as it gets." In many ways, this remains true.

5

the minstrel show

Some months after my initiation into the troupe, I was asked to replace John Broderick in the role of Bones in *The Minstrel Show.* This was either a heartening show of confidence in my ability or represented desperate straits for the troupe, because *The Minstrel Show* was not only a wildly popular piece but also a rare cultural epiphany perfectly in sync with the historical moment.

After much group research into that old and well-loved (by whites) theatrical form, the show had been written by Ronnie and Saul Landau and refined through company improvisation. At one time in America there were more than three hundred companies performing in blackface, singing, dancing, and doing "nigger"-joke routines. The troupe turned the form inside out to use it as a vehicle for investigating racial issues.

Our play was formatted like an authentic minstrel show with six performers (three white and three black) in blackface, curly wigs, sky-blue silk tuxedos, and white gloves. The cast was "fronted" by a white Interlocutor who "controlled" the "darkies," served as the straight man, and represented "respectable" (white) values.

The show opened with a high-stepping, tambourine-slapping cakewalk, accompanied by banjos. This was the commedia warm-up raised to a higher level, designed to boost energy and demonstrate to audiences that they were in the hands of skilled performers. The high-spirited "darkies" frolicked and sang under the relaxed control of the benevolent Interlocutor, then segued into old vaudeville groaners. Nothing scary here:

Inter: Gentlemen, beeeeee seated!

Gimme: (leaps up) Wish I was rich, wish I was rich, wish I was rich!

Inter: I heard you the first time, Mr. Gimme.

Gimme: Did you? But de fairy gimme three wishes, and dem was it.

Inter: Where did you see a fairy?

Gimme: On a ferry boat! (*All guffaw. Gimme sits.*)

Inter: Mr. Bones, are you a Republican or a Democrat?

Bones: (jumping up) Oh, I'm a Baptist.

Inter: Come, come. Whom did you vote for last time?

Bones: Robinson Crusoe.

Inter: What did he run for?

Bones: Exercise! (*All yuk yuk. Bones stays standing with Interlocutor.*)

Inter: Now cut out the foolishness. Are you a Republican or a
    Democrat?

Bones: Democrat.

Inter: And your wife is also a Democrat?

Bones: She was, but she bolted.

Inter: Bolted the party?

Bones: No, just me. When I come home late, she bolts de door! (*All
    guffaw.*)

This traditional cross fire reinforced majority views of black people as happy, expressive children. The dynamics on the stage represented the dynamics in the culture at large.

The first inkling that something was awry appeared during a sentimental rendition of "Old Black Joe." As the "darkies" turned their backs to the audience and bowed their heads respectfully, the Interlocutor began a mawkish recitation: "I hear those gentle voices calling . . ." But not *all* the minstrels stood so respectfully. One in particular (the role I inherited) could be observed mimetically unzipping his fly and struggling to remove an extraordinarily large penis that was obstinately tangled in his underwear. Once freed, he began stroking it surreptitiously with concentrated dedication. This furtive masturbation counterpointed the increasingly passionate declamations of the Interlocutor, who by this time was on one knee, weeping copiously. As the chorus sang, "I'm a-comin', I'm a-comin'," my act of genital worship culminated in an orgasm of preposterous proportions and subsided spasmodically with a bit of stage business involving wiping my white glove on the back of my nearest neighbor as the unwary Interlocutor was being helped offstage in a state of emotional collapse.

This was not Maria Callas at the Met, but it effectively punctured audience expectations, and the howls of appreciation (or the boos and the sound of blunt objects whistling toward the stage) indicated clearly the audience's politics. After this deliberately tasteless (but funny) bit of Brechtian commentary, the Interlocutor began to lose control of the stage. Utilizing additional wigs and masks and wearing agitprop signs to identify characters as "White," "Cop," "Liberal," and so forth, the minstrels "mutinied" and mounted their own scenes, reviewing all of "Nego" [*sic*] history in an acidulous investigation of hypocrisy on both sides of the color line.

"Nego History Week," for example, remembered Crispus Attucks, the first black man to be killed in the Revolutionary War. Our hero, played to perfection by the laconic Willie B. Hart, was pushing a broom when he was killed. Toussaint-Louverture, Booker T. Washington, Teddy Roosevelt, George Washington Carver, black soldiers in Vietnam, and Martin Luther King Jr. were all revisited and analyzed from the perspective of the minstrels' "newly liberated" stance.

Sections of the show highlighted rancorous dialogues between black "liberals" and "radicals" clarifying their relative positions and strategies. In one chilling scene, a white cop killed a black kid for threatening his authority—with a harmonica. When this scene, which began with a lot of jiving and quick street patter, escalated to the point where the cop pointed his gun and stamped his foot on the hollow stage to create the sound of his fatal shot, the previously rollicking audience froze. The silent tableau of Cop, dead Kid, and horrified Friend could be sustained for an excruciating length of time without the slightest rustle from the crowd.

The minstrel show appeared at exactly the right historical moment, when the civil rights movement and emerging black consciousness fused with a social upheaval in the nation's youth to make society appear suddenly permeable and open to both self-investigation and change. Audiences, even uncomfortable ones, of all colors recognized its originality and toughness. Thirty years later, I walked backstage to pay my respects to Anna Deavere Smith after seeing her extraordinary one-woman show about the 1992 Los Angeles riots. I told her, in what must have appeared to be amazing hubris, that I had seen nothing of such aptness, synchronicity, and power since I had had the good fortune to appear in *The Minstrel Show* years earlier. It was clumsy of me to say so but true, and to some degree the success of both shows depended on their appropriateness to the political moment.

Part of the gag of the show was that it encouraged audience members to try to distinguish white from black players. In doing this, they were forced to confront their own prejudices, since all the performers played black stereotypes equally well. As actors, we too had been forced to face these issues in developing our characters; we'd had to answer to one another for our own prejudices and unexamined assumptions, and we used this experience to our advantage in provoking the audience.

We did not skewer only liberals. No piece ripped the scales off buried prejudice as thoroughly as the "Chick/Stud" scene, about a black "Stud" who picks up a white "Chick" in a bar and takes her home. The scene begins just after sex. One of the actors is wearing a White Girl mask with fixed blonde braids and an expression of yearning compassion. Both actors stand on an empty black stage, isolated in single spotlights. The White Girl is fretting and struggling to say something.

> *Stud:* For Christ's sake, if you got something to say, say it.
>
> *Chick:* What's wrong?
>
> *Stud:* Nothin's wrong, baby, you got a problem and I was just solving it for you. Felt pretty good, didn't it? Yeah, the white man invented that problem for black man to solve.

Their conversation oscillates between stereotypical positions, the Chick being more and more earnestly liberal and the Stud more exaggeratedly self-important:

> *Chick:* . . . You may have the body of a man, but emotionally you're a child. You can't know me as a woman!
>
> *Stud:* Woman! Ain't nobody tole you, baby? You ain't nothin' but a white chick. You're status and satisfaction and revenge. You're pussy and pale skin and you know no white man can satisfy

you like I can. Now me, I'm different. (*At this point the Stud begins taking himself incredibly seriously, puffing himself up.*) I'm all NEGRO. I got the *smell* of Negro and the *hair* of Negro and all the goddamn passion of Africa and wild animals. (*beat*) I haven't got the same hang-ups, have I?

When the Chick reaches the inane apogee of her position and exclaims passionately, "You *do* want to love me, you *neeeeeed* to love me," the Stud's response—"Sheeet! You been reading too much James Baldwin"—invariably brings the house to whistles and cheers.

At this point the minstrel playing the White Chick takes off the mask and skirt and, holding the skirt beneath the mask to create a puppet, moves into the spotlight; the rest of the actor remains in the dark so that the illuminated puppet takes on a life of its own. It moves tenderly, provocatively, toward the Stud. He acts cool at first, then becomes frightened as the Chick comes closer, taunting and coming on to him. The Stud responds violently, grasping the Chick puppet and strangling it as the operator lowers it slowly to the floor. When it is "dead," the Stud discovers that the skirt and mask are "empty." The first minstrel, still holding the mask, laughs and is joined by the rest of the cast, also laughing, who chase the Stud offstage, teasing him.

This scene turned audiences inside out, switching sides and points of view too quickly for them to take refuge in canned attitudes. They didn't know where to stand or how to be hip, because the "safe" ground was constantly being chipped away. They did know that they loved it, though—and we were just getting started.

Near the end of the first act, a ten-minute film played in which a watermelon is kicked, stabbed, hacked, run over, disemboweled, and dropped from high windows. It eventually reassembles its parts and drives away its tormentors. The soundtrack, written by avant-garde composer Steve Reich (one of the many talented people the troupe attracted into its orbit in those days), was performed live by the company. Three tiers of minstrels seated stage right of the screen sang the words "Wa-DUH-Me-LON, Wa-DUH-Me-LON," in a four-note round, each tier beginning its "Wa" on the "DUH" of the tier in front of it. The effect was hypnotic, deconstructing the word *watermelon* into a shimmer of rhythms. The film *O Dem Watermelons* won many awards at film festivals and often played on its own as a short.

During intermission, the minstrels assaulted the audience, breaking through the "fourth wall" of the theater by climbing off the stage to dance, tease, flirt, and generally raise hell. This alerted the audience in visceral terms that we were "among" them now and could no longer be "managed." Intermission was also the critical time for touring actors to score dates and places to sleep after the show. Shyness in this fifteen-minute window of opportunity was detrimental to rest.

The show was definitely on the cutting edge, and word about it spread rapidly. One night I was flabbergasted to see Harry Belafonte and Nipsey Russell in the audience, falling out of their chairs with laughter.

Despite these successes, there was no way the troupe could support itself with its current audience. The only way to make enough money to support our members and expand our repertoire was to mount a tour. In 1966 Ronnie decided that the play to export should be *The Minstrel Show* and made it my responsibility to assemble a road company and direct the production. I felt nowhere near ready to do this, but the troupe rarely honored niceties like personal reticence. Motivated by necessity, I began supervising auditions and the complex task of assembling a touring company, melding veterans and new performers to go on the road.

The troupe members were a varied and colorful bunch and attracted similar folk, which made my job of assembling a road company considerably easier. The indisputable stars of the original *Minstrel Show* were two prodigiously talented black actors, Willie B. Hart and Jason Marc-Alexander. Willie was about six-four, very dark-skinned, with an erect, relaxed posture. We nicknamed him "the Prince" because of his natural dignity and unflappable calm. He had a glass eye that imparted a loopy expression to his face that he utilized skillfully in real life and with genius onstage. His fortes were "Step'n Fetchit" characters, apparently stupid as a post. After establishing his character's mental limits, he would shuffle around waiting for the moment to lock his IQ-less gaze on his victim. With no apparent movement or change of expression, he could *intend* you to see a situation as he did and seismically shift the ground of assumptions, highlighting his actual mastery of the situation and the density of the *other* character. It was a magical capacity, and to this day, I do not understand how he accomplished it.

Jason was his perfect foil, as sparky and erratic as Willie was solid and grounded. Light-skinned, with thick hair piled high on his head like a hat, he walked with a springy stoop, like a bobbing question mark. He had an explosive laugh that sounded like something breaking against a wall, and his angular body was always in motion. He was a true clown, and as with all clowns, his humor seemed to be a survival mechanism protecting a deep wound. He and Ronnie fought often and abrasively; arguments ended in tears, with apologies and protestations of affection as sincere as the anger had been moments before. It was Jason who played the Stud with such relish and exaggerated sexual braggadocio that he never failed to win an ovation.

The third black minstrel was played by a different actor on each tour. Earl "Robbie" Robertson was an elegant man then in his late thirties. He sported a tidy goatee and had a precise, slightly effeminate voice and a sardonic sense of humor. He maintained a quiet reserve that discouraged the normally easy swap of anecdotes and personal life histories, perhaps because he was older than the rest of us.

His replacement on the second tour was Ron "the Preacher" Stallings. Ron was a saxophone player who later fronted the band Southern Comfort. His baby face featured large, wistful eyes that camouflaged bountiful reservoirs of impish humor. Like the rest of us, Ron viewed life on the road as an expanded opportunity for sexual search-and-destroy missions. One night just before the curtain rose, he was standing backstage letting his vision graze over an audience generously populated with nubile girls. He turned to me with a transcendent, blissful expression on his face and murmured in a purring, reverent hum, "No survivors."

The "white" minstrels, in addition to me, included John Condrin, a three-hundred-pound bartender with a soaring soprano voice and an eagerness to be loved that hinted at sleeping personal horrors which eventually caused his commitment to an asylum.

Bill Lyndon deserves a book of his own. Small and dapper as a jockey, he was the most irreverent, instinctively antiauthoritarian person I have ever met: a diminutive Lenny Bruce, with equal speed and the same corrosive New York humor. He was playing Pantalone when I joined the troupe, and his character was such a Jewish caricature and so scabrously funny that it was indelibly stamped on my imagination. When I began to play the role myself, I was never able to shake his model and finally surrendered to it as my homage to perfection.

Bill was a gifted criminal, quick-witted and very cool. He supported a deep fondness for narcotics and amphetamines by working credit cards, money orders, and traveler's check scams with consummate skill, sometimes driving four or five hundred miles in a single day to hit stores all over the Bay Area before a card "burned down" on the national computers.

He was married to Anne, a sharp-faced girl with a voice like sandpaper. Love of the wrong side of the street seemed to run in her family—a pistol fell out of her sister's bra at Bill's funeral—and like Bill she loved drugs, sex, and crime in some indeterminate order. Their house was either a three-ring circus or a geriatric ward, depending on whether the drugs of choice that day were uppers or downers. You could drop in at any hour and find Bill and Anne on methedrine chewing their lips and constructing puppets, while someone was injecting drugs in the kitchen and others puzzled the deeper meanings of comic books or fussed with musical instruments over and around someone passed out on the couch.

Not unpredictably, Billy and Annie's trip disintegrated rapidly. When the VW van that Bill was driving ran off the road and flipped, they lost a baby daughter, too presciently named Velocity Anne. Bill and Anne were never the same after that. Though they later had another child—a sweet, bewildered boy named Mikey—chaos and darkness seeped into their lives like stains on the wallpaper of a cheap hotel. Bill was diagnosed with cancer, and I intuit some connection between that dis-ease and his deep grief over his daughter's death.

I helped Bill and Annie move to Santa Cruz, where he began a strict regimen of sunshine, exercise, raw vegetable juices, and fresh air that whipped his cancer into remission. So they moved back to the city, and I went to see him a couple of days after his return. There he was in the center of his kitchen, trembling like a leaf and "cooking" Dilaudids—synthetic heroin pills—in a spoon. He had been celebrating his remission by injecting them for several days; it was clear to me that this was not a man who wanted a long life. His cancer returned with a vengeance, and Billy's last days were hell.

I visited his house shortly after the cancer's return, and the place was a pigsty. Billy was propped in bed hooked to an oxygen tank, weak as a kitten. He was staring through the open door into the filthy kitchen, where the sink overflowed with crusty plates and pots. Annie and some friends were sitting around the table, directly in Bill's line of sight, shooting speed and arguing about the division of the dope. I did what I could that day, which was to wash the dishes and straighten the house, but that Dantean diorama remains as vivid today, thirty years later, as it was then.

The last time I saw Bill, he was in the hospital looking like the leftovers of a burnt offering to the devil. My girlfriend Marilyn (soon to become my wife) offered to scratch his back, and as she rubbed and soothed his tortured skin, Billy sat there, completely whipped and crying quietly. There was nothing to say. As we were leaving, I said reflexively, "I'll see you later," but it was bullshit and everyone in the room knew it.

It is difficult to reconcile this last view of Bill with my memories of his vitality and energy onstage, but it is a valuable exercise to remember that when you live without the limits of law or convention, you must supply your own. If you don't, or can't, formlessness becomes terminal.

The last performing member of the *Minstrel Show* cast was Bob Slattery, a fortysomething longshoreman and socialist organizer with rugged, aristocratic features and a bluff, authoritative manner that was perfect for the condescending role of the Interlocutor.

Because Bob considered himself a "serious" revolutionary, he was perpetually stressed by the rest of the cast's sexual high jinks on the road—especially those of Ron, Willie B., Jason, and me. Bob had reason to be upset. From our perspective, sex was a necessity transcending hormones. Because the company was so poor, we could not afford hotels and normally were forced to camp on the floor or a couch at the homes of our show's sponsors— a good incentive to drum up alternatives of our own.

Our modus operandi was to size up prospects during the opening number. As the singing lines of minstrels cakewalked past one another, claims for intermission conquests would be staked in the pauses for breath. "The redhead in the third row is mine" or "Hands off the blonde with the big tits in the furry sweater." Desperation often breeds competence, and we became skilled at securing berths during the intermission's fifteen-minute hiatus.

This was before the time when America's sisters and daughters were lining up to trade anonymous sexual favors for access to rock stars, and groupies were not yet writing books about their "careers." Sex may have been easy in the sixties, but we were not rich and famous, and for the girls we pursued, sex had to be based on some sort of personal connection, which was not that easy to fabricate in fifteen minutes. We took advantage of our image as a small, dedicated, revolutionary band of players (which we were), and of course we were helped by the show's enormous popularity.

Still, neither the audience's approbation nor our excuses concerning the economics of our situation assuaged Bob's anger. Day after day as we alleviated the boredom of long drives with inventive hyperboles of the previous night's bed-wrestling, Bob berated us as "frivolous adventurers" whose sexual politics were "disgraces to the cause." His hectoring continued until one night a trim undergrad decided that Big Bob was too juicy an Oedipal fantasy to ignore and took him home. The next morning, a freshly showered, impeccably groomed, *beaming* Bob Slattery burst into the coffee shop where we'd assembled, rubbing his hands energetically and exclaiming, "Let's get some breakfast, boys. By *God*, I'm famished!"

The entire touring production consisted of the six minstrels and the Interlocutor, two banjo players, a tech man, six bentwood café chairs reinforced with plywood seats, six tambourines, and some costumes and wigs. Despite the fact that the show had only three technical cues, to my knowledge we never performed a show without at least one technical mishap. There was almost always a standing ovation at the final curtain.

I loved the spontaneity of the road. No two days or nights were the same. I enjoyed the deep intimacy that developed among the cast members. While I'd had black friends in high school, the relationships with Willie, Jason, and Ron were deeper and more intense. We ate together, slept together, performed together, and on occasion orgied together. Living this intimately, we developed empathetic communications, as if we were separated from "civilians" by an invisible shield that allowed us to see them but prevented them from seeing us. Conversation simultaneously covered the practical, political, imaginative, and absurd—something I had experienced in college with my small circle of friends, all deeply involved in our apprenticeships as writers, but we were still students. This was the real world.

It was definitely real. People risked everything for what they wanted. Some were criminals, it's true, but I was lax about moral judgments then because their crimes were against property, and our prevailing politics attributed most poverty to fiscal conspiracy. We were self-styled guerrillas operating behind enemy lines, and petty theft was considered a way of living off the enemy's surpluses. I had known many armchair revolutionaries; now I felt that people like Bill Lyndon were the ones with the requisite nerve and pluck to create social change.

We took these revolutionary intentions seriously, and the style and content of *The Minstrel Show* were among our most potent weapons. At this point in the midsixties, Lenny Bruce had not yet been hounded to death by New York District Attorney Frank Hogan for his political critiques but he *had* been arrested for saying "fuck" onstage. The authorities made implicit connections between bad politics and "bad taste"; predictably, the show was closed and we were arrested several times.

In 1966 we were organizing a second autumn tour: three days in Denver, then on to Madison, Chicago, and Philadelphia, culminating in Manhattan's Town Hall where Dick Gregory was to be our host. We regarded his support of the show as an honor, demonstrating that we had passed the acid test of the progressive black community's review. The review of my own race would be another matter.

The first two performances in Denver were benefits for the Young Democrats, and on the second night, September 8, we played before an audience of judges, Democratic bigwigs, attorneys, and local pooh-bahs. The show was particularly hot that evening, and the audience's appreciation was frenzied. In the middle of our finale, we noticed large numbers of police officers massing in the wings, restraining gasping Doberman pinschers.

We wasted no time wondering whether the dogs simply had a hankering for some soul theater or whether the cops, stuck with dog-sitting duties, just hadn't wanted to miss the hippest theater from California and brought them along. After our third encore, I raised my hands for silence and announced to the audience that the police were poised backstage to arrest us. "We are,"

I intoned, "the San Francisco Mime Troupe, and we do *not* intend to be arrested *backstage!*"

On that cue, the minstrels and the Interlocutor climbed off the stage and began threading our way through the supportive audience toward the exits. The dumbfounded cops ran onstage with their dogs and milled about uncertainly. From the floor, we applauded them, clapping and whistling, yelling "more" and "encore." The audience joined us, cheering the comedy of the police wrestling their writhing dogs off the stage as if it were an intentional performance.

Orchestrating their humiliation did not endear us to the police, and the cops waded into the crowd after us with zeal. To their credit, they managed to capture three of us: Robbie Robertson, Bill Lyndon, and me. (Bob Slattery demanded to go along with us, as I recall.) I was glad I was not the officer who had to explain to his superiors how the *other* three minstrels, made up in blackface and dressed in sky-blue tuxedos, had been able to "slip away in the crowd."

The next morning's *Denver Post* featured a prominent picture of us at the police station, still in makeup, regarding the camera with a "Can you believe this shit?" expression. We were bailed out before noon and represented by a local attorney named Walter Gerash, who had seen the show and who took our case pro bono. His forbearance was sorely tested when he was forced to contend with Mime Troupe standards of behavior in court, such as Bill Lyndon giving the finger to an annoying journalist, which promptly became a front-page photo op. We were eventually found innocent of "lewd conduct" (we were, after all, protected by the Bill of Rights), but we did spend ten days on trial before an all-white, very straight jury. My favorite moment was when complainant George Hussey testified, under oath, that "sex is either holy, or in the home."

Such legal shenanigans were expensive. Even though the lawyers were pro bono, we had to be flown back to Denver to stand trial, and needed financial support throughout the trial's duration. In other cases, lawyers had to be paid. The troupe's business manager, Bill Grishonka (Graham), produced the first four light-show rock-and-roll dances in San Francisco as benefits for the Mime Troupe. They featured such performers as the Grateful Dead, Jefferson Airplane, Quicksilver Messenger Service, Moby Grape, and

The Loading Zone. Each of these events was sold out two or three times over, and Bill was so impressed that he leased the Fillmore himself, quit his job at the Mime Troupe, and became a rock promoter, which made him famous. Ronnie considered this a betrayal and never forgave him.

By late March of 1967 *The Minstrel Show* had been running for two years, and we were bone tired and broke. Ronnie wanted to cancel the show, but Bob Slattery, who was doubling now as our business manager, booked a quick last tour in April—Buffalo for a week at two thousand dollars, and on the way home one-nighters in Winnipeg, Calgary, and Vancouver. Commedia veteran Kent Minault was to replace John Condrin, who had left the troupe by this time.

The prairie province of Alberta is the Bible belt of Canada. The leader of the reigning Social Credit party preached fundamentalist sermons on the radio. A moron might have predicted that sending the Mime Troupe to the University of Calgary could engender trouble. But we had no morons in the troupe, so we forged ahead with our plans to perform.

The week in Buffalo was uneventful and we departed on schedule for Canada. As we were being processed by Canadian customs, our stage manager Lee Vaughn suddenly confided that he had some marijuana in his suitcase. My heart nearly stopped, but miraculously we slipped through undetected. I ordered him to clean out his suitcase, and then forgot about it.

At the university, we were assigned two student guides I'll call Judas and Judessa, who had apparently never considered fun as an operative mode of living. When they heard us (as they later testified) "laughing in the bathroom," they decided we must be high on drugs and called the Mounties.

The company was gathered in our impromptu dressing room under the gym when the Mounties arrived and asked to search our luggage. We raised a storm of protest, citing the Bill of Rights and the Constitution (neither of which exists in Canada) and so thoroughly confused them that they left to get legal advice. We took advantage of the respite to triple-check everyone's luggage for contraband.

We were confident when they returned, and watched smugly as they rifled through our socks and underwear, tie-dyed shirts, and raggedy blue jeans. Confidence changed to catastrophe when one of them discovered a bag of seeds and stems that hard-luck Lee had forgotten he had hidden in his sneakers. He was unceremoniously arrested and taken to Spy Hill Gaol.

When the school administration learned of Lee's arrest, they canceled the show. Without their money, we had no funds to travel to Vancouver. We countered the administration's move by asserting that (a) only the stage manager had been arrested so the company was still prepared to do the show according to contract and (b) it was the *students,* through their student council, who had hired us; we were answerable to them and not to the administration.

The administration resisted our interpretation, and we resisted their resistance. Honed by plenty of such "combat" experience, we had the added incentive of desperation. Each troupe member assumed a role: publicity, legal, rehearsal, show setup, and so on. We located a mimeograph machine and some willing students and flooded the campus with announcements of a rally to be held in the cafeteria the next afternoon to address the issue of student autonomy (essential to our survival). Afterward, we planned to perform off-campus in a downtown theater; the rally would also serve as publicity.

The next day at noon the cafeteria was jammed with curious students. We had erected a makeshift stage, borrowed a microphone and loudspeaker, and convinced two faculty members to join us onstage as a gesture of solidarity. The issue, we explained to the crowd, was that they, the students, were supposed to have autonomy in running their student unions. The administration had arbitrarily reversed one of their decisions. There was much cheering and whistling at this, and things were beginning to percolate when a school official entered the room accompanied by two Mounties in long black overcoats. The official's first act was to pull the plug on our loudspeaker, which couldn't have suited us better. Lack of amplification was no obstacle to actors whose vocal cords were calcified from performing outdoors. Furthermore, by pulling the plug, he graphically reinforced our argument about censorship. The crowd booed him violently, and the harassed official decided to have us arrested.

Reality often beggars the imagination. Picture this scene: the cafeteria jammed with students, surrounding a raised stage on which three young black men (one with a glass eye, wearing a five-foot-long striped knitted cap) and three young white men with long hair, blue jeans, and earrings are sitting, all strangers to the campus. Next to these outside agitators are two tweedy faculty members in jackets and ties, bearing mute, principled witness to their administration's injustices. At the official's signal, the Mounties rushed forward and arrested—*the two faculty members,* while the Mime Troupe members climbed off the stage and slipped away in the crowd!

There was no time to ponder minor miracles. We were stranded and broke in Golgotha—beg pardon: Calgary—with no way to get home. We had to figure out how to mount a show and attract an audience in a strange town while being sought for arrest.

Fifty phone calls later, we discovered Milton "call me Milt" Harradence, reputed to be the Melvin Belli of Canada. He was a flashy dude sporting a camel's hair trench coat who actually owned his own F-84 fighter jet. I'm certain he was the local fixer because he told us so, and we were relieved to know that he could "fix" our troubles. However, he wanted four thousand American dollars before he would lift a finger—and we didn't have money for breakfast.

Some authentic student guides, not the embryonic Rush Limbaughs we'd been assigned, led us to a subterranean student council office and a bank of precious telephones. The office was situated behind two glass walls that formed the intersection of two hallways. We rifled the Yellow Pages, commandeered the phones, and began organizing the myriad details necessary to produce a performance.

After half an hour's intensive work, someone looked up and noticed a small crowd of police officers standing in the hall, observing us through the glass as if they were trying to decide whether we might be the people they had been sent to arrest. Anticipating that they might surmount this intellectual challenge quickly, we segued seamlessly into a group improvisation of "students late to class"—checking watches, gathering notebooks and coats, exclaiming things like "Oh, shit, I can't be late to class *again!*" This piece of foolery actually got us out the door and halfway down a long corridor before we heard someone shout, "Stop in the name of the law" (really).

Our response was to run like hell. Our student mentors ran ahead to point the way. Doors burst open miraculously, yanked apart by students materializing from God-knows-where, indicating escape routes and shouting,

"This way!" and "Follow me!" They led us under steam pipes, through furnace and utility rooms with the police in hot pursuit. It seems funny now, but we were not laughing.

We burst through a final door and were blinded by the glare of sunlight and ice. We bulled our way toward the parking lot through waist-deep snow with the Mounties close behind us, still demanding that we "stop in the name of the law!" As if summoned by prayer, two cars appeared, driven by loyal students, and we divided our group, diving into different cars and speeding off in opposite directions, congratulating ourselves on our escape.

My car got away, but the other, stopped at a red light, was surrounded by Mounties who were, by now, *really* pissed. Kent Minault, Ron Stallings, and Ronnie Davis were taken by the Royal Canadian Mounted Police and searched thoroughly. They found one "seed" in Ronnie's pocket and "residue" in Stallings's and hustled them off to Spy Hill Gaol, without bail, charged with possession, a rap that carried a three-year sentence in Canada.

Ronnie was convinced that we had been set up by the student drivers, yet I was currently being sheltered in the house of mine. When he brought the next day's morning paper, with bold *red* headlines announcing the "drug bust" of the troupe, I imagined downtown Calgary swarming with citizens erecting stakes and piles of faggots to immolate the outsiders who had come to defile their children. I didn't like any of the things I could imagine—and liked even less the events that actually occurred.

Prior to the arrest of Ronnie and the others, Lee had been released and sent home to California on bail. Now he was in a quandary: If he showed up for his hearing, he could be found guilty and sent to prison. If he didn't, there was no chance that Kent, Ronnie, and Ron would get bail. To his credit, Lee opted to return, but Canadian customs purposefully detained him at the border. He missed his hearing and was arrested and thrown in jail with the others for jumping bail. Learning this, Jason, Willie, and I, still free but cut off from all support systems, worked the telephones relentlessly, trying to find help.

In San Francisco, other members of the troupe, spearheaded by fellow actor Emmett Grogan, organized a press conference that put our story on the wire services. Emmett also organized a parallel demonstration at the Canadian consulate in New York City, where poets Gregory Corso and Allen

Ginsberg appeared on our behalf. With its leader jailed, the troupe maintained itself on an emergency footing with actress Anne Bernstein running the office while Sandy Archer and Bob Hurwitt organized fund-raising benefits. Bob Scheer contacted Robert Kennedy's people, who offered strategy and advice. Everyone pitched in except Milt Harradence, our Canadian lawyer, who did nothing but attend press conferences and get photographed in his camel's hair trench coat. As Ronnie said later, "everyone in jail told me he was great. I should have noticed that all his clients were inside!"

Finally, Ronnie's brother contacted a business acquaintance in Canada who vouched for them, and the three were bailed out for $2,500 apiece. The anonymous benefactor who put up the money without a moment's hesitation was Ronnie's "archenemy" Bill Graham, now wealthy from his rock-and-roll light shows at the Fillmore Auditorium. He stood up for us, just as he supported numerous causes and individuals over the years, without regard for his personal relationship to us. We flew home chastened, bankrupt, and despondent about the troupe's future. The Canadian government must have been delighted to forget the whole thing, because the case just disappeared.

In October of 1991, I was in Paris filming *Bitter Moon* for Roman Polanski when a bundle of mail arrived from home for my fiftieth birthday. Included in the packet of cards and notes from friends was a newspaper account of Bill's death in a helicopter accident. Shortly before I had left for Paris to begin this film, Bill and I had passed an evening together, attending a fund-raiser for the Holocaust Oral History Project, run by a valiant cousin of mine named Lani Silver. Her organization has by hook and by crook collected more than 1,200 videotaped interviews with Holocaust survivors, despite being ignored by foundations that tell her they've "done the Holocaust." Bill had walked away from Auschwitz at eight years old. One of his sisters had died in his arms, and *he* was not done with the Holocaust; he was one of the project's staunchest angels.

Bill was ebullient that night. Months earlier, director Barry Levinson had asked him to play Meyer Lansky in his film *Bugsy*. Bill had called me in a panic: "I haven't acted in twenty years, Peter! What do I do?" I introduced him to Harold Guskin, an eminent acting coach in Manhattan, and they worked brilliantly together. Now Bill was proud of his work in the film, relaxed and healthy-looking, and obviously in love with the beautiful woman sitting next to him. When we parted, it was a tad sentimental, and he reflected emotionally on the years and miles we'd traveled as friends on parallel routes. I left feeling that the shadows haunting him had finally turned their attention elsewhere. In Paris on my fiftieth birthday, I learned that they'd only taken a coffee break.

6

growing a new skin

The troupe, although famous now, spent the spring of 1967 clambering out of the economic difficulties engendered by the Calgary misadventure. "Appeal IV," our last rock-and-roll light-show benefit, raised enough money to repay Bill Graham for our bail, but not much more. The shows in the park were barely breaking even, and college tours were not delivering enough cash to sustain us. The escalating intensity of the antiwar movement and the lure of groups like the Diggers was fragmenting troupe energy and commitment.

On May 1, Ron sent out a letter to thirty-five members of the company, firing them in a triage to save the core. When the dust settled (and it settled without rancor or blame, because the situation was so clearly desperate), those remaining began to prepare a national tour of a new show, *L'Aimant Militaire* (*The Military Lover*), a remake of an old Goldoni farce that we had revised to comment on the Vietnam War.

Because this was to be a long tour, we created several other, smaller shows to give ourselves a more varied repertoire. One was *Olive Pits*, another Goldoni adaptation, scripted by Peter Berg and me in one frenetic afternoon; we retired to separate rooms, each wrote a version, and then we returned to the rehearsal hall, where we cut and spliced the two scripts into a show that won the troupe a special OBIE (the off-Broadway awards presented by the *Village Voice*) later that year.

The third show was a small troupe classic, featuring nine-foot-tall puppets designed and built by Roberto La Morticella. The show had a short pithy title, designed to compress all its essentials into two words: *Eagle Fuck*.

Roberto was a stocky, cryptic man with the loyalties (and thick mustache) of an Italian anarchist. A welder by trade, he had a penchant for mammoth projects such as constructing out of telephone poles a children's playground apparatus in the shape of a dinosaur. He loved to make things with his hands and practiced a very direct, no-bullshit approach to issues and ideas.

La Morticella's analysis of the war in Vietnam was articulated by these gigantic puppets, draped in black shrouds and topped with mournful, skull-white papier-mâché heads, representing Vietnamese women. The "women" walked around carrying little puppet babies and going about their bucolic business for a few minutes, before an equally gargantuan eagle puppet with an enormous pink penis entered, fucked them, and killed them. End of show. Five minutes tops. Simple—eloquent even, like hitting a cat on the head with a hammer. We threw that playlet into the mix just to make sure the "great" drama schools of Yale and Carnegie Tech we were about to visit knew exactly where we stood on the issue.

On tour members would receive the princely sum of eighty dollars a week. It seems incredible today, but you could survive on eighty dollars a week in 1967 and have something to spare for marijuana and guitar strings. Life support was always hazardous in the troupe (and remains so today—current troupe members raise families on approximately two hundred dollars a week). We had no government grants or foundation support, no bookers or agents. Our loyalties were to the movement, each other, and our beliefs. We had become what we had intended—a guerrilla theater troupe—and we were totally committed to its roles, on and off stage.

By most measures the tour, which began on my twenty-sixth birthday, October 10, 1967, was a grand success: we made money, won prizes, and garnered extraordinary reviews. But in the midst of this bloom were some presentiments that my path with the company was coming to an end. I had become a peer in every regard. During the tour, for some forgotten reason, Sandy Archer and I were not speaking. In my self-righteous anger, I was aware that she had once appeared unapproachably exalted; the fact that I was now arguing with her and defending something of my own (even if it was stupid) crystallized a sense of my own evolution since our meeting only two years before.

Madison, Wisconsin, was a center of student intellectual ferment, like Cambridge and Berkeley, bustling with smart people and hot ideas. "There was music in the cafés at night, and revolution in the air." You could crash, get weed, meet great girls who would talk with you about books, music, and politics, and sleep with you if they felt like it. Madison was happening!

We were preparing to perform in the 1,500-seat college auditorium when some students asked us to announce a demonstration organized for the next day to protest the presence of recruiters from Dow Chemical (makers of napalm and Agent Orange) on campus. That night after our show, Ronnie made a curtain speech:

> We are from another area but would like to help you all here. We were told there will be a demonstration against the Dow recruiters tomorrow at 12:00, and we thought that you and we might all be there. We have learned through our experience that, after all, this country is our country, and if we don't like it, then we should try to change it, and if we can't change it, then we should destroy it. See you at the demonstration.

These were the types of speeches and sentiments that endeared the troupe to school administrators and public officials everywhere. I missed the demonstration, having overslept after a bawdy night with an undergraduate Valkyrie who was not about to let me go until I had decimated every ideological misconception and physical tension she had accumulated since birth. The demonstration evolved into a full-blown riot and late-twentieth-century readers are familiar enough with riots to render a description unnecessary.

We toured many of the famous Ivy League schools: Columbia, Brandeis, Boston University, MIT, Yale, and Harvard. After the immensely popular show at Yale, the troupe was invited to the inner sanctum of drama professor Robert Brustein, one of the reigning lights of the "new" theater. Brustein, seated dead center in a large, wood-paneled room, surrounded by adoring students in cable-knits and cords, proceeded to give *us* a lecture on guerrilla theater. Since we had struggled the last several years as guerrilla actors without the support of any foundations, stipends, institutions, charities, trust funds, or investments—since we had logged thousands of hours on the road and met with disappointments, accidents, physical abuse, arrest, threats, and danger—we felt that he might have had the humility to ask *us* at least one question on the subject. But I suppose one does not attend Yale to listen to people your parents have sent you there to avoid becoming, and we were all too tired to argue with him. I had played out this encounter one too many times, and the bottom suddenly fell out of my desire to enlist this particular group to our cause. The other actors must have felt similarly, because we reverted to our traditional "if-I-fuck-you-can-I-sleep-in-your-bed?" routine, which probably confirmed Brustein's opinion of us as an inconsequential fringe phenomenon. We left what should have been a memorable evening with a bad taste in our mouths.

The tour culminated in a triumphal visit to New York City, where we played for two weeks at Jonas Mekas's Filmmakers' Co-op and won rave reviews from all the papers. We gave a San Francisco–style outdoor performance of *Olive Pits* on Central Park's Sheep Meadow, for which the troupe was awarded its special OBIE. Everything we touched seemed to blossom, and the troupe's destiny seemed assured. However, the whole experience was no longer as fresh or as satisfying to me as it had once been, and the political and intellectual perspective that had so engaged me on first contact was now losing its edge. After all, if the society you are criticizing gives you a medal, how effective a vehicle for social change can theater be?

The tour ended with a bizarre personal event. After eighty-nine shows in ninety-one days, we finished, exhausted, on the East Coast. I took the cast to Turkey Ridge Farm, the site of my father's cattle business in the Pocono Mountains, to recuperate.

It was a glorious eastern autumn afternoon, one of those days when rainbows appear to have been dusted over the hills. The trees blazed in scarlets, russets, siennas, ochers, lime yellows, variegated oranges, and umbers, one outdoing another in the intensity of its annual good-bye. The occasional white-stemmed birch, bright yellow leaves resembling jets of burning propane, flared against this kaleidoscopic background like a marker beacon. The grass felt electrified, sizzling in the lush fields dotted with plump white cattle—the perfect day to unwind by dropping LSD.

I wandered off to a favorite spot in the far corner of a field. Just behind the stone row separating the field from the shadowy woods, twenty paces into the forest, two Indian grave mounds rested on the leafy ground like hard-boiled egg halves on a tabletop. Each had a pair of pristine white birch trees growing from what I assumed was the head of the grave. As the LSD announced its presence in my system, I stretched out on one, gazing up into the trees. My attention shifted from the twittering leaves to the elastic spaces flexing and contracting between them. My awareness rose like a bubble and burst into those spaces. I lay on my back for an edgeless period of time, letting the wind-whipped leaves sweep my identity away. The tensions and anxieties of the road, no longer contained by a discrete self, evaporated. My mind became wordless, and the husk that had contained it opened wide as a blooming flower.

At dusk, I walked back to the main house and settled on the front lawn to watch the sun go down. The perfume of the grass was overwhelming, and the earth beneath me, warm from the sun, was a comforting support. Bill Lyndon called to me from the doorway of the house. I was still under the effects of the acid, and his cry advanced toward me as if each sound was traveling on its own individual air current.

"Pe-e-e-t-e-e-r. T-e-e-le-e-ph-ph-o-n-e."

I walked through the shadowy kitchen to the bedroom my dad used when he stayed there. I picked up the phone. The handset resembled a petrified embryo, and my father's voice crackled out of its head: "Hiya, son."

I was not in good shape to speak to him. Things between us were generally edgy and complicated, punctuated by dangerous flares of temper as I grew older. My nervous system was too raw and vulnerable from the acid to deal with him at the moment, and I heard myself blurt out, "I'd rather be outside." My censors were drugged; the words had leaped out of my mouth, cruel and clear.

My father's voice was a tiny vibration locked inside the heavy handset. He performed a little pirouette of self-pity. "Jeesus! Well! Sorry I called, son. I was just . . ."

I tried to check this corrupt transaction before it gained momentum. I hadn't intended to make him feel bad. In fact, I had been impeccably trained to protect his feelings, no matter how cruelly or inappropriately he behaved. I stammered, trying to erase the stain I'd made on the moment, and finally, confused by the effort, I confessed, "Listen, Dad, I can't talk to you right now. I've taken LSD. I'm all right, but I just can't talk."

He started to growl, literally, and the telephone swelled with his anger. He began chanting, "The drugs have Got! To! Stop! The drugs have *Got* To Stop! If *you* don't stop them, *I'll stop them. And you know, I can be pretty fucking brutal when I have to be.*"

There it was again, the threat naked and inevitable as an extended talon. Normally, any solidity inside me would have buckled. Perhaps it was the acid, but for the first time now I heard quite clearly, within the armor of his rage, a disabling terror. With his defense transparent to me, I found the language to communicate with him.

"Listen, Daddy, I'm okay. Really. I'm okay. I love you. I'll call you back after this wears off, but I swear, I'm okay, I just can't talk now." Placated by this reassurance, his fear and anger subsided and he began to mumble, "Okay, okay, son. Take care of yourself, all right? Call me back, though. Okay?" He hung up. The rest of my day was glum, the edge definitely off my high.

Sometime later, I returned to the room to lie down. I was straight now but still fragile, and just as I settled, the phone rang again.

"Hello," I said.

It was my mother. "Your father's dead."

My mouth dried and my pulse trebled. I had heard her clearly, but still I said, "What?!"

"I said, 'Your father's dead,'" she repeated calmly, but her subtext was seething anger.

"Oh, my God," I said. "Is he really?"

"He might as *well* be," she said, indicating how grievously I had wounded him.

This psychic terrain was familiar, secured by known landmarks, and now my anger flared. I felt safe enough with her to attack. "You're protecting *his* life with *mine* again," I said, and hung up. I was on fire, as incendiary as the trees outside. I was unhappy. I was *normal.*

I returned to San Francisco with complicated feelings. Life on the road was fun, to be sure, but grueling. There was no way the troupe could be more pointed in its social critiques, yet it was about to be co-opted by the society it wanted to change. The problem seemed to lie with the very idea of theater itself.

My commitment to pursue social change wholeheartedly demanded that I break through the fourth wall of the stage and live consistently with my beliefs, not just during performances. Something remarkable was in the air. "Revolution" and "change" were the dominant subtexts of everyday activity. Even sybaritic members of the counterculture who were not committed to social change measured their personal style and behavior by their distance from the standards of "straight" people.

People were becoming tired of being relegated to watching and reading about the glittering elite who had all the fun and money. Being a "citizen" is a bit like being an audience member at a movie and watching the stars have sex with each other while you imagine yourself in their place. For the price of admission you can get so pumped full of brain candy that you forget you actually spend your days humping rubber at the Goodyear plant or bagging tampons down at the Safeway.

This social arrangement appeared a meager deal to increasing numbers of people, and the soapboxes of the sixties offered plenty of competitive visions for rectifying it. Utopian communalism vied with anarchism, which competed with revolutionary communism, each clamoring for public attention, each proffering its own perspective as the most useful tool for understanding and changing the status quo. But common to all these philosophical can openers was the underlying assumption that radical change was *necessary.*

From the Digger perspective (rapidly becoming my own), theater had been co-opted as another commodity, just as all the arts had become specialized as entertainment and/or decoration. Because audiences paid money at the door, they knew intuitively that what was presented onstage was part of a business and therefore not at all threatening to established values. If you did not like the message of a play, you were free to leave the event as unchanged as you would in leaving a store where you did not like the merchandise. I had come to feel that while an evening at the theater might be intellectually provocative, nothing about a theatrical event nested in the context of economic interchange could challenge the implicit forms and relationships of *shop, shopkeeper,* and *consumer.*

From within, every culture appears as seamless as a dream. To Jívaro warriors, for example, head-hunting is a high social and religious duty, not the barbarity it appears to us. If you accept without question premises of profit and private property and if you pursue those ends, even in the best of faith, then eventually the cultural mall we call America will stand before you, the product of your cumulative actions. No one will know precisely how it was built or for what purpose, and like goldfish in a bowl, we will no longer be able to imagine living outside the aquarium.

The Diggers believed that the antidote to such conditioning was personal authenticity: honoring one's inner directives and dreams by living in accord with them, no matter the consequences. Theater is obviously an appropriate vehicle for experimenting with such ideas, but the discipline appeared more and more circumscribed by the dominant culture's values. If theater had been co-opted and turned into another product in the cultural supermarket, weren't all efforts *inside* the market fruitless? All your skill and ability were just more packaging, and you wound up as just another product, this one labeled "radical." If we wanted to create a culture predicated on different premises, a *counter*-culture, we needed to escape the aquarium.

The option of standing outside the dominant culture and creating an alternative to it seemed achievable at the time. Visions of limitless possibilities inspired the Diggers much as they inspired the early nuclear fission researchers, who imagined a world without electric meters. And as these visions unleashed potent imaginative forces that affected actual behavior, they became *real.*

This line of inquiry evolved, for the Diggers, into the concept of "life acting." *Acting* is the way that humans behave and communicate with one another. You know that I am angry because I "act" angry: my voice sharpens, my movements become violent, my eyes express a hostile intention. The ability to notice these changes in my body and behavior offers obvious survival advantages, and humans have highly evolved skills decoding such signals. We are all experts. However, if I *pretend* to be angry, you will perceive that pretense; it will appear different to you than real anger.

Actors use this knowledge to reflect the life of the mind. When belief in a particular scripted moment fails us, we use our imaginations to manipulate our nervous systems so that we are *not* pretending but expressing actual feelings. Although stimulated by imagined events, these feelings are nonetheless real. The art of acting requires a consciousness of these procedures and the ability to choose or substitute one imaginative premise for another.

The Diggers attracted actors (trained or not) who wanted to employ these skills in their everyday lives, constructing events outside the theater that were "free," financially and structurally, so that they might exist outside of conventional expectations and defenses. A further refinement required conscious creation of a character, a persona for everyday life, who embodied one's highest social and spiritual aspirations; we wanted to imagine our most authentic and admirable self and act him or her out every day. In this way, each of us might *become* his or her own hero, as well as an engine of social change.

For me, this process of forming a new identity developed from an experience during college. At Grinnell, my friends Terry Bisson, George Wallace, Bennett Bean, and I sent away for peyote, a hallucinogenic cactus, from a mail order source in Texas. When the cactus arrived—thick, clotty, and deep green, tufted with cotton—we had no idea what to do with it, so we researched the subject in the library and found mention of a nearby peyote church among the local Powshiek Indians. We drove to the reservation in Tama, Iowa, and traded half our stash for instructions on how to prepare and ingest the cactus.

Peyote tastes something like the green moss at the bottom of a pond must taste. Managing to chew and swallow seven or eight buds apiece was an achievement. Nothing happened for a long while. Disappointed, Bisson rose to leave. Then he turned to the group and said, "Hey, my hands are dizzy." Everyone understood *exactly* what he meant and as if by magic we were all simultaneously transported into a realm where such things can be true. We went outside into a cold, dazzlingly starry night, stunned and shocked by the beauty of the world. We separated, wandering off to follow our own personal predilections. I felt as if I had been transformed into a small wolf and spent the greater part of the night dog-trotting effortlessly through the Iowa cornfields, following scents and colors, marveling at these newly heightened powers. At one point I stopped to look down and was amazed to see little dog tracks in the furrowed ground where my footprints should have been.

This event haunted me for years, and was too palpable to dismiss as a hallucination. Around the time that I left the Mime Troupe in 1967, I met Jim Koller, a fine poet and editor of a respected poetry magazine called *Coyote's Journal*. The logo of the journal was a Coyote footprint, and the first time I saw it I recognized it as the paw print I had seen frozen in the Iowa ground. I realized that the "small wolf" that had come alive inside me was actually a coyote. Not long afterwards, I met a Paiute-Shoshone shaman named Rolling Thunder with whom I became quite intimate. When I told him the story, he regarded me seriously and asked me what I was going to "do" about it. I had no idea what he meant or expected at the time, but during the turmoil of leaving the troupe and pondering my deepest intentions, I concluded that I had been offered an extraordinary gift and felt compelled to honor it. Without fully understanding why, or what it might mean to me, but needing to mark the occasion somehow, I began using Coyote as a last name. The change in identity itself would come somewhat later.

The Diggers were fascinated by what life might be like if lived in a consistently improvisational manner, and we dedicated ourselves to awakening others to this possibility. What might it be like not to be "lonesome for a hero," as Emmett Grogan used to say when describing "civilians" living by proxy, reveling in the achievements and adventures of others as a compensation for the meagerness of their own existence? This idea of life acting was a kind of mental nuclear fuel, and before it was diluted into the weak tea of *lifestyle* (which came to mean *spend* any way you choose), the concept galvanized our community. Our "life actor" par excellence was Grogan, whose response to political, social, and spiritual ferment was to create a unique and completely appropriate personality.

7

emmett: a life played for keeps

One day in early 1966, before Jessie left for good and before the first tours with the Mime Troupe, a lithe, freckled man with flinty Irish features walked in to observe one of our rehearsals. He had an arresting gait with a chiseled face thrust aggressively forward, as if it were impatient with the body behind it. His eyes were a cool blue, his face a mask, suggesting abundant anger and determination. Emmett Grogan had come to audition.

We struck up a conversation that carried us through the afternoon and a long walk back to our respective flats, which, it turned out, were on opposite corners of the same intersection of Fell and Steiner Streets. Emmett was a galvanizing storyteller and a new and immediate friend who subsequently changed my life in ways more profound than anyone I had met before.

If all of us are life-actors to some degree, Emmett was determined to be a life *star*. He carried with him the absorption of a born performer. Men and women *attended* when he arrived, moving through a room with the detached concentration of a shark. He had developed a sense of drama in his bearing, his cupped cigarette, his smoky, hooded eyes, which declared him a man on the wrong side of the law, a man with a past, a man who would not be deterred.

Emmett, born Eugene Grogan in Brooklyn, had been condemned to a life sentence at hard labor with his soul. He grew up in a culture whose values and goals were so sublimated to material ends as to be indivisible from them. As the son of a clerk who served wealthy clients, Emmett felt consigned to an obscure future, to viewing wealth and power from the wrong side of the counter. What do you do when your culture itself is the enemy? Eugene Grogan created *Emmett*. And he helped create the Diggers as the vehicle in which Emmett might star.

The original Digger movement began in England in April of 1649. Oliver "Ironsides" Cromwell, executioner of King Charles I, was now the protector of the empire. Cromwell had participated in the great insurgency that established constitutional monarchy in Britain. For many of his followers, however, this was not enough, and Gerrard Winstanley, a London cloth merchant and dissenting Christian, published a pamphlet, *Truth Lifting up Its Head Above the Scandals,* which established what became the basic principles of anarchy: that power corrupts; private property and freedom are mutually exclusive; and only in a society without rulers can people be free to act according to their consciences. His pamphlet *The Law of Freedom in a Platform* was dedicated to Cromwell.

Winstanley declared that the English civil wars had been fought not only against the king but against the great propertied lords as well and that since Charles had been executed, land should be made available to the very poor. To that end, he led a group of his followers to St. George's Hill, Surrey, to "dig" and cultivate the common land.

Food prices had reached record heights in the 1640s, and the number of Diggers very quickly doubled, alarming the Commonwealth government and local landowners. The Diggers were attacked by angry mobs, their spades taken, their crops destroyed, and their houses and carts burned. They were harassed by various legal means as well, but they abjured the use of violence. Though Winstanley's group was destroyed and he himself disappeared from political life except as a pamphleteer, the principles he espoused remained vital in English Protestant sects and became part of the basic tenets of the socialist tradition.

The San Francisco Diggers originated in the conjunction of the visionary acuity of Billy Murcott, a reclusive childhood friend of Emmett's, and Emmett's own genius as an actor and his flair for public theater. Billy had intuited that people had internalized cultural premises about the sanctity of private property and capital so completely as to have become addicted to wealth and status; the enchantment ran so deep and the identity with *job* was so absolute as to have eradicated inner wildness and personal expression not condoned by society. A quiet, stooped, curly-headed man with a perennially wistful expression and the ability to be completely invisible in a gathering, Billy read voraciously and spent long hours by himself, driving a cab and thinking. (Eventually he became a diamond cutter. Who knew?)

To be *free,* as Billy understood it, was the antidote to such addictions. For most people the word *free* means simply "without limits." Harnessed to the term *enterprise,* however, it has become a global force, intimating limitless wealth; as such it is the dominant engine of U.S. culture. The belief that vanquishing personal and structural limits is not only possible but necessary to successful living is so integral to American ways of thinking that assertions to the contrary are regarded as heretical. In fact, personal freedom, as it is colloquially understood, has lots of limits: it limits aspirations (to adult adjustment, for instance), creates continual cultural and economic upheavals, forces relentless adjustment on an overstressed population, ignores biological and social principles of interdependence and reciprocity, violates the integrity of the family and community, exhausts biological niches, and has strip-mined common courtesy and civility from public life. Freedom within the relentless pressures of a market-driven society appeared impossible precisely because of its stultifying effects on the imagination in all realms but the material.

From our point of view, freedom involved first liberating the imagination from economic assumptions of profit and private property that demanded existence at the expense of personal truthfulness and honor, then living according to personal authenticity and fidelity to inner directives and impulses. If enough people began to behave in this way, we believed, the culture would invariably change to accommodate them and become more compassionate and more human in the process.

There were two important corollaries to this assumption. Since we were all products of this culture and often could not be certain whether our impulses were truly self-generated and not unconsciously conditioned, we expanded the idea of freedom to include, first, anonymity (freedom from fame) and, second, freedom from money as both a clear dividing line between us and the majority culture, and as a test of our integrity. By eschewing payment and credit for what we did, we tried to guarantee that personal acts were never unconsciously predicated on the desire for fame or wealth. After all, if we were getting rich and/or famous from our activities, it would be hard to say that we were doing them for free.

Our hope was that if we were imaginative enough in creating social paradigms as free men and women, the example would be infectious and might produce self-directed (as opposed to coerced or manipulated) social change. People enjoying an existence that they imagined as best for them would be loath to surrender it and would be more likely to defend it. If this were to occur en masse, it would engender significant changes in our society.

From the Digger perspective, ideological analysis was often one more means of delaying the *action* necessary to manifest an alternative. Furthermore, ideological perspectives always devalue individuals and serve as the justification to sacrifice them when the ideology is threatened. As a case in point, consider Robert McNamara, sacrificing a generation of youth in Vietnam after concluding that the war was pointless, because he did not want to tarnish the dignity of the nation's leaders by criticizing them. We used to joke among ourselves that the Diggers would be "put up against the wall" not by the FBI or other forces of domestic oppression but by our peers on the Left who would readily sacrifice anyone who created impediments to their power and authority.

I remember vividly the first day in 1966 that I went to the Panhandle with Emmett to visit the Digger Free Food. Hearty stew was being ladled out of large steel milk cans and dispensed to a long line of ragged street people. Each portion was accompanied by a small loaf of bread resembling a mushroom because it had been baked in a one-pound coffee can and had expanded over the top to form a cap. The morning fog stung my cheeks, and my senses were sharpened by the spice of eucalyptus in the air. Emmett and I stood to one side. The line of waiting people, clutching their ubiquitous tin cups, passed through a large square constructed from six-foot-long bright yellow two-by-fours: the "Free Frame of Reference." In order to receive a meal, one stepped through and received a tiny yellow replica about two inches square, attached to a cord for wearing. People were encouraged to look through it and "frame" any piece of reality through this "free frame of reference," which allowed them a physical metaphor to reconstruct (or deconstruct) their worldview at their own pace and direction.

Emmett asked me if I'd like something to eat, and I said, "No, I'll leave it for people who need it."

He looked at me sharply. "That's not the point," he said, and his words pried open a door in my mind. The point was to do something that *you* wanted to do, for your own reasons. If you wanted to live in a world with free food, then *create* it and *participate* in it. Feeding people was not an act of charity but an act of responsibility to a personal vision.

In John Neihardt's book *Black Elk Speaks,* he describes how Black Elk's village *acted out* the dreams of the shaman, assuming roles and costumes and behaving according to his directions. This realization of a dream in the flesh is precisely what the Diggers sought to accomplish.

The deeper implications of anonymity were lost on Abbie Hoffman and Jerry Rubin, both of whom came to investigate our activities in late 1966. Abbie returned to New York and published a book (for sale) called *Free,* which catalogued every free service in the city of New York that supported truly needy people; these services were immediately swamped by an influx of suburban kids into the Lower East Side. He plastered his own name and picture on the book, thus advertising himself as a "leader" of the free counterculture. While egocentricity may be as authentic as anything else, performing under its influence does not represent a new form of any kind, and we criticized Abbie for confusing the issue.

Abbie was and remained a close friend of mine until his disappearance underground after selling drugs to an undercover narcotics cop, but a friend with whom the Diggers had pronounced disagreements. One morning he woke up Peter Berg by pounding on the door and shouting in his pronounced New England twang, "Petah, Petah, I bet you think I stole everything from ya, doncha?" This was indisputably true. Berg stumbled to the door, regarded the cheerful hairball before him as if he were sucking a lemon, then responded sleepily, "No, Abbie. I feel like I gave a good tool to an idiot." He closed the door, and that was the last time they spoke.

Emmett's personal relationships to the concepts of "anonymous" and "free" were always complex and ambiguous. His notion of anonymity was to give his name away and have others use it as their own. So many people claimed it for so many purposes that eventually some reporters asserted that there *was* no Emmett Grogan and that the name was a fiction created by the Diggers to confound the straight world. While Emmett's largesse was one way of demonstrating lack of attachment, it also made his name ubiquitous, and thus famous, among the cognoscenti.

Life with Grogan was a daily exercise in such contradictions, a constant refinement of my understanding of "truth." I was never sure precisely where and how the hair might be split. Arriving late for a meeting, he might excuse himself by telling a story about being attacked by street toughs out for revenge over some earlier event, the subtext being that *everyone* knew Emmett and had strong opinions about him. His friends usually accepted these stories without challenge, if "with a grain of salt," simply enjoying the drama of his life. If, however, a particularly outrageous claim pushed you to confront Emmett, he would always have a backup ready; he might remove his dark glasses with the air of a smug magician, revealing a blackened eye and wounds. The wounds were definitely real, but was the story? If it *was* true, was it completely or partially true? I never knew for sure.

"Never let them catch you in a lie," he said to me once, alerting me that he was aware of his self-dramatizing and also the extent to which "theater" was necessary to his work.

That work was to "act out" the life of your own hero, to live as you wanted to, to deny defeat and the myriad excuses that most people tender for their inability to be who they want. Since this idea of who we wanted to be was engendered in the imagination, imagination was the primary tool for its materialization.

All artists desire an audience, and while we might criticize our culture, some part of us wants at the same time to be acknowledged by it. For Emmett, this contradiction—this simultaneous spurning and yearning—became the crucifix on which he impaled himself. It does not require much imagination to see in the shape of a crucifix the outline of a syringe, and it is that ambivalent symbol of healing and death that symbolizes Emmett's dark side—his addiction to heroin and the indenturing of his personal autonomy to it.

Inventing a culture from scratch is an exhausting process, since everything must be reinvestigated. When the investigation is coupled to a belief in a noble mission, no limit or taboo can be accepted. If imagination knows no limits, why should we be concerned with the limits of our bodies? Drugs were utilized as tools in the quest for an imaginative and physical renaissance.

As edge dwellers, we were proud of being tougher, more experimental, more truthful, and less compromised than our peers, most of whom seemed more interested in easy assimilations—dope-and-long-hair-at-the-office or the marketing possibilities of the counterculture—than in real social alternatives. If their Hallmark Card philosophies were fueled by acid, grass, and hashish, we had all of these, plus heroin and amphetamines—the allies of such blues-life champions as Charlie Parker, Billie Holiday, foot soldiers in 'Nam, and all others who had faced the beast at close quarters and been consumed in the flames through which they tried to signal.

Hindsight has taught me that there is a ravenous, invisible twin haunting each of us. Despite "good works" and selfless sacrifice for noble causes, without unremitting vigilance, even tiny indulgences will betray high aims and deflect nourishment to this parasitic companion. Unfortunately, not even hindsight frees us from the consequences of such indulgence.

Emmett stuck me with a needle twice. The first time, he pierced my ear. "It'll change you," he said. We were in Sweet William's kitchen, not too long before he became a Hell's Angel. Lenore Kandel, William's olive-skinned poet-lover with her thick shiny braid, inscrutable smile, and fertile erotic imagination, hummed contentedly while she strung beads for the glittering curtains that festooned every window in the house. Sweet William's presence created ceremony; his grave face, with its high Mayan cheekbones and dark eyes, bore solemn witness as Emmett pierced my ear. Today it seems like no big deal, but Emmett was right. It did change me; it marked me as an outsider, drew me deeper into our confederation and a little farther from the pasty grip of civilian life.

The second time was in the living room of a famous bad-boy Hollywood movie star. This time the needle was a syringe, loaded with heroin. "It'll change ya," Emmett said, and it did. It changed a lot.

8

the invisible circus

I returned from the Mime Troupe tour in late 1967 and felt with the changing season a pleasing sense of spaciousness inside myself. Leaves had fallen from the trees in the Pennsylvania mountains bordering Turkey Ridge, and just as one could see greater distances through the bare branches, I felt that my life was revealing itself as new and open. For the first time since kindergarten, I was completely purposeless, rootless. I was free.

The draft was no longer an issue. At eighteen I had applied for conscientious objector status, but my application had been dismissed because my religious affiliations were not formal. In 1965, when I left graduate school, opposition to the war was appearing on all fronts. I had been summoned for my draft physical but a sympathetic army psychiatrist practically told me how to answer his questions so that he could give me a 1-Y deferment on psychological grounds. With that threat removed, and liberated from academia and the rigors of touring, I felt that my life was mine again to invent.

By 1967, San Francisco had become a symbol of freedom and license to the rest of the nation. I was straddling two worlds—still in the Mime Troupe but increasingly fascinated with the free-form, more radical street life of the Diggers.

The Diggers' home turf was San Francisco's Haight-Ashbury, a working-class, pleasantly interracial neighborhood of old Victorian homes bordering Golden Gate Park and near enough to the University of California Medical Center to offer cheap housing intended for med students. It was being inundated with young people from all over the country, and the city capitalized on the phenomenon: the national media were filled with articles about San Francisco, the Haight-Ashbury, and its Psychedelic Shop. The San Francisco Mime Troupe was even on the cover of a chamber of commerce brochure, despite the fact that the city had arrested and prosecuted the company! The counterculture was the "new thing."

Although it had been surfacing in the media for a while, the big announcement of the counterculture's "arrival" took place earlier that year with a major event. The Human Be-In had occurred on a lovely day, January 14, 1967, and newspapers and magazines transmitted photos and stories of the mass celebration into America's most remote communities. The nation knew that something was going on "out there." Paisley banners and flags stenciled with marijuana leaves fluttered in the balmy winds that seemed to be blessing the fifty thousand people assembled before a single stage crowded with celebrities and Haight Independent Proprietors (HIPs). Jerry Rubin was representing the "political aspect" of the counterculture, while Timothy Leary and Richard Alpert represented expanded consciousness and bliss. There were also a few genuine seers and artists like poet Gary Snyder, back from ten years of studying Zen in Japan; his old crony, Allen Ginsberg; and Zen master Shunryu Suzuki Roshi, abbot of the nearby San Francisco Zen Center, solid as a rock, smiling and enjoying himself.

Fifty thousand people took drugs, danced, painted their faces, dressed in outrageous costumes, crawled into the bushes and made love, fired up barbecues, pitched tents, and sold wares—crystals, tie-dyes, hash pipes, earrings, hair ties, and political tracts. Fifty thousand people played flutes, guitars, tambourines, tablas, bongos, congas, sitars, and saxophones, and sang, harmonized, and reveled in their number and variety, aware that they were an emergent social force.

The Diggers doubted that the event would benefit the neighborhood much or change its political realities, but a party is a party. It was our neighborhood and our community and also our receptive audience, so we were there too, giving away free turkeys donated by LSD mogul Stanley "Bear" Owsley. We had underestimated the impact this event would have on community solidarity and self-awareness and the ways it would trumpet the existence of the counterculture nationally. Individual freaks, isolated in heartland hometowns, were delighted to discover that there were thousands like them in San Francisco, who were prepared to embrace them as brothers and sisters; they wanted to be there too. More kids began arriving from everywhere. They served themselves up as sweatshop employees to the merchants and as customers to the dope dealers; they begged, scrounged, and hustled in order to survive. The Haight Independent Proprietors appeared at conferences with city officials discussing the "problems" of the community. People making money off the scene—the rock bands, merchants, and dope dealers—felt that publicity about the Haight would "change people's heads" and automatically generate changes in economic relationships and political structures—a fond hope, easier to entertain than the nine-hundred-pound gorilla of changing one's own life.

Time magazine coined the word *hippie* to describe the new pilgrims, juvenilizing the word *hipster* and trivializing in the same stroke those seeking alternatives to *Time*'s official reality.

The Haight had its own newspaper, the *San Francisco Oracle,* which for all its radical pretensions once refused to print a poem by Gary Snyder because it was "too negative and too political." The *Oracle* was colorful, full of treatises and manifestos, and about equal to any other paper in disguising opinion as fact.

In September of 1966, a week after the first issue of the *Oracle* appeared, a white San Francisco policeman had killed a black youth named Mathew Johnson fleeing in a stolen car. Word went out on the street that the boy was shot in the back, and the black community erupted. Social upheaval had been anticipated since the Watts riots in Los Angeles a year earlier, and when it arrived in the Bay Area, it arrived full of vengeance and wrath. The National Guard was called out as the rioting spread into the Fillmore district, which adjoined the Haight. Curfews were extended over both neighborhoods, sparking a flurry of political responses. Students for a Democratic Society (SDS) staged a march down Haight Street urging people to violate the curfew. The Haight merchants countered with signs urging people to stay out of trouble, and the Digger response was, predictably, "Do what you want." More than one hundred people were arrested on Haight Street for violating the curfew the first night.

Resistance to authority occurred on other fronts as well. Angered at again being refused money from the city's hotel-tax fund, in May of 1966 Ronnie Davis organized a large gathering of the city's artists at our studio to form the Artists' Liberation Front. Dedicated to "collective defense and offense," the ALF intended to bypass "official" city-sponsored art and bring recognition to the work of the community-based artists and people of color who were being ignored. A third of its members were Mime Troupers; the rest were progressive artists who dedicated their work to a broad range of social issues.

In response to the Be-In, the Diggers began brainstorming an event to announce and define our terms of engagement to this emergent youth culture. Our intention was to "assume freedom" as opposed to "winning" it. We agreed that the site of the event would be Glide Memorial Church, centrally located in San Francisco's seedy Tenderloin district. Run by a flamboyant African-American minister named Cecil Williams, who favored Afro "'dos" and tie-dyed dashikis, Glide had a boisterous congregation with a larger than normal representation of pimps, gays, addicts, hustlers, winos, and prostitutes of both sexes. Because of this constituency, Cecil and his church were highly tuned to the realities of the disenfranchised. We simply told them we wanted to have a "happening," which they assumed would be something like the colorful street fairs the Artists' Liberation Front had been sponsoring, and agreed to let us use their building.

The core of the Digger gang assembled to organize the event: Emmett and I, Peter Berg and Judy Goldhaft, poet Lenore Kandel and her lover Bill Fritsch, a couple so charismatic they could stop conversation simply by entering a room. Kent Minault arrived with his pal and psychic twin, Brooks Butcher, a Dionysianly handsome, high-energy fellow with merry eyes and curly brown hair whose life was dedicated to "revolution." Brooks brought his girlfriend Pam Parker, a stunning redhead with fearless humor and a steel-trap mind. An heir to the Parker Pen company, she cemented her relationship with us by springing for a Chevy pickup that the Diggers needed desperately but could not afford. Ever afterward, however, she "paid" her way with her imagination, not her checkbook.

Claude Hayward, dressed in an Italian anarchist black coat, represented *Ramparts* magazine. Nina Blasenheim, Phyllis Wilner, Sam, my live-in girlfriend and eventually the mother of my daughter, and Natural Suzanne (Siena Riffia) were there as well. Earlier in the day, I had stopped to pull the coat of poet and author Richard Brautigan, a tall, mustachioed wraith who wandered the Haight gravely peering at everything through round, frameless glasses. I'd asked him to join us, and now he stood owlishly at the rear of the room, swiveling his head as if he were seeking the sources of sound.

The rest were artists and social visionaries of every stripe, members of the vital community that was making San Francisco the locus of this emerging cultural force. No art or culture flourishes without such a community, and while I have singled out the individuals who were my friends, this is not to suggest that they were more important than the others in that room.

People began volunteering ideas, and before long all of Glide Church had been imaginatively divided into "territories," with people claiming responsibility for what might occur at each spot. Discussions were punctuated by whoops of delight as everyone vied to suggest more improbable and outrageous events. We were animated by a healthy sense of competition with the Human Be-In, hoping to create an event that would more accurately demonstrate what a free city celebration might be.

It was decided that a full weekend was required to immerse people into "assuming freedom." It was also agreed that except for a few handbills to announce the event, now named "The Invisible Circus: The Right of Spring," all advertisement would be by word of mouth.

On February 24, the night of the event, I was confined by illness to my cabin above Dolores Park, where I had landed after moving from Jessie's and my old apartment on Fell Street. The Invisible Circus was described in Emmett Grogan's book, *Ringolevio*, and since I wasn't there, I'll refer the curious to his account. Suffice it to say, the party got completely out of hand, with a couple fornicating in front of a staid Commission on Pornography discussion, naked belly dancers cavorting through the crowd, and the crowd itself practicing every conceivable excess in every available nook of the building. Richard Brautigan and Claude Hayward established a printing press in one room, and Richard wandered the floors, observing the madness, and then rushed back to print and distribute special handbills commenting on and alerting others to what he had observed, linking the participants in a prototypical World Wide Web. Horrified Glide administrators smothered the event in the wee hours of the first morning, but the players were partying in high gear by that time and retired to the beach to continue the festivities until the sun rose.

All the excesses, crudities, fantasies, and experimentation of this Digger party were consonant with the emerging spirit of the times and with our intention to stretch the envelope of cultural possibilities. Permission was the rule, and despite the chaos, the conflagration of taboos and bizarre behavior, no one was hurt, wounded, shunned, or scorned. I don't mean to suggest that bizarre behavior is the inevitable result of personal freedom or violating taboos, but in this case, it was simply like letting the steam out of a pressure cooker: once accomplished, it was not necessary to repeat.

Despite its high jinks and fun-loving spirit, the Haight was experiencing violent social spasms. It had become the geographical locus and metaphor for a burgeoning national movement. New shops catering to the "head" crowd lined the formerly mundane street, supplying the locals and luring tourists with the accoutrements of the new lifestyle: Mnasidika (leathers); In Gear (mod clothes); the Blushing Peony (boutique); the I/Thou (coffee shop); the Psychedelic Shop (enlightened literature and accoutrements); the House of Richard (Mexican drag); the Blue Unicorn (a coffee shop dating from Beatnik times that Bob Stubbs had started for a hundred dollars and maintained by selling used books, records, and secondhand clothes, as well as coffee and staples); and the Print Mint (art supplies and staples). These new shops featured colorful signs and window displays and ubiquitous advertising posters in psychedelic graphics; they transformed the neighborhood.

The merchants had a problem, however, because the burgeoning population of street people had no money. The proprietors accused them of intimidating paying customers by begging in the doorways. (Sound familiar?) Some shop owners, like the Thelin brothers at the Psychedelic Shop and the crew at the Blue Unicorn, remained loyal to the street culture and offered quiet spaces where people could detox from chemical or sensory overload. Other merchants hired street people at feudal wages to keep the rest of the poor away. Various charities like the Haight-Ashbury Switchboard (which located bed space, lawyers, and bail and served as a message drop) and the HIP Job Co-op were established to address the problems caused by the unmanageable influx of new souls and the alienation growing between them and the merchants. These were well intended but essentially Band-Aid measures. The Diggers were particularly piqued with the HIP Job Co-op, which took advantage of the desperation of runaways by offering them sweatshop wages to make the "love" objects sold in local stores.

Tourist buses began including Haight Street in their itineraries, and middle-class people from faraway places began photographing us as if we were exotic natives observed on safari. (The tourism diminished when we responded by spray painting the windows of the buses and the camera lenses.)

The police were rousting street people in a heavy-handed manner. The same kids magnetizing the tourist dollars were being swept off the streets while the media simultaneously baited feature stories about San Francisco with their photos. This galvanized us to action, and the Digger Free Food, free medical clinics, free crash pads, and Free Store were responses to this hypocrisy.

The police response to the problems was the creation of a unit called the S-Squad, shortened to SS by the street people. It developed a well-earned reputation for brutality and nastiness. But the overzealousness of the police exacerbated difficulties for the merchants when customers were arrested along with the indigent. (The two groups were, after all, indistinguishable.) Before long, the Haight merchants were meeting with the police to "improve community relations," and this cooperation with the authorities created some definite advantages for them. Newspapers, reporting on the meetings and the spirit of cooperation among the "good hippies," printed the names of the shopkeepers *and* their shops *and* the merchandise they offered for sale. Greyline tourist buses rolled through the neighborhood once again.

Exploited and divided as it was, the Haight bustled with life for those in tune with it. The street itself was the real scene: a down-and-dirty, do-your-own-thing public stage running between Stanyan and Masonic Streets. You could sing, beg, get high, cruise for sex partners, plot the overthrow of the government, sleep, be mad, or do what you would there. It was liberated turf. One night, fellow *Minstrel Show* performers Willie B., Jason, and I were lounging and singing a cappella on Haight Street near Ashbury. People gathered to listen, and as they clapped in rhythm and expressed their appreciation, the spirit became infectious. Almost imperceptibly, the street filled with partying people who transformed it into an impromptu mall. A volleyball game materialized, using the high-tension bus lines as a net. Groups of black people wandered cautiously up from the Fillmore, testing the atmosphere to determine if they were welcome. Discovering that they were, they joined the party, raising the stakes in the doo-wop competitions, joining the volleyball game and the dancing hordes of people who had claimed the street as their own.

The police were dumbfounded and finally erected barricades at the two "ends" of Haight Street, letting the party roll on rather than risk a riot. Long before Woodstock, dozens of such spontaneous dress rehearsals were expressing people's desires for social harmony and real community.

One morning San Francisco awoke to discover that walls, freeway columns, and fences had been plastered with five-foot-high posters of two enigmatic Chinese men in pajamas, lounging on a street corner in the relaxed and at-home posture of hipsters everywhere. Over their heads was the Chinese ideogram for revolution, and under their feet were the cryptic words "1% Free." The poster was designed by Peter Berg, executed with stencils by artist Mike McKibbon (drawn from a turn-of-the-century photo of tong hit men found in a library book), and a group of us had spent a long night pasting them up in every neighborhood in the city.

The slogan "1% Free" was ambiguously received. Some thought it meant that the Haight merchants should dedicate 1 percent of their profits to the community, while others felt it meant that only 1 percent of the population lived autonomously. The *L.A. Free Press* misread the posters and published a piece declaring the Diggers to be common stickup artists out for a piece of the pie. After the *Free Press* story broke, local media swarmed us like flies, trying to reach Emmett or other Digger "spokespersons." Someone steered them to me at the Mime Troupe. Producer Zev Putterman wanted me for a new TV talk-show pilot to be called *The Les Crane Show.* Bart Lytton, the chairman of Lytton Industries, and I were to debate for the TV audience. "It will be good for your group," Putterman crooned smoothly, ignorant of our intentions, "it'll get your point of view across."

I certainly could not appear on television as a Digger, since offering myself as a spokesperson would have violated the truth and group precepts, so I agreed to appear only as a member of the San Francisco Mime Troupe. I was already familiar with Bertolt Brecht's warning that attempting to use the media self-servingly is self-deception. But my head was turned at the prospect of a national audience for radical ideas, and being a zealous young man with something to say, I jumped at the opportunity. Knowing I was only a cultural Ritz cracker, I smeared myself with myself and offered the tidbit to the maw of television.

Les Crane was an edgeless fellow of the type that TV talk shows tend to favor, the kind of man who demonstrated his hipness by wearing bluejeans below his suit jacket when he interviewed Bob Dylan. Bart Lytton was a thickly built, mischievous rogue. The show was going to pit Bart and me against each other like unequal gladiators: a mature, corporate chief executive millionaire to represent democratic capitalism, and myself, a callow, unknown, penniless actor representing social change. Despite producer Putterman's loading the deck in favor of the status quo, I did not behave as the frothing antagonist they had expected. I managed to hold my ground and be charming and quick-witted enough that, at the close of the show, Bart tipped his head to me on camera and graciously said "touché," indicating that he felt that I had acquitted myself well. Others must have felt that the show was interesting, because it did go on to national syndication. In what might have been a cautionary episode about my future life in show business, I found myself, with Peter Berg and Sweet William, stranded, absolutely broke, and hungry in Los Angeles the following year. I contacted Zev Putterman and asked for a hundred dollars to get us fed and home, feeling that I had contributed in some manner to his success as the producer of a national show. His response was, "I only give money to Synanon" and he hung up. (Synanon was a drug treatment center fashionable at the time.)

As the summer of 1967 (trumpeted by the Haight merchants as the "Summer of Love") approached, a number of older hands realized that the area was poised to become unlivable due to the accelerated influx of new residents. Furthermore, the street itself was no longer necessary as the primary staging area for anyone but the Haight merchants. It was obvious that we could not craft an autonomous life on top of the asphalt, and many people planned moves to the country or, like myself, simply moved to cheaper, less crowded neighborhoods.

9

edge city

My first move out of the Haight was only as far as the intersection of Pine and Divisadero, to a railroad flat, a series of rooms strung on a long hallway in a wooden Victorian two-family house. Karl Rosenberg and I had been evicted from Mrs. Beltramo's Steiner Street penthouse for allowing the tiny kitchen to be used as a Digger galley, and it was here, just before I left for my last tour with the Mime Troupe, that I met a woman who was to figure prominently in my life, and moved her in to share the flat with me.

Eileen Ewing was the firstborn of a prosperous Louisiana doctor who had wanted a son and consequently nicknamed his daughter Sam. She had, in her family's estimation, made a mess of her life, quitting college to run off with artists, freaks, and hippies. She was tall and willowy, proud of her stunning figure, with the kind of Scandinavian coloring and chiseled features that grace fashion magazine covers. The day she accompanied a girlfriend I was seeing into the Mime Troupe office, I knew only that we were attracted to each other. I learned later that she couldn't spell *consequences,* and I couldn't have cared less about them.

In Sam's personality, boldness cloaked confusion and self-doubt, like a massive bronze constructed around a flawed armature. On the day she moved in with me, she borrowed some money to rescue a trunk with all of her possessions. I noticed later that all her departures tended to be messy and abrupt. Over the years, she has moved more often and more precipitously than anyone I have ever known, abandoning homes, property, and plans in a moment as if her psyche were only one step ahead of a repossessor. The sparks between us eventually produced an adored daughter, much psychic turmoil and suffering, and years of estrangement. She attached herself to me with an ardor that was frightening and sometimes suffocating, and I was about as reliable an anchorage for her hopes as a junkie guarding a drug stash. My casual betrayals of the relationship were exacerbated by the libidinous attitudes of the times and the opportunities I enjoyed as an actor. I couldn't have remained faithful to Sam if she had tied me to the bed, and my countless infidelities and her imaginative revenges produced predictable fissures in our relationship. Just how deeply those faults had riven the bedrock of her personality, I only discovered when we got together to talk things over for this book, twenty-five years later.

We began on her back porch with the easy intimacy of people who have shown one another their worst and best and managed to survive. When the subject switched to our personal relationship, however, she became upset as the painful memories overwhelmed her. Her throat swelled with rage, and her speech was venomous and breathtaking in its intensity. I had the lucky intuition to sit silently and let it wash over me like a caustic bath without trying to defend myself. When she was finished, I apologized, sincerely shocked at the extent of the pain I had caused and chastened by seeing my behavior from her point of view. I reminded her that she had always been a special person to me, honored as a skilled artisan and as the mother of our beloved daughter, and that while I had been a young and unconscious fool, my intentions had never been malicious. In that instant, something passed away from her face like the shadow of a cloud racing over a hill, and lightness and youth returned to her spirit; it was a stunning transformation. It made me sad to consider what a fearsome price she had paid for something as evanescent as love, but since that moment, whatever beasts were haunting the space between us moved away for good.

On my return from the final Mime Troupe tour, the character of our apartment changed with the arrival of Claude Hayward, his feral companion Helene, and the Communication Company. Claude was a ferret-faced guy with an easy laugh and furtive manner who had recently left the staff of *Ramparts* magazine. Helene was 120 pounds of condensed hostility; her unmanaged thicket of black hair made her look as if she had just participated in a classroom experiment on static electricity. She disguised her abundant anger behind honeyed bonhomie and an engaging smile, but she could have swindled a shell-game hustler and would have stolen a wooden leg without compunction. After each of their visits, personal possessions disappeared as if they had been rubbed out by cinematic special effects. Helene would steal your sleeping bag!

An anarchist by temperament as well as a skilled thief, Claude had somehow come into possession of Gestetner machines, which electronically cut stencils for mimeographing. Before the advent of desktop publishing, these Gestetners were the state of the art, allowing photographs and graphics to be reproduced cheaply on readily available mimeograph equipment. This technology (and these liberated machines) became the foundation of the Communication Company, the public information arm of the Diggers, a service offered by Claude and Chester Anderson to the larger community. Under Claude's direction, and later for the *Free City News* under the skilled mentoring of Freeman House and David Simpson, these machines produced such stunning documents that even the Gestetner company (from whom they had been stolen) subscribed for the free handouts, incredulous at how their machines were being used to "paint" and wanting to understand the process.

The Diggers printed broadsides constantly: free handouts of exhortation and provocation; analysis of contemporary events from a free point of view; the condensed (or expanded) result of late-night jawboning among Berg, Sweet William, Kent, Emmett, me, and whoever ambled in to join us around the Cribari wine jug of an evening. (While women were usually present at such sessions, they more often than not seemed content to chat among themselves or laugh at us, perhaps because they managed the lion's share of the physical work, a point to be clarified later.)

Digger papers had several modes. They could be as simple as a photograph of a human spine bracketed by the words "INVISIBLE GOVERNMENT"; they could be succinct expressions of true insight or blather that required concentrated effort to decipher. Consider the following:

THERE IS A GREAT DEAL TO BE SILENT ABOUT
Contemporary history is a money conspiracy—the key to the
atom. The facade of present seeming normalcy shows signs of
weathering; each day the cement crumbles a little more—portents
of chaos everywhere as we grow aware of our own nakedness and
impotence, our nothingness—time is shrinking into itself. Only
the present seems to hold possibility. . . . Chaos is real world—
shifting, changing, slipping out of grasp. Meaning only found
beyond experience. Basic impulse always religious—a cold light
on our own incompleteness. Like a debauched child's face.

    printed 5/29/67 by the communication company (ups) chicken
little was right.

At other times they were very clear, such as this response to a pronounce-
ment by a local judge:

MUNICIPAL COURT—DIVISION 12—JUDGE AXLEROD
BLUES
    How many people does Judge Axlerod clothe, feed, house?
    What
    digger
    has
    ever taken
           yr money.
    What judge has ever taken you home?
    Judges are all about property.
    They are a commodity, replaceable, buyable, sellable,
    expendable . . . obsolescent. Stay out of their way as they break
down. Expect no mercy, no grace.
                KNOW THEM FOR WHAT THEY ARE.

    Everything we have belongs to you. . . . .
                The Diggers
          Communication Company

Still others were an opportunity to share a vision and disseminate ideas
for public colloquy, as in the following excerpt:

where is PUBLIC at?
where are PUBLIC streets at?
therefore
an erection in the Panhandle.
the PUBLIC parks—here you can pitch a tent anytime.
PUBLIC streets on riot with truckloads of arms protecting
the private property of super-charging merchants.

the PUBLIC beaches—here you can paddy-cake any old time.

PUBLIC streets where fantasy laws justify the concepts of
LOITERING &
VAGRANCY.
the PUBLIC schools—here you can be conditioned to PUBLIC
opinion in order to express yourself in
the PUBLIC consensus.

the PUBLIC officers—here is the understanding of PUBLIC
service.

WHERE IN THE STREET CAN TWO FINGERS TOUCH
WHERE IN THE STREET CAN YOU GET OUT OF
NEIGHBORHOODS.
WHERE IN THE STREET CAN YOU ESCAPE THE
ECONOMIC NET.
WHERE IN THE STREET CAN YOU TRIP OUT YOUR
DOOR AND SMILE AT SINCERE.
WHERE IN THE STREET CAN YOU HITCH A HIKE
DOWN THE BLOCK.
WHERE IN THE STREET CAN YOU TAKE OFF YOUR
SHOES AND SING AND
DANCE WITHOUT DISTURBING THE DEATH CALLED
PEACE.

Claude's "thing" was to offer his printing services to groups with which he was in sympathy, and one day two young black men came to discuss a printing request. The older of the two and the obvious leader was a sturdy, handsome man of about twenty-five with an open, intelligent face and a passion in his speech that compelled attention. His companion could not have been more than sixteen. Huey Newton, commander in chief, and Bobby Hutton, a foot soldier in the newly formed Black Panther party, had decided that their organization needed a newspaper and had come to see the Diggers about helping them produce one. (Bobby died in a hail of police bullets not long after our meeting.)

We spoke at length, and as a result of that day's conversation, the first and (I think) the second issues of the Black Panther party newspaper were printed by the Communication Company.

The relationship that developed between the Diggers and the Black Panthers was only tangentially political. The Diggers were not "serving" black causes out of ideological loyalty. The Haight-Ashbury district bordered the Fillmore, the black ghetto of San Francisco, and black people mingled freely in the Haight Street counterculture. We shared the same place, followed our respective visions, and were allied by territory and a common love of freedom. Because our visions were congruent at least in these ways, because we faced common enemies, and perhaps primarily because we were neighbors, we forged an alliance.

The Diggers created a series of "free stores," which were little more than bins of take-what-you-like goods. Peter Berg refined Arthur Lisch's original free store on Frederick Street with Trip Without a Ticket, a free store designed to encourage reflection on the relationships among goods and roles —owner, employee, customer—implied by a store. A number of us agreed to help him, and we begged the money from a patron and rented a building at the corner of Cole and Carl Streets. We painted the Free Store interior a tasteful white with donated paint, scavenged counters, racks, and hangers, and began filling them with the available detritus of an industrial culture: clothes, jewelry, televisions, kitchen implements, discarded skis and trunks, tennis rackets, and waffle irons. The store's existence advertised its own premise: "stuff" is easy to acquire; why trade time in thrall in order to get it?

Not only were the goods in the Free Store free but so were the *roles*. Customers might ask to see the manager and be informed that *they* were the manager. Some people then froze, unsure how to respond. Some would leave, but some "got it" and accepted the invitation to redo the store according to their own plan, which was the point. Your life was your own, and if you could leap the hurdles of programmed expectations and self-imposed limits, the future promised boundless possibilities. If you couldn't, you had to understand this either as a natural limit or as one to be remedied. There was no one or no system to blame. The condition of freedom was presented as an actual possibility, not "a message," the subtext of a play or literary tract. Transmission through action, heightened by the reality that we were living in the liberated commons of the Haight, made the situation potent and its implications radical.

One day, on my shift as "manager," I noticed an obviously poor black woman furtively stuffing clothing into a large paper bag. When I approached her, she turned away from the bag coolly, pretending that it wasn't hers. Smiling pleasantly, I returned the bag to her. "You can't steal here," I said.

She became indignant. "I wasn't stealing!"

"I know," I said amiably, "but you *thought* you were stealing. You can't steal here because it's a Free Store. Read the sign—everything is free! You can have the whole fucking store if you feel like it. You can take over and tell me to get lost."

She looked at me long and hard, and I went to the rack and fingered a thick sweater. "This?" I queried. She looked at it critically, then shook her head. "No, I don't like the color. What about that one?" We spent a good part of the morning "shopping" together. About a week later, she returned with a tray of doughnuts, probably day-olds from a bakery somewhere. She strolled in casually, set them on the counter for others to share, and went to browse the racks. She knew which end was up.

More than a few times, soldiers used the Free Store as a trampoline from which they could bounce out of the military. The Diggers felt that the war in Vietnam benefited a class of people who were neither our allies nor our friends. Unlike some who opposed the war, we respected the boys who went over there and did not presume to judge their intentions or morality. We preferred them alive and unscarred, however, so when we encountered soldiers who had changed their minds about military service, we did what we could to help.

Through the antiwar underground, we had acquired a number of draft-card blanks and the coded information for filling them in so that they would pass inspection. We had inherited a couple of "liberated" seals from draft offices in other states, and whispers circulated on the street that if someone from the armed forces felt moved to register a personal protest against the war by leaving the service, the Free Store was the place to go. On my watch, several men entered in uniform, picked civilian clothes off the rack, changed, and left behind their army-issue duds. After a few minutes of elliptical conversation, Billy from Iowa might leave as Phil from Florida, and William from Minneapolis as Robert from Memphis. They slipped into the maelstrom of Haight Street, disappearing into whatever future they imagined for themselves.

The Free Store was only one "theater" in the struggle to create escape hatches in daily life. Others did the same work differently. One morning, Ron Thelin, founder of the Psychedelic Shop, and Arthur Lisch, the Quaker mediator between the Diggers and Glide Church, set up an impeccably prepared breakfast table on the shoulder of Highway 101 during morning rush hour. Dazed commuters on their way to work were startled to see a table with four chairs, lovely crystal and linen, orange juice, coffee, and a full breakfast at the side of the road. Ron and Arthur sat calmly reading the papers, three feet from the flow of traffic. Two empty chairs and full place settings provided an invitation to anyone brave enough to stop the car and reinvent his or her life. No one did.

Another afternoon Peter Berg and Judy Goldhaft filled a flatbed truck with half-naked belly dancers and conga drummers and drove down the middle of Montgomery Street, the city's financial section. The women swayed invitingly, the music pulsed, wine and marijuana were passed around and offered to open-mouthed bystanders. Invitations were extended to anyone who felt like "climbing on the bandwagon."

The instruments of change were not necessarily events but sometimes individuals. One day, as I was helping unload the free food in the Panhandle, a young woman with a radiant smile appeared at my side, waiting to receive a tray of food to pass on. Dressed in a yellow India-print dress, her round face framed by an unruly mop of sandy hair, she radiated a captivating enthusiasm and joy.

"Who's she?" I asked Emmett, whose response was a proprietary: "Stay away from her." I guessed that he had already taken her under his personal purview, or was planning to, or might want to, or might want me to think that he had, but from that day on she and I became intimate friends. Her name was Phyllis Wilner, and she was a first among equals in the Diggers.

Phyllis had fled New York and the chaos of life with a clinically schizo-phrenic mother at fourteen, opting for the safer unpredictability of life on the streets. She possessed a wacky and sunny personality, and the sheer number of fortunate events that occurred randomly to and around her made me believe that she was attended by a magical grace. I remember her leaving the Treat Street communal house one morning, saying, "I wish I had a bicycle." She returned that evening wheeling an expensive ten-speed through the door and recounted a tale of being picked up hitchhiking by a young man (whose life story and metaphysical beliefs she recounted in great detail) en route to deliver his bike to the Goodwill because he was moving out of town and could not take it with him.

She moved a mattress onto the tiny back porch of our Pine Street apartment for a while, radiating optimism and cheer through the house until she moved on to another and then another Free Family abode in nomadic fashion. If a problem existed somewhere in the community, such as Natural Suzanne delivering twins and having no husband, Phyllis solved it by moving in to care for the household until something else could be arranged, even if that "something else" might take months.

After many years of this peripatetic life, which included spending time with the Hell's Angels, homesteading in the New Mexico wilderness, making numerous cross-country jaunts to New York City and then back, baking at the Free Bakery in Oakland, and gardening and looking after babies at Black Bear Ranch in the Trinity-Siskiyou Wilderness, Phyllis returned to school. She took a high school equivalency test, completed nursing school, and somehow made her way to a refugee camp in the Himalayas, where she aided Tibetan refugees. She returned a year later, covered with bangles and carrying presents for almost everyone. (Mine were left in a car she'd hitched home in.) She took a job in the psychiatric ward at San Francisco General. Given her empathy and fluid sense of reality, it was not surprising that she became a favorite with the patients. Once she calmed a man who had been terrorizing the floor, complaining constantly about being cold and damaging his room by building a small fire in his metal wastebasket. Phyllis hunkered over it, warming her hands and talking brightly to him, until he joined her. Having finally been acknowledged, he was open to discourse, and they agreed that he might modify some of the more objectionable aspects of his behavior. This was her technique with everyone.

In 1974 she fell in love with and married John Chesbro, a droll, quiet man with a penchant for carpentry and a demon chewing on the back of his head that had once driven him to a suicide attempt and short residence in a psych ward. Phyllis seemed able to placate it, and they moved north to live near the hip college town of Arcata, California, where they built a fairytale life in a north woods cottage, berrying and harvesting wild clams and mussels.

Some years later, as their paths were diverging, John granted himself a total divorce from everything by committing suicide. Phyllis attended to the sad business of sorting out and disposing of the artifacts of their life and eventually found her way to Lynn, a woman friend, an Olympic-class athlete and professor at Humboldt State College with whom she began to share a house. Today, Phyllis is still "helping out," serving in an emergency mobile crisis center, teaching, helping a sick friend, and keeping herself healthy. She still burns like a sun, and her example informs my anger whenever pundits dismiss the sixties as a playpen for lethargic, self-indulgent people and blame them for today's social problems.

There is, of course, a political agenda motivating such misinformation. Phyllis was one among many, and each one had an equally colorful story and contributed something of worth. Our collective energy was changing the Haight. The free food services had been assumed by a local church; Dr. David Smith had established the Haight Ashbury Free Medical Clinic; The Trip Without a Ticket was serving scores of customers and many local stores had instituted "free" boxes of cast-offs or couldn't-sells free for the taking. The Diggers had created palpable change and were widely respected and regarded. Our advice was sought, we were interviewed and queried for articles and books, and no matter how diligently we pursued anonymity, we were, in the counterculture at least, becoming famous.

10

crossing the free frame of reference

A feeling of potential charged the air like pollen in 1967. It was ubiquitous, random, and shimmering with promise. Ideas seemed nourishing enough to sustain life. I felt as if I had emerged from a chrysalis and was stretching new wings at the edge of a boundless savanna.

As the potentials for change implied by Digger action and philosophy became clearer, it was difficult for me to remain in the limited context of the Mime Troupe. Life outside the theater appeared more challenging, and my talents as an actor were bringing me personal notoriety that conflicted with the Diggers' goal of perfect anonymity. I bade a bittersweet good-bye to Ronnie and the company of dear friends and abandoned myself to an undefined future.

The Digger family released spores everywhere. The call to be "free" was infectious, and people across the country accepted the challenge of playing life in that key. Small communities coalesced everywhere, intuitively connected to the new sensibility and working to express it more fully. The Diggers were only one such.

One of our self-appointed tasks was the framing of large public celebrations for the solstices and equinoxes to embrace disparate communities into the most generous, inclusive frame of reference possible. In fact, the genius of these festivals (and I remember this as Peter Berg's contribution) was the assumption of a *planetary* frame of reference. People often expressed amazement at how thousands of disparate and often antithetical groups—Hell's Angels, Black Panthers, gay collectives, merchants, runaways, soldiers on leave, flower children, deserters, and civilians—could interact so peacefully at our parties. But accepting the planet as the most inclusive frame of reference subliminally unites rather than divides people, giving them all equal standing under the sun, and diminishes opportunities for contested space, status differentials, and violence.

In marked contrast to many large commercial events, the free parties we sponsored in Golden Gate Park had a luminous air about them. It was lovely to wander about and witness imagination made manifest as people turned their minds inside out. Jungians would have had a field day categorizing archetypes, as images from all of human history materialized on the green swards of the park: aborigines, Tonto, Inquistor-General Torquemada, Shiva holy men, cowboy bikers, every shade of gender bender, flower children, urban junkies, stockbrokers with cautiously expressed face paint, dentists on dope, real estate agents disguised as flower children. All the local bands played to their own community for free. Music and dance wove everything into a brocade, and the sky became a common tent for activities ranging from the sweet to the bizarre: face painting and clowning for the children, or Roy Ballard and friends from the Black Man's Free Store, a parallel to the Trip Without a Ticket based in the predominantly black Fillmore district, basting a spitted white mannequin over a charcoal pit.

Dionysus ruled, and in the ample arena that acceptance created, people partied and danced, shared food, made new friends, and otherwise touched the real and common content of their lives. Freedom forced people to improvise at the edges of their imagination in a common quest for transformation. It was not a bad dream; like all utopian visions it was rooted in high expectations about what people could accomplish when working in concert.

The Diggers operated at the edges of the counterculture, expanding it through alliances and recombinations that transformed our core group beyond recognition. We came to refer to this larger, centerless alliance as the

Free Family. One such conjunction, between the Diggers and the Hell's Angels, plays an important role in the next part of the story. It came about in an improbable way.

On December 17, 1967, a parade was held in the Haight called "The Death of Money." Marchers carried a coffin marked with dollar signs and the witness-participants blew pennywhistles, flashed car mirrors into the faces of passive onlookers (to symbolize that they were actually watching themselves), and passed out posters with the word NOW printed on them in large black letters. Phyllis Wilner stood on the back of Hell's Angel Hairy Henry's motorcycle, and they cruised down the white line between rows of stalled traffic.

Traffic was stalled because the authorities had not been forewarned about the morning's "event." The cops were infuriated: there was no permit for this demonstration and no way to disperse the four-thousand-odd people partying and chanting, "The streets belong to the people." Enraged, the cops arrested Hank for riding his bike with Phyllis standing on the back.

Now, Hairy Henry was a very tough guy who had just finished a nine-year stint at San Quentin for armed robbery. He had what the authorities called "an attitude problem"—that is, his attitude was adversely affected by authority. The cops asked to see his license and told him they would return it at the station house. Hank told them to keep it and got back on his bike. When the cops arrested him and started to drag him toward the paddy wagon, another Angel, Chocolate George, leaped into the fray and pulled him out again. George was a big, easygoing guy who liked to hold court in front of Tracy's Donut Shop and was well known and liked on the street. The cops swarmed the two of them and forced them into the paddy wagon; this angered the crowd, so the whole motley assembly followed the cops to the station house in a chanting parade led by Hell's Angel Freewheeling Frank and poet Michael McClure playing his autoharp, demanding the release of the two prisoners.

The cops were flabbergasted when the coffin from the Death of Money demonstration was passed around and rapidly filled with the bail money for the two men. When it was handed over to Pete Knell, president of the Frisco chapter of the Hell's Angels, it was his turn to be stunned, both by the gesture of community support and by the speed with which it had been accomplished. Since it had been a Digger event, the Angels credited the Diggers for the happy result.

The Angels pay their debts: they threw a party in the Panhandle of Golden Gate Park on New Year's Day. They asked us to arrange the details, but they footed the tab, including the free beer, and offered the Grateful Dead, Janis Joplin, and Big Brother and the Holding Company as a huge thank-you to the community. It was the first large-scale free rock concert in any city park, and it was a grand day.

Whatever else they were in those days, the Angels were definitely authentic, and this was the critical denominator on which the Diggers founded a relationship with the club. The Angels respected our dedication to freeness and anonymity (as far as they respected any outsider), but the real beginning occurred, I think, when Emmett and I showed up at Chocolate George's funeral.

I don't remember how Chocolate George died—it was a year or so after the arrest in the Haight in late sixty-eight or early sixty-nine. Emmett came to me one day and said, "We're going to pay our respects."

This idea was a little unsettling. The Hell's Angels were real tough guys, not wanna-bes or guys expressing biker fantasies on the weekends. They roared through the streets on their chopped Harley-Davidsons, dressed in black leather jackets with the club's death-head logo flaunted across the back, and they brooked no interference or the slightest disrespect. I had seen two Angels empty a Mission Street bar in a fistfight, and when they clustered on Haight Street in small, raucous knots, people gave them a wide berth. Those who sought to prove something by challenging them or behaving in an overly familiar manner paid a fearsome price. I had witnessed several incidents where inappropriate behavior had been chastised by a swarm of leather boots and scarred fists. I did not know what Emmett had in mind and was not comfortable with the idea, but I was not about to punk out, and so I agreed to go.

The scene at the funeral home was definitely nerve-jangling. The place bristled with choppers, chrome gleaming like blades. Hard-faced men in greasy leathers and dusty boots paced sullenly in the front yard, smoking and communicating distractedly. The air was thick with anger and the possibility of sudden violence.

Inside, the home was jammed with more of the same. Many of the Angels appeared stupefied and had obviously been dropping "belligerence," their pet name for sodium seconal (reds). All eyes turned toward us, the outsiders, as we entered, and the room grew deathly quiet. I could feel my bowels churning, but Emmett and I "held our mud" (remained expressionless), doffed our hats, and walked over to the coffin. There was George, all right, only he wasn't laughing and shouting "hello" in his booming voice. His skin appeared pale and translucent, incongruous against his dark leathers and vivid patches, stuffed into a silk and flowered crate like an oversize bracelet from a plush jewelry store. No one moved. We stood over him for a while, resisting the impulse to be rushed by the aggressive silence, then saluted George good-bye and left at a leisurely pace; I could only hope no one would notice my pulse, which was pounding so hard that I was sure my ears were flapping. After this time, however, whenever I encountered Angels on the street there was a nod or friendly chitchat. In this way I met Frisco chapter president Pete Knell and became friends, but that belongs at a later point in the story.

The Diggers had seized the imagination of the counterculture; we were news. The following story may illustrate our authority. Not long after George's funeral, Peter Berg, Emmett, Sweet William, and I drove to Los Angeles to confront some music producers who were hoping to stage a "Digger benefit," intending to charge money for tickets but then donate the proceeds to charity. We were not about to be used in that manner.

We scored a car and drove from the Bay Area directly to an expensive house surrounded by a high wall in ritzy Bel Air. Sunken lights in the driveway cast eerie shadows on giant ferns, and a black wrought-iron gate swung open for us by unseen command. We made our entrance into a room full of casually but expensively dressed music-business types, the emerging counterculture aristocracy. White was the color of the season, I believe, intended to indicate refinement and spiritual evolution—New Age Protestantism, which equated material rewards with God's love, I guess. If they were the light, we were the dark—leathers slick with oil and road dirt, edgy, armed, and not about to have our name co-opted by a bunch of Nehru-shirted aesthetes whose monthly tab for weed and cocaine equaled any of our annual incomes.

The house bubbled with self-importance. It was a "heavy" event: everyone there thought of himself as powerful and important, and this included us. As things were called to order, Emmett disappeared (to rifle the coatroom, we later discovered), and Berg, Sweet William, and I were left to impress on these folk that under no circumstances were they to charge money for anything pertaining to the Diggers. I said it nicely, Berg said it coldly, and Bill made it dangerous. There was some consternation and nervous frittering as the do-gooder fraternity realized a major event was slipping through its fingers. Then Derek Taylor, the rep for the Beatles, rose decisively and ended it, announcing over his shoulder breezily as he walked out the door: "That's it, I'm out of here. These guys have always been the hippest. If they say it's not happening, it's not happening. So I'm not playing. Why waste time?"

With a nod to us, he was gone, leaving the event (and the other producers) bereft of the Beatles' star power. The meeting fell apart, and we left feeling flushed with our ability to make things happen.

The Hollywood sun felt langorous and lush after the bracing fogs and winds of the North Coast. Elated by our success, we decided to stay in Los Angeles for a while. Benny Shapiro, sitar master Ravi Shankar's manager, took us in and loaned us his house as headquarters. The Diggers' reputation as cutting-edge social thinkers had spread fairly widely; now our refusal to accept money and our ability to quash or create events had amplified our status as underground "heavies."

There was no reason for Hollywood people to regard us any less cynically than we regarded them; consequently we were "tested" assiduously and often by the wealthy rad-lib community there, who hoped to dismiss us and justify their own lack of commitment by discovering inconsistencies in our ideology or behavior. There were two flaws in their strategy. The first was that we didn't have much of an ideology, and the second was that we were rarely ever consistent. *Authenticity* is a large, whimsical room to run around in.

People tried to buy in by offering "money for the cause," but except for very close friends who were willing to play with us, this never worked. One night in Benny's living room, some lounge-suited trickster offered Emmett $2,500 "pocket money—to help your work." Emmett thanked the guy impassively and, in the next moment, as if he had forgotten something, picked up a telephone, called Huey Newton, and donated the money to the Black Panthers on the spot. We were broke, but Emmett's move was shrewdly designed for the audience (probably to play them for higher stakes later). With one stroke, he reaffirmed our mythology and staged a piece of living-room theater to enhance our local reputations and facilitate further connections.

Ploys like this built our credibility so that soon people competed to host and support us. Since we could take money only from our closest allies without suffering a loss of mystique, we had to determine who in L.A. should be granted access and what the cost of punching their ticket might be—both to us and to them. Show-biz people are nothing if not clever, and the sharpest figured out quickly that while money may not have been the appropriate medium of exchange, drugs and compliant starlets were a very effective substitute, readily accepted by the four warriors from up north. In short, being courted in Babylon was fun. We were young, hip, penniless, and adored for it. With no records on the charts or films in the can, we sashayed from the plushest rooms to the nightspots of the moment, lounging on couches the size of pickup trucks and snorting coke from designer coffee tables.

All I had to do was be myself and do whatever I felt like. How could anyone be unhappy when life was so simple? It would be years before I slowed down enough to ask myself, if I was so happy, why was I loaded every day?

One night Peter Fonda, Brandon DeWilde, and Dennis Hopper visited Benny's to check us out. These guys were our age, sons of the film community, caught somewhere between their home base and their imaginings of free life, seeking to connect with a pure strain of the underground. We discussed "what was happening" for some time and how it might be translated into film (still never accomplished, as far as I'm concerned), and we passed scenarios and ideas back and forth as they picked our brains for stories. Chat was easy and things felt good. Then Sweet William took the floor, magnificent in his Angel colors, his hard-chiseled face and poetic eyes mesmerizing even those of us who knew him well.

"You know what I'd do?" he said. "I'd make a movie about me and a buddy just riding around. Just going around the country doing what we do, seeing what we see, you know. Showing the people what things are like."

This was the germinating idea for the hit movie *Easy Rider,* a film about which I have complicated feelings. Of the three actors who visited us at Benny's that night, only Dennis Hopper would leave the safe havens of his known haunts and run around with us during the rest of our stay. I came to think of the others as beautiful hothouse flowers that could not withstand the rigors of unprotected environments.

Dennis was connected to the Diggers by an alternate and more substantial route, however. A serious art collector, he was an old friend of Billy "Batman" Jahrmarkt, whose San Francisco gallery had championed such young artists as Bruce Conner, George Herms, and Wally Berman, creators of uniquely Californian visual statements that were not necessarily derived from the art capitals of New York and Europe.

Knowing Batman made Hopper family, a distinction he may have found dubiously beneficial. Some time later, Emmett, Peter, Billy, and I were cooking smack in his living room forest of pop and op art when his wife at the time, Brooke Hayward, walked in, appraised the scene, and left for good, precipitating a long downhill spiral for Dennis. His dark time at the bottom of the well made his eventual success in Hollywood that much sweeter for me, because he possesses the honesty and generosity that makes you root for him instinctively.

Offscreen, in those days Dennis was a passionate and half-crazy seeker of truth, something like the photographer he played to perfection in *Apocalypse Now.* I liked him. One afternoon, he, Michael McClure, and I were having lunch shortly after the opening of Michael's controversial play, *The Beard.* Michael was telling a wonderful story, filled with colorful obscenity, when a flushed-looking fellow walked over, muttered something about having a date in the back of the room, and punched Michael in the face three times with impressive rapidity. We leaped to his defense, and Dennis terminated the matter by jumping onto the table and adroitly drop-kicking Michael's assailant into unconsciousness. It's hard *not* to like a guy like that!

Despite good feelings for Dennis, *Easy Rider* remains a sore point with me. Peter and Dennis had seen and been excited by the Mime Troupe and suggested that I write and direct a scene with the company for inclusion in the film. I was excited by this prospect and pleased because it could funnel a little cash into the pockets of my fellow performers, who were still subsisting on a five-dollars-a-show salary.

Several months later, they called with an offer: twenty dollars a week and a place on Fonda's couch for me, but nothing for my friends—"because this is a real low-budget thing, we're doing it because we *believe* in it" (as if we did not behave that way daily). I wrote them off angrily as spoiled brats and refused to play. Even in the realm of low-budget independent films and even in 1968, twenty dollars a week was a beggar's wage.

The finished film added insult to injury when the two protagonists visit a commune in the Southwest where sincere and drab hippies, the kind of nutless townfolk John Wayne might have protected in a corny western, are given the full Hollywood spin as "good people," as if they were Franciscan monks who just happened to smoke dope and dress funny. The community entertains itself by watching a clutch of dodos clump through a mindless commedia-type stage play announced by a crudely lettered sign as "Gorilla Theater"—an obvious travesty of the Mime Troupe's guerrilla theater and a backhanded slap at the communards, who are less hip than the individualistic, wandering biker heroes.

This was an inaccurate, smug, and insulting reflection of the life my friends and I were creating out of hard labor, with minimal assets and comforts. It was galling to see our style and our intentions misunderstood and misrepresented to the vast cinematic audience. What elicited my enduring scorn, however, was the film's ending, where the two "free spirits" are blown off their motorcycles by rednecks in a pickup truck. This ending was more than infuriating and dishonest; it was counterpropaganda that suggested that the cost of living free in America was death—so if you don't want to die, boys and girls, stay home and be audiences; *real* adventures are for charismatic, handsome people like Hollywood actors. But in fact, people were living "free" all over the United States at that time, dealing with the tough issues of subsistence, making peace with their neighbors, and developing appropriate spiritual and community practices while this sorry-ass subtext was being promulgated by guys who were queasy about leaving their safe haunts in their own hometown! This was the status quo in hip drag, and I was disgusted with it. I did not see Dennis Hopper for many years after that. When I did, we had both been resurrected as actors and men, and the joy of seeing him healthy and well (and the clusters of memories we shared) wiped away all my bitter associations as if they had been fog.

Years have gone by since that film made a fortune and introduced America to national treasure Jack Nicholson. Peter, Dennis, and I have grown and changed, and I have no desire to chain anyone to an identity they've since transcended. However, that slow-motion cinematic death still burns in my mind as a betrayal of the sensibilities it capitalized on. Far fewer people will read these words than have seen that film, I am sure, but at least I've marked my objections, and I can drop that chip from an overloaded shoulder, leaving it in the road behind me with those crushed bikes, sprawled actors, and fake blood.

By the summer of 1968, some of the problems associated with living without money began to chafe. I was restless. It was far more entertaining to pitch Digger philosophy or create spectacular events than to scrounge for money or car parts and move flats of food and vegetables from one place to another interminably. Emmett and I set off for New York City to check out the scene, see what we might accomplish there, and, we hoped, have some adventures. Janis Joplin, a good friend, sometime lover, sometime dope partner, always steady pal, was in New York when Emmett and I arrived. We ran around for a few weeks together, taking her out to hear great jazz and blues singers she might have otherwise overlooked because they lived far afield from her rock-and-roll milieu.

After she and her band left to continue their tour, Emmett and I stayed on in their rooms at the Chelsea Hotel, pretending to be "managers." That ruse wore thin, and we were forced to move from room to room, jimmying the flimsy locks to find an empty room and greasing the palms of the maids with the bottles of Southern Comfort that well-wishers sent Janis by the case and she had left behind for us.

Anyone who has ever tried to pitch anything over the phone can understand the daily routine we invented to establish social connections in a strange city. You begin with a name and a phone number—perhaps you got them at a party or from a friend of a friend. You have just enough legitimacy to keep the other party on the phone long enough to begin a pitch. Then, to keep the person engaged, you have only your imagination and skill—stock in trade for improvisational actors.

By the end of the summer we had created a network of apparently unlimited horizontal and vertical social mobility, with access to virtually every room we wanted to enter—from the Park Avenue mansions of the wealthy and celebrities like Baby Jane Holzer to the "shooting galleries" on the Lower East Side, recording studios, Italian social clubs, and rock stars' living rooms; we had drinks with columnist Jimmy Breslin, shared joints with Puerto Rican gang leaders. Each personal encounter enhanced our ability to set up the next meeting, where we could encourage people to participate with us in our grand revolutonary scheme. Each "score" increased our prestige and in turn made the next round that much easier. This was not social climbing but social *spread,* the recombination and intermarriage of previously separated "networks" of people in order to create the condition of a free society we described.

One example of our summer's work was the brokering of a peace meeting between New York detectives and Puerto Rican gang leaders. Emmett and I used our status as outsiders to create a neutral turf where the antagonists could meet and talk. We did this, surprisingly enough, through Albert Grossman, the avuncular Ben Franklin–lookalike manager of Bob Dylan and Janis Joplin. Albert had given us the run of his office, and his assistant, Myra Freedman, was generous with her time, full of bonhomie and edgy New York wit and extremely useful to us, taking messages and allowing us to turn their offices into a command central. For this particular meeting, Albert made a few calls and arranged for us to use the penthouse boardroom of the CBS building after hours.

The police and the gang leaders met outside the sealed and darkened building. They were escorted upstairs and into the room by the doorman, who had to unlock the front door of the immense skyscraper for them. There, at the head of an impressive hardwood table with seating for twenty, were Emmett and I, in blue jeans, with our long hair, earrings, and leathers, waiting for them as though this was our living room, reveling in the confusion and shock apparent on their faces. It was a classic Digger ploy—hard politics conducted with a style that put us in charge of the meeting and gave us the authority to ensure a successful rapprochement. This was our art, a miniature perhaps compared to the vast canvas of the media event in Chicago, but it was substantial and we were becoming very good at it.

We were given Paul Simon's apartment for another meeting. Emmett told me that David Padwa, a wealthy stockbroker, wanted to "give us ten grand" and asked me to "pick it up." Of course, receiving such donations was one of the inevitable internal contradictions of the Digger position. Money was necessary to operate at all, and if we were to be able to create "free" events (or sustain ourselves to create free events) the cash had to come from somewhere. We viewed our wooing of donors as an opportunity to engage them in a new social arrangement as much as an opportunity to get funds for our work.

Emmett himself had another engagement that night, so Danny Rifkin, manager of the Grateful Dead (also Paul's houseguest), and I agreed to stay and meet Padwa. Leaving the apartment with Emmett, Paul Simon walked into a large wooden horse from an old carousel he had mounted on rockers. Rubbing his shin, he said, "God, I hate that damn thing" and limped out. Emmett was right behind him.

Padwa arrived shortly afterward with poet Leonard Cohen and Andy Warhol "star" Ultraviolet. They appraised us coolly and listened politely as Danny and I told them about the Diggers. Suddenly, Leonard Cohen leaped to his feet and announced dramatically, "David, these men are lying. This is not a leaderless group at all. I am a novelist and reader of men. These men are *leaders*," stressing this last word as if it were a communicable disease.

It occurred to me that Cohen (a poet and songwriter whose work I admire) was probably hustling Padwa for something himself and feared competition. Danny and I ignored his rant and continued, offering, "So what we'll do with your ten grand is . . ."

The room temperature dropped perceptibly when Padwa interjected in an icy tone—"What ten grand?" I was about three stammers into a confused response when I realized that he had not visited intending to give support to the Diggers but had probably been invited simply to meet us. The situation was a classic Emmett move. He had guessed that David *might* give us money, and rather than risk his *own* status by asking, he had sacrificed Danny and me to the task, so that we could be written off later if it became a problem between David and Emmett.

As this revelation crystallized, shattered, and fell apart in me, Padwa rose gravely, said, "I don't *give* money," and he and his entourage walked out, leaving Danny and me as embarrassed as if we had been caught masturbating in front of a mirror.

Three hours later, Emmett stormed in. "Hurry up, the truck's downstairs. Gimme a hand!" he said, barely concealing his delight at some mischief he had planned and effectively changing the subject before Danny and I could confront him about the evening's betrayal. Emmett had arranged for a truck, and we loaded Simon's hated carousel horse onto it, piled in behind it, and drove north to Woodstock, New York, where we deposited it in the early morning hours on Bob Dylan's front porch as an anonymous gift to his children. Dylan was Simon's bête noire in those years.

Twenty years later, I saw Paul Simon across the room in a New York restaurant. I had the waiter slip him a note that read, "Didn't you ever wonder what happened to the rocking horse?" I saw him read it and scan the room for the sender. Recognizing me, he asked me over and introduced me to a journalist interviewing him for the *New York Times*. I told him the story, and he confessed that while he had known that we had taken it, he hadn't known its destination until that moment. I imagined the journalist framing a mini-headline in her mind: "Other Shoe Takes 20 Years to Fall."

The partying, hustling, and scamming were fun, but they were, after all, a sideshow to the real work of the Diggers, which was to create free life amid the desert of industrial capitalism. New York was too large, too anarchic, too entrenched in various levels of corruption and territoriality for us to gain much of a purchase on the city beyond our person-to-person travel through it. We required a more manageable stage and a larger support system, and that meant returning to San Francisco.

11

biker blues

At the end of that summer of 1968, Emmett and I returned to San Francisco. Sam and I had separated during one of our innumerable spats, perhaps because I refused to take her with me to New York. She had moved out of our small cabin overlooking Dolores Park and was staying at Paula McCoy's classy Victorian across the street from the Grateful Dead house on Ashbury Street. She had taken our nine cats with her, which bizarrely died of distemper one after another soon after she moved into Paula's. On each visit there, part of my time was spent poking through the garage (where the cats always seemed to prefer to die), seeking the source of a stench.

Emmett and I had been using large quantities of hard drugs in New York and I was in bad shape, passing out often and unexpectedly, finding myself suddenly on the floor looking up at the bottom of a sink. One night, on a visit to Paula's, I was flirting with a woman there, much to Sam's displeasure. Sam was stalking me (which of course made this pursuit extremely difficult), emanating murderous vibes. I don't know if it was the vibes or my weakened state, but at one moment I was on top of a long stairway and in the next moment I was lying at the bottom, looking up at Sam towering above me, with her hands on her hips and backlit as a glowing silhouette. She regarded me long enough to see that I was still living, then turned and walked off without a word.

I was drifting, with no fixed abode or relationship, and if I disregarded being loaded or drug-sick, I was having a wonderful time. Our reputation and family were expanding. There were places to visit, people to see, comrades to assist, music to make, and women to love. I decided that a motorcycle would be a dashing addition to my life.

Pete Knell of the Hell's Angels lived in the bottom half of a dilapidated two-family house. Billy "Batman" Jahrmarkt lived upstairs, with his wife Joanie and children, Jade, Hassan, Digger, and Caledonia (referred to collectively as the Bat People). It was an unlikely but highly workable arrangement. Pete respected authenticity, even Billy's all-consuming dedication to heroin, and the arrangement suited the Bat People too, because Pete had a gigantic dog named Eckloff who guarded the house unremittingly. Eckloff was a monster. He appeared to me about the size of a lion and Pete's downstairs dwelling, always cool and shadowy, made a suitable cave for him.

Pete's living room featured a high-backed thronelike chair, a small bar, and a bed in one corner suspended from the ceiling by heavy chains. The decorative motif was strictly functional, since most of the functions held there would have played havoc with furniture and decorations anyway. Steel mesh over the windows protected against retaliatory bombings from rival bike gangs and gave the interior an otherworldly feel. A short corridor led past the bathroom to a small, unfinished back room attached to his garage shop. It was furnished with several mattresses, which Pete offered to let me use while I built my bike. I accepted.

Pete was an impeccable worker. He built chopped-down Harleys that were light, fast, unobtrusive, and reliable. He was also a very patient teacher. I had recently inherited three thousand dollars from a grandmother's will. I had given Sweet William a thousand dollars toward his bike, Freeman House and David Simpson something toward building *The Bare Minimum*, the Diggers' free fishing boat, and with the remainder, I bought a brand-new 1969 Harley Davidson FLH engine. While we waited for it to arrive, Pete and I located an old but sound 1937 Harley "rigid-frame," so called because it had no shock absorbers. I spent days sanding it smooth, and Pete showed me how to prime and paint it expertly with spray cans. "Watch the surface," he said. "Make it shiny and wet, but don't let it orange-peel or run." I practiced and soon possessed an electric-blue frame gleaming with kinetic energy.

Pete showed me how to disassemble the heavy-duty Harley transmission and grind and bevel the locking lugs on the gears so that they *clicked* rather than *clunked* into place when shifting. We rebuilt a clutch and bought new discs and a chain for it, then took the clutch cover, the "grasshopper" (a spring-loaded assist for a manual clutch), the tool kit, the headlight, and a few more odds and ends to be chromed. Such errands led me to the fascinating industrial section of the city, south of Market where replaters took dingy bumpers, valve covers, fuel pumps, and pulleys and resurrected them as the gleaming fantasies of hot-rodders and bikers. Out of these grimy places with oil dirt yards, wormy dogs, and filthy facades the sorriest-looking parts emerged pristine as museum sculptures.

The San Francisco Harley dealership was managed by a terse, bald fireplug of a man named Dave. Pete described him as "a guy who don't *like* to fight, but if he does, you know that he'll take care of business." Pete's guarantee was enough to establish my credit for the purchase of taillights, foot pedals, brake and clutch clamps, and the myriad pieces of hardware necessary to build a working "putt," as Pete referred to his bikes. This extension of Pete's credit was nothing to be taken lightly. Though an "outlaw," Pete was strict about obligations that the Diggers often dismissed casually. He paid his bills to the penny, while—to name one example—we took advantage of substantial traffic in telephone credit cards. For us, it was a victory to "liberate" a famous politician's or a corporate telephone card for "free" calls. Ditto for gasoline and bank credit cards, which often underwrote our long journeys and deliveries of supplies to the growing number of Digger family houses. Scruples about such behavior were anesthetized by our image of ourselves as guerrilla warriors living off the enemy. This was not a position that would bear overmuch scrutiny, and it was definitely not shared by Pete Knell. He was an outlaw, but his life outside the law was marked by a fixed, though contrary, relationship to it.

Like most people, I consider myself an honorable person. What strikes me in hindsight about my ethical transgressions at this time is not the revelation of a flaw in my character but the ease with which anyone can sweep away ethical concerns in pursuit of a noble goal. The facility with which I performed these sleights of mind informs my caution today when I review the noble utterances of politicians and reformers. If I was able to justify personal misconduct as a way of redressing systemic wrongs, I suppose anyone can, so it no longer surprises me when prevalently high-sounding goals become transformed into justifications for malfeasance.

Pete identified with the country, its goals, and its institutions. While he thought that much of its behavior was rife with self-serving bullshit, he did not consider these critiques to be excuses for *personal* dishonesty, and I was chastened by his example. The irony of being tutored on civic responsibility by an outlaw was not lost on me.

The time I spent at Pete Knell's was unnerving and stressful. Having to be preternaturally alert all the time around the Angels was exhausting and required even more self-medication. Freedom from the responsibilities of the Mime Troupe and a stable relationship left me ample opportunity to use heroin and methedrine whenever I wanted (which was often), and consequently my health was suffering. Signs of liver trouble appeared, and I chewed 90 percent protein tablets all day long as a junkie's tonic for avoiding cirrhosis.

My status at Pete's house was curious. Because I was not a "prospect" seeking admission to the Hell's Angels, there was much club business that I was not privy to. When three or four Angels congregated in his living room and the wooden soup bowl of pills was passed around, it was never long before someone wheeled around demanding to know just "what the fuck" I was doing there. I learned to discern pretty accurately when to get lost.

There was some dissension among club members about Emmett's intimate access as well. He had his own relationship with Pete and we were friends, so he was around often. For him, like me, the Angels were a kind of test to pass, a way of measuring our courage as well as forging an alliance that supported our social agenda. One night several members decided to give Emmett a beating as a warning to the rest of us about getting too close. They invited him to ride with them to Santa Cruz, and were drinking in a bar there when something triggered Emmett's receptors to danger. Excusing himself to get something from his bike, he walked outside, rode back to San Francisco without hesitating, and lay low until things cooled down.

Pete liked me and trusted me to keep my lip buttoned. When some mem-

bers inquired whether or not they could steal the parts of my bike being
stored in his garage, Pete stood up for me. One of the reasons he liked me, I
think, was because of our free-ranging discussions. While not formally educated, Pete was razor sharp, well informed, and very curious. He liked to test
his ideas against mine. We had many discussions about politics and he could
never understand what he perceived as the "carelessness" of the Diggers. He
felt that we were reckless in assuming that our *intention* to construct a counterculture would protect us from failures of strategy in dealing with the majority culture. He discounted all leftist revolutionary rhetoric, pointing out
that most people calling for the revolution failed to live alertly and cautiously as warriors and consequently were no threat to anyone. He did not
understand how we could be unconcerned with organization and structure,
though he had to agree that it was the Diggers' lack of structure that made
infiltration by government programs like Cointelpro impossible. He appreciated my interest in his life and in motorcycles but was ambivalent about
Bryden Bullington's painting on my gas tank: a voluptuous bare-breasted
blonde angel with flowing white wings, creating a pentangle at the tip of
her index finger. The image sparked Pete's proprietary concerns about the
club's identity.

"It's an *earth* angel, Pete," I assured him, but he was never totally satisfied,
uneasy that it was an infringement on the motif of his blood brotherhood.
This issue of our intentions continued to reside below the surface of our relationship. Poet Michael McClure was riding a yellow and black chopper that
Pete had made for him, and Emmett had one as well. Pete must have wondered whether we represented friends, pretenders, or potential adversaries.

The issue was not enough to create a breach between us. He encouraged
me to participate openly in his living-room discussions and to challenge
his fellow Angels intellectually and philosophically—not a particularly easy
thing to do when they were loaded. The Angels were not given to dialectical
subtlety and were often happy to resolve dialectical tension with a quick
punch. Later, Pete encouraged younger Angels to stay at the Diggers' Olema
commune periodically, though I was never certain whether he wanted them
to study us, report on us, or learn from us. Still, it was always clear that they
enjoyed being treated as intelligent men whose ideas mattered, and they
understood such treatment as a mark of respect.

Anyone who comforts himself with easy clichés about "bikers" is deluded. During the years that I had access to the club, I met sculptors, master chemists, machinists, economists, physicists, and poets. I met individuals in the Hell's Angels who were as brilliant and incisive as anyone I have met since. Generally, they held themselves to a higher standard of honesty and commitment than most civilians I knew. Like the Diggers, they lived life as they imagined it possible. Unlike the Diggers, however, their aspirations and hopes for success extended no further than themselves.

The Hell's Angels were a conundrum and a challenge, and to none of the Diggers more so than to Bill Fritsch, our brother known as Sweet Willie Tumbleweed. He perceived in the Angels a standing rebuke to his integrity, because he loved and admired their fearlessness and lack of compromise. He confronted the issue for himself by joining them. What follows is his story, which is once again also mine.

12

sweet william's story

Sweet William, born Bill Fritsch, came by his passionate, poetic, inflexibly self-confident spirit genetically. His father was a sullen Hungarian house-painter for whom family life was purgatory, and his mother was a devout Russian Communist who had once refused to sell breast milk to the aging J. D. Rockefeller, who, according to Fritsch family legend, spent his days lounging in a motorized chair that tracked the sun in his penthouse atrium, sipping breast milk because he believed it would keep him healthy and vigorous.

Bill's parents divorced when he was three, and his mother married a merchant marine left-winger who shaped Bill's political instincts and class antagonisms quite early. The remainder of Bill's early education was contributed by children of the Philadelphia Mafia. It was one of them who crystallized the dynamics of capitalism for Bill when he said, "Free enterprise is as far as your father rules."

At New Town High School, an all-boys school in Philadelphia, Bill remembers himself as "an average kid with middling talents." He tells me this with unembellished honesty as he struggles to get a Camel out of a flattened pack with his good hand. I am uncomfortable watching his difficulty, but Bill handles the moment with aplomb. A few minutes ago I watched him approach, on his way to our meeting in a little San Francisco hamburger joint, a solitary figure framed against a white wall, one arm and one leg flapping uselessly as he placed each foot and his cane with fixity. Despite this physical infirmity, his face still bore the commanding, determined expression I remember from the days when he could have stopped a mob on his own personal authority.

In the early fifties, Bill left home at sixteen to join the merchant marines and worked his way into the role of union delegate for his ship. When he shipped out, he met Richard Marley, a man who would weave in and out of both of our lives in years to come. Richard was born in England, the son of a famous militant Communist mother. On Bill's maiden merchant marine voyage, Richard delivered long lectures to him about boycotting the whorehouses in ports. Richard explained how the girls were exploited by the capitalist class and how workers, in solidarity with them, could not participate in their degradation. This was depressing to Bill, whose libido seemed to orchestrate most of his decisions. He is an extraordinarily sincere man, however, and when the boat docked in Manila, he gave up his liberty and remained on the boat for three days and nights, tormented by the tension between his conscience and his body's desires. He broke on the fourth night, sneaking off the ship like a guilty dog, streaking into the closest whorehouse. There he found Richard Marley in bed with *three* whores, laughing uproariously as they serviced him with thoroughness and imagination. This was perhaps the last time Bill was susceptible to ideological manipulation.

He was cooking in the ship's galley the day the captain sent his eggs back for the third time. Bill heaved the plate of food in the captain's face and was fired on the spot. He took his hundred-dollar discharge pay and flew to California.

Bill gravitated to the bohemian haven of San Francisco's North Beach in the late 1950s. He was parking cars for twenty-four dollars a week, so broke that he was picking cigarettes off the sidewalk. In a bar one day, a guy named Roy Miller noticed his pack with all the different brands of butts in it and asked, "You into making some money?" Bill answered affirmatively, and Roy asked if he could get a gun. Bill could not but managed a butcher knife and with it the two robbed a Safeway for $3,400. Bill was exhilarated by the experience, "hooked on the rush," as he put it. Walking down Market Street afterward, the wind kept whipping his long hair into his face, so he bought a celebratory Panama hat. That hat became his trademark, Roy followed suit, and before long, he and Roy became known as the Panama Hat Bandits.

High style was a pronounced trait of Bill's personality, which was generously endowed with charisma. He resembled the actor-director John Cassavetes, but his face was, if anything, more masculine, less softened by conflicting sensibilities. He was cocksure and apparently fearless. His fidelity to his impulses was so absolute that for people like myself, awash in ambiguities, he was a beacon of certainty and personal power.

"We'd dress up on weekends," Bill remembers, "and rob those Tahitian Hut tonga-wonga bars. It was a great life." Until one day four guys entered the motorcycle shop where he worked. Bill looked up, read the vibes, and thought to himself, "Flash, I'm dead." He assumed that the men were Italians who owned the tonga-wonga bars. Luckily, he was wrong. They were cops.

Because Bill was only twenty at the time, he was sent to the Youth Authority at Tracy while Roy did time at San Quentin. While Bill was incarcerated he took an aircraft mechanics course and became certified. When friends inquired about prison, he shrugged it off: "I did a hundred sit-ups a night, a hundred push-ups, and jerked off the rest of the time."

When he was tripping on speed, Bill could keep you spellbound, examining the cosmic potentialities of a small stone he'd found somewhere or reviewing his last act of lovemaking in staggering detail, explaining precisely what had occurred in the minds and bodies of both participants. His was egotism at its most innocent, assuming that his personal explorations had universal resonances. He regarded these explorations as his work.

When he was released from Tracy, Bill went to work in the prop shop at Pan Am. By 1962, he had married Richard Marley's sister and had two boys. His life appeared stable and normal, but this was an illusion. His family and personal plans were about to be disrupted by the social seizures and generational conflict of the decade.

East-West House was a San Francisco writer's cooperative hangout. Marley brought Bill there one day and introduced him to poet Lenore Kandel. Bill fell in love immediately, went home, got his clothes, said good-bye to his wife and children, and left.

"It was the only honest thing to do," he says flatly. I ask him if he has seen his children since, and he just shrugs. It makes me sad to think of that broken family. I wonder how different Bill's life might have been if he had stayed with them. Where he lives now, in a tiny room in a decrepit old boarding-house, there are no children's drawings, no photographs of him with a woman and children, no tarnished trophies and yellowed high school year-books. If he misses such things or regrets his choices, he will never say. Like a wolf who has chewed off a paw to escape a trap, only he knows how much the paw is missed.

It was fitting that Bill and Lenore Kandel should have fallen in love. They were extraordinarily beautiful people intimately tuned to their bodies. Their skin looked as if it would taste delicious. Bill was fire and lava, given to volcanic explosions and sudden insights that rocked him like seismic tremors. Lenore was a giggling dakini (one of the feminine consorts of the Buddha). Her psychic center of gravity appeared to be located in the earth's core; nothing perturbed her rock-steady equilibrium. Already an established poet, she was also an accomplished belly dancer who earned pocket money making beaded jewelry for a foreign import store.

Their bed filled almost a whole room and was an epicurean marvel. Both sides were lined with boxes of cookies: Oreos, pecan sandies, and various whipped-cream and chocolate confections. There were dirty books, scented oils, and things to drink. It was a bed you could live in for days, and they often did. Their coupling seemed like a universal principle, a melding of dark and light forces. They moved into a flat on Chestnut Street that they inherited from a friend. Bill went to work on the waterfront, Lenore modeled for the Art Institute, and the world appeared to be in order.

In 1966, Ronald Reagan was elected governor of California, promising to punish the mouthy students acting up in Berkeley and to fry the inmates on San Quentin's death row. His victory signaled a sea change in the social climate, and about a week later, the Psychedelic Shop was raided by the police, who seized copies of Lenore's erotic poems, *The Love Book*. These graphic paeans to monogamous love and sex had been published before, and since you could walk to any street corner and buy hard-core pornography or open a men's magazine for steamier stuff, our community perceived this as Reagan's attack on the psychedelic culture.

Lenore and her book became the center of a very public pornography trial. I had not yet met her, but I felt that she should be invited to attend the initial Artists' Liberation Front meeting, so I found her phone number and invited her. When she and Bill appeared, they galvanized everyone's attention in the packed room. They were dressed, respectively, in bright red and cobalt-blue leather Levis, radiating the charisma and self-assurance of natural leaders. Their style was effortless, authentic, royal. You could imagine them at ease in a French café or at an embassy ball; they would know people who were never bored or plagued with self-doubts. You felt yourself sinking a bit in your own estimation by comparison.

They certainly raised the mark by which I measured myself, and I was not the only one to notice them. "Emmett and I pinned each other right away," Bill laughs, "recognized each other as rivals, right off." They began to hang around together, and through Emmett, Bill and Lenore gravitated into the Digger orbit.

Sweet William loved the Diggers. "They were a challenge. It was somethin' I didn't understand," he says. "Everybody was winging it." He rose to the challenge, assuming roles with the Free Food deliveries, the truck repairs, and guarding our treasury and its record, the Free Bank book, with characteristic dedication. The Diggers respected Bill's fearlessness and dignity similarly. He was too proud to lie. He was indisputably *somebody*. I felt that way about many of my friends then; though their fame was strictly local, they had an authority that rested on character and ability rather than on wealth or social status. One of the defining attributes of the sixties was the collective impulse to reveal yourself candidly and publicly, confessing your inner visions as your daily life. It was as if the participants at a costume ball suddenly found the event too silly and simultaneously dropped their masks. Farm boys from Nebraska were writing poems, preppy girls from Grosse Point were throwing the Tarot and studying herbs. Kids with no idea of who they wanted to become could idle on the teeming streets among people who would not judge them for their confusion. Personal style counted more than a pedigree, and even within this community of dedicated life actors, Bill was a star.

In retrospect, it appears inevitable that Bill would have joined the Hell's Angels. His masculinity was so pronounced and his sense of honor so demanding as to require constant testing. One day he and Emmett were leaving an event at the University of California extension on Laguna Street and they noticed a chopped Harley Davidson parked by the curb. Emmett and Bill said, "That's my bike" simultaneously.

"I just kept saying, 'Bike, bike, bike,' everywhere—everywhere," Bill remembers. "Everywhere I went, whoever I ran into. Lenore did some kind of spell. Took some blood out of my finger. I don't know what the fuck she did with it, but the next day, you had some inheritance for me, and Jon and Sarah Glazer had an aunt who died, and they gave me money."

The bike that Emmett and Bill saw belonged to Pete Knell. During negotiations, they liked each other, and Pete offered to be Bill's sponsor if he wanted to join the Angels. When Bill returned to Peter Berg's and announced his decision to do that, Emmett spat, "What a waste!" dismissively. At the time I thought he was jealous. I did not realize that he had made a prophecy.

Bill "prospected" with the Angels for seven months, a period of apprenticeship during which he spent time with each member of the San Francisco chapter in order to win approval. He was tested in every way imaginable. Two votes against him were enough to keep him out of the club, and every member had his own criteria for passing or failing a prospect. Failure could be costly. Shortly after being turned down for the third time, Gordon Westerfelt, a dapper, handsome man with the cocky swagger of a World War II ace pilot, was slipping the key into his apartment lock one night when someone stepped from the shadows and punched his brains into jelly with a small-caliber bullet. His bike and personal possessions, including his girlfriend, subsequently circulated through the club. My mentor at that time, an Angel named Moose who had "adopted" me as a personal friend, told me shortly afterward that he was putting out a reward for the killer. Since I was not an Angel and he did not have to tell me the truth, and since he knew that

I knew this, I have no way of knowing whether this was a rumor he wanted disseminated.

Twenty odd years later, when I ask Bill about Gordon's death, he shrugs and asks me who I thought might have done it. I tell him that I suspected that perhaps he or Moose might have had something to do with it. He looks away, and I remind him that *something* changed his fate dramatically, *something* had unaccountably punctured his impenetrable good fortune, and that I had never understood how he had moved so abruptly from the realms of the charmed to the luckless. By way of explanation to myself, I had imagined an act with terrible karmic consequences.

He looks at me levelly, without blinking, and I feel as if I am in an empty room in an abandoned house. A door creaks open and then closes. I can almost hear the rustle of something moving behind the walls. Bill takes a drag on his Camel and changes the subject.

"Everyone had their fears and fantasies about the Angels," he says, referring again to his probation period years ago. "But as long as you approached individuals and were all the way honest, you were okay. The testing is about honesty—what you are and what you're really about."

One night, during his prospecting, Bill and some friends were drinking in a bar when an Angel commanded Bill to punch a guy at the end of the bar for no reason. Bill turned to him and said, "Anybody who tells me to go punch somebody gets punched in the face." This was the candor and intuitiveness that ushered him, member by member, through the portals that closed civilian life behind him forever. Bill entered the realms of hell, and Lenore followed willingly. Their bright jeans were replaced by black leathers now, and they raced together through the streets on Bill's barking machine like two close-coupled feral dogs.

The Angels' scene made no allowances for females or poets. One night Lenore was accidentally smashed in the face by a thrown glass beer pitcher. Another time, she crashed on the bike, injuring some vertebrae and leaving her in chronic pain. Walking was almost impossible for her, her hands and feet trembled, and she became nearly a total recluse. Eventually she bailed out.

"Lenore was a good, loyal woman with me. She did the best she could,"

Bill says gravely. Our community was shocked when they broke up. When I heard the news, I had an eerie presentiment that the balance in Bill's life had tipped into darkness.

There was a gathering dusk in the streets as well. By the early seventies, the Haight was tattered and worn, the original careless exuberance shadowed. The perfect expression of the change was a murderous rock-and-roll concert remembered by the name of the site at which it took place: Altamont.

The Rolling Stones were coming to town, and the Grateful Dead management wanted to throw a party in honor of their high-status rock star friends. Emissaries from the Dead requested the Diggers' help in creating the event. Both Peter Berg and I suggested events framed by multiple bonfires, each of which would be the locus of music and activity, rather than a central stage. This would ensure a collaborative frame of reference and minimize divisions between the community and its entertainers, a point we both stressed. Before the hype and marketing concerns of the music business dominated the culture, bands understood that they were of the community in which they performed and responded appropriately to that reality, rather than as objects of veneration acting out for faceless nobodies.

Our ideas did not seem elevated enough for Sam Cutler, the neurasthenic Englishman working in some managerial capacity for the Dead, so he approached Pete Knell and the Hell's Angels and told him that the Stones "wanted to do something for the people."

Sweet William was in the room when this conversation occurred, and he remembers Pete's response: "Tell 'em to come. We'll pick 'em up at the airport, bring 'em to the Panhandle, and let 'em do a free concert." Pete went on to guarantee that the equipment would be set up and ready for them and that all they would have to bring would be their guitars. The Hell's Angels knew what "free" meant too.

Sam asked Pete how much the club would want to serve as "security" at the event, and Pete told him, "We don't police things. We're not a security force. We go to concerts to enjoy ourselves and have fun."

"Well, what about helping people out—you know, giving directions and things?" Cutler queried, angling to have the Angels attached to the event in some official capacity. When Pete agreed that they could do that, Cutler returned to the question of price, and Pete said, "We like beer."

"How does a hundred cases sound?" Cutler responded, and a deal was struck. The Angels intended to give the beer away and felt that this would be good for their club's image.

Weeks went by while site after site was investigated and rejected before they settled on Altamont, farm country in the rolling hills between Oakland and the Central Valley. In Bill's words, it was "a goddamn, fucking, bereft pasture. In the middle of nothin'. Couple of barbed-wire fences. Cow shit. Not even a barn." This was the environment in which the Rolling Stones' "gift" would be tendered and received.

Bill remembers his shock on arriving at the site on the day of the concert. A stage with three stories of scaffolding had been erected, festooned with mammoth speakers, lights, and equipment. The place was teeming with people from the lip of the stage to the horizon, a churning, roiling sea. "With my misguided sense of responsibility," Bill says, "I was crazy trying to look after people . . . see that this one didn't get crushed or that that one knew where to go."

He looked down from the stage to check his bike and was amazed to see someone sitting on it. "I couldn't believe it," Bill says. "I told him to get off the bike, and he wouldn't. I said it again, and he wouldn't. I grabbed him so hard I heard every bone in his body snap. I was so angry I would've ripped his fuckin' head off and thrown it in the pasture. The bike fell over and I went crazy. I started stompin' him. I didn't even want his ghost around." This was how the party began.

From the beginning of the event, people insisted on "crashing" the stage. They were not used to "free" events being hierarchical and proprietary and could not understand why there were off-limits at a free concert or why guards were required, and it rankled them. The event so resembled a massive commercial concert that perhaps the audience became confused and felt as if they had been demoted to nonentities and wanted to get closer to the heat and glow of the luminaries. They had, in fact, been unwittingly enlisted as extras in a commercial film and should have been paid. The concert was not free at all but had merely waived admission. Its real organizing principle was a merchandising event to create a live album and film—and a dynastic marriage between the Grateful Dead and Rolling Stones' families.

Whatever the reason, the crowd was whipping itself into froth; somehow it fell to the Angels to protect the stage and keep it clear enough so that the concert could continue. "We did it 'cause it had to be done," says Bill. The Oakland Angels arrived. Unlike their party-hard San Francisco brothers, this chapter had the reputation of heavyweight gangsters with a penchant for violence. Moving slowly and precariously through the crowd on their roaring, spitting bikes, creating a cacophony that overwhelmed the music, they edged up to the stage. Bill pulled the Angels' national president Sonny Barger up next to him. A warm-up band was playing. "I feel this shudder next to me," Bill says. "I look over and it's Sonny. He turns to me and says, '*We're* keeping this stage? Do you realize that if all these people had their minds together they could crush this whole thing?'"

Sonny's perception of reality broke through Bill's preoccupations, and he too realized that their pitifully small cadre of Angels had been slicked into the role of defending the stage against hundreds of thousands of unruly people.

The crowd was impatient for the Stones, and its surges forward were becoming wilder and harder to control. Even from among so many, Bill singled out Meredith Hunter. "I shoved Meredith Hunter off that stage *myself* three times," he says. "Big tall fucker. Three times I had my hands on that guy. I shoved his fucking ass back. I *told* him. I tumbled him off the stage three times. How clear do I have to be?"

Sweet William was desperate. He went backstage for the Stones, fearful that delaying their appearance would unleash a maelstrom. "They were tuning up," Bill recalls. "Chatting. Their *little* band. I recognized Mick Jagger. I didn't realize he was just a little fart. I told him, 'You better get the fuck out there before the place blows beyond sanity. You've tuned up enough.'"

Jagger told him that they were "preparing" and would go when they were good and ready. "I'm getting really pissed at this little fuck now," Bill says. "I want to slap his face. I told him, 'I'm tellin' you, people are gonna *die* out there. Get out there! You been told.'"

Bill returned to the stage and was standing there when Hunter's murder took place, recorded for all to see in the Maysles brothers' film *Gimme Shelter.*

"All of a sudden there's a scuffle off to my left," Bill says. "I saw a flash, the gun going off, but it [the music] was so loud you couldn't hear it." Meredith Hunter was standing there with a pistol, stark naked, loaded out of his mind, when Allen Pizzaro made his move.

Allen was a strange guy from San Jose. He had been a member of a club called the Gypsy Jokers that had been obliterated by the Angels. He had prospected as an Angel with the San Francisco chapter for eight months, but never owned a bike. On the night he was to be voted in, he answered an ad in the paper for a Harley Davidson, beat the owner senseless, and took the bike to his initiation. "He was a wild guy," Bill says. "He'd do anything." Not too many years later, his dead body was fished out of a reservoir, where he'd been dumped for some "anything." This day, however, he was the star, center stage, on film.

Allen grabbed Meredith's arm. "He fired one shot with Allen holding him," Bill says. "It's what saved Allen from the death penalty." Allen twisted the arm away, at the same time reaching back with his free hand and drawing his hunting knife from a belt scabbard. He swung Meredith around—"a classic street move," Bill calls it—and stabbed him.

The music stopped for a moment. A girl screamed, "a forlorn, wailing scream, like a rabbit dying," Bill remembers. "You never forget it. Then they were passing his body over the crowd. It was bobbing and floating like a body going downstream in a riptide. It was like a Greek play. Everything was classical. The hunger of the people for somethin' that didn't exist. Why come on the stage? Why!?"

In the ensuing melee, my friend Denise Kaufman, a local musician with the all-girl Ace of Cups band, was hit in the temple by a thrown bottle, fracturing bone and causing a severe concussion. Denise was eight and a half months pregnant at the time, and the Stones were approached for permission to use their helicopter to carry her to a hospital. They refused. Denise was ferried on a long grueling trip by car, after which, due to her advanced pregnancy, she was operated on without anesthetic. Both she and her daughter survived undamaged, but for those who know and love her, the same could not be said of the local reputation of the Rolling Stones.

The Angels took the heat for Hunter's murder in the press, but they felt betrayed by Cutler. Word circulated for a while that Cutler's life was to be forfeited and he moved to Texas abruptly. The bizarre, appropriately show-business finish to events occurred a few days later when the Maysles brothers visited Paula McCoy's house, where Bill happened to be staying at the time, to see what "piece" of *Gimme Shelter* the club wanted. They obviously had no idea of the organization's mood when they described the film enthusiastically. "We knew the Angels were a draw," one of the brothers said breathlessly, "but we didn't know that we'd get *lucky*." At that point, Angel Jerry Genly rose and kicked him square in the balls. "I think that was the end of the meeting," Bill says, laughing.

If you were forced to select an event that "ended" the optimistic promise of the Haight-Ashbury era, Altamont would be as good as any. After that, the party was definitely over, and what ensued, in the streets, in the Hell's Angels, and across America, was harder, colder, and all business.

Pete Knell used to say, "If you wanna know anything about America, look at the club. It's a reflection of America on all levels: high idealism and murder." The club was a cross section of blue-collar values and neuroses, and something murderous was afoot in both nations.

Janis Joplin and Jimmy Hendrix were dead of overdoses. Hell's Angels Terry the Tramp and Harry the Horse were murdered. Vietnam veterans were returning from the atrocities of jungle warfare, some with psyches ablaze with what they'd seen and had to do there to survive. A new element had risen to prominence in the club. A San Francisco homeboy, back from 'Nam crazy-dangerous, had opened a bike shop, prospected into the club, and climbed the ladder of power there with murderous ruthlessness. Little Bill, a physically sweet and beautiful club member, an amateur magician, got into a fracas in a Mission District bar one night. As he was leaving, three guys followed him to the street, bent him over his bike, and summarily executed him. The Angels retaliated by blowing away one of his killers in nearby Precita Park. Members stopped wearing their colors in the streets and affected jean jackets and hooded sweatshirts. Things got closer, tighter, more dangerous. "It was a cut-dog rotten bunch of shit" is all Sweet William will offer about that period. Murders became endemic. Expediency became the law.

Sweet William was running around with a girl from Fresno and biked down there one day to sell some cocaine. Pete Knell warned him not to go alone, but Bill was fearless. He and the girl ended up at a house party organized to raise money for the African Student Movement. Bill must have felt bulletproof to enter the all-black party alone in full Angels' colors, for the Angels were an unabashedly "white" organization that would not even allow black people who were personal friends of members to sit with them in public. He was led through a gauntlet of curious stares in the suddenly silent room and down to the cellar. He remembers a table and a drug scale and about a dozen men crowded together watching the count. After weighing out the cocaine, one of the black men said, "We're taking you off, white boy."

"No, you're not," Bill answered, and the fight started. "I wrecked that fucking room," Bill says, "fighting twelve niggers by myself. Then one of them reached over the top of the crowd that was piled on me and 'boom,' it was like a white flash. When I woke up I was in the Fresno County Hospital."

The "students" had shot him and left him for dead. Someone upstairs heard the ruckus and called the cops, and the cops discovered a pulse in Bill and called an ambulance. The bullet had entered his brain, ripping a path to a nest where it remains today. It was an expensive ticket for a trip of just a few inches: it paralyzed half his body.

When I visited him in the hospital shortly afterward, he was a wraith. His hair had been shaved off. He was blue-white, his face as taut and translucent as the skin of a drum. He was suffering terrifying hallucinations and felt that he was on the verge of comprehending secret profundities that evaporated just before he could own them.

He left the hospital a hero to the Angels, bought a three-wheeled motorcycle, and continued to party with them, but his life was shrouded in darkness. He moved in with Dee, a crazy, Faye Dunaway–lookalike witch from Georgia, and they grew so psychosexually drug entwined as to be indistinguishable. Bill began shooting heroin again, in direct contravention of Angel law.

In late October of 1980, Bill crossed the path of Pussy Paul, who owed him money. Bill held him prisoner in his apartment all night, and when he released him the next day, Paul "dropped a dime" and turned Bill in to the cops. Several nights later, on Halloween, the cops broke into Bill's place and beat him so badly that they fractured his hand and shoulder. The cops were just punctuating a lesson to Bill, but it makes you wonder what kind of men would kick in the door to pummel a cripple.

He was recovering from these wounds when a fellow Angel, Flash, called to inform him that Moose had rolled over for the police and was testifying against the club. The Angels needed Bill at the trial to verify a piece of information for the defense.

Bill refused to believe that Moose, an archetypal Angel, had rolled over. Everyone loved and admired Moose. He was fearless and roly-poly, with flaxen hair and a wispy blond mustache; when he arrived in his white Cadillac or on his white Harley with the red cross on the tank, it invariably signaled festive occasions. Moose was married at our Olema commune in a ceremony performed by poet Gregory Corso. My conversations with him had sometimes continued for days. He would often arrive at night and kidnap me with no warning. Once we left so quickly that I had no shoes, so he stopped at Tattoo Larry's house and commandeered a fine pair of Chippewa work boots that I still use.

Moose (real name Lorenzo) had been running an amphetamine laboratory, manufacturing white-crossed tablets from his home where his mother, his hillbilly Uncle Charlie, and Moose's slightly retarded son lived. One story he circulated about his arrest was that the police had discovered his laboratory. Another was that the cops had learned his mother had soaked the stamps on letters she sent him in LSD. He said the cops had threatened to put his mom and Uncle Charlie away, so he rolled over and gave evidence against his brothers in more than a hundred cases.

When Bill heard Moose say it with his own ears—"I rolled over in February"—he was shattered. "I couldn't fuckin' believe it!" he stammers. "It was like the blackness of the sky opened up and swallowed me. I wept for that. Really. I wept and thought, if that could happen to Moose, to *Moose*, there but for the grace of God . . ." As in all matters like these, only Moose knows what really happened. Those who had observed Moose's lethal side, including myself, suspect that the police must have had a much heavier beef over his head than a simple dope bust—big-time heavier.

I got a sense of the fear Moose could inspire some time later, about 1970. Our part of the Free Family was organizing a caravan, and I was forced to sell my bike to raise the funds to ready my truck. A couple of San Rafael bikers came out to Forest Knolls in Western Marin County to appraise it. They were tough rummies, but rummies. One fellow's pistol fell out of his pocket when he squatted down to inspect my oil pan. It fell in the soft dirt of a flower bed and he didn't notice it, so I retrieved it and stashed it in my pocket until the negotiations were over. I had been asking $1,200 for the bike, a fair price, but these guys were disparaging it as a prelude to bargaining. One of them walked over to me threateningly and then noticed my earrings with little fox toe bones dangling from them. Few people wore more than one in those days, and three in each ear were distinctive.

He stopped short and asked, "Ain't you that guy that runs around with Moose?" I nodded. The two looked at each other, something wordless passed between them, and they pulled out a wad of hundreds, peeling off twelve without another sound. We signed the papers, and I kicked the bike into life one last time. Just before the one fellow rode off, I handed him back his pistol. It was a nice moment, but orchestrated by Moose's power, not mine.

We are at the boardinghouse. Bill is sitting on the fetid bed in his undershirt. Tattoos on his chest of the Hell's Angels' winged skull and the Tibetan *dorje* thunderbolt on his chest have blurred with time. Under the Angels' death's-head are two words, too small to read, and next to them, slightly larger, "Out 8/23." "Protocol," Bill says, referring to his ouster from the club after four-teen years. I question him about it, and he looks away. "It was on me," he says. "I was tied up with a woman with a bad reputation for drugs and shit. They told me to drop her and I said I did. But we were tied together economi-cally and in some other crazy fucking ways and I didn't. When they found out, they booted me out. I gave my word and broke it. It's as simple as that."

Whatever life is, it isn't simple. I look at him, grim and grizzled, sur-rounded by obscure mementos, one arm lying useless on his lap. He used to laugh often and easily, with a smile so luminous it felt like a reward. Now when I manage to slip through his defenses and catch him off guard with a funny memory or remark, his face lights up again, shedding its haggard mien, splitting into creases and an engaging, shiny-toothed, Cheshire-cat grin. All his old power resides in that smile, just below the surface. It is hoarded now, no longer spent exuberantly. We have both changed that way, have both learned that errors have costs and that nothing is replenished forever. There are limits. Bill's are simply more obvious because he wears them on the surface of his body.

I know deep in my heart that had the Angels not changed, Bill would never have broken his word to them. His action sounds to me like one of those things we do when we desire a certain result but are not prepared to take responsibility for it. The Angels took Bill's voracious hunger for truth and manliness, his health and wholeness, and he offered them willingly to a vision of camaraderie and autonomy in which he wholeheartedly believed. When that vision soured, I believe it was too much to face, and drugs supplied the necessary anesthetic. On my lap lies a book of Bill's poems, and I am rereading one I'd first read nearly twenty-five years ago when he was still hale and whole.

The Image Role
(Thinking of All My Digger Friends)

Lookee where you put me up on an image of myself gaping in the yawn of your
lazy afternoon.
Lookee where you found me up on a pedestal
drowning in the fog
of your own blind eyes.
Lookee here, I'm a hero now
I got it made
I even remember panty raids
   coolin' it behind my Hollywood shades
   Yeah, I'm a jelly bean, sweet and mean
   I'm a hero, famous—a myth in my own time
   A father mother figure outta line
   A swingin' singin' holy man set afire
   The gun in my pocket ain't for hire.
I've got this image of myself pasted up on all the walls
I'm a gypsy a tramp a healer and a vamp
Everywhere I go people stop and stare

I'm known everywhere.
I was invented by MEDIA
a name that's pretty trippy
Even my friends ain't sure
who they are anymore.
They've all got a hundred
million faces
just like me.
Whose brand name are you?
Or do you see
I've got this image built on solid air
of no name and fame and tricky business games.
But I'm going, the child is getting old
and everything it ever was
is all getting sold.
The tumble is to! astonish! Oneself!

13

the red house

Our family joined the general migration from the Haight that began in 1967, after the Summer of Love. We were concerned with creating a more durable economic base for ourselves. The practice of doing things "for free" was fine social theater, useful for highlighting values and relationships to commodities, wealth, and fame; appropriate, too, for many transactions, but not a practice that would support what was now a loose confederation of several hundred people. Furthermore, remaining in the Haight was preaching to the converted. We needed land bases from which to integrate ourselves into new communities, to expand our resources and our reach. Since we had no money, we substituted cooperation and energy and helped one another establish a series of camps that we hoped would evolve eventually into networks of support.

A good deal of the time was spent visiting one another at these family houses: Willard Street, Carl Street, the Red House, Black Bear Ranch, Olema, Salmon River, the Bakery, Trinidad House, Garberville, Arcata, and Willits. By the time this chain of camps was established, we had begun to refer to ourselves as "the Free Family" as often as "the Diggers." Our diaspora spread north out of San Francisco, and Highway 101 resembled the thread of a beaded necklace that connected us to family sites along its length.

At every location people were perpetually busy repairing old trucks, locating food and goods to sustain themselves, and making deliveries to more needy family members in remote locations. Large "runs" were required to gather supplies to enable thirty people to survive a hard winter in isolated communes like Black Bear. We spent weeks scrounging necessities: oil, flour, kerosene, matches, toilet paper, powdered milk, dried fruit and nuts; hustling money and goods; and scouring wrecking yards for parts to prepare our old trucks for the taxing journeys.

The vehicles of choice were 1949 to 1954 Chevys and GMCs. Not only were they plentiful and the parts relatively interchangeable but the six-cylinder Chevy 235 engine was a paragon of reliability that could be fixed in the dark and tuned without sophisticated tools. Trucks heading north would meet trucks coming south, near Hopland, Healdsburg, or Cloverdale, and pull off the road for an impromptu picnic. Presents and gossip were exchanged, supplies traded, vehicles repaired, and parts swapped. Kids frolicked, impromptu jam sessions materialized, and camp was made and broken at the road's edge, while the straight world streamed by, intent on being somewhere before sometime, regarding our rowdy assemblages with curiosity while we became increasingly comfortable in the timeless.

One of the fundamentals of our early economy was the Free Bank. *The Free Bank Book*, a thick, hand-stitched blue Chinese notebook with lined pages, recorded group finances and personal transactions. Always an imperfect system, flawed by the comic vagaries of our contradictory relationships to money, the Free Bank lasted at least the first three years of the Diggers and served as an organizing principle for numerous debates about group economics and personal character.

Obviously a Free Bank is an imaginative fiction, so our relationship to it was necessarily imaginative. Consequently, it was a perfect mirror of personal ethics and attitudes toward money. Some people made meticulously honest entries like "$49.50—flour, olive oil, kids' shoes, canning jars, honey" (you could get a sixty-pound tin of honey for $9.00 in Weed, California), or "$2.10—fan belt." Each entry would be signed by the person who took the money from the group cookie jar. Then there were others, like Emmett for instance, decidedly less meticulous. Emmett's entries, day after day, read "$20.00—truck parts." Everyone knew the money was going for heroin and no one would have countered his right to the money or his use of it. We were touched that he *only* took twenty dollars and hustled the rest of his needs elsewhere. He could have been honest about it, but perhaps the evasion was not directed toward us, but toward himself.

The meager funds were allocated at group meetings where men and women struggled individually and collectively to win financing for competing interests. Since everyone knew everyone else's business, it was difficult to bullshit, and decisions were made by perceived consensus.

Roles were generally divided along traditional male-female lines, with the women looking after the food, houses, and children and the men looking after the trucks and physical plant. The roles were chosen according to personal predilections, however, and there were women who worked on trucks and men who preferred the kitchens. Everyone helped with the children, but out of necessity, the Digger women, specifically Nina Blasenheim, Judy Goldhaft, Phyllis Wilner, Myeba, Siena Riffia (aka Natural Suzanne), Roselee, and Vicky Pollack, attended by a rotating "staff" of allies, perfected the art and sustained the effort necessary to glean surpluses from the various grocers at the Farmers' Market. The Italians who controlled the market simply would not give free food to able-bodied men, and consequently the women became our conduit to this basic necessity, which afforded them power and high status in our community. Judgments about inequality and injustice, loafing, slacking, cheating, and stealing were usually vocalized at the moment, and no one braved the ridicule and scorn of Digger women for long without shaping up or shipping out.

The women's movement was beginning to coalesce, and the new consciousness was forcing reconsideration of sexual patterns and stereotypes. Much of the women's movement, as reported in the media, seemed (to this observer) more concerned with winning a share of the economic pie than with altering the status quo toward one in which women's particular skills and genius would be appreciated, by creating alternative forms of work and social and personal relationships. We were so removed from the marketplace that our concerns were different. We had *chosen* this life and accepted its consequent hardships more or less good-naturedly. There was so much work to do and so little money with which to accomplish it that everyone was equally pressured to win the rewards of a free life. It was this sense of free will, and of being under equal duress, that protected our households from the internecine gender warfare emerging as women understood that their lot in life was an arbitrary social convention and not a preordained natural state.

Survival takes work everywhere, but it seemed more interesting than a "job" to spend half a day in a junkyard dismantling an old truck for parts, replacing something broken with something close to new, lovingly cleaned, repaired, and repainted. The investiture of time conferred value, and for this reason many of our trucks were perfectly running specimens, whimsically decorated and impeccably cared for. Who but a free person had the time to wire brush and lovingly retrofit each old part necessary to the reassembly of a vehicle? We were happy to live with society's garbage because we had the time to recycle and reclaim it.

Each Free Family site had its own genesis, stories, and movable feast of characters. The folly of trying to unravel even a small part of our collective history is clear to me every time I make the attempt. Each house took on something of its own character and tone, attracting consonant people. Each house had its particular predilections and modalities of work and play. There were common denominators, however, so perhaps the best way to express the variety of communal life is through some specific examples, beginning with the Red House, in Forest Knolls, owned by brothers Ron and Jay Thelin, the founders of the Psychedelic Shop, and Ron's wife Marsha.

Ron Thelin was a San Francisco native son. His father was the manager of the Haight-Ashbury Woolworth's, directly across the street from what would become the site of his sons' Psychedelic Shop.

In Ron's senior year of high school, he met Marsha Allread, a perky, optimistic freshman with a wacky sense of humor. They were to be primarily together for the next thirty years.

Ron possessed the kind of archetypal American face Norman Rockwell might have drawn. He and his brother Jay won Bibles for attendance at church. They were white-bread, all-American boys in all but one critical degree, which is that they didn't care fuck-all about material wealth.

Ron took his first acid trip in 1965, swallowing one of master LSD chemist Stanley "Bear" Owsley's sugar cubes given to him by Allen Cohen, editor of *The Oracle.* Ron's frame of reference for the event was spiritual—the literature of Aldous Huxley had placed psychedelic drugs in that context—and like most early voyagers he undertook these journeys with the highest of intentions. His experience was transformative, blissful, unifying, and instructive—and Ron wanted to spread the word.

In January of 1966, he and Jay took their five-hundred-dollar savings and leased a storefront at 1535 Haight Street. They covered the walls with burlap, assembled crafts from local artisans, and offered books by Richard Alpert, Timothy Leary, Joseph Campbell, Aldous Huxley, and the Wassons, the latter famous researchers of the mushroom, including psychotropic varieties. They were, to say the least, in the right place at the right time.

In the summer of 1966 Ron and Marsha were living with friends on Clayton Street when one of their roommates, John Detata, had a particularly bad day. He had just flunked out of San Francisco State and broken up with his girlfriend. He had a virulent case of poison oak and a broken arm in a sweaty, moldering cast. It was definitely not a day for him to take LSD, but he did and became the three hundredth person to leap to his death from the Golden Gate Bridge.

Marsha was frightened by John's death and wanted to leave the city. Ron began to look for a new home and discovered the sleepy west Marin town of Forest Knolls. They located a large shambling red house on Resaca Street, the dream home of a retired ship captain, with several outbuildings. They bought it for $24,500, and Ron, Jay, Marsha, her brothers Gary and Artie Allread, her sisters Susie and Charlene, and Charlene's daughter Holly moved in together.

It took forty-five minutes to drive from Forest Knolls to the store on Haight Street. Ron would fire up a joint, get high, and enjoy the drive, speculating about what miracle the day might hold.

It was about this time that Ron and I met. Walking on Haight Street one day I discovered the Psychedelic Shop. The walls were dotted with photos of local musicians posed in front of a wall of faux hieroglyphics, the shelves stacked with interesting books, and Ron seemed like a nice chap. I mentioned that I had a friend named Duane Benton who made arguably the world's loveliest candles; I thought Ron might be interested in them. We chatted for a while, and our friendship began.

Ron met Peter Berg about the same time. Obsessed with seeking forms that might foster new social relationships, Berg challenged Thelin about the Psychedelic Shop. "Does this store express the [psychedelic] experience?" he demanded. Berg, as always, possessed the power to stimulate people to see things anew, and Ron had an epiphany, understanding instantly that "storeness" did not interest him.

On October 6, 1967, laws against LSD went into effect. On October 10, my birthday, a "Death of Hippie" event was held in the Panhandle of Golden Gate Park. Janis Joplin and Big Brother and the Holding Company performed, and people brought bells, beads, bongs, and plenty of acid to commemorate the event. A procession marched down Haight Street carrying a black coffin with the words "Hippie, Son of Media" painted on the side; at the parade's end the coffin was cremated.

Ron kept the store open all night and gave away every single thing in it. "Everything went," Ron remembered later, laughing. "Even the stuff on consignment."

Two weeks after closing the shop, Ron cashed in his life insurance, bought a white panel truck he christened the Free News, and took off with a gallon jug of wine and two friends to join the "Exorcism of the Pentagon" in Washington, D.C. This antiwar event would produce the indelible images of young women placing flowers in the muzzles of rifles held by equally young soldiers.

When Ron returned from Washington, things at home had deteriorated. Marsha had grown tired of his drinking and philandering and moved to a commune in Placitas, New Mexico. Ron stayed behind, consoling himself with the affections of Lynn Ferrer, an *Oracle* staffer. They created a baby together, later named Deva Star, but according to Ron, "everything had changed. It wasn't there. It was over." It, to Ron, was the promise of the Haight-Ashbury and its dominance as an influence in his life, and he foresaw the end even before the Summer of Love had begun.

Ron was living in the Red House, as the home in Forest Knolls was known, along with the members of the Sons of Champlin rock band, who had moved in after Marsha fled. Marsha returned one day with a new boyfriend, Richard Farner. She had come, she said, to sell the house, and she refused to leave. She moved into a room with Richard. Ron stayed in his room, drinking red wine all day and playing the piano for hours at a time. When the atmosphere in the house became too intense, Marsha moved to San Francisco for a while. Ron shuffled over to visit her one hangdog night, and something about his loneliness and dislocation must have touched her, because this was the night their son, Jasper Starfire, was conceived. They moved back to the Red House together, and poor Richard moved on.

Jasper was the glue that cemented their relationship, but their life together was not an easy ride for Marsha. Ron's stubborn and quixotic sense of personal freedom was deeply ingrained, and they had barely returned to Forest Knolls when he became committed to the Diggers. Soon, Diggers were coming by at all hours to talk, play music, or crash in one of the many rooms or on a vacant couch. Meals might be for four or thirty, and there was no way to know in advance. Even after the Sons of Champlin moved out, the house was jammed to the rafters and extremely chaotic. No consensus about what "free" meant existed, and the Red House was transformed into an early laboratory seeking the answer. "You couldn't go backward, and forward was where?" Ron told me later. "We had to learn how to do this."

David Simpson and Jane Lapiner—Mime Troupe members now Diggers—moved into a Red House outbuilding that resembled the prow of a ship. Mime Troupers Kent Minault and Nina Blasenheim and their infant daughter Angeline (a new mother herself at this writing) lived in the Red House proper. Kent was tall and patrician, read the Bible in Greek for relaxation, and was dedicated to complex and daunting projects that often involved liberating tons of lumber from building sites. Chuck and Destiny Gould converted an old barbecue shed into a one-room apartment for themselves and Destiny's daughter Gilian and their child-to-be Solange. Tom Sawyer, a quiet reader, managed to perch like a bat in a cranny somewhere. Gary and Sidney Allread, Marsha's brother and sister-in-law, built a loft in the Sunshine Room. Roselee, once an NRA sharpshooter, moved in from the Willard Street house in the city. Digger, our eccentric and brilliantly inventive shade-tree mechanic, joined the entourage with his step van and tools. John Albion and his wife Inga migrated down from Black Bear Ranch, while Balew lived with Marsha's other sister, Charlene. Mary Gannon, the bass player for the Ace of Cups, joined the party with her dewy-eyed lover, Joe Allegra, father-to-be of their baby. Judi Quick, ex of Barton Heyman and a former member of the Mime Troupe, staked a claim on a room with her paramour, Samurai Bob, a taciturn and sardonic ex-marine incarnated into a shamanic drummer who smoked dope continuously and dedicated his days to plotting the overthrow of all private property. Pragmatic and acid-tongued Joanna Bronson left her husband John (who subsequently became a practicing Muslim scholar), and she and her two children became a unit with Vincent Rinaldi, the dark, bearded, whimsical heir of Dionysus and Pan, a lovable source of music and mad antics.

I mention these people by name because most will appear in this narrative again, surfacing haphazardly as the tapestry of our relationships grows increasingly complex. Kent and Nina play a particularly important role, and after my father's death, along with Samurai Bob, Joanna, and Vinnie, would become the core group of our final commune at my family homestead, Turkey Ridge Farm.

Babies were born in the Red House: Kira and Jasper Thelin, Mary Gannon's daughter Thelina, and Danny Rifkin's daughter Marina. The architecture of the house, as well as the large number of blood relations in Marsha's family, promoted the social cohesion that was the hallmark of this particular Digger camp.

It soon became obvious that the credo of "do your own thing" did not work in an overloaded household. Too many conflicting impulses and intentions in too little space created havoc. Ron and Marsha did not want ownership of the property to be the criterion for their authority, but neither did they want their lives continually disrupted. Various experiments were tried and discarded, but what seemed to work most effectively and least oppressively was the recognition that in any situation, one person in the group was best suited for the leadership of that particular task. "Group intelligence" consisted of the ability to recognize and use individuals' skills appropriately. A corollary of that insight was that you could not be attached to leadership. Consequently, twenty-five rotating leaders existed at the Red House.

There was one toilet. Setting aside the inconvenience to household members, there were neighbors, who eventually complained about the septic overload seeping down the street. In Marin County, the soil is primarily a nonabsorbent clay, and septic tanks do not leach very well. The ordure of thirty people had drenched the impermeable earth around the commune with enough unpleasantness that in response to complaints, the county placed a lien on the house until the problem was corrected. The Red House was forced to begin what would become a series of numerous and gargantuan public works projects, accomplished in typical Red House fashion.

A sympathetic neighbor donated five hundred dollars to buy a twenty-five-foot strip of land on the south side of the property to make room for additional leach lines. The Red House crew, wielding picks and shovels over many long, beer-swigging, pot-toking afternoons, dug a six-by-six-by-ten-foot-deep gray-water sump beside the house and filled it with discarded kitchen appliances, crank shafts, engine blocks, and domestic flotsam. The "gray water" from dishwashing, baths, and laundry collected here and was siphoned down a thirty-five-foot drop to drive three RAM pumps, which use the fall of the water from some height to power the pumps without electricity. They transported the more offensive effluent two hundred feet to the leach field created in the newly purchased twenty-five-foot strip. The construction of the leach field itself was the excuse for another extended party, and on that day, other family members joined the Red House and hand dug 140 feet (forty feet per legal bedroom) of ditches to bury the leach lines.

Jim Jurick, the county health inspector, a kind and patient man who is still a friend of the Thelin family, dutifully inspected each stage of construction. If he wondered why twenty or more people were always available to work on the project, he never asked, which allowed Ron and company to maintain the fiction that they were simply a single family repairing a single-family house . . . with a little help from their friends.

The total economy of the Red House was sustained by three welfare checks that arrived for the children of the "Big Moppers"—Marsha, Joanna (Bronson) Rinaldi, and Nina. This was a minimal amount of money to support thirty people. The Welfare Department would never have sanctioned a single-family home with so many inhabitants and, to protect taxpayer dollars, the department performed periodic inspections. Had inspectors applied the same diligence to fraudulent and wasteful military expenditures that they did to our living arrangements, the national deficit would not exist. These inspections prompted energetic responses. One family's bedroom would become the Yoga Room for the day; another's would become the Music Room, the Workshop, or the Barbecue. People extraneous to the legal definition of "single family" would disappear so that the welfare workers would always discover and dutifully scrutinize three indigent women, living a life filled with rustic but imaginative amenities. As soon as the bureaucrats' car had disappeared down the hill, inhabitants of the dwelling spaces reappeared to reorganize their possessions and reclaim their homes.

The overriding concerns of these family houses were to learn how to live communally, to expand and deepen the sense of community, and to diminish our per-capita consumption of natural resources and energy. These were no easy tasks. Furthermore, American individualism made unanimity and collective cooperation difficult. We challenged ourselves to create systems in which each of us could maintain personal authenticity and still participate in a social unit. Though easy to express, such creations required constant discussion, checking, and rechecking.

The Red House did this more effectively than the more anarchic, end-of-the-world mob that assembled around me at the ranch in Olema. Perhaps because there were so many siblings under the same roof or perhaps because Ron and Marsha were such generous people, things at the Red House always seemed easier and less choleric—chaotic, certainly, and Dionysian at times but without the grudging resentments and flares of ill temper that seemed endemic at Olema. Yet even the best collective life can wear thin. Some people would use anyone's toothbrush, and objecting to this might be regarded as bourgeois. Vinnie unilaterally removed the bathroom door at the Red House one day, asserting that "the fear of being observed" was a neurotic vanity to be banished.

Who will empty the garbage, clean the toilets, and do the dishes are mundane but vital questions. Ron noticed my lover Sam washing only the tops of the dishes and setting the dirty bottoms on the clean tops below them because she "didn't want to be bothered." Differences in personal aesthetics became sources of friction. If I prefer washing my face in a clean sink and someone else doesn't, it is a difficult issue to resolve from an ideological position, and hours were often wasted in the vain attempt.

Being "bothered" is what the responsibility of living together is all about, whether in a family, a commune, or a village. Extending the standards of care and support you hold for yourself to others requires a lot of energy and commitment. It involves increasing rather than diminishing your sense of responsibility. The leap from our heritage of single-family homes to intense communal living was an extreme shift, and we often discussed the fond hope of establishing a small village, where each family might have its own household and maintain its personal environment to its liking.

But the struggle with these issues, enervating and irritating as it sometimes was, felt like necessary work. We knew that if we were to build a new culture from within the old, it would require time, patience, and practice to resolve obstacles and create habitual responses that were based on community well-being rather than merely personal preference. We were in uncharted territory, and for better or worse, the people working with you were your tribe. There did not seem to be any better place to be than with them then at the edge of the world.

But by 1971 the only people remaining at the Red House were those with nowhere else to go. The place was degenerating. Ron and Marsha had moved away and into the city sometime earlier, having gone to live with Ciranjiva, an eccentric, silver-haired, dope-smoking, coke-snorting Indian holy man who insisted that he and his followers were immortal. Lou Gottlieb, founder of Morningstar Ranch, a famous local commune belonging to a parallel tribe to the Diggers, had met Ciranjiva in India, been impressed, and brought him home. Chanting "Bom Shankar Bolenath" at the top of his lungs, Ciranjiva would inhale huge draughts from a *chillim*, a small clay pipe for smoking marijuana and hashish, and then, wreathed in smoke, would begin lectures saturated with impenetrably baroque Hindu imagery. Although I was not drawn to him, Ron and Marsha adored him, and his followers were a lively, intelligent, energetic, and happy bunch, still interconnected and mutually supportive today.

At a certain point, however, the communal chaos of the Ciranjiva community must have grown somewhat tiresome, because Ron and Marsha moved back to Forest Knolls and decisively claimed the Red House as their own. No longer sensing a contradiction between ownership and freedom, they filled a fifteen-ton dumpster with garbage from the house, jettisoned everyone and everything, and assumed personal responsibility for their home. The failure of collective discipline allowed privatization to invade the heart of the counterculture. "I had always been off the hook before," Ron said. "It wasn't *my* house so I never had to be responsible for it. As it degenerated, I suddenly understood something about freedom leading to responsibility."

They cleaned, washed, and scrubbed the house, creating there a model of the luminous, orderly universe they perceived. "I had learned a lot from communal living," Ron admitted. "A twenty-five-mile-an-hour speed limit is a cooperative agreement. It is a tool designed to do certain work. You can't exceed the nature of the tool and call that freedom.

" 'Do your own thing' made authority impossible, even *legitimate* authority," he continued. "We *reacted* to false authority, which demeans true authority. True authority is skill, insight, and knowledge."

For the rest of his life, Ron's political activities centered around his home and community in the San Geronimo Valley. He maintained a subsistence wage as a cab driver, raised his children and grandchildren, and became a respected participant in local issues. In 1995 he was diagnosed with a small cancer in his liver, which failed to respond to treatment. He grew thinner and visibly weaker, but never complained, fretted, succumbed to self-pity, or stopped enjoying his life. The Red House became a festive center as people dropped by, partied, discussed politics, kept company, and contemplated future plans while Ron awaited what he called "my passage."

A week before he died I paid a visit. Ron was sitting in his pajamas before one of the wood-pellet stoves his brother Jay manufactures. Food was being readied, women chatted amiably in the kitchen, and occasional laughter tinkled like wind chimes. Small groups of visitors dropped by, and the breadth of care and concern for this wonderful man was movingly evident.

Ron told me he had no regrets. "I've been so surrounded by love and care," he said. "I've had such unbelievable good fortune." He was thin and yellow as a pencil except for the swelling in his stomach where the tumor gave him the appearance of a malnourished child.

He died March 19, 1996, on the eve of the vernal equinox.

A month later there was a celebration in his honor in the Redwood Grove in Forest Knolls. Three or four hundred people showed up: politicians, family, friends, some I had not seen in twenty years. The day was sunny and leisurely, redolent with pot smoke and the sound of popping beers, laughing kids, speeches that few attended, good music, and the solid coherence of a community honoring itself by honoring one of its stalwarts. There was no more appropriate way to honor Ron Thelin than with a party.

My contribution to the event was an original song performed in his honor. It was called "I'll Be Back as the Rain":

> My friend and companion went out to go walking.
> He didn't bring his shoes, he didn't carry a cane.
> He passed through the gate on the day the plums blossomed,
> Said, "Don't you wait up, I'll be back as the rain."
>
> The tobacco smoke's cleared and the wineglass is broken.
> The ashes are cold where there once was a flame.
> Outside in the green hills a wild bird is calling,
> Singing, "Don't you wait up, I'll be back as the rain."
>
> *Chorus:*
> So dust off the keys of the upright piano.
> Slap tambourines while the saxophone blows.
> The blossoms don't mourn in the ices of winter.
> We don't mourn for a man who lived life as he chose.
>
> There's a new glass in the roof and the light comes in streaming,
> You can lie in the bed and see star-shot domains.
> In the dreams of the wife, he's there fair and handsome
> And his children are singing, "He'll come back as the rain."
>
> Fog is the breath of the mountains at morning.
> We're passengers all on a runaway train.
> The buck in new velvet and the baby a-bornin'—
> We're all standing in line to come back as the rain.

14

black bear ranch

The Red House was one among many Free Family camps, shaped in large measure by the character of Ron and Marsha Thelin. The most remote of our community houses was Black Bear Ranch, and its particular culture was always the most extreme. While it would be inaccurate to say that Elsa Marley's personality was emblematic of Black Bear, it is fair to say that Black Bear was the perfect place for a woman as talented, eccentric, and free-spirited as Elsa, and so I'll tell the Black Bear story through hers.

Elsa Marley's life has embraced enough avant-garde movements and events, from friendships with abstract expressionists Willem de Kooning and Franz Kline in New York to painting in China during the demonstration in Tiananmen Square, to fill a small library. I met her shortly after she married Richard Marley, the merchant marine who instructed Sweet William not to patronize the Manila whorehouses. Elsa was a founding member of the group that created Black Bear Ranch.

Black Bear was at the dead end of a nine-mile-long dirt road in the Trinity-Siskiyou Wilderness, one of the most remote habitable places in California. The goal of this group was to create a commune and "family trust" there, and they did. It exists to this day, and I am still one of about two hundred owners.

Elsa is Canadian. After a prolonged and colorful youth that included time in New York, Majorca, Yugoslavia, and London, she found herself in Berkeley supporting her two kids by modeling for the Art Institute. One day, she had an epiphany that linked her "quick-action posing" for artists with an idea she felt might make her some money. She designed a series of veils to wear while dancing nearly nude under psychedelic lights as someone read aloud from the Book of Revelations. *Revelations* was a smash hit, featured in *Playboy.* It played every Thursday night for almost a year, and people traveled to Berkeley to see it from all over the Bay Area.

The show's popularity made it a successful agent of cultural cross-pollination. Through it Elsa met Bill (Sweet William) Fritsch and Lenore Kandel. Peter Berg, John Robb, and Lynn Brown came by from the Mime Troupe, and by that happenstance Elsa entered the gravitational field of the Diggers.

Elsa began to see a great deal of Lenore and Bill at this time, and Bill's friend and former brother-in-law, Richard Marley, came around often. Everyone seemed to know everyone else. Ideas flowed as copiously as wine and as ubiquitously as marijuana smoke, creative projects were engendered over lunch, and the world appeared waiting to be reconceived.

Elsa glows when she remembers these times: "I was interested in seeking out people of creative genius. Imagination could solve *anything.* Everything was possible. Potential for instant change—always on the edge of illumination. It was like standing on line in the post office and suddenly someone says, 'You're next.' It was even more exciting than actually *doing* it. [That feeling of] being Next! And suddenly, too, your heroes are interested in what *you're* doing!"

A friend of Elsa's gave up all his worldly possessions. (In this materially fixated time, people might be surprised at how often such things occurred during the sixties and seventies; when I moved to Olema, for instance, I gave away 1,200 lovingly collected records, convinced I would never again live with electricity.) Elsa moved into this friend's Victorian house full of furniture on Eureka Street when he abandoned it to pursue some spiritual path. "Another perfect street for another 'Eureka!' experience," she laughs. Her roommates included her two kids and Richard Marley's girlfriend, Eva.

Shortly after moving into her new digs, Elsa performed at an artist's party at the home of Margo St. James, a big-time San Francisco madame and something of a performance artist herself. Margo went on to form the prostitutes' union, COYOTE—an acronym for Cast Off Your Old Tired Ethics—and later ran for political office. Richard Marley was in attendance, and when Elsa performed *Revelations,* he fell in love. The next day he called on Eva, his girlfriend, who was out, stayed for a cup of coffee with Elsa, and then another, and Eva was history.

The day after the party, Elsa took a trip to Sonoma with Janis Joplin to help Janis discuss some problem she was having with her band. Adhering to contemporary psychological protocols, *everyone* took acid—including Elsa's two-year-old son Aaron and the dogs. She and Aaron spent a glorious day together chasing wild horses and braiding daisies, until they stumbled on Janis sitting near a large pile of cow shit humming with flies, utterly bummed out.

Elsa laughs and reminds me, "That was *so* like Janis. Out there in the middle of glory, sitting in the shit. I moved her next to some flowers."

When Elsa and Aaron returned home exhausted, she found a small shoe box on top of her bed. On top of the shoe box was a tiny pair of earrings and inside the box were Richard Marley's worldly possessions. He stayed until 1980.

Richard and Elsa had not fully entered the Digger community yet, but their domestic arrangements were definitely in our style. They were sharing their house with the Bat People—Billy, Joanie, Jade, Hassan, and Caledonia (this was before the Bat People moved upstairs over Hell's Angel Pete Knell). Friction due to differences in temperament and internal chemistry produced an anarchic boil. Richard ran around upstairs wired on speed, while Billy Batman stayed downstairs, zonked on smack, immobile as a table, while their children raced between the two levels like fluids in a heat exchanger.

Peter Berg focused his persuasive powers on convincing Richard to join the Diggers, a tall order. Marley's natural cynicism led Peter to award him the uncannily accurate nickname of Harpo Bogart. His curly blond hair greatly resembled Harpo Marx's, while his raspy, deadpan voice and unflappable attitude were pure Humphrey Bogart. "I don't get this *free* shit" was his litany in response to Digger theater. Richard was still employed as a longshoreman, taking speed to wake up and go to work on the docks. He would return at night worn out and enter a house full of babies, flutes, feathered fans, lace, bangles, beads, crystals, and Elsa and her friends stoned on grass or acid. "It's a good thing we were in love," Elsa observes drily.

Tracy, the only name I ever knew her by, and Scott Hardy, a psychedelic light-show artist, joined the Marley circus that winter. The two lived on the road, perpetually in transit among New York, San Francisco, and Los Angeles, crashing with friends. Kirby Doyle, a mad Irish poet, moved in. He had just published his novel, *Happiness Bastard,* and although not yet certifiable, he was working toward his credential, shooting speed and spending his nights discoursing in erudite, epic rambles. Before long he and Tracy were keeping company and Scott had moved on. Ten years later, after Tracy died of an overdose from swallowing her stash of drugs while she was jailed for a minor traffic infraction, Kirby went to pieces and disappeared for a time. He was seen preaching on street corners in San Rafael, calling himself Radio Doyle. By 1985 he had pulled himself together again. I encountered him last in 1993 at a poetry reading in San Francisco; he was fit and hale and just beginning a series of readings that would hopefully introduce a new generation to his wondrous, wild, and funny poems. Experience has taught me never to write people off; there are second and sometimes third acts in America, and each trough of a wave is seamlessly attached to a crest.

Peter finally convinced Marley to help Sweet William hauling the garbage from family houses in his truck, to save the fees for city service. Richard's contribution was minimal, however, because he was never overly keen on manual labor. Elsa was expecting their child, Indira, and the two crossed the line into the Digger fold at the "Invisible Circus" event at Glide Church, where Elsa appeared as one of the nude (and, in her case, pregnant) belly dancers. From that time on they were family.

In the late spring of 1967, Elsa and Richard left their house in charge of Digger friends (a *big* mistake) and headed north to the Klamath River to have their baby. They settled into a little cabin with friends and had not been there ten days when Elsa went into labor. An hour later, the police broke down the doors. The cops found some raspberry-leaf tea, a long-muscle relaxant very useful for childbirth, and assumed that it was marijuana. They found a birth kit, given to Elsa by her doctor, containing a syringe and some powdered vitamin C, which the cops assumed was cocaine. They arrested Richard and Elsa and took Elsa's children, Yoni and Aaron, to a foster home.

Elsa was sent to jail, and her water broke twenty minutes later. When the other inmates informed Elsa that the baby would be taken away from her, she was shocked and sat bolt upright in her bed. Her contractions stopped. She remembers thinking, "They already have two of my kids—they're not getting this one!"

In the meantime, all tests of the police seizures proved negative, and the charges were dropped. Richard was released and managed to free the children. Elsa was released. Indira (named after the East Indian queen of the gods) Star (scientists had recently discovered a new star) Marley was born on December 27, much to Elsa's disappointment. "We wanted the first *Christmas* baby, to show those fuckers," she said.

The authorities did not want hippies in Siskiyou County. They could not know that within ten years northern California would lose its logging industry and be crushed by the national recession and that yesterday's upright local merchants, vociferously supporting the harassment and expulsion of hippies, would be today's welfare clients of the billion-dollar market in illicit marijuana. It is, in fact, California's leading agricultural cash crop, produced largely in the deep woods and hidden recesses of the northern counties. Soon, those good ol' boy sheriffs, merchants, and supervisors would be soliciting campaign contributions from the hippie growers even while they were milking Uncle Sam for federal handouts from the CAMP program (Campaign Against Marijuana Production) in order to eradicate the same marijuana that was underwriting the local economy.

Richard and Elsa left the hospital and returned to San Francisco to find that the Diggers had not only liberated their house but all their personal possessions. This was a definite downside to life in a free family, but they took it in stride and moved in with Sweet William and Lenore.

Black Bear? We're coming to it. Elsa's meander takes us there.

A lusty, voluble Italian from Los Angeles named Michael Tierra—trained in classical piano and composition—had moved north and taken a place on Rattlesnake Hill in Dunsmuir, California, where he met John and Inga Albion. Richard and Elsa arrived to visit him in the spring of 1968 in search of a country base, bringing with them the motto "Free Land for Free People" emblazoned on mental banners.

Driving around one day, they passed the Big Sky Realty Company, and on impulse Elsa said, "Stop the car." She gave the realtor their criteria: eight to one hundred acres, isolated, good water, a house and outbuildings. The realtor did not hesitate; he went directly to his file and pulled the information on Black Bear Ranch, an abandoned gold mine in one of the area's most remote canyons.

The ranch and mine originally belonged to John Daggett, lieutenant governor of California during the gold rush. Appropriately, he was also director of the San Francisco Mint. Due to his exalted political position, he was able to enlist three hundred indentured Chinese laborers to build a nine-mile road from the nearest one-store town up to the crest and then down three hair-raising miles of reverse-camber switchbacks, dead ending at the ranch: eighty acres of forest, buildings, gold, rushing trout streams, and a few spacious meadows.

For sale: twenty-two thousand dollars.

Elsa, Redwood Kardon, a tall, handsome, steady brother from the L.A. Free Clinic, conscripted into the family by Berg and myself, and Phyllis Wilner camped there for a weekend, poking around the old but serviceable house and outbuildings, the abandoned orchards, and the meadows and cooling themselves in the frigid creeks. They concluded that the Free Family had to own it. The down payment was $2,200, and while this amount seems minuscule today, it will place things in perspective to realize that collectively they were having trouble raising their monthly rent of thirty-five dollars or that between 1966 and 1975 my approximate annual income was $2,500.

But Elsa has always possessed an optimism that exists independently of objective criteria. "I believe that if I have a righteous need for something, it will come," she says even today. The group drove nine hours nonstop to San Francisco and spread the news of their glorious find to friends at the Willard Street house. Dour, bespectacled Eva "Myeba" Bess listened in silence and left the room. She returned moments later, stone-faced, and handed Elsa a two-thousand-dollar check. Richard was unhinged. Selfless generosity was so foreign to his orientation as to be inconceivable. Eva's simple act permanently anchored Richard's belief in the Free Family, and he left immediately to seek the rest of the money necessary to outfit a homestead. With the fanaticism of the newly converted, perhaps he took things a bit too far when he left Elsa and their new baby as collateral with a dealer who advanced him a large amount of LSD to transform into cash.

Group schemes for raising money proliferated like legislation in Congress, as our various subsets and clans began the process of making Black Bear our own. Michael Tierra, Redwood, Marty Linhart, Peter Lief, and Elsa traveled to Los Angeles to raise funds in Babylon. Elsa was ecstatic. "They *all* became my lovers," she remembers, "except Peter, who was stoned on acid every day and never came out of his room."

Tierra had a list of celebrities who were either sympathetic to their goals or terrified of invasion by his wild friends and paid them to leave. When actor James Coburn was recalcitrant about supporting this vitally important revolutionary endeavor, Michael burned an American flag in his house. The ensemble was royally received by designer Charles Eames, who took a particular fancy to Elsa and her work. Peter Tork of the Monkees generously offered a place to stay while Elsa and the others worked the town. "He was sweet," says Elsa with some chagrin, "and I felt bad because the boys ripped him off for everything that was liftable."

Film director Michelangelo Antonioni wrote them a check in an elevator; Steve McQueen gave a little. Their rap appeared bullet-proof. Elsa, wild-eyed and idealistic as a hippie Joan of Arc, prophesied fervently that "a new world will be born." The boys came on hard, relentless and mercenary. Even Grogan, who was not traveling with them, scammed a great deal of money for Black Bear Ranch, but predictably to those of us who knew him, it never reached ranch coffers.

This traveling dog-and-pony show epitomized the conflict of high idealism and unprincipled selfishness that characterized many Digger activities. Elsa's vision was an unsullied white, straight from the tube. I'm sure the boys were believers too, but the colors of their visions were not as pristine.

Elsa's group raised about fifty thousand dollars—serious money and hard work at any time. Because the title had to be in someone's name, Richard signed all the papers. They assembled tools and supplies, bought and repaired an old Coors beer truck to transport them, and prepared to depart for their new life. When the core group—Richard and Elsa, Mike Tierra and Gail Ericson, John and Inga Albion, Eva Bess, Roselee, Redwood, Peter Lief, and Efrem and Carol Korngold—rolled down the dirt road and parked at the ranch house, they were shocked to find people already camping there who refused to budge. It was, after all, free land, wasn't it? Some stayed, some drifted on. Richard and Elsa's party set up housekeeping in the barn because the main house was already full.

It would be hard to overestimate either the isolation of Black Bear Ranch or the collective inexperience of this initial group of pilgrims. With the exception of John Albion, a miner's son from Colorado, no one possessed even the most basic skills for rural living, let alone *primitive* rural living.

Richard decided to take the bull by the horns. One day shortly after they had arrived, he called a meeting in the main house for the following morning. Donning an old school band uniform (for authority), he placed a large blackboard at the head of the room and, reprising his experience as a labor organizer, set to work organizing his friends into shitter committees, food-prep committees, janitorial committees, planning committees, and so on. As cleverly as a latter-day Jefferson, he laid out a blueprint of an enlightened community, and then, pleased with the design, order, and probity of his model and awash in optimism, he rested.

By the next day, the blackboard had disappeared, nothing had changed, and Richard was crushed. It was bad enough that the title to this impending disaster was in his name, but winter was approaching and the idea of being snowbound with this crew in an isolated canyon plagued Richard's mind with Donner party fantasies.

Kirby Doyle arrived high on acid with a truck full of plywood and geodesic dome materials. The next morning he told everyone how he had spent the night listening to the spirits of the old miners weeping—a bad omen. Despite this gloomy premonition, Richard and Kirby assembled a geodesic dome in what had once been the garden of the main house. Elsa, Richard, Yoni, Aaron, Indira, and Jeannie Di Prima, daughter of poet Diane Di Prima, and her dog spent the first winter in that fifteen-foot-diameter dome, which also served as the family kitchen and art studio.

By January, they had run out of kerosene for the lamps and even matches. The house was freezing. No one knew how to chop wood, and only one or two people knew how to cook. Everyone was stiff with cold. The babies were sniffly, the grown-ups crabby. Oblivious to such trivial temporal concerns, Michael Tierra would wander into the kitchen in a silk dressing gown, famished after a morning's piano practice, and wonder aloud, "Where's my breakfast?"

At the first thaw, county crews plowed the road. Richard and two others took the old Coors truck into the tiny town for the first mail run since the snow had trapped them. Three days later, they had not returned and the ranch members panicked, imagining them lost over a cliff. In fact, they had driven to San Francisco, where other Diggers raised money to stuff the truck with grains, cooking oils, flour, raisins, dates, nuts, granola, kerosene, cornmeal, and enough staples to get the ranch through the rest of the winter. When they returned six days later, they were celebrated as heroes.

It was one of the worst winters in California's recorded history, with more than four feet of snowfall. The roads were so impassable that Mark volunteered to walk out for critically needed kerosene and matches on homemade snowshoes. He completed the grueling eighteen-mile round-trip in one day, returning home with twenty gallons (about 120 pounds) of kerosene, which leaked en route, burning his skin painfully.

Emergency situations are often an excuse for suspending democratic processes, and several members at Black Bear proceeded to take advantage of this time-worn political tactic. The general population was aware that something needed to be done but didn't know where or how to start. Richard joined forces with Efrem Korngold and Marty Linhart to form the "Let's Get with It" political party (read "junta"). Using combinations of revolutionary rhetoric, blandishments, and threats, they organized firewood crews to fell, cut, and split wood for heat, cooking—and sex, for that matter, since the women had begun withholding their favors out of general disgust with the men's ineptness (or perhaps because they were simply too cold). Responsibilities for kitchen, cleanup, and children's duties were assigned in similar fashion. Affairs became more organized, although "organized," in this context, does not mean *normal*.

Since the inhabitants of Black Bear were urban people who had never lived in the country before, their imaginations were prey to horrible inventions. The surrounding area was truly wild—canyons brimming with black bear, cougar, and lynx—and the presence of such carnivores became magnified in their minds into dire threats. Some were afraid to let their children out of sight; others spent all day, every day, indoors. Gradually a consensus emerged that since they *had* moved to the country, they ought to be out *in* it occasionally. Timers were set, and once every hour the coffee-klatching and the bitching were suspended, and everyone ran outside to do laps around the house, screaming at the tops of their lungs to frighten away potential predators.

The group survived the first winter somehow, acquiring the minimal skills necessary to exist outside the support systems of urban life. As it evolved and prospered in the next years, Black Bear became an integrated component of the Free Family network, a situation not always to its advantage. "Family" members would often arrive like invading birds, dropping seeds of conversation and random political ideas from the distant city, which, in that isolated environment, sometimes engendered genetic mutations barely resembling the parent notions that spawned them.

There was, for instance, a period of time when everyone abandoned their tiny single-family dwellings and individual rooms to sleep together in the main house in order to subvert what had been diagnosed as "growing factionalism." All clothing was suspended from pipe racks in the center of the room, and everything was free for anyone else to use. There was no private property. Monogamous couples were disparaged as decadently bourgeois by a faction that held sway for a season, decreeing that no one could sleep with the same person for more than two consecutive nights because that would encourage "coupling."

I was visiting then and smitten with Geba, a magnificently zaftig earth mother who, to my fevered imagination, had stepped directly from an R. Crumb illustration. She maintained an outside bed on a hill she called the Eagle's Lair. It was lovely to be there, under the stars and rustling trees, and the idea of having to report to the main house as a sexual conscript was unappealing, to say the least. On the day that my allotted time with Geba was up, I sought refuge with Richard and Elsa in their diminutive creekside house. They somehow managed to float above all institutional rules, and I spent a heartbroken day in bed with both of them, making love to Elsa, taking Nembutals with Richard, and, according to Elsa, moaning rather undecorously about my crush on Geba.

By 1969, Black Bear was becoming famous in the counterculture. Sociologists Glenn Lyons and John Salter visited, observed, and took notes, and finally abandoned scientific objectivity and moved in. Psychologist Herbert Marcuse's daughter, Yeshi, lived there with her husband Osha and their daughter Rainbow. Sociologist Don Monkerud arrived to prepare a book on the fledgling community and fell into its clutches. There exists a wonderful photo from this time in which John Salter, pad and pencil in hand, is standing fully dressed beside the hole that Babo, stark naked except for boots, is digging for a fence post while John questions him about Black Bear life.

Children were born at Black Bear, and gardens were planted and tended seriously. Local Indians—Karoks, Yuroks, and Hoopas—attracted by the novelty of this zany community with its bare-breasted women and the copious amounts of elderberry wine we made, brought freshly caught salmon as trade and gifts and generously taught people how to smoke it. Once they brought a dead cougar, a protected species and consequently as illegal to possess as drugs but much more difficult to hide. We destroyed the evidence by eating it. "Not so many people have ever eaten cougar," Elsa points out fairly.

Jon and Sarah Glazer, two rotund and indefatigable Digger foragers, appeared one day with their Chevy pickup bed filled to overflowing with quivering red whale meat, donated by the experimental whaling station at Point Richmond. Black Bear chefs concocted ingenious recipes, and for months people ate whale-a-cue, canned whale, broiled, steamed, sliced, diced, chopped, ground, pressed, smoked, and sun-dried whale until some people imagined that they were living underwater and that the swarm of gnats before their eyes were krill on which they should be feeding.

"We ate a lot of placenta," Elsa adds as an afterthought, referring to the group custom of ritually tasting the afterbirth of infants born on the ranch.

The ranch had a way of eroding standards of scientific objectivity. Sociologist Don Monkerud once became so incensed by Kirby Doyle's lack of physical labor and ceaseless sermonizing about the Bear Flag Republic and how northern California should secede from the south that he shattered a half-gallon jar of honey over Kirby's head—and then spent the rest of the day crazed with guilt over wasting precious honey.

It was easy to get out of touch there. Free Family members came and went often, bringing food and drugs, stopping to visit and help out, but remaining relatively immune to the site-specific madness. The collision between inside and outside realities became markedly obvious one spring when Marty Linhart appeared in the city after an isolated winter, wearing a dress, covering his long pigtails coyly with a scarf tied as a babushka. Marty was a muscular, very hairy, bearded Jewish guy with a broken nose, curiously illuminated eyes, and manic enthusiasms. There was absolutely nothing effeminate about either his appearance or sexual predilections. He just happened to be wearing a dress. City family members were reassured that he was only "exploring his gender" under the tutelage of Black Bear women. They had collected money, quite a lot of money, actually, and sent him to the city to have a vasectomy. Marty thought that this was a capital idea. He was copulating his brains out up there, and if the price tag was tying off his seminal vesicles, he could hardly wait.

In the same way that one behaves gently so as not to unduly startle a sleepwalker, several of us elected to chaperone Marty around the city, trying to subtly help him remember "normal" life. We smoked dope and ate Chinese food. We visited friends and remarked obliquely how interesting it was that he was the only man we encountered wearing a dress. Our perspective prevailed, and we convinced him to use the money to get his teeth fixed, which he needed to do. He did, and he threw away the stupid dress and returned to Black Bear like any other ordinary, messed-up man, to face the wrath of the women whose money he had misappropriated.

In 1993 I was swimming at the Salmon River, visiting Black Bear alumni who live in the environs or who return there every August to keep family bonds tight. One day Marty appeared sans beard, hale and hearty, with an effervescent and charming wife and a dazzlingly precocious and beautiful sloe-eyed daughter whose presence provoked my nine-year-old son into a frenzy of attention-getting activity. She was a stunning reminder of the potential cost of being too quick to trade the future's possibilities for a momentary fancy.

And, of course, there had to be a bear.

On one visit to Black Bear, I learned that a bear had been marauding through the ranch, violating food stores, scaring people, and generally making life miserable. Efrem was planning to shoot it. I didn't know Efrem well at the time; I had not yet learned to love and respect him. I perceived him as a dyspeptic, analytical fellow who affected a blue Chairman Mao hat, and his natural dryness and reserve gave him a rather officious air.

I felt that killing the totem of the ranch could only bode badly for us. Furthermore, it seemed like a poor way to announce our intentions to the other species we were learning to cohabit with, so I volunteered to do something about the obstreperous bear. I elicited a promise from Efrem to give me three days, and I jumped into my truck with Tattoo Larry to find some native people who, I hoped, would know the appropriate thing to do.

I had made some good friends among the Tripps, an old and established Karok family on the Salmon River. We began our mission by visiting first Hambone and then Willis Tripp. Each person they sent us to referred us to another, and everyone seemed shy and diffident about advice. By the end of the second day, Tattoo Larry and I were tired and frustrated. On the third day, we were referred to a small hardscrabble farm where an old native man was milking a solitary cow. He listened to our story in silence, rose, and walked away, and we waited there an hour, uncertain whether or not he had even understood us.

"The bear doesn't have any sense of danger in the noise of a gun," he said when he returned. "That's why you can't frighten him away. Fill a shotgun shell with rock salt and shoot him in the butt. He'll get it then." Larry and I were elated; at last we knew what to do. We leaped in the truck and began our return to Black Bear.

When we arrived the bear was dead. It had entered a cabin, and after this worrisome escalation, Efrem had spotted it grazing on berries and killed it with a rifle shot. I was crushed and angry. All our efforts had been for nothing, and to my mind, our family claim of being other than exploitative settlers had been seriously compromised.

Infuriating me further, Black Bear people were flaunting bear claws, teeth, and fur as talismans, as if they were hunters who had felled the creature with a spear and earned the right to display its power. I was sick. Only Zoe Leader—Malcolm Terrence's partner, a beautiful girl with dazzling eyes, now a merchandising executive at the Walt Disney Company—had thought of Larry and me. She had wanted each of us to have a tooth of the bear to honor our efforts and had buried the skull to hide it; however, she could not find it again. This was fortunate for me, because I would have coveted a bear's tooth. Its loss saved me from what would have been a morally indefensible contradiction—judging others while doing the same thing myself.

I felt estranged from Efrem after that. In time, he separated from his wife Carol and moved in with Harriet Beinfeld, a sunny woman, the daughter of an eminent surgeon. I lost track of them when I left Black Bear the last time.

When I saw them next, I was living on my family farm in Pennsylvania, attending to affairs relating to my father's death. They arrived on a blustery winter night in 1972 or 1973 and I learned with astonishment that they had been living in England, studying acupuncture. Efrem appeared radically transformed. He was calm, self-collected, and very gentle. But the bear still stood between us.

Years later he explained how he had tried his normal procedure of clicking the rifle bolt to frighten the bear away. It had not worked as usual that day, and the bear stood its ground, gazing at Efrem with a disquieting directness, until he grudgingly killed it with a single shot through the heart. When the bear was skinned, its body looked so human that Efrem was shaken to his core and resolved never to kill anything again. In that moment he made a decision to forswear violence and change his life, and he credits his career as a healer partially to the *bear's* intention to sacrifice itself for his awakening.

Efrem and Harriet returned to California and began a medical practice that expanded to include the sale of Chinese herbal tinctures to other acupuncturists and the training of Western doctors in holistic medical theory and techniques. Efrem became a member of the state of California board that certifies acupuncturists for state licenses.

In 1975, not so many years after the bear's death, I returned to California from the East. I inherited a tiny flat from Michael Tierra over a garage directly behind Efrem and Harriet's light and orderly apartment. Their newborn son had a hole in his heart requiring immediate surgery. Furthermore, he had a curious malformation of his thumbs and fingers that made his hands vaguely resemble paws. Efrem and Harriet were anguished about the impending surgery and the shots, catheters, and suffering they would inevitably inflict on a child too young to understand the pain he must endure. I was sitting with them during this crisis, wordlessly lending support, when Efrem turned to me and said softly, "Did you know his name is Bear?" He turned away, and I had to catch my breath to choke off a sob.

I was ashamed of my bitter thoughts about Efrem, ashamed at how easily I had judged him and imputed to him motives less beneficent and noble than my own. I too had used the bear, to some degree, as a way of suggesting that I cared more passionately and deeply about living in harmony with other species than he did. Without referring to it directly, Efrem let me know that he sensed that the spirit of the bear had entered his son and that it would take not only this suffering but also his lifetime of care and parenting to redress the wrong he had committed by taking the bear's life. By acknowledging its spirit in his son, he was apologizing to the bear itself. The generosity and humility of his act and the depth of his commitment made me ashamed of my harsh and self-centered stinginess.

He has remained my doctor all these years, even after I moved away from the city. Often as I lay wincing at his needles, I would marvel at the curious karma that had connected us—and not only him and me but all the various factions and subsets of the Free Family—and wondered at the bizarre, unpredictable, and often tortuous routes on which we have, as a group, lived and died, groping our way to maturity.

Year after year, like a tree accumulating mass that includes scars, bolls, and torsion twists, Black Bear Ranch became more organized; people became more mature and responsible, and relationships lost their adolescent raggedness. Homesteaders overflowed the borders of the ranch proper and migrated along the Salmon and Klamath Rivers, making individual homes there, creating smaller cooperatives to board children of more distant family members to facilitate the children's schooling. Some hired on to the Forest Service, while others staked small gold-mining claims, panning or digging just enough gold to justify homestead requirements.

Recently, the Forest Service has been driving people off those claims, without mercy trampling gardens, burning the houses where the home-steaders have lived for years, and for extra measure destroying the bridges to their homes, which cross over the turbulent river. The rangers have specious legal excuses, but the real reason is that this community has become the backbone of environmental resistance to and criticism of Forest Service poli-cies. Such policies have raped this area in the name of political and economic agendas that serve no one but corporate shareholders, allowing logging on totally inappropriate soils and slopes. The resultant runoffs and siltation have collapsed roads and decimated fish and wildlife habitats, and the Black Bear people have been articulate and educated on-site witnesses to this be-trayal of the public trust.

They were also active in the struggle to stop the Gasquet-Orleans road, an asphalt spike piercing the heart of the country most sacred to the Hupa, Yurok, and Karok Indians. Incredibly, in reviewing the case, the Supreme Court rejected the concept of *land* as a basic spiritual necessity protected by the Constitution. It would be interesting to know what a spiritual necessity might be and why, if a building can be protected as a place of worship, the land it stands on should be exempt.

Elsa is a grandmother now. One of her children lives in Paris, pursuing a master's degree in French. Her daughters are both mothers, and Elsa has re-turned from a three-year sojourn in the People's Republic of China, painting with a Chinese artist named Chen Ke Liang who came to America with her. They work together on fine Chinese paper, he with traditional inks and she with acrylics and oils. They call their large, abstract, intensely beautiful can-vases "Joint Projects" and see them as a marriage of Eastern and Western sensibilities, precursors of deeper understanding between the two cultures.

Elsa is still an edge dweller. Her eyes have never lost their excited opti-mism about the very next moment. She dresses stylishly and imaginatively, with her bohemian traditions still visible in her choices. Her hair is gray, and she appears grandmotherly, plump as a succulent blueberry muffin. I am cer-tain that her young art students have no idea of the wild life their presently decorous and soft-spoken professor has lived.

15

dr. feelgood's walking cure

Closer to San Francisco, things were marginally less bizarre than at Black Bear. Our reputation as edge dwellers and visionaries was solid and we were widely credited not only with understanding the counterculture but also with having the insight and skills to help shape it in positive and more radical directions.

Would that my personal life was as exalted and impeccable as these visions of the future. Sam and I had gone East to visit my parents and things had not been good. The issue of "other women" kept appearing with regularity (and with good reason) in our discussions and I was feeling suffocated by the intensity of her attachment and the commitment she wanted in return. She announced her intention to have a child "with someone." My response was a classic of ambiguity: "And I suppose you're just going to go off and have one then?" She reminded me pointedly that it was *my* child she wanted, and somehow I managed to reconcile my desire for space between us with our sleeping together. By the time we returned to the West Coast, Sam was pregnant with our daughter Ariel. We were soon estranged again, though, and Sam moved in with Paula McCoy, the Diggers' wealthy and elegant hostess, who maintained a salon in her beautifully refurbished Victorian home on Clayton Street across the street from the Grateful Dead's house. Sam's two most enduring memories of that time are Paula retiring to her bedroom with *all* the men at six every night to watch the news "and laugh," and foraging for food in the stuffed refrigerator only to discover that every container in it was empty.

Things got so crazy at Paula's one morning that Vinnie Rinaldi, a temporary immigrant from the Red House, ran through the rooms shirtless and barefoot, screaming "Chick-a-dee, Chick-a-daa" over and over again at the top of his lungs. He threw open the sliding doors and ran up and down Clayton Street chanting his crazy, shamanic healing mantra of mood-altering nonsense, which actually worked because everyone collapsed in laughter watching him.

The scene was too much for Sam, and she hitched a ride out of town with a friend of Paula's named Phil, a tough labor organizer who took her to Ward, Colorado, where he subsequently disappeared; it was believed he was murdered in the course of his work.

I moved to an abandoned ranch about an hour north of the city, in Olema, California. I was living in isolation with my buddy Bob Slade and his girlfriend, Eileen Law, when, in the winter of 1968–69, I was invited on a trip to England by the Grateful Dead, to accompany Emmett, Paula McCoy, Ken Kesey and some of his Merry Pranksters, and Hell's Angels Sweet William and Pete Knell. The Dead had mounted a cultural mission to "check out" the Beatles and determine if they were as socially inventive and progressive as their music suggested.

I realize that it sounds arrogant to assert that a famous rock band might enhance its status by association with an impoverished band of anarchists, but the social climate in the sixties was nothing if not complex. The Dead were a "people's band," proud of their dedication to psychedelic illumination, the premises of the counterculture, and their relationship to their community. They were also wealthy and successful, and a consequence of that was that they had moved to elegant digs in Marin County and were now somewhat removed from the cutting edge and hardscrabble life of the streets, the theater where the Diggers excelled. The Diggers, like our counterparts in Holland, the Provos, were internationally known within the counterculture at this point, and bringing us along would reinforce the Dead's bona fides, "sending a signal" in the parlance of politics, about the

Dead's affiliations. At the same time it would afford the Dead access to our analysis and social inventiveness. It seemed like a good arrangement, and since the Dead were picking up the tab, I decided to go. The only problem was that I had a serious case of serum hepatitis from shooting drugs and my body had the color and integrity of an overripe banana. The Dead provided an apparent solution by bankrolling a trip to a notorious celebrity doctor in New York, famous for his "walk around" hepatitis cure.

His waiting room could have been glassed in as a diorama labeled "Geriatric Preservation Practices, Park Avenue, 1920–50." The room was a collage of tatty Empire reminiscences and patterned silk wallpaper. Four or five desiccated older women overwhelmed by lusterless furs were immobilized in chairs with small, apparently mummified dogs at their feet. None of them betrayed signs of life. The room was petrified. The only apparent motion was the dust motes suspended in the winter light gumming its way weakly through the gauze curtains before collapsing onto the ravaged cheeks of Dr. Feelgood's patients.

I was no picture of beauty either. I am six foot three, and my weight had fallen to 170 pounds. My hair was long enough to sit on. I sported a Charlie Chan mustache and goatee and was dressed per usual, in stained leathers and a cutoff jean jacket with a silk-screened photo of Malcolm X sewn on the breast. The women might well have wondered what they were doing in the office of a doctor who would even *see* someone like me.

A tall and exaggeratedly curvaceous blonde wearing what appeared to be a miniskirted nurse's uniform summoned an elderly patient into the inner sanctum. A few minutes later the old woman emerged, amazingly reanimated, chattering like a canary, bright-eyed, and gay. Even her fur coat and musty dog were transformed, the coat gleaming and the dog's claws clicking animatedly over the wood floor as they passed out the door onto the streets of the living. This transformation was repeated with each patient until the room was empty, except for me.

My turn. Dagmar (as I'd named her in my erotic fantasy) admitted me to a spacious, blue-tiled room. On my right were two industrial-sized stainless steel refrigerators. In the center of the room was an expansive desk behind which Dr. F. sat in a white Marcus Welby uniform with (I swear) a round dentist's reflector on his forehead. He was magnificent, with an imposing head topped by generous amounts of styled silver hair like the television evangelist Dr. Robert Schuller.

"So," he said in a thick German accent (again, I swear it's true), "you vant some speed?"

I was dumbfounded. "No," I said. "No, not at all. I'm sick! My liver is messed up."

"Methedrine does not hurt ze livah. Ze livah loves speed," he said confidently.

I thought, "Where the fuck am I?" But he was the doctor, so I told him of my pending trip to Europe and my present physical difficulties.

The doctor listened, nodding sagely, then crossed the room to one of his refrigerators and began selecting small vials of injectable vitamins from its stocked interior. He filled a syringe the size of a baby bottle, instructing his nurse to write down the contents and amounts so that I could duplicate the procedure on my own in England. When the behemoth was almost full, he turned to me and asked in a kindly tone, "Do you vant a little speed in this?"

"Is it okay to do that?" I asked, thinking to myself, "How often do you get drugstore methedrine?" (Much too often, I was to learn.)

"Absolutely!" he said emphatically and opened the second refrigerator, which was filled to overflowing with row upon row of small *bombillas* (glass ampules) filled with methedrine, resting snugly in Styrofoam containers of a dozen each, like the eggs from a druggie's fantasy of the Easter Bunny. He sucked the contents of one of these into his vitamin cocktail and instructed Dagmar to tie off my arm for an injection.

As he squeezed the contents of this horse syringe into my bloodstream, the niacin and B-complex vitamins announced themselves with a hot flush and sweat, making me dizzy. The effects of the methedrine followed like a dog chasing a rabbit, accelerating my pulse as if it had been turbocharged. My breathing became deep and rapid, and I started sucking air like a marathon runner. I must have looked like I was enjoying myself, because the good doctor clutched my arm, placed his lips close to my ear, and in a deep, upwardly inflected, sexually charged whisper, said not once but twice: "Niiice? . . . *Niiiice?!*"

London's Heathrow Airport bristled with police and special services, having been forewarned of the arrival of our entourage. British customs invited me to "stand aside" in a little room they kept available for strip searches and other formal unpleasantries. They were alert for contraband but couldn't have been prepared for the loony-tunes idiot who appeared before them, carrying his in a brown paper sack under his arm. After an interminable wait, while they investigated seals, checked prescriptions, and questioned me at length, they must have decided that I was too nutty to be smuggling and allowed me to pass into the austere gray charm of a London winter.

The meeting with the Beatles was inauspicious. The management at Apple Records was understandably nervous when our entire group of twenty-odd rockers, bikers, and street people invaded their offices. John and Paul were out of town. Ringo was sweet and quietly loopy, and George made a nervous appearance before us in the Apple foyer to recommend a hotel where "they take anybody."

Instead of a hotel, we chose to rent a large flat in the Prince of Wales Mansions between Kensington and Battersea Bridges and declared open house. European hipsters, hippies, and freaks from several countries heard of our arrival on the grapevine and came to call. The house was a maelstrom of activity. Stanley Mouse, designer of many Fillmore rock-show posters, was decorating the gas tanks of the Hell's Angels' bikes in the foyer. Our salon mistress Paula McCoy, *House and Gardens* elegant, glided among the rooms, naked under a full-length mink, serving drinks, drugs, and snacks with grace and consummate skill. Pete Knell and Sweet William scoured the streets of London in search of the club's first English "prospect," whom they eventually found in the person of Buttons, a sweet Cockney who returned to America with us for his initiation. (Buttons completed his initiation and did become the first English Hell's Angel, but it didn't take deeply, and he eventually left the club.)

I developed a crush on a delicate little English wren of a girl, appropriately named Jenny, and passed the days and nights in high spirits, meeting and greeting our European peers. I particularly remember the visit of Simon Vinkenoog, a pale, angular Dutch poet who waltzed in with his tall, dark wife Reineke and her girlfriend. The two women were true exotics, intertwining their arms constantly, laughing easily, humming Mozart while the men talked. Their clothes were constructed of intricate brocades and sashes, and small flowers were woven through their hair. They were groomed to an impeccable finish and appeared to have stepped directly from the canvas of the wonderful Whistler oil *The Princess of the Country of Porcelain.* They seemed distant and more sophisticated than any women I had ever encountered.

As a diplomatic mission, the trip, on the whole, was a bust. The low point, perhaps, was the Apple Christmas party, to which we had been invited by Beatles' publicist Derek Taylor. There was no food. Pete Knell wandered around the elegant old London drawing room in his cutoff Levi colors with a pair of tiny white baby booties dangling inexplicably and ominously from his lapels, asking for food with increasing irritation. We were all hungry and had, after all, been invited to a Christmas feast. Pete was pissed off at the cool British aplomb and also at what he perceived as an insult to him and his friends, surmising that the Beatles might be hoping that if we were not fed we might leave.

At a certain point in the afternoon, Pete, Bill, John Lennon, and I were sitting in a corner. John sat on the floor with his hands wrapped around his knees, transfixed by Pete's story about Charlie Manson visiting the Angels in the early days of the Haight and urging them to enlist on his side in a pending racial Armageddon. Pete was recounting how he had told him to peddle his bullshit somewhere else, saying, "If you want a race war, start it." He suddenly seemed to remember his appetite and said, "Where the hell is the food? I'm hungry."

An English twit, blond hair angling across his forehead, aristocratic nose, and pale lemon-colored ascot, took a drag off his cigarette and said, "Oh, really!" in that dismissive English way. "Don't you know it's uncool to be hungry?"

The words were barely out of his mouth before Pete's fist was in it. The guy went down like a demolished building and stayed there, holding his burst lip and paralyzed with fear. Lennon leaped to his feet alarmed and addressed me, "Whut's the mattuh with him, then?"

Bill had already assumed a defensive position at Pete's shoulder, "covering his back." Sensing Lennon's motion behind him, Pete wheeled around, jerked his thumb at Lennon, and commanded me, "Tell him: he's next!"

I rose to my ambassadorial appointment and assured Lennon that it was an isolated—furthermore, past-tense—incident. The guy *had* been rude, after all, to one of John's guests, and we *had* been invited to Christmas *dinner* and had waited five-plus *hours* for some food without even being offered as much as a crustless cucumber sandwich. This seemed to mollify Lennon, but he retired soon afterward, consulting with Derek Taylor, who finally produced food and spirits.

London had other diversions. I particularly remember King's Road and a below-street-level joint named the Baghdad. Sweet William and I arrived about midnight, and thirty Arab men were dancing arm in arm, with champagne glasses on their heads, celebrating the end of Ramadan. At around 2:00 A.M., the owner locked the doors and produced large silver water pipes stuffed with chunks of hashish and accompanied by sweet mint tea and honey-rich baklava. This was the "high" life on a grand scale, and I returned often. Mick Jagger and other popular rockers dropped in and out, and the atmosphere was thick with the buzz of a "happening" place.

One night I arrived to find a Slavic beauty named Ulla dancing on a table in the center of the room, decked out like a character from a Russian novel in knee-high boots, a fitted wool coat with fur trim, and a fox-fur hat. She had high cheekbones, fierce eyes, and luscious lips that when parted revealed glimpses of broken teeth, which contrasted with her styled tailoring and dusted her image with a fine overtone of savagery. Sweet William and I were both smitten with her and bullied our way to the edge of the table to watch her ardently. My desire must have burned particularly brightly this night because in the midst of her dance, she looked directly into my eyes, cocked her hip, rested a gloved hand on it, and said, "Vy nut?" Ulla and I ran off for several days, sequestering ourselves in her apartment. The only time we left each day was for Ulla's required trip to the police station because the authorities had seized her passport for some reason that she never explained, and she was commanded to appear in person once a day to sign in.

Near the end of our tryst, Ulla and I took a train to the country to visit Derek Taylor, the publicist for the Beatles who had walked out of the Los Angeles meeting discussing a benefit for the Diggers the year before. Derek was perhaps the only person at Apple Records who was neither repulsed by nor afraid of our group. A small, lively man, very precise, with a hint of something feral quivering below his urbane and polished surface, he had a keen eye for bullshit and a lively and bottomless curiosity. He was as comfortable discussing fine arts as current affairs, and he went to some lengths to recompense us for the anxiety and timidity of his employers, extending innumerable small courtesies to our group and opening his elegant country home and grounds to Ulla and me.

Things began to pall after a month or so. Heroin was legal in Britain at that time, and Sweet William and I were using it a lot, tying up various bathrooms for long periods of time while people pounded on the doors to get in. We were falling away from the group purpose, whatever the hell it had become. I was still sick, understandably. Dr. Feelgood's cure had apparently intensified my problem, and the little white English "jacks," tiny pills of pure heroin, made their contribution as well.

It was time to go home. The only problem was that I had no home, having just dropped my stuff off at the Olema farmhouse shortly before our departure. Sam was pregnant and, no matter how callously I chose to ignore the fact, I must have unconsciously known that I would have to deal with that reality before too long. For the moment, narcotics anesthetized me to such concerns, and I joined my fellows on the plane for a triumphant return to California. *We* had been to see the Beatles.

16

slipping to the edge of the world

Bob Slade, a Kansas City friend I'd met when I was with Jessie Benton, found the Olema ranch sometime around 1968 through his friend Vicky Double-day. She had been living there with her two husbands, Mark and Cecil, making them both crazy by demanding that they be sexually faithful to her. Their household disintegrated at about the same time that I decided to leave the city.

Olema—"Coyote Valley" in the indigenous Miwok language—is a quiet intersection of two roads and swampy pastures bordering the fog-shrouded Coast Range of northern California at the inland end of Tomales Bay. The "town" of Olema is simply a post office and a store, and the nearest community of any size (perhaps eight or nine hundred people) was Point Reyes Station, a mile to the north.

The ranch itself consisted of three hundred acres located about three-quarters of a mile north of where Sir Francis Drake Road from San Rafael passes through the still-pristine San Geronimo Valley and Samuel P. Taylor State Park with its rushing creek and thickets of oak, bay, and madrone, and it snubs its nose against Highway 1 running north along the coast. From the Coast Highway a dirt road veers sharply uphill to the right and meanders for a mile and a half before spilling into the courtyard of a single-story, nineteenth-century ranch house. Once owned by the Gallagher family, whose heirs ran the Point Reyes post office, it then belonged to Doc Ottinger, a retired physician who leased the land to local cattle ranchers and the house, which had no electricity, to whoever would take it. Doc was locally famous for the spotted Asian deer he had introduced to this bioregion. I doubt that he anticipated that white people with feathers and amulets tied into their long hair, purified in sweat baths and using wild psilocybin mushrooms to sandpaper their nerve endings, would one day creep through the fog-moistened coyote brush and *Ceanothus* bushes stalking his deer for dinner with silenced rifles.

The ranch house was romantically picturesque—smothered in unkempt old roses, with small paned windows, and a lichen-covered shingled roof extending over the front porch. It was flanked on two sides by an abandoned garden and orchard whose silver-barked apple trees blossomed exuberantly each spring. The whole complex was surrounded by a weathered picket fence and nestled among a barn, a corral, and several silvery-gray outbuildings, bleached by the salty coastal wind.

The three hundred acres were half usable pasture and half steep hills, flanked on the east by a mountain referred to locally as Old Meatloaf. The back of the house faced a broad flat table of grass that splayed out toward the road, dipping once into a deep, stream-coursed gully thick with live oak and bay trees, continuing directly into the dark, timbered Coast Range. I called them the "Chinese hills" because the early morning fogs settling in the clefts between the ridges transformed them each day into living Chinese landscape paintings. "Fog is the breath of mountains"—the mushrooms told me that one day, and it seemed right. Still does.

From our elevation, we could see Tomales Bay, the little town of Point Reyes Station to the north, and most of the winding dirt road separating our romantic hideaway from the rest of the world's realities.

Bob Slade was not a Digger, but a friend from an earlier time of my life. He and I moved in and spent days walking the rolling green hills and exploring the abandoned structures. It was a perfect score—the archetypical outlaw hideout—and we were primed to put it to good use, but the trip to London intervened. I barely had time to stake a claim to a room and to drop off my things and my new dog Josephine before I left for Europe.

When I returned from England, I was sick as my dog. Dr. Feelgood's prescription had, if anything, exacerbated my hepatitis, and I was daisy-yellow and weak as wet paper. Olema was practically deserted, and Slade and his girlfriend, Eileen Law, were off gallivanting. Since I could barely navigate the distance to the bathroom unaided, I lay in my corner room, staring at the scraps of faded wallpaper peeling on the redwood walls and the gleaming sun-drenched life beyond the windows, and wondering how I had come to this pass.

Michael Tierra had brought me a coyote puppy from Black Bear as a gift, which I had named Eeja, a Shoshone word for coyote. He lay on the porch just outside my window, too wild to touch but civil enough to my attentions and food to remain just out of reach. Next to him was my white pup Josephine. I had found her at a commune at an old hot springs resort called Harbinger colonized by freaks and turned into a lunatic's idea of the sensual life. Ron Thelin and I had visited the place in the autumn before my trip to England and thought it a pigsty. Naked and willing nymphs did pour hot water over us in the soaks, but the place was so filthy that anxiety about noxious microbes tainted sexual fantasies with dread.

There I saw what appeared to be a small, albino coyote with blue eyes. She was unmistakably feral and hyperalert but also obviously ill, with runny eyes and nose and a curious twitch in one eye that made her appear to be winking. I fell in love with her immediately and determined to take care of her. I found the owner, a young girl from Colorado, who told me that her father had dug up a litter of coyote pups and killed all but one, which he had mated with his Australian shepherd. This dog was a pup of that union. When I pointed out how sick the dog was, she said, "Yeah, bummer, isn't it?" and offered no resistance to my taking her. I named her Josephine, in honor of the queen she would become, and except for the trip to England, we were never apart for even one week over the next ten years. She became a psychically tuned companion who would slip silently into restaurants and hide under my table. I could stop her at a distance with hand signals so she would not cross streets against traffic, allowing us to travel effortlessly in cities.

Once when we were separated in Manhattan, I backtracked twenty-six blocks to find her waiting under my car. She was my most trusted companion (which no doubt comments on my human relationships). With her I felt that I could fall asleep in a public park with a hundred-dollar bill in my mouth and be perfectly safe.

She lay next to Eeja on the wooden porch, and the two of them were luminous in the sun. Their fur shone, their eyes sparkled, their teeth were glistening and white. Their beauty and fitness were indisputable. A thought crossed my mind—literally crossed it in moving red lights, like an electronic banner quoting stock prices—spelling out the words "Health is beauty." Not a profound insight, perhaps, but I was sick enough (and vain enough) to pay attention.

I reviewed my life choices up to that point, reviewed my friends with sallow skin, nicotine-stained fingers, and bad teeth. For all our brilliant social invention and hipness, were we *healthy?* What did freedom and liberation *mean* without freedom from illness? I had lots of time to ponder because my speculations concerning limitless invention had finally collided head on with their first inalienable limit: the integrity of the body. Abuse of it had flattened me like foolscap.

One day, Rolling Thunder came to visit. He was a curious amalgam of contradictory qualities: a Shoshone medicine man, political activist, and opportunistic carnival huckster who had appeared in the Haight several years earlier, announcing that he'd had a vision of the Diggers as the reincarnation of white soldiers killed at Little Big Horn. He attracted a lot of attention in the counterculture community. A fellow named Doug Boyd wrote a book about him, and actor Tom Laughlin featured him prominently in his Indian-Zen-mystic-karate-Western *Billy Jack* films.

Rolling Thunder and I had become close when I spent some time at his house in Carlin, Nevada, fixing his cars and machinery as an admission ticket to his world. His best tobacco was always available to me, and in later years whenever he came to town, usually at the behest of the Grateful Dead, he'd stop by Olema and we'd smoke and talk before he left to doctor someone who needed fixing. R.T. may have been showy, but he also had the real goods and could definitely heal the sick.

So this day, when Rolling Thunder stepped into my room and then stepped out again quickly, saying, "There's a rattlesnake in here!"—I paid attention.

Besides, there *was* a rattlesnake. Camping in the Nevada desert one day, I had killed and skinned one and tanned its hide for my hatband. I took to wearing the rattles on a thong around my neck as a talisman. If I had been less dense, I might have remembered a pointed incident the year before at the Bear Dance, a large pan-tribal gathering in Susanville, California. I liked the dances, the all-day gambling games, and the festive atmosphere. Moreover, I had Native friends who usually showed up at these events, and it was a good time to talk politics and trade gossip. I had walked around the grounds with Eeja tucked under my arm. The Natives loved him and wanted to touch him for luck, and I was an instant celebrity and honored with an invitation to sit with the gamblers. I developed a flirtation with a Native girl that was approaching critical mass until I bent over to put the puppy down for her and the snake's rattles fell out of my shirtfront. She recoiled as if she'd been struck, raised her hand the way actors ward off vampires in bad movies, and said, "No!"

"No," she repeated, backing beyond the reach of any protestation I could muster, and then she disappeared. From that point on, there was a decided chill in the air, and I realized that I had made a serious transgression. I stopped wearing the rattle, apologized to it, and even buried it ceremonially. I thought no more about it afterward, however, and continued to wear my hat with the snakeskin band.

It was the hat in my closet Rolling Thunder was sensing before I even told him about it. He seized my arms, reviewed the rows of puncture marks along my veins and said, "That's where the snake bit you." He may have been speaking metaphorically, but he had a way of making his point. He made me pray over the hat, "wash" it in tobacco smoke, and apologize to the spirit of the rattlesnake aloud. When that was done, I had to gather certain twigs and herbs and make a fire to burn the hat and the band. He gave me some teas to drink daily, including one called bitterroot, which was the foulest substance I have ever put into my mouth.

Ten weeks after those prayers and teas I was cured, and I resolved to keep my excesses within more tolerable bounds, as well as never to dismiss any living thing again by reducing it to a crutch for my vanity. I kept the second of those promises.

This resolution didn't, of course, apply to women. There was something about that farmhouse with a single guy in it (even sick) that served as a magnet for women. To this day I do not understand the phenomenon, but at least twice a week some lovely girl wandered up the road with a bundle of food and curiosity, and stayed for lunch and an afternoon's frolic. Most I never saw again (which might have led a less deluded man to assume the frolics were not that transcendent). But the fact that they came and went like breezes amazes me to this day. How did they find the place? What homing instinct did they follow up my red clay dirt road, and once there, what possessed them to minister to a sick guy with yellow skin and wild dogs for companions? Sometimes I assumed that they were by-products of Rolling Thunder's cure, bizarre phantasms sent to fill me with healing energy and whip my body back into shape. I might have remained faithful to this theory if *none* of them had ever stayed. Among those who did stay was lithe and lovely Nichole Wills, a sunny girl with a captivating smile, an abundance of sexual energy, minimal demands, and a few very dark secrets. She assumes prominence in the narrative later, when our family stew was in full boil at Turkey Ridge Farm, and I'll allow her to surface in her own time.

At first, Olema's only other inhabitants were Slade and his girlfriend Eileen, a tall, slender, maternally calm girl with the kind of deep auburn hair and eyes you might not notice at first glance, but on the second you'd stay for a good long look. Slade would leave in search of adventure each day, and Eileen would clean and putter softly about the house while I remained bedridden. I did not know at the time that her ardor for cleaning was fueled by secret dips into a speed reservoir, but the upshot of her tippling was that the house, though rustic and simple, was always immaculate. Slade had it made. He would run out in his polished chestnut boots, crank over his snappy MGB, and tool off. No matter what time he rolled back in, no matter where his center of gravity had shifted, Eileen was there with food, an orderly house, and a warm body for him. If he didn't show up for too damn long, why, then, occasionally she might be there for me too. It was a sweet deal, and I thought Slade a fool for not treasuring her.

It was easy to be sensitive to Eileen because I had no responsibility for her and she wanted nothing from me. Sam was another story. She had moved into Olema for a while while I was in England, asserting her proprietary rights, I suppose, and looking for a nest for her expected child. She ran afoul of Eileen and her friend Diane, a quiet, capable blonde girl with a subtle smile and a vicious black German shepherd, and they "vibed" her away.

She bounced around various musical communes for a while, the Grateful Dead ranch in Novato, and then a place that some of the members of Crosby, Stills, and Nash maintained, becoming progressively distraught. During that time, she ran into Paula McCoy, who, thanks to Emmett, was just starting her terminal flirtation with heroin. Paula said to her, "If you get through this, you can get through anything," but, Sam remembers, "she wouldn't touch me [or help me] because she knew I needed too much."

She made her way to the city as her term approached and settled for a while with Linda Gravenites, roommate and spiritual center-of-gravity for Janis Joplin, who was on tour in Europe. Janis sent word that Sam could have her baby in her bed, if she could have it before Janis returned. "That was more than most people gave me," Sam recalls drily.

It's hard for me to remember if I was simply heartless or oblivious or heartless *and* oblivious concerning Sam's situation. I honestly can't remember. I was sick and confused, Olema was peace and quiet, and despite numerous positive attributes, Sam and I together never generated peace and quiet.

My Digger friends soon transformed this little idyll at Olema. Scratch a Digger and you find thirty-five others. Slade had difficulty relating to some of the people who showed up from time to time, especially my close friend Chuck Gould, a lone-wolf uncle to a lot of our kids and the perfect running partner. Chuck's style is East Coast Jewish tough and very smart. He is one of the funniest people I know, and also trustworthy and loyal to his core. (In later years, after he became a successful businessman, Chuck continued to generously support Digger kids with tuition money and allowances.) He would help me with the chores that were too mundane for Slade, who made no secret of his disdain for Chuck. "He doesn't play jazz," Slade would say;

he usually left when Chuck arrived. "Not playing jazz" was shorthand for saying that Chuck (and people like him) consider issues and others as designed for purposes other than his own amusement.

I had trouble with some of Slade's pals too. Spider, for instance, was a limber young thug with a quick smile full of bright teeth, a handsome, swarthy face that resembled Omar Sharif's, and an instantaneous readiness to fight. If someone in a supermarket, in the midst of scanning the soup, the dried herbs, the toothpaste, and the Q-tips, accidentally caught Spider's eye, that dark face, grinning with malicious intent, would be in his before he could disengage his eyes, saying, "Do you wanna fight or what?" It was startling and effective and was backed up by training as a boxer. The few times I ever saw anyone take him up on it were disappointing, because the other guy invariably lost.

Another endearing quality of Spider's was that he had no conscience or sense of responsibility to others—a garden-variety if amiable sociopath. He could drop acid in your orange juice in the morning, steal your car, fuck your woman, and then eat your lunch with the same crazy smile and infectious giggle. His idea of a culinary ne plus ultra was a bacon sandwich composed of two slices of bread and *one pound* of bacon. He would stand at the stove cooking the whole pound, oblivious to the spattering grease (or numbers of people to be served by the available bacon) and rap: "You know how when you were a kid you could never get enough bacon? You know how there would just be a couple of pieces on the plate, or like, when you go in a restaurant, or whatever. I mean, YOU CAN NEVER GET ENOUGH BACON. Well, I can. So this is why, how, I make my bacon sandwiches."

Danny Rifkin had come to stay a while. The manager and, as far as I was concerned, the true conscience of the Grateful Dead, he resembled Haile Selassie's kid brother—curly Ethiopian hair and beard, pronounced Semitic nose, and cinnamon-brown skin. Unable to accept the easy spiritual homilies so in vogue at the time, Danny spurred himself—as well as, by example, the band and all that knew him—to be a better person.

Spider, in his infinite wisdom, had secretly poured LSD in Danny's morning tea. It was a bright blue day, Danny was in the garden tending his mounds of corn and beans, and I was off somewhere on one of my endless runs for auto parts to keep my truck running. Consequently what follows is Danny's story:

A horse and rider approached. It was Del (not his real name), a highway patrolman who came to the ranch often to shoot and to talk guns and hunting. I assumed that his curiosity might be related to official espionage duties because he always brought reloaded highway patrol–issue ammunition for our pistols so that we could afford target practice together. As a group we had little other than recreational drug use to hide, and being equally curious about him, I drank coffee with him, smoked cigarettes, and discussed the issues of the sixties, the effects and dangers of different drugs, the relationships among culture and economy, politics, and ethics. He was intelligent and provocative in his questioning and appeared to be nonjudgmental and honestly curious. Although he never appeared in uniform, he was clear about his identity, and I respected him and protected him from witnessing anything that would have put him in conflict with either his job or his personal principles.

There were other cops around as well, however. Tony Veronda was a barrel-chested, good-natured, simple-as-cow-flop cowboy on the surface but shrewd and unsettlingly watchful underneath. He thought that his visits, disguised as neighborly bonhomie, were the epitome of undercover operations. He mentioned once that he was an assistant sheriff's deputy, and his conversation was peppered with the type of jocular remarks about drugs that a white bigot might make to black people about watermelon.

One day he was rambling on about a sheriff's department surveillance of a particular type of plane whose unusual name spelled "acrobatics" backward or something. The subtext of his story was that the police were omnipresent and omnipotent and had tracked the plane from Mexico to San Diego and from San Diego to somewhere else, where they were waiting for it to arrive with its cargo of marijuana.

Since I knew a friend who owned such a plane (and pursued such a livelihood), I called him and mentioned my conversation with Tony. He instantly hung up without saying good-bye. Three days later, he called back and said that I'd saved him a lot of grief and money, and was there anything we needed at the ranch? I mentioned our ten-gallon, sawdust-insulated hot water heater's insufficiencies, and two days later a Sears Roebuck truck delivered the largest, slickest, hot water heater known to humankind, replacing our little improvised job with a behemoth that must have held ninety gallons. Thanks to Tony, we were in hot water.

On the day of Danny's "dosing" by Spider, Del arrived on horseback, riding solo over the hill. He was ill at ease and uncharacteristically cold. "There's more behind me" was all he said tersely to Danny, without hesitating or looking right or left.

The LSD was just turning Danny's brain to scrambled eggs, but it didn't require brains to figure out what Del meant. Though he had some difficulty assessing the exact population of the ranch, getting distracted by whether or not to inform the bushes and trees as well, Danny managed to get the word around and started everyone on the task of hiding their guns and personal stashes of dope. Everyone but Spider, that is, who decided that the moment was perfect to leave for Sausalito and exercise his overpracticed hand at seducing teenyboppers; he pursued them with the same directness he used in challenging people to fight, following his time-tested adage: "Ask enough people to fuck and you may get slapped a lot, but you get fucked a lot, too."

No sooner was the last Smith-and-Wesson wrapped in plastic bags and buried in the whole wheat flour or stashed in the compost to cook with the horseshit and decomposing salad greens than the air swelled with an escalating pulse. Red dust trails appeared down the road just as a helicopter rose from the gully and slipped low over the hill. A grand assemblage of state, county, local, and federal law enforcement agents swarmed us, converging from every direction on this tiny gaggle of underfed, impoverished citizens. The women stood around absently, half naked, babies suckling, nervous systems resonating with the harmonics and dissonances of so many engines whining, whistling, groaning, and roaring simultaneously. Because the group knew that it was doing nothing that might warrant one-tenth of this police attention, the event was interesting public theater, not a cause for alarm.

The police hit the decks running: SWAT types in body armor carrying M1s, crouching low under the thudding copter blades, highway patrol and county sheriffs, DAs, and the obligatory FBI guys. They presented Danny with a botched and inexplicit warrant of sorts, which might have been useful had Danny been able to read it. It mentioned something about an LSD laboratory in the barn and marijuana plants in the garden and was so far off the mark that the spectators lost interest and let the lawmen go about their searches as they chose.

When the revelation occurred, perhaps serially, perhaps simultaneously, that *"there was nothing there,"* the event fizzled to a sodden finale worthy of the cast of *Police Academy.* The place was what it looked like: a rundown ranch house, overcrowded with old trucks, ramshackle outbuildings converted to living quarters, and desperately poor people.

When that revelation penetrated their group consciousness, they organized a military evacuation with a great deal of busy huffing and stern warnings, chest puffing, some mediocre glaring, and not one word of apology for disturbing the day. They even refused an offer of fresh mint tea, which Ananda brought out of the house, naked from the waist up per usual. They squeezed into their idling vehicles and motored off in dark, oily clouds of disappointment.

The overcrowding, the poverty, and finally the police were too much for Slade, and around this time he transferred his base of operations to the Grateful Dead ranch in Novato. Compared to us, the Dead were rich, and their scene was full of great toys and props—more Slade's style. We saw one another after that but not as often and across a subtle divide. I lost track of him for a while until I met his daughter at Danny Rifkin's fiftieth birthday party, and she told me that her dad was a guest of "Uncle Sugar" in a new prison in Colorado. A letter from Slade followed shortly thereafter, and it was great to hear from him again, tough and cool as ever. One line of his letter caught my attention:

> I'm so sick of living with whining white bankers and S & L looters and young, totally fucked-up black crack dealers that I'm almost ready to take the pledge and promise forever to stay in my own lane and never cross the solid yellow line again. . . . Not quite, but almost.

That was pure Slade, and perhaps I had been lucky to have lost track of him. His edgy boredom demanded placation in curious and unsettling ways. I walked into the yard one day, for instance, just as he was convincing Arlene, a statuesque redhead with more courage than sense, to allow him to shoot a cigarette out of her mouth. She walked off ten paces and stood there, neck craned forward so the cigarette would clear her remarkably prominent breasts, and Slade sighted down the barrel of his black, hammerless, snub-nosed .38 Special. I held my breath, but my imagination raced ahead and rode the small slug ripping Arlene's lower jaw off and flecking the fence with bits of tongue. There was a sickening clap of shock as the gun fired . . . and nothing moved—not Slade, not Arlene, not the cigarette. Slade regarded the gun blankly, shoved it into a pocket, and walked away. Arlene looked down her nose at the intact cigarette, took a drag on it, and followed him, while I remained transfixed, chilled in the shadow of what might have transpired.

I had no idea where he was headed that last day when he packed up his goods and he and Spider headed down the road in his sporty MGB for the last time, churning up a trail of dust that finally obscured them like a smoke screen. Olema was mine, collectively speaking. The last "foreign elements," the last dissenting voices to the Free Family experiment, had left and we were now commencing . . . *something*. I did not know exactly what, or how to describe it. But just because Slade and Spider had left did not mean that things would now be more harmonious.

Ruth and Morris Cohon at their wedding breakfast.

Wearing my "actor's suit and shoes," with Jessie Benton and her son Anthony, 1964.

Jessie Benton, daughter of painter Thomas Hart Benton. A natural aristocrat at Chilmark, Martha's Vineyard. 1963. (Author's photo)

Emmett Grogan, Harvey Kornspan, and Richard Brautigan at the first Artist's Liberation Front meeting in San Francisco, 1966. (© Lisa Law)

Bill Lyndyn, Mime Troupe puppeteer, master con, and . . . I suspect on LSD here.
(© Chuck Gould)

Sam and me posing for Tom Weir around 1966. I'd have taken my clothes off too, but probably couldn't get those damn boots off. (© Tom Weir)

Judy Goldhaft (Berg) preparing one of her grand tie-dyes. (© Chuck Gould)

A Digger house food run—Judy Goldhaft in the print dress, Nina in the white shirt, and Ron Thelin in plaid. (© Chuck Gould)

Freedom House, not the best photo, but no history of the day could exclude him, and this is what we had.
(© Chuck Gould)

Sweet William, after joining the Hell's Angels.

Pete Knell, President of the San Francisco Hell's Angels. A truly great guy who taught me much.

Freewheelin' Frank—poet, artist, incendiary being. Brought into the fold by Michael McClure. (© Chuck Gould)

Natch'l Suzanne, pregnant with her twins Taj and Gamilah. (© Chuck Gould)

Nina Blasenheim, Angeline, and Kent Minault. 1969. (© Chuck Gould)

Paula McCoy,
the Digger hostess.
A shooting star.
(© Chuck Gould)

Billy "Batman" Jahrmarkt and Kirby "Radio" Doyle, pondering the mysteries in 1968
or 1969, before Billy left for, and died in, Afghanistan. (© Chuck Gould)

David Simpson's house-home towing "The Bare Minimum"—the Digger's free fishing boat. (© Chuck Gould)

In front of their truck, named "The Albigensian Ambulance Service": (left to right) Judy Goldhaft holding Ocean, Destiny Gould holding Solange, Peter Berg. (© Chuck Gould)

At Olema, 1969, recovering from hepatitis. Note: snakeskin now gone from hat band.
(© Chuck Gould)

The Digger poster we pasted up all over San Francisco, designed by Peter Berg and artist Mike McKibbon. The H.I.P. merchants considered it a shakedown.

Olema Gothic, 1970: Ariel, Sam, and me on the Olena Commune. Ariel's now a PhD with a daughter of her own. (© Casey Sonnabend)

Vinnie Rinaldi, the cosmic clown, laughing at Ron Thelin working. (© Chuck Gould)

With J.P. Pickens,
musician,
artist, "Beat"
elder, in 1968.
(© Chuck Gould)

"Dog-eater"—this is what I
looked like rolling up to my
mother's door after Morrie's
death. The photo was snapped
by a photographer who
bought my dad's cameras at
the fire-sale of my mother's
possessions. (© Martin Cohen)

Chuck "Mooneagle"
Gould—running partner,
photographer, "uncle"
to all the kids.
(© Chuck Gould)

Top row (left to right): Photographer Chuck Gould, Jane Lapiner (and Omar's eyes),
David Simpson with Sierra, Judy Goldhaft, Peter Berg, Destiny Kinal. Bottom row:
World's dumbest dogs, unknown boy, Aaron Rosenberg and Ocean Berg, Gabrielle
Cohen holding Solange Gould with Gillian Kinal, unknown. (© Chuck Gould)

*Hardcore Digger,
Samurai Bob,
at Turkey Ridge,
not too long
before he died.*

*The house, shed, and barn looking toward the mountain which makes half of the
Delaware Water Gap.*

Nicole Willis—the Turkey Ridge "time bomb." 1982. (© Leslie Landy)

Poet Gregory Corso, the derelict who called out to me, "Pierre! Oh, Pierre. Coyote-man!" when I was working on Wall Street.

As Chairman of the California Arts Council, 1976.

Hanging out with Gary Snyder, around 1998.

17

free fall

By now Sam had had our baby, Ariel, and moved back to Olema, asserting her right to be there by pointing out, "It's free, isn't it?" Because of its isolation, the ranch was a perfect laboratory for the exploration of absolute freedom, and before long was overflowing with eager pilgrims who devised ways to forge small niches for themselves in the already overpopulated environment. I nicknamed Olema "the Fool's School" (including myself as enrolled) because by and large, most who came up the road knew less about group life, hygiene, and labor than I did. However, since I had been blundering around there longer than they had, my stature was automatically elevated to the formless and far-from-invested role of patriarch. Among my self-appointed responsibilities was the struggle to instill a rudimentary sense of responsibility into each new arrival.

> *Some Pearls of Wisdom from the Leader*
> • If you let the baby shit on the floor and then eat it, you'll have a sick baby *and* a shitty floor.
> • Free food doesn't mean that I cook and you eat all the time, asshole.

- It's fine if you want to take speed, just don't talk to *me*! I don't actually care that the insects are communicating with you.
- I *know* the Indians used moss for tampons, but you're picking poison oak.

People usually stayed long enough to get their acts together before leaving to present themselves as seasoned communards elsewhere. Despite the turnover, lack of hierarchical leadership, and aggressive libertarian values, we did learn a great deal about living together. Large meals were prepared more or less on a schedule; trucks were kept running; a garden was planted and harvested. There was pretty good music daily and usually an easy amicability reigned. This last was not inconsiderable when you consider that sometimes twenty people were living in and around the one-story ranch house with one bathroom and, until the gift from our dealer friend, a ten-gallon hot water heater.

Revolutionary experiments are fine in theory, but in practice they could frazzle the nerves of a mummy. My old Haight Street partner J. P. Pickens, had moved his wife and three children into the barn. J. P. was a true original—musician and composer of great feeling, an older bohemian whose life was dedicated to spontaneity and social experiments. He was a devoted father and loving husband to his sensitive and rather ethereal wife, Mary Anne. Unfortunately J. P. had a pronounced predilection for methedrine. He used it as a creative fuel and would sometimes stay awake for days on end reducing himself to a raw and vibrating bundle of nerve ends. His methedrine-driven obsession with collecting had not abated; it now threatened to overwhelm the barn. He would disappear for days and return with his stake-sided pickup loaded to the top rail with impossible amounts of Industrial Age flotsam: ring-and-pinion gears, dental equipment cabinets, plastic tubing, soggy cardboard boxes filled with pipe fittings, and random Formica samples—all of it, by his estimation, invaluable and "too great a score to leave, man!" Trying to deter him was like trying to arrest a force of nature. One bizarre midnight, I heard an unusual low rumble outside. I calmed Sam, rolled out of bed, and looked out my window to discover next to the barn a full-sized tractor-trailer truck, idling and rattling like a ball-bearing factory in an earthquake. J. P. was standing on the running board urging the driver in a hoarse whisper, "Be *quiet*, man! These people are a little uptight about my stuff." Something snapped and I ran outside stark naked, screaming at J. P. and the driver to get the fuck out. J. P. threw the man a look begging him to understand, as if he had brought a friend home for dinner only to find his wife having a tantrum. The truck executed a noisy, laborious three-point turn and shambled down the road. J. P. turned to me as if nothing had happened, grinned happily, and said, "You want some speed?"

J. P. had also colonized half of an old shed beside the kitchen. Bryden had claimed the other half. Bryden was working on a large painting of the *Four Horsemen of the Apocalypse*, a vivid and arresting canvas featuring four skeletons riding white horses and enjoying the hell out of themselves. Bryden's model was a human skull with a candle on the dome of its head, resting at eye level on a stepladder. Since Bryden's drug of choice was heroin, he would nod off occasionally, then glide back into the present moment with a little bob, and paint a bit more.

It might have been cozy except that Bryden and J. P. loathed each other. Bryden considered J. P. a noisy speed-freak dwarf and accused him of stealing (conveniently forgetting that Bryden himself had swindled some irate teenagers out of marijuana money, leaving them to await his nonexistent return in *my* house while I was on tour, which resulted in the theft of my guitar and guns). He would later gut my daughter's piggybank and leave an IOU.

J. P. thought Bryden was a "junkie fuck" (if I remember the exact phrase), and the misunderstandings between them eroded their mutual civility until they painted a white line down the center of the shed, and each commanded the other to stay on his respective side. One morning, carrying my first coffee of the day out of the kitchen door and into the anemic morning light, I observed J. P. tiptoeing around the corner of the shed, alert as a weasel, pistol in hand. He slipped stealthily along the wall and around the corner, nodding a greeting at me. No sooner had he disappeared than Bryden showed up, similarly armed, stalking J. P. It was a Keystone Kops routine with dangerous potential. Being a skillful leader, I intercepted the pending catastrophe by inserting myself between them, screaming "stupid motherfucking dirt-bag assholes" at the top of my terrified lungs and demanding their weapons, which, amazingly, they delivered.

Like it or not, I was considered a leader at Olema, or at least impartial enough to be called on to arbitrate disputes. I was painfully aware that I had little vision or wisdom to offer my "followers" and was, in fact, the victim of a dynamic I had unconsciously allowed to develop. As the "leader" I had permission to define the game, set the vocabulary, pontificate about it, and inspire others with fervid visions of what we were accomplishing collectively. "Followers," at least those who paid any attention to me at all, were more than willing to pitch in and bring these compelling visions to glorious fruition. The flaw in this system was that if the leader did not consistently supply visionary energy and inducement, the followers dropped everything for the predilections of the moment, and the brave new world faltered and then stopped dead. I had so appropriated the collective vision that I deprived others of the opportunity of developing their own; I had unwittingly assumed the full responsibility for actualizing Olema's potential. If that potential failed to materialize, Olema was little more than a grubby, overcrowded dirt farm with a large, licentious, dysfunctional family alternately groping for sanity and destroying itself in small increments. Since I refused to see myself and my efforts so minimalized, I was forced to keep everyone else on track with "the big picture."

Consequently I was already exhausted when J. P. pulled an ugly little nickled pistol on Dick the Burglar and demanded that he keep away from his family.

Dick was a handsome, muscular, Nordic type Bruce Weber would have loved to photograph. He had spent approximately nineteen of his twenty-six years in institutions and had been toughened to the core by it. What saved us all from being at his mercy, besides a certain innate sweetness, were his insecurity and difficulty with speech. When he did speak, which was a rare enough occasion, words tumbled out of his mouth and over one another with such intensity that they spent their energy in a formless avalanche. Also, since he had been raised under absolute authority his entire life, he overestimated mine and never challenged it.

Dick was with J. P.'s family because J. P. was not, and though his relationship with J. P.'s wife Maryanne was purely friendship based on a mutual need for kindness, J. P.'s speed-shredded nervous system read their camaraderie as a personal reproach. So one night, sweating and shaking, he pointed his pistol at Dick, screaming, "Stay the fuck away from my family," while Dick faced him down, chanting over and over again, "So who's got the gun? Who's the cop, J. P.? Who?" until I intervened, standing between the gun and Dick, hoping that J. P. would remember that we were friends.

I had to mediate again when Dick, for unknown reasons, began head-butting Tattoo Larry around the living room, trying to provoke sweet, shambling Larry into throwing what would have been a decidedly ill-advised punch. I feigned indifference, stalling for time, while I tried to figure out how to rescue Larry without putting myself directly in the path of Dick's bad intentions. I did not want to lose whatever meager authority I possessed by being beaten to a pulp under Dick's hammer fists.

"Why don't you split his head open with the axe and save your own, Dick?" I asked casually. "Or better yet, if you've got all this energy, why don't we go haul some firewood?" This non sequitur derailed him long enough for Larry to disappear, and like a cat leaving a dead mouse, Dick turned his attention to something else.

Another explosive ingredient appeared one day in the form of a swarthy, handsome, and very streetwise troublemaker named Gregg. He had a practiced charm and soon inveigled a place for himself and his girlfriend among us. He set up a small camp under the trees in front of the house. He had a penchant for heroin, so occasionally we would get high together, and during these hiatuses he revealed his personal history: a long stint in reform school and a hustler's life on the streets.

Gregg was definitely not a follower. He soon developed a very pronounced intention to inhabit my role as chief and proceeded to test me and the security of my perceived position. One day I noticed that a set of my axle stands—steel tripods that hold a truck securely aloft in order to provide space under it for work—had moved from inside to outside the barn where I'd stored them. I marked it in passing. A day later they had moved again. One now rested about ten feet away from Gregg's camp, and he was using the other under his truck.

"Stick 'em back inside when you're done with 'em," I said, a bit piqued that he had not asked permission to use them. Despite our intention to abolish private property, it was a generally respected principle that personal possessions and particularly tools were exempt from collective ownership.

"Sure thing," he answered noncommittally, and continued with his work. The next morning the axle stands had been joined by my four-ton hydraulic jack. All three were plainly visible but had been moved quite definitely within the invisible boundaries of Gregg's camp. I couldn't accuse him of stealing because they were in plain sight, and I didn't have any use for them at that moment that would justify taking them back. Making a big deal out of his using them would have appeared overly concerned, but I did know that a play was being made, and I was determined to do something about it.

I mentioned my conundrum to Moose, my Hell's Angel mentor, during a visit several nights after the second "move" of my parts, and he looked at me as if I were an idiot. "They moved once," he said. "They'll move again."

The next day, the axle stands and the jack were gone. I asked Gregg about them, and he said he had returned them and hadn't seen them since. He was packing to move because he and his girlfriend had made themselves unpopular, commandeering the kitchen to fix their meals and barring others from entering while they cooked. They hoarded and labeled personal supplies and threw tantrums if they suspected that they had been disturbed. The tension between us had become thick and corrosive, but I didn't know how seriously the situation had deteriorated until it was almost too late.

It had been a tough day. Gregg and I had been arguing a lot, and the place felt emotionally chaotic. A Hell's Angel friend named Larry had come to visit and had returned from a walk with the body of a great horned owl he had shot out of a tree. I felt like my insides had been ripped open. I knew and revered that bird. It was the totem of J. P.'s son, Owl, and an unspoken agreement existed that nothing was ever hunted on our land. I set out feed plants in the cattle ponds for the migrating ducks and had appointed myself God's own janitor of the local roads, removing dead animals from the right of way, smoking tobacco ritually and praying over them. In return I took whatever feathers, fur, bones, or talons I needed to make talismans. If they were exotic, like the occasional red fox or badger, I would tie ribbons around the legs, wrap the body in chicken wire, and bury it in the oak leaves for a year. The shiny black beetles (the same species they use to clean museum specimens) would strip and polish the bones until they gleamed, and I would convert them into jewelry and power objects for friends.

More important, the owl was my daughter's namesake. The stormy night Sam went into labor, Chuck Gould and I raced from the city over the tortuous coast road to the tiny town of Marshall at the edge of Tomales Bay, to get the midwife who was to attend the birth. The night was extremely blustery and rainy, and animals were crossing the road in such numbers that Chuck and I remarked on it.

When we reached Marshall, Tracy, the midwife, was feverish from hepatitis and could not come. I was panicky, and as we raced back toward San Francisco, a doe deer stepped into the glare of my headlights and forced us to a complete stop. She looked at me directly, I thought, and it was as if someone had thrown a switch in my mind, shutting down the internal dialogue. She turned away in a leisurely manner and stepped off the road gracefully. Just before she disappeared into the brush, she looked at me again, and her expression gave me the distinct impression she was informing me, "This is where I have my babies." All my anxiety fell away, I relaxed, and we continued our journey at an easier pace.

A few minutes later I turned to Chuck and said, "God, what am I gonna *name* this baby?" As if punctuating that sentence, a large, dark mass materialized out of the storm. It was a great horned owl, flying so low that the knuckles of its talons actually grazed the hood. Chuck and I laughed in astonishment. Although my daughter Ariel temporarily changed her middle name to Lowell in an attempt to blend into the "big-hair" girls in the Texas social landscape of her university, her totemic name, given to her even before her birth and recognized by her extended family, was Low Owl.

Now this owl lay lifeless before me on the kitchen table. I couldn't explain all this to Larry and was dumb with sorrow for the great bird and the meaning of its connections to my life. Larry lived in a world of petrochemicals and steel, a world where a nine-sixteenths nut fits a nine-sixteenths bolt. If I could have made him understand the fuzzy mysteries of my world, he would only have felt ashamed. I said nothing directly, except that "we usually don't hunt here, Larry," but he could tell I was crushed and spent the rest of the day sitting disconsolately under a tree with his black and white bird dog. When I stumbled past en route to my cabin, he looked at me mournfully. "Nice dog," I said to be polite.

"Yeah," he said kind of abjectly. "But I pushed him too hard and broke his spirit." I wondered if he was speaking about me or the dog? Was this an oblique criticism, or was I inventing things? I was too confused to pursue it; the day had turned rancid and I was tired of putting the best face on things and wanted off the hook.

As if on cue, Doc Holiday came by later with some very strong heroin. I got so high that I could not hold my head up at dinner. My incapacity was impossible to disguise, so I excused myself and returned to my cabin. It was dark and cold. I built a fire and sat in the dark musing about the cacophony and disorder around me, trying to reassure myself that it was to be expected, that we were breaking new ground, building something in the ruins of an exhausted old system. Errors, bad habits, and indulgences would be part of the process. "Still," I told myself, "we are moving forward."

My efforts at self-hypnosis proved futile. I had practiced this rap success-fully on other people in the past, explaining inconsistencies between present realities and visions of the future as a process. But it was not working that night, and I was glad that the heroin had kidnapped me from myself.

I awoke some time later, still sitting in my chair, disturbed by an urgent whispering, "Don't. Moose! Don't kill him!" I spun around to find Moose and Sweet William pinioning Gregg between them and the rear wall. Moose had a long Nazi dagger he had wrested from Gregg's hand poised over Gregg's heart.

Gregg was gibbering with fear, "I was just gonna *show* the knife to Coy-ote, I swear to God." Neither he nor I nor Sweet William had a doubt that Moose could have snuffed out his life as he'd stub out a cigarette. "I swear to you," he continued, panic choking his voice, "I swear to you I just wanted to *show* it to Coyote!"

Moose kept the war-trophy dagger and let Gregg leave. He and Bill had arrived earlier and heard something about my condition. They had come to my cabin and had been sitting behind me in the pitch dark (waiting for me to wake? guarding me?) when Gregg had slipped into the room carrying a dagger with a swastika crowning the handle. I have no doubt that had they not been there, I would have been murdered. From that night onward, the Hell's Angels took on a special resonance. They *were* angels to me—but if so, then surely I was in hell.

Just before Gregg's final departure, Sam noticed that her treasured trea-dle sewing machine was missing. We suspected that he had ferried it to the new camp he was making, and after the knife incident I was in no mood for charity. I assembled a couple of loyal pals—foremost among them Rolling Thunder's foster son Nick Fosmo—and I woke Gregg just before daylight by sticking my pistol in his snoring mouth.

"I want the sewing machine" was all I said, and that was the last word anyone uttered for a very tense hour. He and his girlfriend threw on some clothes and woke Frank, their muscular sidekick, and we left the ranch for their new camp near Inverness. There, we loaded the treadle machine, the axle stands, my jack, and several other purloined goodies and backed out carefully, leaving Gregg and company to whatever fate the road would bring them.

Events like these were wearing me down. My confidence in my ability to help anyone was now so insubstantial it could blow away; what I needed was the weight that an infusion of real knowledge might offer.

Fosmo and I decided that our problem was that we were stupid, or more accurately, I decided that *I* was stupid (he is one of the sharpest men I've ever known) and Fosmo didn't argue with me. Rolling Thunder had sent him to me immediately after he deserted from the Marine Corps. Fosmo was seventeen, but so practical and grounded, so fearless, that we became close friends quickly. His natural talents, and our friendship I suppose, promoted him into my vague circle of leadership at Olema. But we were being looked to for direction and didn't know "shit from shinola," as he put it. We loaded a newly repaired Ranchero (assuring the hapless owners, who had intended to camp with us only long enough to fix it, that we would return in no more than a few days), summoned my dog Josephine, and bid our farewells to Eeja and the others. The populace of Olema assembled in the yard to wave good-bye, a family portrait of simple rural folk, bare-toed in the dust, clutching the young 'uns: *Dysfunctional Gothic*. They knew we needed a rest, and we knew we had better return with something of value.

While writing this book, I rediscovered the journal I kept during that trip, which had been lost for twenty years. Some extended quotes from it will convey my state of mind and the particular flavors of that journey:

First Day
Gone. Olema can sink or swim without me. Fresh wind in our sails. Smoke cigarettes, good talk and good silences straight through to Pyramid Lake [Nevada]. Bed down on the twinkling desert. Stars so clear they shout. Small fire crackles and smell of sage. Stretched out to sleep and a couple of cowboys ride up in a truck. Revolver under my pillow.

"OK, boys, just checking," they say and drive off.
I uncock the pistol, ease the spring on my California mind.

Second Day
Light comes onto the desert from the inside of things, golden and warmed by their
dreams. Morning glistens like the first day of Creation. I hunt the rim of the lake
looking for rabbits. Josephine prances and dances in circles on her back legs—ghost
Coyote doing the sagebrush shuffle.

Fosmo warns me that we'll be busted hunting on a reservation, so we hide the
rifle. We pour a gallon of Olema springwater into Pyramid Lake as an offering.

Drive around Lovelock, choky-dry town made of dust and wind-burned wood.
Fosmo points out sites of childhood adventures. Buy a pail and supplies, window-
shop the whorehouses in Winnemucca where the glitter girls turn cold when we try
to play with them: "Pay you? Hell, honey, fucking a cowboy would be my idea of
work too, but getting high and fucking a hippie? Darlin', you should pay us!"

We drive past Battle Mountain. Bad town for longhairs and get to Carlin late to
see Rolling Thunder and his lady Helen. They are Fosmo's foster parents, and we
are given a swell welcome.

R. T. tells us about a group called the Disciples of Thunder who have started
a commune in Elko and are trying to live by his teachings. The local cops have
rousted everyone badly, and they're dispirited and want to leave. He has put his
house up as bail for some of them and is worried, asks us to check it out. . . .

[On the way there] a car full of thick-necked young cowboys ("beef-priests,"
Gary Snyder calls them) starts tailgating us. They are haw-hawin' each other as
they tap our bumper, trying to scare the piss out of a couple of longhairs they
assume to be flower children. We speed up, so do they, slow down, so do they.
Bump, bump, they tap us, at speed high enough to be scary. Fosmo reaches under
the seats without a word and gets out our two pistols. Lays mine in my lap. He
braces his legs against the front [fire wall] and nods at me. I jam the emergency
brake, locking the back tires, and cut the wheel so that the truck skids in a full circle, facing backwards in front of the amazed shit-kickers. Fosmo and I jerk the
doors open and draw a careful two-handed aim on the car full of suddenly pasty-
faced beefers maiming each other getting clear of the line of fire. They skid around
us, burning rubber and fishtailing down the road, while Fosmo and I collapse in
the dirt, laughing convulsively, wondering what stories they'll tell in the local bar
that night. Perhaps the next hipsters who may be flower children will be left alone.
Throughout the day we laugh each time we remember their expressions.

The Disciples of Thunder commune is disgusting. A crash pad filled with pim-

ply dopo-winos disguising sloth behind proto–New Age bullshit. I overheard someone actually say, "Oh, God, that was cosmic, man."

One fellow there named Harvey, a dignified, self-possessed biker type, seems
truthful. We hit it off and drink wine together. The main mouth of the place, a
skinny kid with corrosive sensibilities and a bad attitude [probably the Peter Coyote of Elko] starts playing mental marbles with Fosmo and me.

"You Californians think you're so far out, so macho and physical. You don't
understand the New Age at all. Your stories sound like bullshit to me, bullshit,
and I'm not going for it."

I had been chatting about California with Harvey and a few kids who were listening, just trying to get the feel of the place, and this rodent starts chewing my
lips, getting progressively ruder and more belligerent. I try calming him like you
would a riled-up terrier, but he has his own leash in his teeth and is behaving as if
I'm threatening a position he has to maintain in front of the others. He crosses the
line when he sticks his face right into mine, and I smack him in the jaw, not bru-
tally, just kind of a lazy sock, to say, "Get outta my face and wake up."

He erupts, screaming hysterically, voice rising to a sustained falsetto, "You hit
me. You hit me!"

People run around uncertainly, knocking over tables and ashtrays. Some are
screaming at me, some at each other, others are trying to calm everything down.
I back up against the sink, waiting to see what the next move will be, and am
pleased to see Harvey jump to his feet and stand beside me. When nothing but
noise materializes, we drink some more wine.

Soon I'm half in the bag and angry at these shiftless people sitting around calling Elko a hole, ranting about the "pigs" while they have made no apparent effort
to get their own house in order nor paid any attention to the jeopardy in which
their behavior places Rolling Thunder's property and reputation. I tell them
exactly how I feel. Things calm down. I'm tired and finally too drunk to talk,
so I go outside and play guitar and sing to myself.

Fourth Day
R. T. returns from work and we go to see Oscar Johnny, respected man of the Shoshone tribe. He has a Ford Falcon with a blown engine and needs help. Lots of men
there standing around forlornly. Not much work getting done. I have tools with me,
so I check the car and offer to help. They look at me and look away. The wind kicks

up dust devils and sighs. *No one moves. Something's going on. I fade back into the crowd. Later that afternoon we learn that Oscar's younger brother had just murdered his sweetheart and then killed himself.*

Stop by the commune again. The place is bustling. Everyone is cleaning, cheerful. The girls have made curtains and papered the shelves, the place is swept clean and been put in order, bright blankets cover the threadbare furniture, pictures are on the wall. The yard is picked clean of trash, and everyone greets us warmly, even motormouth.

Sixth Day
Long, abandoned dirt road between Willetstown and Gardner, Colorado. Two tires go flat. We sit and cook breakfast in the road. Hoping to see elk, but six mule deer pass in stately procession, curious about the lumpy, lopsided vehicle. We force our way into an abandoned summerhouse to call for help. A scumbag up the road wants thirty dollars for a tire, twenty dollars just to come and look—half of what we have between us. We change one tire and nurse the car at a creep about three miles to town, aware that we are ruining the tire but unwilling to abandon the truck and all our camping gear to whatever predators might come down the pike. In town, small Portuguese fellow named Raymond changes the tires with two tire irons— zip-zip, it's done . . . one dollar!

We head up the road to Libré, a famous Southwestern commune. The clay road is like a mud river that we're forced to negotiate at speed, hammer down, fishtailing right and left, Fosmo spread-eagled over the load as ballast, struggling for purchase on the back bumper. We lose our momentum and stick fast about a mile from our destination. It was spring when we left California, and we're dressed for that weather in the cold Colorado snow, trudging in the mud and suffocating in the thinner air thousands of feet above sea level.

At Libré I meet Steve Raines, someone I remember from the Haight. He has a fine adobe house and fireplace. Huge tree trunk in the center holding up radiating vigas supporting a wooden second floor. His wife Pat, though complaining about how many visitors they've had, offers us a place to spend the night. We sleep in their fireplace for warmth.

Seventh Day
Meet Peter Rabbit, a reserved, tall, slender man who looks at you as if he's gazing down from a great height, trying to decide whether or not you're worthy of his inti-

macy. We have been visiting various houses at Libré a full day, and no one but Steve and Pat has offered food, water, or a place to dry ourselves. We are nobodies.

The distributor rotor has broken in our hard-luck Ford and resists my pathetic efforts to tape or glue it together. We are standing disconsolately at the edge of the road when a young guy in a truck approaches. He tells us that he has "nothing to do, nowhere to go," but will not give us a lift and thinks nothing of letting us walk ten miles down the dirt road to hitch thirty more miles for the rotor we need. He refuses to turn his car around on the grass because he "loves the earth." We browbeat him into running us at least to the main road. Waiting for a ride at the county road, a dusty old VW bus full of people pulls up, and my intimate college friend, Terry Bisson, fellow traveler from my first peyote trip at Grinnell College, pops out. I haven't seen him in years and discover that he is living nearby with a commune called the Red Rockers, many from Beverly Hills [among whom was David Ansen, currently film critic for Newsweek]. They are occupying an old house, waiting to move onto their land.

We buy a case of beer and lots of cigarettes as a welcome gift and go with them. There are eleven people living in a three-room house. Terry's girlfriend is Mary Corey, a New Yorker from the world of fashion with a high-speed mind and dangerous mouth. We get in an argument while I am drinking, and she is running rings around me until, in frustration, I say something rude and intemperate. She responds directly in my face with "Fuck you," and I've hauled back to smack her when I realize that everyone is looking at me aghast. I am defenseless before my own crassness. I have never hit a woman before, but cannot explain this or expect to be believed at the moment. I try to explain myself, insist that words have meaning and relationship to life, are like acts, but I have crossed the line and am no longer consequential enough to be attended.

Terry and I stay up all night talking about the event. He says, "Relationships with women are the last bridge to freedom."

Eighth Day

Fosmo, up early, lays a boardwalk over the muddy slough. He and I make a bin to store grains and try to order their kitchen a little, while the others are busy making preparations to move to the land. Terry tells me everybody in the house thinks that Fosmo is very "high" (slang for enlightened) and that I'm "together" but a shithead. [Together was one of those imprecise terms that meant some combination of competent and responsible.] The family loves Mary and is angry at the bad feel-

ings that I generated in their home. I apologize honestly to Mary and the family. This is easy because I am honestly chagrined, and things mellow out. Terry explains to the group about our peyote journey together years ago, how I turned into a little wolf, and how appropriate it is to him that my name is now Coyote.

Eleventh Day

Walk around the plaza in Santa Fe. Indian women all want to see the cache of fox pelts I've tanned from roadkills and call us over. I say that they're not for sale, and as if that were a signal, trading is initiated. A one-legged Indian man is selling peyote ritual paraphernalia. He indicates my fox skins and tells me they stink. I tell him he's smelling the tour buses.

The Santo Domingo Indians are hustling, working the tourists for money. The unwary may buy bits of Clorox bottles and glass for turquoise, old 78 records for onyx. Old women, wrapped in shawls, stony-faced, eyes askance, always observant. One woman offers one necklace for two fox and wants more. I tell her I have to go for the others, and she wheedles and tries to get me to leave them with her. They run white-boy numbers on us. It's our first day, so we fade back to our camp.

Twelfth Day

Back to the plaza and trade all day. Today there are no more numbers; the Indians are ready to trade. When they discuss our goods in their native language, Fosmo and I converse in tutno, an impenetrable kids' language like pig Latin. The trades get down, hourlong, back and forth, placing and taking away things on the colored blankets. Stopping to smoke. This is the season of the Green Corn dance, where young men of the pueblo are initiated and must wear fox skins as part of their sacred regalia. I trade skins for three necklaces, a bracelet, and earrings, all good silver and turquoise. We shake hands. Everyone is happy, and it's a good trade.

Miss Sam and Ariel, far away at Olema. The Ranchero is sounding like steel balls bouncing around in a concrete mixer, boiling over consistently. Daydreams of assassinating all Ford heirs.

Fourteenth Day

Go to Albuquerque attempting to fix the fucking Ranchero. Radiator and water pump are okay. Decide the head gasket must be blown or the radiator plugged.

It's easier to pull the radiator, so we do that again and it's still okay. We time the fucker, check the thermostat, pull the housing, and see water move when we start the engine. We conclude that the head has cracked, a thought too horrible (and too expensive) to contemplate. We discuss abandoning the car or rolling it off a cliff.

We limp back to Placitas, both a town and the locale of a funk city commune by the same name: adobe buildings, tinned-in windows, chickens, burros, horses, cows, big gardens. Our host there, named Ulysses S. Grant, has a problem. Ulysses, an infamous local freak, is running for governor of the state and urges us to support him. We learn from others that half the communal garden is dedicated to feeding the horses on which Ulysses campaigns, and he has inveigled the other communards to do the planting and tending for him. His leverage to accomplish such things is implemented by the fact that he is also the sheriff and his wife is the judge. Furthermore, we are told, he occasionally busts people for possession of marijuana and other chickenshit beefs as a way of maintaining power in the community. That's their problem.

Grant's problem is that his neighbors are taking him to court because his horses break into their yard continually and are ruining their fruit trees and garden. He enlists Fosmo and me to talk to the neighbors and see what can be arranged. The envoys in our delegation of peace are Ulysses, Jerry (a singer with an unnerving, constant giggle), Fos, and me.

As we approach the neighbors' house, four giant cowboys emerge, carrying pool cues. One fellow is an ex–bone breaker for the Chicago Bears whose legs are as big as my waist. Ulysses had not informed us that their relationship had deteriorated to the edge of violence, but these men are serious and could be very dangerous. Fosmo and I are, as usual, armed, but the others don't know that. However, we didn't come here to shoot anyone, and certainly not over a beef for someone like Ulysses.

Chicago Bears opens the dialogue by declaring that "hippies are air pollution." We listen in silence while he fulminates and ticks off a long list of grievances. Fos and I look at each other, and it is clear that we agree that the neighbors have a righteous beef. Grant's untended horses are waking them at night, pushing through unrepaired fences, and wrecking their neat yard and garden. Every attempt to negotiate a solution has been skewered by stoned freaks laughing at the neighbors about being uptight.

Ulysses has the worst political instincts of anyone I have met. Insisting stub-

bornly that he's correct, he gesticulates wildly and speaks inappropriately and disrespectfully at the top of his lungs. He strains my patience.

Finally, I tell Ulysses to shut up, and I paraphrase the problem impartially. The cowboys are so startled by a nonpartisan restatement that they mellow, and after a bit more to-and-fro, we manage to work out a compromise. Ulysses will post "close gate" signs on his side of the fence and deploy some of his awesome legal authority to instruct others to mind them. We negotiate a two-week trial period, after which if things have not changed, the neighbors will sue Ulysses in court.

Back to the tent for a nap. Dream of a woman leaving earth in a golden rocket ship. Miss Sam and Ariel, my tousled blonde daughter. Fosmo misses his horse.

Fifteenth Day
The Ranchero is so decrepit that we decide to return to Santa Fe and maybe home. The heater has blown out, we're freezing, and the car boils over every fifty miles. My daydreams are filled with lurid fantasies about impaling Christina Ford on a manure fork and spreading her entrails along the road while I smash the door (with the sprung lock) on her husband's balls. At Jim Koller's in Santa Fe, we review the truck inch by inch once more and discover an almost totally obscured collapsed water hose. We cut a new length of hose from the useless heater, attach it, and start the engine, and the heat gauge drops to normal immediately. The problem is solved; we are ecstatic and decide to celebrate.

Koller and his lady Cass are preparing for a poetry reading with their friend and neighbor Drummond Hadley and don't want to come with us, but Cass tells us about a college bar nearby, "full of women," she says. "A real pussy place."

We walk down the road. It's dark and crowded with honking cars and fractious energy. Somebody shouts, "Blow it out your ass," and begins shooting. Fosmo and I are in the line of fire and run into an alley. Cars screech and hump, pedestrians scatter in panic, and the car with the gunman continues down the street, driver leaning out the window, firing with his left hand—a dull pop-pop-pop-pop like drumbeats at an execution.

We arrive at the bar full of adrenaline, but it's so crowded the bouncer won't let us in. We cruise the teeming weekend sidewalks for a while and wander off the main drag into a darker, emptier street. Four cars filled with Chicano guys drive by, check us out. We look ahead, and like a nightmare, the street in front of us is *blocked by men, fanning out to form a net. There is nothing to catch but us, so we run for our lives. Eventually, we find Koller's house again. "Thanks, Cass," I say, "Real pussy bar."*

Eighteenth Day
Dream that I'm in prison.

    Wake up completely frozen in the only shade for a hundred miles. We are in the desert outside the town of Gallup, New Mexico. The Ranchero refuses to start, is immobilized in the middle of the sagebrush, miles from nowhere. I am feeding Josephine the balls of male Ford heirs to the tenth generation while Fosmo sodomizes the daughters with a post-hole digger. We should never have stolen this car.

    Fosmo and I pull the starter, which is ruined, walk the three miles back to town to exchange it, walk back, and it doesn't fit! We pull it again, walk back to town, exchange it for one with a bolt pattern that is different by about one millimeter, and start back. My foot is hurting from a motorcycle accident and sore as hell after walking nearly twelve miles. No one responds to our hitchhiking attempts, only a fat Indian cop in a white Jeep who takes swipes at us each time he passes, forcing us off the road and making hitchhiking perilous.

    Gallup is the toughest town I've ever been in. Indians here so fucked up and over they'll kick anyone's ass for a drink. Pawnshop shysters buy their visions and heirlooms for nickels and get rich selling them back to art merchants and upscale tourists going "spiritual." Pawning work to raise the capital to finance new work is traditional Navajo practice, but the obstacles stacked against Indian people ensures that one event or another will make it impossible for them to reclaim their goods, so they pass into the white world, transformed into "merchandise." Millions of dollars of wealth float around the Southwest, based on native culture, and the Indians participate in practically none of it.

    [This is truer today than it was then. On several occasions I have suggested to friends who are Indian art dealers that dealers might make some minimal restitution to native peoples by applying a portion of pretax profits to some nonprofit entity for native welfare or education, and the idea has been dismissed as ludicrous. Meanwhile, at the native arts shows where rugs and fine crafts are sold for stratospheric amounts and discussed knowledgeably by well-dressed and well-spoken men and women who exude culture and sensitivity, it is rare to encounter

even one native person because they cannot afford to buy back their culture as
"art."]

We repair the car and depart for the Hopi Indian reservation in Hotevilla, Ari-
zona, arriving at dusk. The three mesas where the Hopis live stand upright from
the flat desert floor like grand ocean liners in a calm sea. Hotevilla is the most traditional of the villages, where elders systematically uproot water and electricity
lines that progressives try to install. Hopis live in land so difficult that they are
almost the only people who can live there, and they claim that they are able to do
this due to the sincerity of their prayers and the simplicity of their way of life.

During World War II, when the government drafted enough Hopis so that there
were not enough men left to perform a rain dance, it never rained until the con-
scripts returned and performed the ritual again. The Hopis live a monastic, wor-
shipful life, and Fosmo and I believe that if anyone knows about communal living
outside the premises of the industrial paradigm, these people might. We have somehow arranged an introduction to one of the tribal elders, a Snake priest named
David Monongye.

We follow the two-lane blacktop road up the mesa, past the stick fences, stone
and adobe buildings ancient as sand. Little plots of corn, beans, and squash, kids
yelling "Hippieeees" until we turn off on a dirt track and reach the village itself, a
cluster of small, flat-roofed, rectangular stone houses, connected by alleyways car-
peted in deep, soft, stoneless dust. Round kivas, spaced intermittently throughout
the village, appear like the visible tops of pegs fixing the village to the mesa bedrock. The long ladder rails emerging from inside the kivas pierce the sky like
staples.

We find David's house, and a woman responds to our knock and asks us to
leave while they eat. "Come back in an hour," she says. When we return, the room
is packed with rodeo-riding Indian dudes, tough and dusty, close-cropped black
hair, high cheekbones, pitiless eyes. The vibes inform us that if we are inappropriate with this old man, we might not leave the mesa in the same shape we
arrived.

We stay soft and silent. They feed us red beans, tortillas, coffee with milk and
sugar, and say that it's all right to smoke. David is slight, neat, self-contained. He
wears a pale green bandanna around his forehead, keeping his snow-white hair
out of his eyes. He seems very cheerful and gives an impression of sophistication.
There is nothing frail or distracted about him, even though we have been informed

*that he is well over ninety. His wife resembles Madame Khrushchev, and she hums
to herself softly and constantly.*

*The differences between our two cultures (if I could risk calling our Olema proto-
type a culture) are extreme. Inside the Monongye's home, the walls are bare plaster,
devoid of decoration. Only a basket, a rattle, and a paho, or feathered prayer stick,
lend any semblance of color, and they appear to be placed for reasons of storage and
not decoration. Small bundles are tucked neatly in the rafters. The house possesses
no contrived aesthetic; everything is completely functional. Yet the behavior of the
Monongyes' guardians leaves absolutely no doubt that some invisible spiritual treasure permeates every inch of this couple and their house.*

*We finish the meal in silence, smoke, wait patiently for some sign of what to do
next. After about an hour, David asks a few questions about why we've come. We
answer as honestly as we can, and about fifteen minutes later, as if on cue, the
hard boys file silently outside, into the night.*

*We offer them a beautifully tie-dyed sheet that Sam has made, an intricate
piece that took her days to tie and dye. As Mrs. Monongye opens it, I'm embarrassed to see a two-inch notch neatly and inexplicably cut out of one corner. Our
flawed gift appears bright, gaudy, defiant, ebullient, confident, and vain in the
environment of their home. She blesses it [the tie-dye], then rises and makes some
popcorn while we continue explaining to David why we have come.*

*I am at a loss but, even in my normally erratic condition, would have felt his
genuine authority. I explain what we have been trying to accomplish during the
last several years, explain our experiments and points of view, our trials and
errors. I speak candidly about our failures, collectively and personal, and express
my heartfelt desire to bring something of worth back to my own people.*

*David listens, his wife listens, and it feels as if the walls listen, without judg-
ment. It feels like the experience in a psychiatrist's office where one's own statement of the problem is a prelude to understanding. When I am finished, he begins
to speak, while his wife offers him the bowl of popcorn she has blessed.*

*He says something that is obviously a prayer in Hopi, blessing the corn, which
he then shares with us, making some sort of invocation. He talks at great length,
initiating us into the universe of Hopi mythology. Particularly compelling is his
recital of predictions of what he calls "the last days," the period when a world age
dizzy with incoherence and indulgence was about to disintegrate. Signs marking
the end of this Fifth World included:*

- *Hopi lands, the least valuable on earth, will be coveted. [Coalmining at Black Mesa]*
- *Spider woman will have covered the world with her web. [Phone and telegraph lines, etc.]*
- *Men will fly.*
- *Demons will be on the trails, and travel will be unsafe. [Would you let your children hitchhike?]*
- *The end will be at the hands of Red Men from the East, who will be pitiless.*

David invites us to stay with him. We are shocked because we have been repeatedly warned that white people are not allowed to spend the night in Hotevilla. He offers us his guest room and, smiling broadly at me, tells me that it's perfectly okay for my "beautiful dog" [whom I had locked in the car and he had never seen] to sleep with me.

He ushers us into a tiny room overwhelmed by a large metal-framed bed. The room is painted a cool green and has only a dresser with a mirror over it and some sepia-toned photos on the walls.

Nineteenth Day
We fall into a deep sleep, and when we awake, the outside room is full of old men having a meeting of some kind and talking in low, guttural voices. We try to remain invisible as we take our coffee and watch surreptitiously. Bright desert light pierces the windows and smoky air, pasting rectangles on the floor. Men sit everywhere; some doze, some seem completely attentive. When one man speaks, no one interrupts in any way until he is finished. Except for grunts or nods of assent, the speaker has the floor and can take as long as he needs to think. No one pays the slightest attention to us.

How different it is from the chaos of our communal life. Children line the walls in respectful silence. When they get restless, they rise and slip outside like shadows, and only after the door closes quietly behind them do you hear the cries and screams of play, the aural tracks of children everywhere. I am chastened and amazed. Steady parents raise steady children.

I don't remember now how many days we stayed—long enough to hear David sing often and tease us about white people's music, which, according to him, is only about "love." He observed that the Hopi have many songs about water, which they consider the rarest and most precious of resources, and then asked, with feigned innocence, if white people sang so often about love because it was equally rare in our world. He did wicked and witty parodies of cowboy songs and seemed genuinely pleased that I had written songs about owls, the hills of Olema, and other forms of life.

One day, shortly before we left, he walked me around the mesa, offering me precise directions to the sites of abandoned Hopi villages, explaining to me why and under what conditions each had been built, which had good water, and which did not. As he marked each site he asked me to be sure to remember. I did not understand why he was being so particular.

We left with his blessings, rested and full of energy. It was hard to acknowledge and comprehend all I had learned. At the time, I felt that he had offered us these empty villages as bomb shelters for some future Armageddon, places to hide our people if we needed them, and I was flattered and touched. Today, I realize that the most important gift we received was the opportunity to witness and participate in an ancient, ordered spiritual life, for our bodies to experience what such an existence felt like. We were afforded a glimpse into a self-sufficient system that had taken thousands of years to develop. The lightness of their personal lives, the absence of demands they made on the environment and each other was chastening and elevating. For all its hard lessons and physical difficulties, the trip had succeeded. We had a high-water mark to aspire to, and I returned to California with that fixed as firmly in mind as my mind could fix anything then.

Fosmo and I drove hard, excited by what we had learned and anxious to begin the work of renewing Olema. We entered the front yard of the main house just as Maryanne Pickens entered the third day of a total nervous breakdown. Everyone had been sleepless for days, jarred by her nerve-wracking screams, afraid to leave her unattended. People were strung out and exhausted. Maryanne was a babbling wraith, laughing, trying to seduce the women, and occasionally standing stock-still and shrieking at the top of her lungs. People were too distracted to do more than react to our return as an opportunity to transfer the responsibility for Maryanne into fresh hands. By the end of the next day, it was apparent to all that the Pickens would have to move. Maryanne, in the only way available to her, had finally created a condition that forced J. P. to pay attention to her.

My last wrenching image of their departure was J. P.'s two-and-a-half-ton house-truck lumbering off and Maryanne's pale arm waving frantically through the barred window in the back door, while she begged, in a voice raw as bloody meat, for the aid and understanding that we were unable to provide.

While I was away, the Gypsy Truckers had arrived, and they gathered around me now, in a corral full of new trucks, unknown faces watching Maryanne's departure. The Gypsy Truckers precipitated the final bloom and eventual decay of Olema.

18

full bloom

On my return I moved Sam and Ariel out of the overcrowded Olema ranch house into a small, abandoned outbuilding, a tiny horse barn about ten by ten feet square, with an old Dutch door and feed stalls that had to be removed. We tar-papered it against the winter, insulating the windows with plastic and the rough wood floors with old carpets. I put in a wood-burning stove and built a loft for sleeping. Though the shed was tiny, it sufficed for the three of us and our two dogs. Eeja was roaming farther and father afield, drawn by coyotes yapping on the distant ridge. One day, she simply did not return.

It was a low-rent shanty with wooden battens nailed across the black tar-paper skin outside, but it was warm and dry. The old wood glowed in the kerosene lamplight, and it was lovely to lie there and listen to the dull comforting murmur of rain spattering on the slate roof. The stage was set, the play was cast, and if Sam and I were not exactly blissful together, we were not unhappy and intermittently in love—about par for most relationships, I suspect.

Meanwhile the Gypsy Truckers had moved in. I think Vinnie ("Chick-a-dee, Chick-a-daa") Rinaldi met them at the Orange Julius stand in San Anselmo. They were a dashing troupe of *bandidos,* mustachioed, long hair tied back with bandannas, with *conchos*, intricately stamped buttons of silver, running up the seams of their leather pants. The women wore long skirts over their boots and scarves around their heads; dozens of bracelets made their arms tinkle and ring. They had beautifully crafted flatbed trucks with ornate wooden houses built on the frames sporting nifty gingerbread trim, giving them the ornate jewel-box complexity of fine fairy story illustrations. Vinnie told them about Olema, and they pulled into the big corral en masse and circled their wagons. They needed a place to put up for the winter, to ready their vehicles and gather supplies before moving north. After exploratory consultations and some meals, herb, and music, we agreed that they could stay.

Olema at this point (the autumn of 1969) was in full flower, jammed to the rafters with divergent souls, intentions, needs, visions, and aspirations, all feeding like aphids on its nourishing stem. Does a flower intuit that when its bloom is at its peak, it is preparing to die?

I was still the nominal "head man" by virtue of having been the first to colonize the place and perhaps because I had the overarching vision of how Olema dovetailed with the rest of the Free Family; however, my authority was strictly based on persuasion and personal regard. People came and went at Olema and were accepted or rejected according to mysterious consensus. It was commonly agreed that Olema was "free turf," that one could do and be whatever one chose to be, an anarchic social experiment designed to discover alternative modes of living and working together based on personal authenticity rather than economics.

My daily routine in the morning was simple: slip on my coveralls and amble out of the cabin, fire up my Coleman camp stove, and make a pot of coffee. More often than not, I might pad down to the main house and see if anyone else had done it before me. There was usually a can of Top cigarette tobacco on the kitchen table, and it was nice to sit in the weak light, roll a smoke, and contemplate what comedies the day might produce while my coffee steamed beside me on the porch stoop.

Babies would wake, cooing and gurgling. Mothers, steamy from sleep and smelling of talc and breast milk, shuffled into the kitchen on maternal call. Usually someone had made bread, and there might be a pot of jam or honey nearby to smear on it.

Little by little others woke and threaded their way to the kitchen through the prior evening's abandoned guitars, clothing, and accessories, and the intricate ballet of assessing one another's morning moods began. Talk was initially minimal. People gravitated toward the coffee, condensed milk, sugar, and tobacco, and pursued their somnolent wake-up rituals. Before long the thick silence in the house would be dispersed by buzzing energy: children bumping into tables and rolling in the dust, mothers chatting on the stoop, elbows on bent knees, soft curves draped in faded skirts and hair caught in bandannas, bangle bracelets and earrings jingling, all glad for any hint of sun to drive off the morning fog.

Discussion centered on the needs of the day: laundry, flour, gaskets, fuel pump, welding rod, weeding, gathering mussels at Tomales Bay. Runs to town were consolidated, baby-sitters designated, and the parceling out of always-insufficient money for gas and supplies was usually negotiated with ironic goodwill:

From the men: "Well, if we don't *have* money to fix the truck how will we *get* to the bulk food store?"

You could feel the invisible chords of communication among the women, who had no need to look at one another to agree. Someone might look down at the ground or laugh into her palm before responding, "Fine. *Fix* the truck . . . and while you're at it, fix dinner too, because there's no food."

These ripostes oscillated back and forth until temporary equilibrium was achieved. There was generally not too much anxiety because, despite lack of money, we had all the time in the world. What we had lost in material surplus we more than made up for with the luxury of unstructured, free time.

By the second cup of coffee, cigarette at the halfway mark, a musical instrument usually appeared. Jed Sherman was a handsome, mustachioed, longhaired Gypsy Trucker with a laconic good humor; he and I were the two dominant guitar players. Jeff (of Jeff and Carla) was an up-and-comer, but the best musician at Olema was a wiry, goateed young man with an extremely sardonic manner and eccentric personal style named Freeman Lockwood, professionally known as Steamin' Freeman.

Freeman played violin and spent almost every waking hour practicing jigs and reels from a thick fake book of traditional Irish music. He would play six to seven hours a day, every day. He and I commandeered an abandoned room next to the chicken shed and built bunk beds for visiting musicians to use after late jam sessions. Before he died of an overdose, Michael Bloomfield would come from the city to play our cracked old upright piano all night. Olema was his hideout from the high-pressure rock-and-roll life that interfered with his joyful music and enthusiasm; on one occasion, harmonica player Paul Butterfield joined him. But excellent as these musicians were, equally skilled anonymous players drifted in off the road, and the standard was elevated and demanding.

Music was one of the social arts, and we took musical skill and etiquette seriously. Good players would travel from commune to commune, or house to house, to play and learn and teach new songs. Skill was highly appreciated, but show-offs and stage hogs were cold-shouldered until they understood that the most valued talent was the ability to create inclusive ensembles. There was space for both the individual and the group, but all had to work cooperatively.

When people returned home after a trip, they brought gossip, adventurous tales, presents, new goods, staples, and enough energy to generate stupendous parties. The men gathered wood and built a fire or set up a barbecue if there was meat. Depending on the scale of the event, we might build a sweat lodge, drag out the home brew and slice up the hash brownies.

Skirts rustled, metal bowls clanged, flour dust hazed the air, and the house was permeated by an incense of lentils and cardamom, marinating meat, and rising dough. Sam was clearly a leader among the women there. She was imposing, and her entrance could dominate a room, but her self-confidence oscillated between impervious and absent. She had a grand style and witchy powers. Though, like most of us, she was picking her way through the rubble of her own psyche, she could, especially to the younger girls, appear to be a goddess, fully formed and worthy of emulation.

It was Sam who taught the Olema women to tan the deer hides we retrieved in numbers from the Point Reyes garbage dump during hunting season; to make an oatmeal-thick mash from wood ashes and water so that the hair could be rubbed off; to pickle the skin in sulfuric acid and water or rub it with brains, then break it to softness over a fence post or over the back of an ax jammed into a stump. Though the ultimate utility of such skills might have been marginal, they contributed to our sense of independence from the larger culture and supported our intentions to be in continuity with indigenous people who centuries earlier had lived where we were living. Such skills also enabled us to create trade goods and currency out of found objects, personal skills, and time. We could create wealth by redefining it in a game that was not stacked against us.

Lew Welch was a frequent visitor to Olema. A tall, freckled, sad-eyed Irishman whose face was often suffused with childish wonder and delight, Lew was already famous as a Beat poet. He lived sporadically and stormily with a thick, powerful Slavic woman called Magda; when she would tire of his drunken escapades, he would move out of their Marin City pad and up to Olema. He loved jazz and Magda's two children and was proud of tutoring their musical abilities. He introduced me to Magda's oldest, Huey, when Huey was ten years old. Lew beamed with delight as the child scatted tricky jazz riffs Lew had taught him. He might well have been proud. Magda's Huey became Huey Lewis of Huey Lewis and the News and honors Lew's memory to this day by maintaining his stepfather's bardic traditions and catholic curiosities.

I was pleased to have Lew at the ranch because I felt his presence conferred on us a legitimate descent from the Beats. I was extremely proud that Lew had dedicated a poem called "Olema Satori" to me.

One day he was sitting on the floor of the Olema living room, cradling his ever-present gallon jug of Cribari red wine in his lap. He was deep in his cups. The room was pulsing with music and dense with marijuana smoke. Tall, fulsome Carla, the world's most voluptuous seventeen-year-old mother, was utterly abandoned to sinuous dancing, naked from the waist up, and glistening with sweat. Lew was watching with undisguised lust. He turned to me, grinning crookedly, raised one finger, and said very slowly and very clearly, "The . . . worst . . . Persian . . . voluptuary . . . could . . . not . . . imagine . . . our . . . most . . . ordinary day." Having managed this, he pitched over, unconscious.

There was no hint in Lew's joy that day that not long afterward he would leave his wallet and a note in Gary Snyder's kitchen and walk into the Sierra foothills with his rifle to commit suicide. If he hid his private griefs in life, he remained consistent in death. To this day, his body has never been found.

Lew was fascinated with Snyder lore. Grinning and sitting cross-legged, the softness of his moist eyes contrasting with his chiseled Irish face, he would recount story after story about Gary in a manner that was at times incredulous, at times awestruck, and at other times tinged with a note of competitiveness. It was easy to see that Gary exerted a powerful hold on this singularly intelligent and talented poet, but it was not until sometime after Lew arranged an introduction to Gary that I understood the power of that attraction.

It's embarrassing to remember my first impression as I watched Gary's pristine Volkswagen camper pick its careful way over the rutted road to our ranch house. "How could Gary Snyder be driving a *new* camper?" I thought. "So bourgeois!" It came to a stop under the willow tree at the edge of the yard, Lew hopped out with his customary manic enthusiasm, and I ambled over, lord of the manor. Salutations were exchanged, and Gary threw open the side door and invited me inside. Before I had climbed on board, he had already opened some peanut butter and a box of crackers.

He was wearing an old straw hat that shaded his eyes, and I remember him cocking his head to one side to look at me. His look was so clearly appraising, so without social camouflage as to be startling. The visit was uneventful. We ate crackers and talked. Gary was not overweening, and he made interesting conversation—in the parlance of the time, he was "together." His body was muscular and lithe. His eyes crinkled pleasantly when he smiled. His voice was cultivated, and his speech was very precise and peppered with geological terms like *schist, upthrusts,* and *substrate.*

I was a little crestfallen by this initial encounter. He had not congratulated me for carrying the banner of Beat liberation struggles onto new battlefields, nor acknowledged me as a peer, nor questioned me in any way about my revolutionary lifestyle and politics. All he had done was look me over as if asking himself, "What's this guy about?" He did not find it necessary to locate me philosophically or politically. In fact, he did not seem to find it necessary to define himself in relationship to me at all! I had shared some peanut butter and crackers and a pleasant time with him, and that was that. After he had driven off, little remained in my memory except that initial penetrating visual query. It made me squirm mentally and I did not know why.

In the torrential rains of the winter of 1969–70, during the last year of Olema, my father came to visit. It had poured relentlessly for days, and the road to the ranch was a quagmire. The house was overcrowded with restless people irritable from their damp, steaming clothes and enforced idleness. Some Hell's Angels were visiting. My parents appeared out of the storm in a clay-smeared rented car. My father's pockets were stuffed with Seconals, he was lugging a case of Scotch for the weekend, and he was already drunk.

They dived into the turmoil of the farmhouse, and it could not have been easy for them. People were stacked like cordwood. Joints were rolled and passed around continuously, chased by jugs of red wine. There was a sullenness in the atmosphere: too many people trapped in too small a space for too long.

Morris sat at the table, punching holes in his Seconals with a pocketknife, sharing them with a couple of the Angels. "When I need 'em, I want 'em to work in a hurry," he explained to one who asked why he punctured them. When people stood too close to him, he jerked his shoulders as if to shake them off; he muttered, "Faggots" under his breath when a Hell's Angel's swagger got on his nerves. He was pushy and belligerent, and I was certain he would provoke a fight. I considered that this might be his preferred way of dying and was preternaturally alert because I knew that if a fight broke out between him and the Angels, I would have to go down with him.

At one point, Morris collared my friend Gristle, one of the Gypsy Truckers, and said bluntly, "Get Peter for me."

"Get him yourself," Gristle replied blandly. He laughed when he recalled for me how Morris had then propped a hand on his shoulder, fixed his feral eyes on him, and said, "I like you, fella. You know why? Because you're not afraid to die!"

That night, Morris fell out of the loft bed that someone had surrendered for him and my mother. Stoned on Seconals, he climbed out the wrong side, fell six feet, and cracked a toe. He was cranky about it but otherwise resigned. Perhaps he was too stoned to notice. Ruth was acutely uncomfortable and uncharacteristically silent during most of the weekend. God knows what she felt about the shabby environment, her adored grandchild Ariel picking her way over stupefied freaks and bikers, the women dressed like girls she had been taught to avoid. Olema was always as raw and vulgar as hunger. My mother was refined; she spoke in a deep, cultured voice like Claire Trevor and years earlier had traded in her home in the Jewish ghetto in the Bronx for the "modern" world and a starring role in her own personal Fred Astaire film, smoking elegantly and referring to people as "darling" as she soaked up the culture she had longed for as a girl. She obviously preferred the glamour of the thirties and forties to the squalor of our sixties commune, but she never ever missed what was under her nose.

On the Sunday they were to leave, my dad and I were sitting together at the kitchen table. The kerosene lamp cast a yellow pallor on his skin, and the storm outside offered a subdued howl as a score for the scene. His eyes were hooded, and his hair, only recently streaked with gray, was combed straight back in his usual Latin manner. He was half in his cups when he caught my attention by saying, "You know, son . . . ," and then drifted off on a nod before he'd finished the thought.

There was a long pause while he appeared to be checking the insides of his eyelids for news; then he lifted his head abruptly and looked at me squarely. His face was completely serious. "I gotta tip my hat to you, boy," he said roughly. "You're a better man than I am." He looked away, perhaps politely, so that he wouldn't witness my confusion. I didn't know how to respond.

He continued, as if addressing the wall, "If I was your age again, this" (indicating the environs with a motion of his arm) "is what I would be doing."

I was stunned. I had never received such direct and unequivocal approbation from him before, and certainly not for something about which I had many ambivalent feelings. I mean, the *idea* of Olema, the *idea* of the Free Family, revitalizing and reinventing the culture and the economy, was compelling and seemed the only worthwhile thing to be doing with my life. The *actuality*, however, was full of contradictions, embarrassments, and confusions. I might excuse our imperfections as those of a work in progress, but compared to my father's standards of elegance, Olema was a pigsty. I could not imagine how he had construed this swirling chaos in order to justify what he had just said to me.

I told him how pleased I was to hear this, and how moved, and then confessed my own lack of direction and insight. I asked him for advice. He hunkered down for another long silence, and then he uttered what were, in effect, his last words to me. More than twenty years later I remember them vividly:

> Capitalism is dying, boy. It's dying of its own internal contradictions. [*He was, after all, a Wall Street financier, so I listened carefully.*] You think that the revolution's gonna take five years. It's gonna take fifty! So keep your head down and hang in for the long haul, because I'll tell you something. The sons of bitches running things don't give a shit about their children or their grandchildren, and they certainly don't give a shit about you! They've paid their dues, and they want to get out with theirs! They're gonna sell off everything that's not nailed down to the highest bidder. Don't get crushed when it topples down. Take care of yourself and your family. If you can make a difference, do it, but there are huge forces at work here, and they have to play themselves out according to their own design, not yours. Watch yourself.

As far as I can determine, everything he prophesied has come true.

There was another "free land" commune in nearby Marshall, called Wheeler's Ranch, and when its members came to visit we would feast and party and take LSD and make music for nine or ten hours at a time. Once we improvised a sweat lodge for fifty people; usually, we dragged an old cattle trough over a fire pit and heated water to make a rudimentary hot tub for ten or fifteen people in shifts.

Once a group of Hell's Angels arrived at the same time as our Wheeler's Ranch friends. It was an uneasy mix, and many of the Wheeler's people were frightened by the ominous bikers and their hard intentions. Alisha Bay-Laurel, a good fiddle player and author of a popular cookbook, and I, and several others, began to play music on the porch. The music created a fragile cohesion between the dissonant groups, as if the rhythms and melodies were stitching together a protective shield beneath which nothing could go awry. The musicians sensed the incipient tension and played as if possessed, attempting to forestall what felt like a gathering storm of potential violence.

We carried the responsibility consciously, playing for nearly eight straight hours, barely pausing, until our blistered fingers and sore throats could no longer follow the peaks and valleys of melody.

At one point, Angel Pete Knell burst onto the porch. "Coyote," he yelled hoarsely, "a nigger's following your old lady around!" I had no idea what he was talking about and continued playing, but he was insistent. "I *said*, a nigger's following your old lady." I looked through the door and sure enough, my old Mime Troupe partner Willie B. was following Sam, talking to her while she was preparing food. I shouted over the fiddles, tambourines, and guitars that it was okay, that he was a good friend, and a look of total incomprehension crossed Knell's face, so pure it was painful to behold. He looked at me, then at B. again, shook his head incredulously, and reentered the house, which was pulsing with dancers and overflow musicians who could not fit on the porch.

A visitor jumped onto a table in the living room and began an Elvis Presley routine, definitely grabbing the role of Mr. Centerstage. Some Olema people hollered for me to join him, wanting their own champion to contend for the spotlight. Before I had a chance to decline, Pete and two Angels filled the doorway, looking at me levelly. Pointing derisively with his thumb to the exhibitionist behind him, Pete challenged me: "Is this [self-aggrandizement] what it's about, then?" The Angels never kidded around about personal authenticity, nor did they ever stop testing it. They knew I was very high, and they wanted to learn what my unguarded response would be.

I checked out the guy's Vegas moves, shook my head, and returned my attention to the group with whom I was playing, reaffirming my dedication to preserve the day, which continued to be punctuated uneasily by such acerbic ruptures and challenges.

At dusk, Little Mike, normally a happy-go-lucky Hell's Angel, beat someone senseless for refusing to gather firewood for him. This tipped the balance irretrievably, and the Wheeler's people left while the Angels partied among themselves, oblivious. It had been the type of party for which Olema was locally known: eclectic, unpredictable, free-form, and high risk. We were proud of this reputation—until the day the Angels dramatically redefined "high risk."

In the late winter of 1970 Sweet William was about to be released from the hospital where he had been recovering from his near-execution, and Moose asked me if the Angels might throw a welcome-home party for him at Olema. I had been involved with the club for so long that I didn't think twice about agreeing. I should have. I had been a fly on the wall for too many conversations not to have been aware that there were people in the club who resented my access and might make it an issue. As Emmett used to say, "life is hard for the stupid."

On the appointed day, approximately forty bikes rumbled up the dirt road in a dense, ominous phalanx. Eeja, my coyote puppy, now almost full grown, danced and whined on the hill, made nervous by the approaching roar of so many engines. I did not recognize over half the riders. Before greetings could be exchanged, automatic and semiautomatic weapons were being fired into the air and ground. Bullets tore into the hillside, kicking up the dirt around the terrified coyote, sending him fleeing for his life and me running directly in front of the muzzles of the guns, waving my arms to stop their fire.

Events skidded out of control instantly. Fosmo and I had hunted the Coast Range for two rainy days prior to the party, killed and dressed a deer and constructed a large fire pit to barbecue it whole for Sweet William. But he was not there; he had been taken to a motel somewhere else for the real welcome home. This event had nothing to do with Bill and everything to do with distancing the club from its hippie "friends."

The night was a horror. The corral fences were torn down and used as fuel for bonfires. Fights flared up everywhere; men wrestled, grunting, through the hot coals and then wandered about, dusted with ash, spectral as ghosts. Our bedrooms were colonized by stupefied bikers. Tiburón (not his real name), a short, round, homicidal Latin Angel, sauntered around casually lighting cherry bombs and dropping them behind people to check their "mud." Sam's nervous system was threatening meltdown. "Make him stop," she pleaded. I hesitated. Tiburón was a man who had terminated an argument with his wife by firing two bullets through her forehead. (Amazingly, she lived and refused to press charges.) Once, discussing possible scenarios in some future Armageddon, he had confided to me, "I'm not worried. I'd find some farmhouse and blow away the farmer. There'd be plenty to eat." Now he was at Olema, and I was the "farmer."

Nevertheless, I approached him and requested that he stop because "it was making the women nervous." He looked right through that piece of patent bullshit, said genially, "Oh, really?," and dropped a cherry bomb between my feet.

Gunfire was sporadic, erupting unnervingly from the darkness beyond the firelight. Barbiturates were ubiquitous, and it was easy to trip over unconscious bodies in the dark. Sam retrieved a biker's false teeth from a pool of vomit in front of his comatose form and saved them, "To shame him in the mornin'." Occasionally a dog barked or shrieked as if kicked. Sometime near false dawn, Sam and I retreated to our room, hoping to sleep until the nightmare was over. A blind drunk couple crashed into the room, unhinging the door. They stumbled out when I challenged them, but we were awake for the duration, watching the glow from the fires flood the ceiling with eerie shadows to a soundtrack of explosions, roars, and the heavy thuds and cheers of combat. *Walpurgisnacht.*

Morning slunk in, gray, damp, and cold. The house stank of stale alcohol, vomit, and tobacco. People were passed out on every plane surface, and the house and yard were a filthy shambles. Three of the dogs had been stabbed and were limping and shivering with the shock of their wounds.

I was humiliated and angry but not too angry to miss the message. Out in the yard I spoke to the leader of the chapter from another city they'd enlisted for this job. Like me, he was up early, a bearded guy with a hard face and the thousand-mile stare I'd seen on some Vietnam vets. I'd never met him, but he appeared sober, so I called him on class: "This was our home and you were our guests. You abused it. You stabbed our dogs. You burned our fences. There was nothing that we could do to stop you, but I'm calling it for what it was. You guys behaved like trash, and I never expected it from the Hell's Angels."

He knew I was right and listened without responding. He'd been called to do a job. Perhaps he knew the reasons for it, and perhaps he didn't. Whether or not the job was consonant with his personal inclinations, his first allegiance was to the Angels, and we both knew it. He did have the grace to apologize sincerely to me, and then, as if disgusted, he suddenly announced to all within earshot, "Whoever stabbed those dogs is a sick fuck, and if I catch him, he's hurt!"

I walked into my room as the bikes were revving up to leave, and there, next to my bed, was a brand-new candy bar. I perceived it as a gratuitous insult, someone calling me "a candy ass." During my sojourn at his house, when I was building my bike, Pete Knell had invited me to prospect for the club, and I had been flattered and thought long and hard about it. I had decided not to, primarily because so many of my friends were frightened by the Angels and because I could not imagine being blood brother to a man who would hospitalize someone for not gathering firewood for him or who would hate someone simply because of his race. I had decided not to because I felt that my predilection for books and solitude would not be understood or respected and, finally, because I was afraid of the mindless violence and blood feuds. I had remained friends, however, with several Angels and in the past had been protected by those friendships. This candy bar was too much, though, and some self-protective instinct in my psyche shredded. I ran outside, beyond caring that there is no such thing as a one-to-one fight with a Hell's Angel.

"Who left this candy bar in my room?" I demanded with what must have appeared insane vehemence. Flash, a San Francisco Angel I knew well, was astride his chopper, revving the throttle and preparing to leave. His black glasses made his expression impenetrable. "I did," he said without affect.

I barely had the time to shift my weight toward him when he reached into his breast pocket and took out an identical candy bar.

"Candy," he said, grinning appreciatively. "I love it. You want some more?"

I was frozen by the ambiguity of the situation. Had I been insulted or not? Had he just double-trumped me? Confusion replaced my anger; I didn't know what to do, so I chose to accept the surface reality and tried to retrieve my dignity. I shook my head and stood silently watching the bikes move away, spitting and barking.

Before he left, Flash looked at me long and hard, and in his expression I read the challenge to shit or get off the pot: ride with the wolves as a wolf, or get lost. My choice had already been made, and I watched them leave without regrets. Except for an occasional chance encounter, I never saw the Angels again.

19

approaching terminal velocity

pochteca—Nahuatl word referring to
a mysterious band of pilgrims
who wandered the Mexican empire
in search of the land of the Sun

In April of 1970 we were evicted from Olema. A new cowboy had leased the pastures and didn't want to share them with thirty hippies. We cleaned the house and grounds down to the last cigarette butt and bottle cap and left the Olema ranch as meticulous as an altar, as an expression of appreciation to it.

We paid every outstanding bill in the town of Point Reyes Station, even those falsely charged to our name by transient guests. The citizens of the town understood and appreciated the gesture. While we were definitely "outsiders" to the local people, they had liked us. We had been honest in our dealings with them and had certainly supplied them with ample entertainment and gossip. Tom Quinn, the brother of the new lessee of the land, was a commercial artist. He made an elegant wooden sign with a coyote footprint on it. Under the footprint he wrote ". . . and company have gone." As we drove out for the last time, I wrote the word *on* after the "gone." Six months later I returned and took the sign itself. I still have it.

Sam and I were "off" again, despite an intervention by the Hell's Angels. Hairy Henry and Moose had picked me up one day and drove me to get Sam, and then they refused to let us out of the car until we promised to get back together. I have no idea why it was important to them, but we agreed to do it—and as soon as we were let off, we resumed our separate ways. Sam went to New Mexico to see her beloved friend Cass, ex of our mutual friend, poet Jim Koller.

Sam, in her own words, was "way crazy." Koller gave her a vision to take two horses and go to Big Mountain at Four Corners in the Southwest. I agreed to help her and sold my motorcycle and gave the money to Fosmo to go to New Mexico and get her horses, but he spent it en route, according to Sam, on drugs, trying to enlarge the original stash.

In Colorado, she traveled with Ben Eagle and Chipita, friends from a New York wing of the Free Family. Ben and Chipita had been living on horseback, wintering in the Rockies in a tiny canvas *wikiup*, surviving by foraging and hunting. They moved Sam and Ariel into their camp for a while but the weather was too severe for the baby. Sam left in her pink VW van and drove to the Red Rockers commune. She set up camp there in a little canvas-covered lean-to, determined to conquer her devils or die trying.

Back in California things were grittier and rougher, too. We were homeless in a colder time. The struggle to keep an extended family functioning with only minimal resources was exhausting and draining. We were getting tired. A change of scenery was called for, and this apparently insignificant impulse produced the Free Family Caravan.

The idea was to travel to far-flung locales and use our neutrality as newcomers to create meetings, détentes, and political alliances among people who should know one another but did not. It was apparent that the counterculture was growing; every state had pockets of people living as we did, creating relationships and new communities within their regions. Each of us in the Free Family had a friend somewhere else, so it seemed organic and evolutionary to begin weaving these places together, expanding the base of our economy and spreading the cultural word.

Travel was so necessary to our community (with distant houses in Black Bear, Olema, Oakland, and San Francisco) that the idea of a caravan evolved out of our normal life. The initial plan was to celebrate the summer solstice at Libré, the Colorado commune where Fosmo and I had been so coolly treated on our Southwestern journey to Hopi land. I don't remember whose idea it was, but judging from the panicked responses to our queries, I am certain that it was not Libré's.

Prior to the caravan's departure, I took a road trip north to Black Bear as a shakedown cruise for my truck. Rereading a journal sharpens my memories of how serendipitous, comical, and turbulent life on the road could be. After so many years, the journal's rediscovery is like opening a sealed time capsule.

Coyote's Journal
Sun in Gemini—1971

After months of labor "Dr. Knucklefunky" is reincarnated as the Meat and Bone Wagon: '49 Chevy one-ton, new brakes, rebuilt steering, suspension, engine, wiring. Everything touched, looked at, rebuilt, or replaced. Wooden sides added to the bed, metal strapping made into bows supporting a canvas cover; welding tanks chained to the running board. Phyllis, Natural Suzanne, and her twins, Taj and Mahal, head out with Josephine and me on Saturday, 22 May, to Lost River, Salmon Creek, Trinidad, and Black Bear to gather wild herbs and medicines to carry to Colorado for summer solstice celebration at Libré. Truck loaded with bulk honey, raisins, milk, flour, cheese for the family at Trinidad.

At Little Robert's, we see maps of the Siskiyou lumber cuts threatening Black Bear and learn about the Indian resistance. Stopped at Forest Knolls [the Red House] and worked on the exhaust, rerouting it to save the lives of Suzanne and the children riding in back.

North of Ukiah on 101, run into J. P. [Pickens, with a now-healthy Maryanne and kids], Bergs [Peter Berg and Judy Goldhaft], Albion, and Chris convoying

south from Black Bear. J. P. has a new 1948 Chevy two-and-a-half-ton we nick-
name the Circus Wagon. Stop and picnic. Pull out and repair J. P.'s gas tank. Berg
planning to winter in the East. Reach Lost River around midnight, miss the turn to
David and Jane's [Simpson and Lapiner, former Mime Troupers], camp in a
meadow.

Sunday
David has finished a new wing on his house, all reclaimed wood. Goats, chickens,
horses, machinery, new corral. We walk through the mutilated forest: crushed
trunks, trees lying around like discarded condoms. A chain saw buzzes up the hill
somewhere. The reason hippies are allowed to live on this land is precisely because
it has been ruined. We are the second crop.
. . . David shows me his plans for a shower/sauna bath-truck. It's amazing.
Hot water heaters mounted over a fireplace of old tire rims. Laugh at the notion of
the huge thing lumbering through strange towns, filled with naked people. What a
brilliant idea: to appear at backwoods homes with hot showers.

Monday
. . . Pick sacks of chamomile and lemon balm, leave for Salmon Creek. Stop at For-
est of Arden and pick wondrous mint. At Salmon Creek, Gristle and Carol [Gypsy
Truckers] are there. Gristle still looking like Crazed Dr. Sivana from the Captain
Marvel Comics, kinky hair, wild eyes. He's torched the roof off his '49 Ford school
bus and wedged a Chevy V-8 into the engine compartment. It barks like a wolf
when it starts. I weld some linkage for him with my torches.
Natural Suzanne is down in the dumps, self-conscious about being dependent
because of her twins. Her body is probably complaining from all the work, and per-
haps my sense of urgency is pressing her.
Drive on to Trinidad house, modern tract home in the middle of a subdivision.
You can tell which place is ours from a mile away, looks like a red-ant heap. [The
Trinidad house population, as best as I can remember, consisted of Freeman and
Ivory House and Jim and Sue and their five kids: Danny, Luna, Dave, Jonny, and
Mad Anthony. Some Free Bakery people lived there as well.] The Free Fishing Boat
is finally in the water.

Tuesday
Up at 5:00 A.M. to fish—me, Owl [Pickens], and Freeman. Take a rotten alumi-
num dory out to the thirteen-foot wood skiff, which looks lovely, restored and
repainted. Few fumbling minutes attaching the umbilical cord from the engine to
the fuel tank and we're off, to sea in a rowboat! We pass the Head, into open water.
Gray sky. A dolphin, the curve of his back like a fall of hair. Birds appear out of the
swell and thrum like sine waves across the mind of the sky. High and holy out here.
Seals look us over. Beside Flat Iron Rock, I hook something heavy that runs all my
line out and then rips the hook loose. Rebait and hook something even heavier that
snaps sixty-pound test line like a strand of spit. We all look at each other. Good
God, it's the OCEAN! There are things down there bigger than men!

Cap'n Freeman notices that the fog has come in. Hard not to notice because we
can't see beyond the prow of the boat. He starts the motor and we improvise a direc-
tion home, arguing among ourselves about where the edge of the continent is. We
pass a rock almost obscured by sea lions and their harem. They trumpet at us, and
I holler back exuberantly. The rock appears to explode as the sea lions scream and
throw themselves and their ladies off the rocks. We grip the gunwales of the boat,
terrified that they are intending to capsize us.

The fog lifts a moment and reveals that we are dead on course for China. Owl,
prudent eleven-year-old, fastens on a life preserver. . . .

The kids make dinner while the adults rap about problems. Everyone wants to
fish, no one wants to tend to the house. Freeman admits that the boat brings in no
money or food yet, so it is "fun" and everyone wants a share of that, regardless of
the fact that some people are seriously studying fishing. He reminds everyone of the
necessity of food gathering as a focus. Plans are made to gather mussels tomorrow
and fix a dome for the children [to sleep and play in] to relieve the strain on the
house.

Quiet night. My loveliest sisters here: Natural Suzanne, Phyllis (whom I lean
against, writing); Nichole is singing "My Cherokee" a cappella, sweet and soft.

Wednesday
Something has changed in the atmosphere of the house, and everyone awakens
happy as clams. Dave (who escaped from San Quentin and lived with us almost a
year before getting drunk one night and returning to his hometown to brag about

being the only living escapee) builds five bunk beds today. The children had cleaned the house for us before we woke. Windows are being washed, floors scrubbed, the house being made love to, turned into a home. I've seen this cycle before. Beginning with houses too small for the size of our group needs, people live in them unconsciously, minds elsewhere, thinking of moving out. The space becomes cluttered and unloved, problematical, ugly. Then the inevitable flash occurs: this is it! This is not a rehearsal for life, this is my life, and people assume responsibility, banish the filth, and make it a home. . . .

I feel outside the main flow of things, so work with the kids today. I like their natural inclination to deal openly with real work: shooting out ideas and suggestions, using what works and dropping the rest. They imitate as faithfully as mirrors. Makes me reflect seriously on what am I actually teaching them—explicitly and, more important, implicitly.

. . . Natural Suzanne feeling better today. Things a bit awkward among the three of us. We are not lovers this trip: some other relationship is being developed, but we don't know precisely what yet. Phyllis—holy, magical, beautiful woman who sometimes forgets to view herself from the same charitable perspective she uses for the rest of Creation. Nichole here, body and spirit apparently dedicated to random sexual encounters, moves in my life like a warm summer rainstorm, satisfying and nourishing. Natch'l Suzanne getting it together for the road. The trip has shaken her out of her set a bit. Truck travel is hard for everyone, but for a real princess, with twins, it's grueling. She bounces back dark, foxy, and mischievous. My good fortune at knowing these women overwhelms me. The fact that they love me is a constant challenge to deserve them.

Thursday

Sheriff comes. Someone pissed outside again, and a neighbor, who just happened to be watching, called the heat. One-eyed Orville drops in. He is the patriarch of the straight community—fisherman, crafty, mean, politic old man. Warns us to respect our neighbors. The sheriff even tried to tell us that the babies shouldn't be naked but couldn't pull it off with the requisite seriousness.

John, Dave, and Charlie return with two fish. A better day than yesterday. Charlie caught both of them so there was a long discussion about making him captain when he turns twelve.

Discussed an idea called Planetedge, a nonprofit corporate form we could learn to handle as a tool without necessarily identifying with the corporation. Might be the family's economic base—an office and depot in Arcata, clearinghouse for the caravan, and a central information depot.

Friday: Sun in Gemini, Moon in Cancer
Early morning plans stretch out to noon departure for Black Bear. San Quentin Dave's final words, said to me personally: "Don't hurt anybody." They puzzle me for hours. He was up for murder.

We take Nichole and Vicky to 101 so they can hitch south, then drive down 299 over the Coast Range, fogs and firs, convoluted hill road, to Willow Creek. Two outlaw bikers putt past, Misfits from Eureka, dark, wild-looking men. They regard us coldly as they pass, and I get a shiver at how dark and pitiless the road can be.

After Wetchipec and Forks of Salmon, we're stopped on the road by a twinkling old Indian man named Les Bennet in a green pickup. Clear skin, bright eyes, copper bracelets on each wrist. He laughs softly, talks easily, scoping us out. It occurs to me that he is guardian of the road. Spots the elk-tooth necklace I am wearing and asks ingenuously, playing with my head, "Don't it make you sleepy?"

We drive on, engine overheating, convinced we're on the wrong road, until we crest the summit and begin rolling down into Black Bear. Everyone's on the knoll. The ki-yi-yi's and ululations start as soon as they recognize Josephine, dancing in ecstatic circles on her back legs. They all look illuminated and happy. We make camp for Suzanne, who is exhausted, and I cross the creek to see Richard and Elsa [Marley] where we celebrate our annual Yellow (Nembutals) shoot, surrounded by the sound of the rushing creek and the rustling leaf-breeze music.

Saturday
Leveled ground with John Cedar and Richard, set up tent in the woods at the far end of the meadow, whose five acres is being terraced by hand. Looks like China: rushing water, green shoots of plants, the turned earth, berry-brown bodies, naked, bent, working rough-handled shovels and hoes. Fir trees, high hills, everything flexing like the bodies.

Michael Tierra lays out herbs he's collected for the caravan: omolé [native name for soap root, a great shampoo and fish poison], wormwood, verbena, vervain, wild onion, sweet cicely.

Bonfire meeting this night to discuss the caravan. I try to interest people in my notion of Planetedge, but they're "edgy" about anything that would engage us with the bureaucracy. [A nonprofit entity would have to be registered legally.] This precipitates a long discussion about revolution. I am cranky with their recalcitrance and macho posing, insist that armed revolution is a mental pet, not reflected in the daily strategies of the community. It is a mythic superstructure lending an edge of danger and self-importance to activities that are revolutionary enough in their own right.

In the midst of this discussion I learn of Lew Welch's suicide. It grieves me deeply. I remember how he considered himself a failure and yet how much support and encouragement he gave me [and so many others] when I really needed it. His death puts all our bullshit into perspective. We have many good words and prayers for him.

Sunday, Second Week
Elsa gives me a large black book covered with the hide of the bear Efrem shot. It is being filled with recipes, herb cures, and information about the five years at Black Bear to hopefully educate and inspire others. The entire ranch has participated in its creation, and I am moved and proud of the effort that these overburdened friends have made to participate with [the Caravan]. They have given me the charge to be their eyes and ears.

Monday
Natural Suzanne tells me she wants to leave. She's unhappy and wants to go home. She tells me I've been a bummer, no help to her, and full of bad vibes.

Go for a long walk with Smilin' Mike and Tierra to collect herbs and roots. Have a long talk about the difficulty of maintaining relationships with many different people; with the comings and goings, closures and intimacies have to be perennially redefined or they evaporate. I say that it makes me feel good to know that everyone else is . . . (pause, searching for the word) and Tierra laughs and says, "Suffering."

Tuesday
The cow is dead. Someone chained it on a hill and it slipped and strangled itself while we were off picking herbs. Danny and I turn it into ribs, steaks, chops, ham-

burger for a meadow lunch. Whole kitchen buzzing. Everyone singing my song,
"The power of sweet, sweet music." Finger-popping and taking care of business.
Zoe [who buried the bear skull to save it for us] is half naked, improvising a beauti-
ful ballet to [Michael] Tierra's Bela Lugosi wake-up piano. Wonderful dark Italian
passions in his music, the piano straining to express his anger, confusion, funky
shuffle, delight, running together, interpenetrating, and breaking out of each other
like the rivulets and streams beside the house. I get a very graphic image of fucking
Zoe on top of the huge mound of raw, red cow meat piled high in front of me. Taste
and delicacy prevail, however.

Wednesday, Second Week
Suzanne announces that she's having a great time and in no hurry to leave. Our
departure has been put off three times now and is becoming something of a joke.
Each day we tarry adds something to our swelling larder, which now includes more
than two hundred pounds of acorns, small tomato plants, more roots and herbs,
and several new passengers.

Thursday
Owl and I work all day welding a rack to secure my three-drawer tool chest on the
running board. I teach him how to use the cutting torch, and he works beside me,
steady as a grown man. . . . At one point, he disappears and just as I'm beginning
to grumble to myself about kids, he returns with two hamburgers. I promote him on
the spot from Punkus Minimus to Punkus Maximus, and he's proud of his new
nickname.
     . . . The Black Bear Book begins to look like the Torah, growing daily as people
expend enormous amounts of energy adding information to it. Elsa's drawings
are wonderful. Each time one is completed and passed around the room, you can
mark its route through the crowd by the smile illuminating the face of the person
holding it.
     . . . Stay up most of the night with Geba. Met her last year and didn't get time
to know her. Large woman who would have driven Rubens berserk—big breasts,
hips, high-cheekboned face, flat honest eyes. Quiet. True. Her soft questions search
for my heart. She is deft, lifts the corner of word-curtains and peers underneath.

I am nervous, like a deer. I tell her many secret feelings, shadows, doubts about myself, this family, and its future that are hidden behind my public face. Liberated women will save us all.

Sunday, Third Week

Departure is a bungle. Smilin' Mike and his son Timmy want to leave with us. My truck is loaded down so heavily the springs are bowed. Mike is no help; he can see that but does not defer and, passive-aggressive, rests the weight of decision on me. Sensing the tension, Phyllis offers to hitchhike, and it is so obvious that he should be hitchhiking and not her that it angers me. I offer to take his son to Trinidad if that will help. He muddles around. Something about him doesn't feel right. He smiles too much.

In Orleans we spot [Karok Indian] Willis Bennett and his friend Darvin—short, stocky, 1950s pompadour, massive build. Darvin is drunk, but a high intelligence flashes through the smoke screen of the whiskey. They insist we stay and go eel fishing with them. Willis says it might be a year before we see each other again. I check with the girls and they say okay. . . .

Later, drinking and making music. All the kids playing volleyball. Willis likes my buckskin vest with the leather handprint of my daughter sewn on it. He wants to trade for a fringed, shiny black, three-quarter-length vest his daughter made, a Vegas cowboy number. I try to squirm out gracefully, but he is insistent. "What, it's not good enough for you?" he demands sullenly. When I refuse, he sulks off and drinks alone. Willis passes out, and his young nephew Moose, chasing a ball, runs into the corner of my truck and splits his head open. I drive him and his mother to the Hoopa hospital over forty miles of dirt road. Nice people there. Doctor teaches me how to stitch, and Moose, ten or eleven at most, never flinches or complains once. I'm struck by the thoughtfulness of the staff. Different than the city.

Monday

Stop at Trinidad house. Everyone happy. Been pulling in sixty to one hundred pounds of fish a day, small smokehouses up all over the yard. Neighbor relations still difficult. One-eyed Orville comes around, malicious, insinuating, dropping veiled allusions about our being burned out. San Quentin Dave watches him blankly. I watch Dave. Orville has no idea that Dave was sentenced for murder.

Ivory [Freeman's wife at the time] is weaving a blanket from the men's hair. Freeman talks about a solstice ceremony at Trinidad Head to reinvoke the spirit of Surai, the old Yurok fishing village that used to be there.

Tuesday
Stop at Salmon Creek. Libré has sent a letter reneging on the invitation, telling us that they are helpless and lame, working on their own problems. Everyone at the Trinidad house enthused about the caravan. More and more people planning to go. I send Peter Rabbit and Libré a fifteen-cent get-well card.

Before leaving, David Simpson takes me aside. I've confessed my ambiguities about the trip to him and that the idea of continuing some of the craziest aspects of our life on the road leaves me cold. I feel like being alone. He tells me, "A man is no better than his time. To try and be better means being worse."

David pleases me by saying that after Olema, I now travel as I would have liked others to have moved through my place. He laughs commiseratingly at the burden I've taken on, and I leave feeling much better.

Driving south, we pick up an old hitchhiker named Elmer, a white gospel singer from Oneida, Tennessee, sixty-nine years old but "sexually, just like a young boy," he says often, darting his tongue about like a monkey and eyeing Phyllis. He's got emphysema and black lung from coal mining. Tells us all about it while he eats Wonder bread and drinks Dr. Pepper. He sings gospel songs in a strong nasal voice.

We drop him off and pick up a stringy Okie named Walt, coming from Oregon where he got rolled and robbed. All he's got are his coat and a bottle of wine. His hobby is jokes, he says, and he tells jokes without a repeat for seven hours. Good jokes. I laugh till I cry. He sings like Hank Williams, yodels, and plays harmonica. He used to be a warm-up comic for the Grand Ol' Opry but "couldn't take the pills" and left.

Back in the city, Berg is at Treat Street. He has warmed to the idea of the cara-van and tells me, "Everyone is going to Colorado." I'm pleased to know that he con-siders the trip worth his time, since his attention can close down as rapidly as a blown fuse if he is not interested in what's going on.

Our departure date keeps being postponed. The summer solstice is celebrated on Mount Tamalpais [in Marin County]. Sam appears with my pixie-daughter Ariel, delivered [to me] by a proud Jim Koller, who regards Sam as a Valkyrie and seems to feel that our destiny, hers and mine, is to be shared. [Sam had an extraordinary

story. *Her friend Cass had left Koller and was weird to her when she visited.
Unhinged by grief at their estrangement, Sam sheared off her hair with a scissors
and went to the Huerfano Valley in Colorado with some names I'd given her. She
arrived just as the peyoteros returned with peyote from a trip to Texas. She had
set up a small lean-to covered by a large canvas Drum Hadley gave her. Carelessly,
with no ceremony or prayers, she ate an extremely large peyote button and fell
asleep.*

*She woke in the pitch dark, terrified. Her black Great Dane, Crow, was growl-
ing and trembling, ears flattened. A number of dogs walked stiff-legged around her
camp, growling and spitting in the dark. She got her feathers and a bag of cornmeal
and made a circle of the cornmeal around the lean-to, lit a fire, and prayed all night
long. Something turned around for her.*

*She made a beautiful camp and lived rather idyllically for a month or so with
Ariel, teaching her to build fires, use needle and thread and scissors, and cook.
According to her, "for the first time, I began to feel myself as whole." Ariel began to
grow restive at their solitude. Sam realized that Fosmo wouldn't show up with the
promised horses and said to herself, "I've had enough." The next day Jim Koller
appeared magically and announced that he was going to California, inviting her to
go. "Can you wait an hour?" she said, which was how long it took her to break
camp. They drove straight back to the Red House, where the caravan was preparing to leave for Colorado.]*

Sam looks beautiful, long blonde hair cropped short and her eyes clear. Ariel
has lost her infant look and is taller, very quiet, and demure. I am excited to see her
after a long time and lift her up to plant a kiss on her downy butt. She startles me
by smiling shyly and saying, "Don't do that, Poppa." I set her down, thrilled at
being called "Poppa." Sam is not certain what her plans are, and I wait, giving
her space to decide whether or not to travel with us.

A long procession treks up Mount Tamalpais carrying drums, trombones, and
wine, winding through a rustling, hissing expanse of waving, knee-high grass,
cresting the hill where the ocean extends before us, glittering and vast beneath a
dense awning of clouds. We blow horns, shout encouragement at the departing
Sun, expressing neither neoprimitivism nor anthropomorphism but improvised
ceremony. The gaily dressed children moving as randomly as milkweed spores blow
horns and whistles and sing continuously, accompanying the sun on its long trek
toward winter.

The Red House population is reaching critical mass as family members from different communal bases crowd the grounds preparing their vehicles. A sign in a woman's hand appears on the front door asking people to consider why they are here and what they are doing to help. Numbers have swelled to nearly forty people, and the neighbors are incensed. "Why's" are swarming like hornets:

"Why should I have to wait to pass on a public street?"

"Why are there children playing in the road?"

"Why isn't that septic tank fixed yet? It's disgusting."

"Why don't you go to fucking China?"

"Whatever happened to our sweet suburban community?"

Cops visit daily, tagging vehicles for parking on the street. The night after the sign appears on the door a group meeting goes unaccountably well. People bare doubts, grudges, and misgivings, but the group mind keeps it light and tight so that no one becomes a victim. Each person is called on to declare why they want to caravan and what they think they can do for the group. Crazy Kevin [who had locked himself in his room at Olema, shitting in newspapers and throwing them out the window, emerging only at night to pace through the main house after every-one was asleep, carrying an axe and screaming about "Dr. Death." He was "cured" by Rolling Thunder during one of his visits and was now only odd.] declares that he is pursuing the wisdom of madness. No one disagrees there. Each conversation continues until everyone's reservations have been aired, clarified, and dispersed. People feel fine.

The next day, I am up early, soliciting contributions of welfare money, gasoline credit cards, and food stamps as final provisions for the trip. I am overready to leave. J. P. Pickens gets into a fistfight with a friend's ex-landlord who, for some rea-son, had called the police on J. P.'s buddy. The guy is threading his car between our vehicles trying to pass when J. P. begins screaming at him, calling him a "scum-sucking pig" and shouting, "You stink like a dead dog." As the man's vehicle is forced to a crawl to pass between several of ours, J. P. spits in his face. This is too much, and the guy leaps out to fight, even with thirty of J. P.'s friends standing by. J. P.'s behavior is so bizarre, and the reasons for it unknown to the rest of us, so we stand back to see what will happen.

J. P. is ready. His dilemma is that the methedrine residues in his system misfire some critical synapse, because he misses with his first swing, and the guy flattens

J. P. with one good punch. J. P. rises from the ground, one eye split and bleeding copiously. He offers a zany giggle and says, "Showed him!" Work resumes after some discussion.

Finally, on a Friday morning, all was ready, and according to my journals, with the "sun in Cancer and the moon in Gemini," the first wave prepared to leave.

Word from Libré had come yet again, emphasizing that we were not welcome. They were totally panicked. They said that we were not "together," were too ready to teach and not ready enough to learn from them. There was some truth in this assertion, but much of their information was probably related to my failed ambassadorial visit the year before. The group decided that Paul Shippee and I should go ahead as envoys, since two people hardly constitute an invasion. (Paul was an old friend from Actors' Workshop days once married to Sandy Archer of the Mime Troupe. He had moved into our community in step with me.) We would try to dissipate Libré's paranoia. By the time we left, however, the modest scouting party (also charged with reporting details about routes and campsites) had swollen to include Peter Berg and Judy Goldhaft, their children Aaron and Ocean Rush, and their truck, the Albigensian Ambulance Service. Traveling with them was a slender, boyish woman named Suki, conscripted to operate the video camera that Peter had scammed from a producer who had provided it to purchase a safe way to interact with the Diggers. Paul Shippee and Mai-Ting, a Chinese woman doctor we nicknamed the Dragon Lady (both for her no-nonsense approach and her exotic beauty), would ride in Paul's green Chevy panel truck. Sam, Ariel, and I would travel in the Meat and Bone Wagon.

After a fine birthday breakfast for Judy and Ocean Berg, we piled into the trucks but were halted yet again for a serenade by the Valley Liberation Band, which wanted to dignify our send-off. The band was the raunchiest group of rotten-royal losers imaginable and did nothing to allay my queasy feelings about the impression we might make on strangers. J. P., one eye swollen shut and bandaged, played banjo; Digger, in a filthy L.A. Bikers' Club T-shirt, played tin can; Marsha Thelin's temporary lover Willem, clad in shredded coveralls, played guitar; Smilin' Mike played something as a drum; Vinnie, naked to the waist except for copious amounts of body hair, played trombone; and a crazy woman who appeared from Mexico with a parrot on her head did a loose double-boogie in the middle of the street. We drove all of about seven miles into San Rafael, where we retrieved good radishes, lettuce, tomatoes, and squash from a garbage bin behind the Safeway supermarket.

Our first "official" stop was to be Gary Snyder's place near Nevada City, and the first night we camped on the Yuba River under stars like small tufts of popcorn in the blackness of the sky.

We arrived at Gary's place carrying bay and Yerba Buena leaves we'd stopped to pick as gifts. Gary was walking around in a loincloth, cutting madrone yokes to hang pots over his outdoor fire pit. He didn't stop working when we arrived, and his greeting consisted of "You again." I hadn't seen him in several years.

Later in the day, he thawed a bit and took us to a clean and shaded pine grove near his place, announcing, "Let this be a family camp." We explained our visions of the trade route and caravan, how we hoped to stitch together various regional economies into a larger network. We expressed hope that he and his friends would participate.

The next morning, Gary woke me and Berg early and brought us to his house for coffee and talk. He told us that the people in their area were committing themselves to articulating a sense of place and understanding its species diversity. They planned to be there for the long haul, to serve as its guardians. They had reservations about travelers. Furthermore, he added, they didn't need much.

We had anticipated this response and looked forward to a meeting where we could express ourselves directly to the community and hopefully put their reservations to rest. When we returned to our campsite, Crazy Kevin had tendered us a gift of a latrine, using a hatchet to carve perfectly true rectangular walls in the granitic soil, an act of monumental dedication.

We reclaimed a muddy spring at the site by removing clay, water, quartz, and old pine needles and constructing a spring box from heavy cedar boards, fashioned with carefully dovetailed corners. The box was placed on four inches of white gravel hauled from the nearby Malakoff Diggings. We packed the outside of the box with more gravel and stood back to watch the water rise and the silt settle. We were rewarded with a deep, clear pool to leave for those who followed us. We felt good about our work and hoped it would say more about our intentions than words.

That night, members of the San Juan Ridge community visited our camp: Gary and his family; Zack Reisner; Joel the potter; Doc Dachtler, local schoolteacher, craftsman, and singer; and his pregnant wife Shelly. They wound their way through the trees, halloing as they came.

Our camp was beautiful: lanterns were strung through the trees and around the grounds. A meeting place had been marked out with blankets. Greetings were exchanged warmly, but there was an undercurrent of reserve. The community members addressed us formally, expressing fear that welcoming us would place their still-fragile community in the path of a hippie migration. They explained that they were making a serious effort to live tribally, maintaining separate households village-style but meeting often for group work and policy discussion. They were pursuing systematic, organized research to combat gold mining, irresponsible logging, and exploitative real-estate practices. They were relearning "life in place," as people had lived on San Juan Ridge for thousands of years, and worried that nomads would not be sensitive to local practices and spirits. I liked them for their gentleness and concern, admired their unity and discipline.

We traded songs, and the night was good, but a gulf remained between the two tribes. I was not sure whether it was a difference of intentions or of personal development. They were more settled that we and, in many ways, more accomplished. A thought occurred to me that made me lonesome: "They are the Earth and we are the Wind."

The next day, Doc and I traded songs. He asked to learn my "Rainbow Woman Song" and taught me a "Corn Song" I'd admired. Bearing his song as a gift, we said good-bye and pushed on—over the Sierras, down the eastern slope, into the picturesque town of Sierraville, homing into the magnetic spiritual pulse of Pyramid Lake.

The next day, we entered the lake's force field through the north end. It shimmered before us, a perfect turquoise oasis in the rusty, dusty earth. In the town of Sutcliff, Berg remembered some people we had helped during the Indian invasion of Alcatraz. He proposed asking them for recognition as pilgrims, to clarify our posture toward the lake. In the general store at Nixon, a man steered us to a campsite on native land in Dead-Ox Canyon.

In Nixon we met Dora García, secretary of the local tribal council, who seemed disposed toward us and invited us home. Berg and Suki fascinated Dora's family by showing videotapes of their children over their TV. Dora expressed curiosity about the utility of this (then relatively new) instrument for preserving tribal customs. She agreed to put our petition to the tribal council the following night and then to visit our camp to inform us of the response.

It was technically illegal to camp on Indian land, but we were buried out of sight in the chaparral of a sandy canyon flanking the Truckee River—and we didn't care. Pyramid Lake is one of the continent's magical and holy spots, and we considered our being there totally correct.

We fashioned trotlines (long lines from which dangle multiple baited hooks) and ran them across the river. I spent most of the day making fish gigs out of an old iron rod I found in the desert, heating it with my torches, beating it flat, and filing barbs and a blade on it. Shippee fashioned an exquisite Zen spear, while mine looked as if it had been made in a kindergarten for mentally challenged students. We spent the day spearing the fat, bony carp introduced by Europeans, splitting them open and drying them on the rocks to make jerky for the road. They glittered on the rocks like the wings of gigantic iridescent moths.

Berg returned at sundown, elated with the discovery of abundant cattail shoots. Steamed in the sheath, they are delicious and taste like asparagus. The air was tangy with sage. The children plashed contentedly in the river, and when we weren't lazing away the time discussing alternate economies and self-sufficient communities or how to reconfigure cities to be biologically continuous with their larger environments (versus the present condition of obliterating and poisoning them), we cleaned the campsite for hundreds of yards in every direction as our ritual of respect for the place, gathering the discarded beer cans, cardboard boxes, disposable diapers, tangles of abandoned fishing line, and bottle caps that thoughtless campers had jettisoned.

Sam was cranky and complained that she was not doing what she wanted. When I inquired what that might be, she said, "Hunting," so I prepared the lever-action .22 rifle I'd had since I was a boy and sent her off to hunt jackrabbits while I spent the day fooling around with Ariel. Dora came by and told us that the tribal council had refused our request. We decided to wait and see what their next move would be.

At dusk Judy Goldhaft was cooking Navajo fry bread over the coals when a police car pulled up. A short, squat, reservation cop with a buzz cut and a tough face squeezed his pistoled, belted, and black-sticked body out of the vehicle and sauntered over. We acknowledged him casually but said little. The first move was his. We observed him eyeballing our camp and were confident that it was tidy. He noticed Judy's fry bread and inquired after it, took a piece and seemed to enjoy it, offering that his mother used to make it too. We chatted a while. He told us that he'd received some complaints about our being there but could see that we were camping nicely.

We explained that we didn't want to go over to the official campground and set up next to the tourists and the mobile condos and the TVs on the picnic tables—all part of the culture we were fleeing. We suggested that in lieu of site fees, which we could not afford, our cleaning and care of the area might be considered payment enough, and we showed him the sacks of garbage we had collected as evidence of our intentions. None of this seemed to strike Phoenix (actually his name) as out of the question, but he explained that he did not possess the authority to make policy. He confessed a bit sheepishly that he was under orders to tell us to come to the tribal council office to discuss our occupancy.

After he left, Suki, Kevin, Ariel, Aaron, and I walked over to visit Stone Mother, a large, dome-shaped rock formation at the edge of the lake. At the top of the rock are man-sized holes that made me wonder if they might have been used as meditation chambers. From inside these holes, the horizon-to-horizon arc of the sun's passage is visible. Pelicans glided unperturbed around us, and as we left, a formation of five crows flew low overhead. Kevin raised a stick into which he had stuck a crow feather. He whistled and one of the birds broke away from the pack and soared directly over him. I tipped my hat and saluted them, and another rolled out and did the same to me. They followed us most of the way back to camp. I no longer cared what the tribal council had to say—we had been made welcome by the spirits of the place.

The next day we followed Phoenix into town, a slow and dusty place with streets too hot to walk on barefoot. An old-fashioned, sweating Coke cooler with a heavy lid dominated the porch of the general store, floating its thick glass bottles in icy water.

We met with Teddy James, chairman of the tribal council, a pompous bureaucrat in a crisp polyester plaid shirt and spanking-new cowboy hat, whose attitude informed us that he did not suffer hippies at all. He talked only about money and could not or would not find a place for us in his imagination. When we proposed our trade of groundskeeping for fees he became indignant. "Are you saying that Indians don't keep their lands clean?" he demanded, as if insulted.

I debated showing him the the fifty-gallon sacks of trash we'd hauled into town with us, but I knew it was a lost cause. We should have known better than to use the word *pilgrims* with a man who was still pissed about the landing at Plymouth Rock. He told us to pay up like everyone else or get out.

As we walked back to our trucks, Phoenix, silent during the chairman's harangue, caught up with us. He didn't look at us directly but addressed the landscape, saying, "That guy never leaves the office. You people are welcome here as long as I'm the cop." It was comforting to know that we had been recognized.

Still, it was time to go.

Outside of Austin, Nevada, after crossing a seven-thousand-foot summit and a flat alkali valley, we stopped at a Texaco station called Middle Gate where a rugged-looking man with a gentle manner named Vance made us feel very much at home. Among the five or six Indian men sitting on a bench, gazing over the flats, was a Shoshone named Irwin who knew Rolling Thunder. Irwin volunteered that he disagreed with R.T.'s use of peyote, but he seemed to like us enough to share directions to a favorite campsite called Cottonwood Creek.

Such casual generosity occurred so often on our travels that I am surprised I never took it for granted. Life "on the road" must touch archaic memories for Americans, so many of whom are either descendants of migratory pioneers or personally able to remember their own travels during the Dust Bowl and Great Depression days. Let one example suffice for many:

During an earlier road trip, our group had paused at the edge of a medium-sized highway town: clusters of gas stations, car washes, and industrial restaurants, the kind of place where disappointed locals are surfeited with strangers. Our kids were cold, overtired, and hungry from a long day's haul when we pulled into a House of Pancakes, one of those plasticine roadhouses with Formica counters, twin dispensers whirling industrially colored liquids masquerading as "punch" and "lemonade," and pies and confections that appear to be made from hair gel, resting agelessly in chrome-edged glass cases.

Our group had filled all the counter space and the adults were conferring, pooling small amounts of loose change to determine what we could afford. The kids' heads were swiveling, ogling the oleaginous pies and steaming plates of burgers and fries passing tantalizingly near them en route to flusher customers.

Our counter waitress was a hard-bitten, apparently humorless woman who'd served the migratory public for too long. Her face was set in a permanent scowl, and her "don't give me any shit" attitude was clear as a warning flag. I was irritable and tired myself and the thought crossed my mind that she might be an easy mark for some teasing to entertain us and distract the kids from their glasses of hot water their mothers were mixing with ketchup to make almost-tomato soup.

Our discussion concerning what we could afford must have continued longer than I thought, because it was interrupted by plate after plate after plate of pancakes and eggs and sausages in front of each and every one of our places, accompanied by frothy glasses of orange juice, steaming mugs of coffee, and hot chocolates peaked with whipped cream for the children. Some ghastly error had occurred; some child must have spoken out of turn or something, because I knew that we did not have the money to pay for such bounty. I envisioned a confrontation and the summoning of police when the bill was presented.

I hastened to inquire about the mistake and practice some evasive diplomacy, but the crusty waitress read my intention from six feet away and held up one hand to stop me.

"It's on me," she said. "I got a kid out there somewhere too." Then she smiled—a whipped, ironic, commiserating wrinkle of lip—refused the little money we did have, and shuffled off to take care of some paying customers. I was left with the coppery taste of shame in my mouth, considering by what a minuscule chance I had missed targeting her as the butt of a cheap joke. It requires only one or two such experiences before you realize that on the road, assumptions are a handicap, best left in the rest stops with the trash.

We continued across Nevada. A lovely couple from nearby McGill, Chuck and Beverly Hansen, dropped by our camp at Cave Lake. They'd liked my singing the night before and returned in the morning to offer us two brown and three rainbow trout for our breakfast. Sam spent the morning tanning a badger skin I'd taken from a roadkill the day before.

Later in the day, the campsite swelled with weekend campers, expanding like popcorn in a closed pan, and we were collectively inspired to leave. Occupants of Winnebago City watched in amazement as our sprawling amalgam of tents and laundry, kitchen hearths, cook pots, kids, and dogs disappeared into three trucks, leaving only a pristine beach behind.

As I collapsed my tent, I caught a small brown snake resting beneath it. I told him aloud that I'd let him go, but (as in the fairy stories) he must first tell me something I needed to know. I talked to him calmly until he stopped struggling, then I tested our bargain by opening my hand. He remained coiled on my palm, flicking his tongue and fanning his gaze left and right across my body, gauging my intentions toward him, which were good but deliberate. I had asked a question respectfully, but I expected an answer.

The snake turned away and then back, regarding me fixedly. My thoughts stopped completely and a clear image formed in my mind: red letters wriggling against a black background forming three distinct words—"Anger is panic." The words were appropriate to domestic difficulties I was experiencing with Sam, difficulties that according to her, resulted from my insistent and inadequately suppressed anger. I said, "Thank you," released the snake, and have dedicated some of my time since to regularly considering exactly how his injunction might be appropriate to me.

We camped our way across Utah, following Highway 180 toward Provo and then Highway 40 east through Heber. Torrential creeks thrashed beside the road. The Uintas, spurs of the Rockies attempting to reach Idaho, were rich, green, bristling with quaking aspen, pine, and fir. The mountains appeared to have stubbed their noses against something at high speed, since the strata flex at ninety degrees to the horizon.

Near Strawberry Lake, at the edge of a fine grassy valley sheltered by aspens, I called my mother from a phone booth and learned that my father was ill. This had been such a common experience in my life that I paid no mind to it. My father often escaped the stresses of work by checking into the hospital with an armload of books, the way some people check into health spas. When we made excuses for him at family functions, my uncles winked and said, "Bullshit" to my stories about his "not being well." However, something about my mother's anxiety this time left a residue on my mood.

Sam and I stayed up late struggling with domestic problems. She announced that her work in the world was learning the uses of plants to heal people. Since she had never broached this subject before, I was suspicious and short with her, distracted by the news about my father. I told her about his illness, and she confided a dream of the previous night, in which my father was offered the choice of dying or living damaged; he chose to die.

The next morning I awoke to see Cheryl Lynn Pickens's face pass by framed in the window of a truck. The rest of the caravaners had arrived from the Red House, tired of staying behind. They were rolling up the road in a long line of gaily painted vehicles, canvases flapping, buckets tinkling, motors roaring, drivers and passengers saluting and cheering our reunion. So much for a delicate entrance at Libré.

Bob Santiago and Nichole appeared a day later, and Sam's bile rose. Her pique was prophetic: the next afternoon, Nichole and I sneaked away to go swimming together. After an invigorating splash, a catch-up visit, and a romp of bare-assed desert bouncing, we returned to the water's edge to retrieve our clothes and discovered them gone. Nichole and I were stranded; our only option was to walk back to camp buck-naked. So much for my attempts at discretion. When we returned (with what I considered a great deal of aplomb, considering the circumstances), Sam's expression of hostile triumph made it clear who had stolen our clothes.

Sam's ability to detect my dalliances with other women was uncanny. No haymow was secluded enough, no grove, streamside, tent, closet, or hilltop aerie safe from her sudden appearance. A few nights later in this caravan summer, in the mountains above Boulder, Nichole and I tiptoed into the forest long after everyone was asleep. This was, after all, the pre-AIDS sixties, and the mores of our community decreed that if two consenting adults wanted to pair off for sexual research and development, there was little reason why they should not. Feelings of anger and jealousy were the legacy of a decadent bourgeois heritage and were not to be acknowledged—unless of course, they were one's *own* feelings, in which case their status was immediately elevated to critical importance.

My personal sexual behavior must have been inspired by our country's scorched-earth strategy in Vietnam. "No survivors" aptly describes my dedication to have sex with all the women I wanted. While post-AIDS realities have rendered such experimentation terminally dangerous, at that time the risks seemed minimal, and my recollection is that both sexes found fun, random tenderness, and thrills in such encounters. This is not to suggest that there were never any karmic kickbacks, however.

On this particular night, Nichole and I prepared a bed far from camp in a breezy glade of firs. We were in the gaspy near-crescendo of lovemaking when Sam appeared in a ghostly white nightgown with wind-whipped hair, trembling, like Lady Macbeth, with rage and jealousy. Her antennae, even in sleep, had somehow locked onto my arousal with unerring accuracy. Her presence made continuing difficult, certainly tasteless, and probably dangerous, since Sam is not a woman to turn your back on when she is angry.

Nichole put her arms around Sam, and the three of us sat together in the suddenly chilly night, trying to pick our way through the emotional rubble of conflicting loyalties and desires. Finally, after an hour or two of tortured explorations, confessions, and recriminations, everything suddenly appeared stupid, and we began to laugh hysterically at the improbable slapstick idiocy of the incident.

A day or so later, the caravan pulled into Speedmaster's motorcycle shop on Pearl Street in Boulder, where Julie Boone's lover Carl was working and where we were to rendezvous with friends. We hobbled in, fatigued and cramped from long hours of driving. Julie was standing by the far wall to greet us: lovely Julie, lusty, voluptuous Motorcycle Julie, who had aroused such ardor in Hell's Angel Hairy Henry that he had built a beautiful chopper especially for her. She looked at me and tipped her head back quizzically.

"Oh, Peter," she said casually, as if she'd just remembered something, "Morris died."

I looked at her blankly. I felt nothing. My father? Such a thing was beyond comprehension. How could a man of such vitality and power pass through the veil without creating some celestial disturbance, some ripple? She must be mistaken. There would have to be a rent in the sky, a rush of wind—at *least* a tattered sheet flapping beside the road as a sign I might later recall and think, "Ah, *that* was it."

I turned away and lit a cigarette. I saw her telling others. Berg came over and threw his arms around me. I felt nothing. I was in a motorcycle shop in a strange city, and a beautiful woman, a lover and friend, had just informed me that my father had died—and I felt nothing.

I found a phone and called my mother. She was distraught. Morris had already been buried. The police had searched the country for me for days and could not find me. Ruth hadn't even known what state I was in. "How could no one *find* you?" she demanded, as if that were the entire source of her problem. Yes, she was all right. Yes, relatives were with her. I told her that, of course, I would come home. Did she need me immediately? I would have to drive. I told her I had some affairs to settle up. I didn't know what I should do. I knew I should be there, but Morris was already gone, my mother was in good hands, and I felt I had to finish what I had traveled this distance to do. I was spinning in place. I had no father. The ground had eaten him. I was 50 percent closer than a moment ago to being an orphan.

I hung up the phone and breathed in and out. For a long time afterward, my life felt as it did in that moment: detached and out of touch, just breathing in and breathing out. Perhaps it was the cocktail of drugs I was always imbibing, perhaps the defenses I'd erected as a boy, or the impossibility of feeling loved by him. Some chamber where clearly expressed feelings might live and flourish within me had been sealed tight as a bank vault. The combination to open the locks and spring those heavy doors was not to be commanded by anything as commonplace as a death.

It has been my experience as an actor that the more particularly and specifically a personal experience is relived, the more universally it may be appreciated. Individual events are hardly personal property; they participate in something larger and more profound that people share, understand, and can empathize with. Consequently, my behavior, when learning about my father's death, while apparently bizarre, has antecedents and root causes that may be quite ordinary and not at all surprising to others. Recurrent memories from childhood intrude into the present, overwhelming it—

I am sitting at a desk puzzling over a series of incomprehensible high school math problems. A large, dangerous man, my father, is screaming, "You stupid, dumb son of a bitch!" at me. And then, again, I am being twisted, pummeled, bent, suffocated, and choked under the guise of instruction in self-defense.

Even though my body, as I experience these memories, is the storehouse of all that charged information, I cannot describe what the incidents *felt* like. I can describe the chalky green blotter on my desk, and its patterns of pressed concentric squares where I directed my attention during these homework diatribes. I can describe the gossamer curtains and cherry spool bed, the patterns and textures of my father's clothing. I can recall the mélange of scents in the purple and beige patterned carpet my face was ground into when "wrestling." But I cannot remember feeling anything other than numb— and perhaps an itch of anger, banked like hot coals deep in my muscles.

The nightly drama of homework, for instance, is indelibly imprinted but stripped of emotional content. It was as predictable as a dance. "Let's see what you're doing here," Morris would mutter casually, walking into my room to check on my progress. He would talk his way aloud through the problem I was daydreaming over. Since his calculations were impossibly fast, I was an audience, reduced to muttering "uh-huh" and nodding like a drinky-bird bowing over a cup of water. Inevitably he'd make a mistake, correct himself, then challenge me, "Why didn't *you* see that? Are you paying attention, or what?"

Next, he'd offer some variant of "Okay, I've shown you one, you do the next." I had no idea how to begin, or why if bus A headed north at fifty-two miles an hour and bus B headed south at forty-seven miles an hour, anyone cared *when* they would meet. Inevitably, Morris would become impatient with my fumbling—and then abusive. His fervent unanswerable questions—"How can you be so fucking stupid? How can anyone be so fucking

stupid?"—paralyzed me, and my inability to respond in turn stimulated his
fear that I might actually *be* stupid. Panic provoked threats to "snap your
fucking thumbs" or "break your knees" or, most chilling of all, send me to
reform school.

His yelling invariably attracted my mother, who entered the fray on my
behalf, moved by maternal pity and also convinced by reading Freud that
childhood traumas produce lasting emotional damage (and sometimes alcohol and drug abuse!). As she got older she was less intimidated by Morris
and found the courage to intervene, however ineffectively. Grateful as I
might have been for her intervention, there were now *two* of them, book-
ending me and screaming at one another like harpies.

"Morrie, you're making him crazy!"

"Shut up, Ruthie, you're using up the oxygen in the room."

My role was reduced to sitting there, looking out the window, studying
the other homes lining our street, wondering if each had a similar quotient
of domestic horrors—or was mine unique?

As I matured, I discovered that my childhood experiences were not all
that different from those of many others, and far milder and less damaging
than many. I offer no excuses for my personal faults and shortcomings, nor
do I blame my parents, who did their best with what they had inherited from
their own parents. During the time these stories took place, I was older than
my mother had been when she bore me, and consequently fully responsible.
Fairness, however, demands that I point out that millions of young people
did not *accidentally* or spontaneously express a decade of rage and disappointment like gas after a bad meal. My generation's disillusion over social
injustice and its fervent desire to make the world a more compassionate
place must have had some antecedents. It does not seem foolish to search
for that evidence inside the nation's homes, where the young were bent,
stretched, folded, stapled, and stressed by the social and political costs of the
Cold War and the seductive, ridiculously inflated promises of Midas-like
wealth. One way or another, such forces took their toll, and my household
was no exception.

My father, for all his excesses and fulminations, was a decent, honest
man. But after a lifetime of habitually closing myself down for fear of arous-
ing his ire or violence, it's not surprising to me that his death did not im-

mediately release a flood of feelings. They appeared about eight years later, the first time I could bring myself to visit his grave, after I was forced to acknowledge that I had failed to save his beloved Turkey Ridge Farm from the debt to which he'd mortgaged and remortgaged it and failed, too, in my attempts to rebury him there, at his favorite place on earth.

One day in 1978, I drove to the cemetery in New Jersey where he was buried in a subsection of his brother-in-law's plot. What an affront his fierce autonomy and pride would have experienced had he, the family patriarch, known that his presence was indicated by a shoe-box-sized granite plate in the lawn, shadowed by his brother-in-law's far grander standing tombstone. Death does play tricks like that on self-importance.

When I finally located the site, I was stunned to find his grave bare—nothing on its surface but lumpy dirt. When I inquired, I was told that it had sunk several days before and the groundskeepers had stripped the sod and refilled it to ground level. The engraved letters on his stone—

MORRIS COHON
1904–1971

—and the title of his favorite poem by Dylan Thomas—

"Do Not Go Gentle into That Good Night"

—were clotted and obscured with dried clay from the groundsmen's boots.

I dropped to my knees and began prying the dirt out of the letters with a twig. It was not until drops were muddying the granite beneath me that I realized I was crying and speaking aloud. I had not recognized my own voice: a high, keening, tiny sound, strangled in my throat. It was the voice of a frightened, disappointed child, nakedly entreating his father for affection and respect. I was telling him how much I loved and admired him and how much I needed him to love me the way I was, even though I might not be as smart as he was and didn't enjoy hurting people. I cried and talked and chipped at the clay for over an hour. I didn't think a body could warehouse such an inventory of tears.

Vivid memories flooded me. Occasionally at Turkey Ridge, when the sky was lowering gray as the afternoon rains of summer swept in, my father would summon me to one of our barns to nap with him. It was usually the bull barn that he had designed and built of pungent rough-milled beams sawn from our own native black and white oaks and covered with aluminum sheeting. We would climb into the haymow together, and he would wrap the two of us deliciously close in an old horse blanket. He would drink pear brandy, and I would rest against him, overjoyed to be tucked against his massive body, protected rather than assailed by the crook of his arm. He would sleep that way while I tried to stay awake, relishing the pattering of rain on the metal roof. In those rare moments, I felt content and proud, the way I imagined other boys felt when I watched them playing with their fathers. My world was loving and, better still, safe.

The fact that so much of my childhood was wasted trying to make him notice me does not blind me to the fact that in his own way he treasured and appreciated me more than I realized at the time. Now, beside his grave, I could acknowledge that his spot in the universe was empty, and I was engulfed by a profound sense of loss and frailty, as if I were a helpless witness to the sight of a loved one slipping irretrievably into quicksand. The cause of both my joys and terrors was gone, sucked away with the pitiless neutrality of a Kansas tornado chewing through a trailer park.

Little of this was apparent to me that day in Boulder, however. It would be nearly two months more before I reached my mother's house in the East, two months of playing out the caravan, finishing the hand I had dealt myself.

20

top of the arc

Two nights after I learned of my dad's death, we were camped in the mountains above Boulder in a big wooded meadow. The trucks were parked in a large circle, and we'd constructed a camp kitchen and fire pit in the center. A friend from the East, Lewis John Carlino, appeared unexpectedly, mysteriously out of place. He had met my parents when he'd arrived in New York from Los Angeles about ten years before, a penniless writer. He needed a place to write, and my folks had given him Turkey Ridge gratis for a winter, where he'd composed two one-act plays, *Snow Angel* and *Epiphany,* both dedicated to Ruth and Morris, and then a three-act play, *Telemachus Clay,* which had won an Obie and brought him to the attention of Hollywood. Later, he went on to direct several films, *The Sailor Who Fell from Grace with the Sea* and *The Great Santini* among them. He made good money and bought his own farm near Turkey Ridge in the Delaware Water Gap, where he lived with his crazy wife Natale and their three children. To this day, I do not know what Lew was doing in Colorado or how he found our camp.

It was Owl's birthday, and I'd made him a necklace of deer bones as a gift. Local people dropped by our campsite throughout the day, curious about this gathering of strangers who had appeared from nowhere. We began to drink, and as a party developed I declared the night a wake for my father.

The music that evening was inspired and the women's dancing powerful, their bellies glowing ember red in the firelight. Carla in particular was possessed. She sweated and shone like chrome, giving herself away to the gods. Gristle passed out LSD-dosed marshmallows that kicked the night into overdrive.

Sometime later, I was lying with my head in Gristle's partner Carol's lap. She was sucking my fingers. Gristle appeared in the periphery of my vision demanding to settle some previous argument with Carol immediately. A fight started between them, and Sam stepped into the middle of it to arbitrate. The savagery of Gristle's response terrified her, and she stayed close to me, gasping like a fish out of water until she finally fell asleep. I sat on the tailgate of the Meat and Bone Wagon, watching the stars turn, trying to comfort Sam, listening to Gristle smash things and Carol screaming at him. The congas and guitars were an insistent pulse. Clouds and trees jittered before me, and everything in my field of vision writhed and folded on itself. An unquiet spirit raged through the camp. It was a fit memorial for my father. "Do Not Go Gentle into That Good Night," indeed, old man.

The next day I was up at dawn, still high from the acid, running through the camp nearly naked, hair tangled with twigs and down from somewhere, wiggling my finger and speaking like Pantalone, transmitting his essential insight into the nature of reality—"It viggles, it viggles." I was referring to the universe, of course—making people laugh, and easing our collective re-entry into the day.

(Years later, in Hollywood, working on a film called *Heartbreakers*, the art director, David Nichols, approached me one day. "This may sound weird," he began, "but were you ever camped out in the mountains above Boulder partying with a bunch of trucks and crazy people?" When I admitted that I was, he told how he had walked out of the woods by chance the night of the wake and stumbled into our camp. "I was terrified," he confessed. "I'd never seen a group of people that wild. It changed my life." I could believe him; it had changed mine.)

We lolled around Colorado a while longer and encountered former Mime Trouper Charlie Degelman living in the remote mountain town of Ward. Sam had lived there for a while when she left me the last time, and this was enough of a connection for a couple of good parties, where we swapped

songs and stories. True to our intentions, we introduced Lew Carlino to the
Ward people and the Ward people to folks we'd met while camping near
Summerhill and Gold Hill. Intragroup tensions evaporated, and by the time
of the last party, the caravan people were in high spirits as we prepared to
leave. At that party, while I was playing congas, driving the dancers, I saw
Sam and Mai-Ting dancing together like light and dark Gemini twins. Mai
was shaking her whole body like a flapping rug. She was strong as a camel,
with a funky-toothed grin; she and Sam were locked onto one another with
a magnetic witchy energy. Their mutual appreciation was hypnotizing, and
the Ward people seemed stunned by the rawness of their feelings for each
other; feelings that could and would spin out of control shortly. By evening's
end, I was drunk, my fingertips split and bleeding, and Sam drove me home.
I fell asleep, and in a dream, Hell's Angel Moose drove me around in a
ghostly shimmering Cadillac, instructing me about women. I woke up with
one of his admonitions lingering like a glaze on the morning: "Get rid of the
one who isn't having a good time."

After final good-byes and a hair-raising public fight in the street between
Mai-Ting and Sam about a spoon, the caravan crawled toward our final destination, the Huerfano Valley in southern Colorado.

We drove together as far as Boulder, where we made a long, insane gas
stop: eleven kids running around the station, baby clothes washed in the
water fountain, nine trucks being filled nearly simultaneously, and the yokel
attendants too mesmerized by the confusion to check the hot credit card.
Then, just as we coalesced into a coherent unit again, several caravaners decided to travel to Paonia on the eastern slope of the Rockies to pick and dry
apricots so that we would have a gift to bring with us to Libré. Some other
vehicles required minor repairs, and their riders said that they would catch
up later.

Near Pueblo, Jeff and Carla's truck collapsed a valve lifter and I pulled
over to help them. While repairing it we received word that Gristle had
blown his starter motor, so someone was sent back to fetch him, while J. P.'s
truck was sent forward with the children to scout for a campsite. By the time
Jeff's vehicle was repaired our two trucks were alone. We cruised the towns
of Walsenburg, Gardner, and Farasita looking for our companions or signs
of them, but to no avail.

The next morning, we cooked breakfast by the side of a dirt road, and Peter Berg passed by in a strange pickup driven by some Chicano guy. He waved and flashed his necrotic, crack-toothed grin but didn't stop. "He must have found a way to score here," I marveled to myself. We followed his tracks backward and found Judy Goldhaft also making breakfast by the road. We were snacking on her fried potatoes when the psychedelically painted school bus of a local commune, the Triple A, pulled up with everyone aboard still wired from an all-night acid-rock party in Pueblo.

Expecting hostility after our communiqués from Libré, we were surprised when this group greeted us warmly and made us welcome. They told us pointedly about an abandoned commune called Ortiviz Ranch not far away and suggested that we camp there, recommending it as neutral turf. They also announced a birthday party for Peter Rabbit at Libré, and we decided mutually that I should attend alone and announce the caravan's arrival and our intention to camp at Ortiviz, hoping that this might diffuse Libré's anxiety about our presence.

The consensus of opinion at Libré too was that the caravan should move to Ortiviz Farm. They intimated that there were problems there that we might be able to help sort out. I returned to camp to discuss that possibility. Caravan folk felt that it was not our job to sort out the valley's problems but that since we were guests, we should accept the space we were offered.

In the midst of our discussion, Gristle arrived and recounted the story of Ortiviz Farm as he had learned it from local people. This is the condensed version:

Four hippies from Cambridge, Massachussetts, had come west to implement a vision of a self-sufficient truck farm. They bought the "Ortiviz place," couldn't make it pay, and got bailed out of down-payment trouble by the Red Rockers, the commune nearby where my old friend Terry Bisson lived. At that point, Ortiviz Farm became the focus of a regional counterculture vision to "help the valley get it together." The three communities—Libré, Red Rockers, and Triple A—pooled their auto wrecks, tools, and spare parts and sent volunteers committed to making the place work. Dissension arose, and Gristle told us authoritatively that the "villain" was one of the original four hippies, a certain Tom—a "male chauvinist pig who likes to sit on his tractor." Tom had made the unforgivable error of "holding out against a collective vision of the place for a *personal* vision." Now everyone but Tom had abandoned the farm, which had become a symbol of everything wrong with the Huerfano Valley.

While we were pondering our decision about where to locate, we traveled en masse to visit the Red Rockers, who had finally moved out of their overcrowded temporary house and onto their land. They had built an extraordinary geodesic dome there in a high canyon, a huge silver bug eye, sixty feet across and thirty feet high, rising starkly in front of the jutting red butte formation for which their land was named. The floors were rough wood, and a huge sleeping loft on stout log pillars commanded three quarters of the dome's circumference. They had a well-built kitchen with brick counters and four inset double-burners, as well as a very clean shop area with a VW engine in the process of being surgically reassembled. This was the first house I had ever seen specifically *designed* for the way we lived, and it was light, airy, and extremely functional.

From their front porch, you could see the entire expanse of the Huerfano Valley, including its bordering mountains: the Huajatollas (Breasts of God), the Sheep (Little and Big), and the Sangre de Cristos.

Bisson was away for the moment, but I remet Red Rocker Binjo, whom I had dismissed as a low-riding street hustler the first time we'd met. He was quite different now—simpler, stronger, less cynical, and very friendly. He told me he was "on the peyote road"—had been attending the Native American Church's peyote meetings for a year and taking it very seriously.

Our two groups mingled easily, and we spent the day with them explaining our intentions. We played a couple of volleyball games in which their tight teamwork annihilated our anarchic individualism.

At day's end, dinner was prepared, and their process greatly impressed our caravan. Their gathering exhibited none of the greedy scramble of our camp, where people normally behaved as if food not under their dominion might be lost forever. After a leisurely preparation and a silent moment, dinner was served calmly and elegantly. Compared to us, they were formal, but their house was easy with good feeling and cheer. They were relaxed and unguarded with each other, and for a moment I compared my own people unfavorably, as cranky, eccentric, and self-centered.

Later in the evening, the subject of the Ortiviz farm surfaced in conversation. That the Red Rockers' community was riven by competing political and spiritual visions of the world became apparent during the discussion. Some members regarded the situation through a political prism and could not separate their feelings about Tom from how they judged his history and behavior. Binjo and the more spiritual *peyoteros* felt that they should pray for help in loving the malefactor. Some Red Rock women viewed traditional peyote ceremonies as "male chauvinist bullshit"; others participated in them. Sexual liberation was a dominant theme in their community, and men and women seemed equally committed to transcending role lock. Except for my earlier encounter with Red Rocker Mary the year before, I had never diligently analyzed sexual politics. Digger women, like the men, "assumed" freedom and did not discuss it overmuch. The Rockers' diligence proved instructive, although it sometimes approached mania, as when one of the women turned to me and complained, "We noticed that some of you were served your dinners by your women." She had mistaken courtesy or affection for oppression and would have seen the roles reversed just as often had she observed without prejudice.

The Red Rockers were much wealthier than the Free Family (most of them were originally rich kids from Beverly Hills, in fact), and they had none of our ideological conflicts about easing their labors with technology. They argued that they did not buy enough merchandise to offset the energy gains made from collective living, but they were not forthcoming about where their money came from, and we didn't ask. I guessed trust funds and inheritances.

The day of our move to the Ortiviz farm arrived, and in Digger style, it was a comedy of errors. Trucks became separated, half our people had no gas, and hours and gallons were wasted siphoning fuel from one truck and driving miles to deliver it to another.

The Ortiviz farm appeared to be a breeding ground for wrecked automobiles and rusted farm implements. The sole building was a heavily weathered but well-made adobe farmhouse that we eyed warily until it began to rain, and we jammed inside posthaste. The house was not much: a large, whitewashed kitchen and a back room filled with drying onions laid out in a crisscross pattern on the floor. However, it was ours; it was free, and we had made do with worse.

Shortly after we arrived, Tom pulled up in a blue pickup with the words "I-Am-You" painted on the side. He regarded us cautiously as we pored over the house and grounds, cataloguing resources. He talked to me for a long while. He was long-boned, as spare as a piece of sun-bleached cottonwood, with heavy wrists, and his eyes behind his rimless glasses reminded me of the darkness inside a hollow log. He appeared stubborn and psychologically entrenched.

Our initial conversation concerned two local hippie haters who had been frightening people and forcing them off the roads with their trucks. Just before we arrived, one of them had shot a bucket out of a man's hand in front of his son, and the boy was still afraid and sleeping badly.

It turned out I had met the other. Gristle and I had stopped by a small ranch on the way to Ortiviz Farm, where we found the owner repairing a smashed propane tractor. Clad in stained khakis, he was a dark, skinny man with a brooding face that reminded me of a crushed olive. In response to our query about work he replied, "Yes, I *do* need help, but I don't hire your kind."

We discussed this situation and I suggested a trap for the hippie haters but Tom chastised me obliquely and sagaciously, saying, "If you're going to live somewhere, you have to keep peace with your neighbors. When a man steps out of the bushes and points a gun at me, I tell him to shoot straight so I don't feel it. Sometimes that changes things more."

I admired this courageous resoluteness and had to admit to myself that my image of our riding in and cleaning up other people's dilemmas was a masturbatory fantasy. There would be serious consequences to any violence we initiated, and it would be wreaked on the people who lived here after we moved on.

The next day we pitched our camp in the old house and transformed it into a lovely space that astonished the Red Rockers and Triple A folk when they came to visit. That night we were invited to play the Starlite, a local bar in Walsenburg, as a coming-out party for the caravan's arrival. Sam washed my hair with yucca root she had dug that day, and by the time she was done I felt clean and shiny as a new enamel basin. I shaved and put on a fresh white shirt and the pants Sam had made for me with silver studs running down the legs. She brushed out my hair and tied it behind my head in a bun with a strip of crushed velvet, Navajo style, and I dusted and polished my cowboy boots.

I was ready to rock and roll. As usual, it took hours for the group to depart: gas had to be siphoned yet again, instruments loaded, kids fed and tended, and it was dark by the time we began the forty-mile drive to Walsenburg.

The Starlite was a revelation. It was packed wall to wall with freaks, Chicanos, old cowboys in stained and dented hats, and women in demure polyester frocks or gypsy finery. Everyone was hooting and jumping up and down to the music of the Triple A band, a tight, funky, and extremely professional group. (In fact, they *were* professional; several members had made records.)

As we entered en masse, someone shouted, "The caravan is here!" and the room offered us a loud cheer. This was our moment, an acknowledgment that we had accomplished what we had promised. We surged into the Starlite proudly, everyone looking great in the bar's amber light: white teeth, clean, sun-browned skin, silver rings, bracelets tinkling, swaying, swaggering, and laughing. I was proud of my people.

During a break, the Triple A bass player, a lovely L. A. rock-and-roll girl with a thicket of curly hair and the improbable name of Trixie Merkin, invisibly palmed me a ten-spot. I was touched by her consideration and with her gift was able to buy enough beers to get our people up to room speed. It was not at all unusual for us to be so far from home with less than ten dollars among twenty or thirty people, yet somehow things always seemed to work out.

Turning from the bar to deliver the suds, I bumped into Susanka, a tall and sensual belly dancer from San Francisco. I had pierced her ear and the nose of her friend at the Treat Street house months before. Susanka informed me boldly that they had both been waiting to sleep with me to say thanks. She offered a smile suggesting that inconceivable delights lay in store for me, then faded into the crowd, mouthing "I'll see you later" silently.

Carla began to dance, and the crowd made room for her. My God, that girl could dance! Her eyes were closed and the energy of serpents, earthquakes, magma flows, and torrential winds flowed through her body like spurts of hot oil. The Triple A trombonist was laying down syncopated, double-tongued riffs over the drums. Mai-Ting danced like a motor whose governor had snapped. Suddenly my spine was seized by the music's insistent force, and I was propelled into the crowd, dancing the broken-breath boogie. Beers were passed over our heads, flecking the dancers with froth. Old women smiled ecstatically, flapping leathery limbs with abandon, while the old men snatched at the young girls. You could change dance partners simply by facing a different direction. The room was braiding itself into ecstatic recombinations of multiracial, cross-generational possibilities. I had never seen a whole town high before.

The Triple A set ended and they offered us the stand. None of us were used to electric instruments, but we were game to try. With Owl on drums and Richard Evers, one of the caravaners, on electric piano, I was playing guitar and trying to sing but couldn't hear myself over the monitors. The music wasn't working, and I hated to let down my team and the collective high spirits. David from Triple A sat in on drums and encouraged us to try once more, refusing to let us leave the stage on a low note. I began to sing "Devil Dance," a song of mine that was emblematic of our view of reality and very popular in jam sessions:

> If you weep, it's only skin deep,
> If you weep, it's only skin deep,
> Because—every skeleton wears a grin.
> Your bones are begging you to give in.
> Every skeleton wears a grin.
> Your bones are begging you to give in.

The song took off and the room was high and happy again, and the caravan band powered the room for a successful set.

Stumbling into the street at closing time, I looked up and noticed the constellation Orion, a premonition of winter. Just as I was about to crawl into my truck, a stranger approached and gave me a paper printed by our people at Black Bear, concerning a pending clear-cut of timber near our borders. The silt from the cut would choke Black Bear Creek, and they were preparing their resistance. This planet bulletin had reached me without postage or address more than a thousand miles away.

(Some things never seem to change. Black Bear was unable to stop the first cut, and the consequences were predictable. The creek was jammed by the crushed granitic soil that washed down after the trees no longer held it in place, and the road into Black Bear was washed out as well. After that debacle, logging was prohibited in the drainage until 1995, when the Forest Service decided that these severe slopes and endangered species' habitats could be logged again, restarting the struggle among Black Bear, the progressive community, and the government.)

We paid for our triumphs at the Starlite the next morning, crawling out from underneath our trucks with tongues swollen and eyes running, decimated by hangovers. Everyone was so wretched, the morning's amusement became determining who was in the worst shape. The emergence of each new victim of excess provoked waves of laughter. We assembled a triage center and began passing out strong coffee, nicknaming it the "sacred herb."

I had promised to help a fellow from Triple A named Harmonica Jack work on his Chevy truck this morning; it had been immobilized on blocks for months. I was crippled with a hangover and not looking forward to the task when Susanka, the belly dancer, and her friend Pat drove up, grinning like Cheshire cats and primed for sexual play. They were both scrubbed shiny clean and appeared unfazed by last night's debauch. My already wavering devotion to Harmonica Jack's truck began to oscillate wildly. I bullied young Jeff into helping Jack and had just crooked my arms through Susanka and Pat's, prepared to run off with them, when Sam walked out of the house and immobilized our trio with a "Hi, ladies" that could have snapped the nipples off a stone statue. I stood by watching stupidly while Sam assessed the efficacy of her initial salvo. Sensing that Susanka and Pat were appropriately disarmed, she holstered her weapons and enlisted them to go pick sweet corn with her.

I slouched away to help Harmonica Jack, and by afternoon we had his truck off the blocks and almost roadworthy. A Chicano in a blue pickup stopped and asked if we needed help. In the back of his truck was a freshly dead coyote.

I asked him what he was going to do with it. "Sell it," he said, with a curious, sheepish smile. I offered to trade for the body, and we assessed tools and various items until Harmonica Jack pulled a fluorescent-red foul-weather jacket from his truck. The Chicano, a woodcutter named Raymond, liked it and a deal was made.

The home folks were cooking venison over an elegant adobe fire pit that Paul Shippee had constructed in the Ortiviz front yard. Bob Santiago was cutting the meat by the light of the Coleman lantern. I laid the coyote in the stark glow of the hissing lamp, and all conversation stopped. The light pattering against skin and fur linked us in common mortality: the coyote, lips curled away from his teeth in a death grin, eats the deer, now roasting savory on the fire, which we, the humans, will consume, all of whom will one day die. Everyone stood still, quiet, respectful before this truth.

I took the body inside and Jeff held the front feet while I skinned it. The coyote was a fat and healthy male, and I worked attentively, careful not to cut the hide, passing it successfully over the ears and head. I saw the purple hole behind his ear where the bullet had punched out his life. Children and adults filtered indoors and watched in silence. I was absorbed in my work and in my prayers to this little cousin, intent on expressing my respect and allowing no frivolous thoughts to intrude on my concentration.

When the skin was free, I rubbed his body with cornmeal, pierced his ear with my turquoise earring, and wrapped him in white muslin to bury later. I tacked the skin to a board and salted it so the hair would not fall out. By the time I was finished, almost everyone was asleep. I wandered outside. Crazy Kevin was sitting with a woman before the fire. Over his right shoulder, in the glow of the firelight, gleaming in the darkness, was a bleached coyote skull. I blinked, startled—and it was revealed to actually be a wild sunflower bush. (Three other people had the same experience that night.) Orion was brighter and higher in the sky. I returned to the house and hung blue corn everywhere. I took the clock off the wall: I knew what time it was.

The next morning all the children and several adults told me they'd had coyote dreams. This didn't surprise me. Sam was affected as well. In response to my criticism, she admitted her hostility to the Sirens (Susanka and Pat) but then skewered me by declaring that she had been through her last changes about my lovers. "I learn to love them," she said, "and then, when you lose interest in them, you blame the breakup on me. I'm tired of it." She told me she was now "straight with everything": my pleasure was her pleasure, and consequently I couldn't hurt her anymore.

I was dumbfounded by her accuracy and her gift of freedom, which I construed conveniently as unconditional love and permission to live true to my predilections (no matter how adolescent). I was overcome with gratitude, feeling as if she had released me from the conflict of loving her and other women as well. We fell against each other laughing and talked intimately and affectionately—at least for the rest of that day.

The summer passed in this manner: fretting and feuding over personal dramas and public politics; fixing trucks, playing music, and frolicking; taking care of the children; and following an easy organic sense of time.

At the first hints of autumn, people began to crystallize their plans. Shippee decided to stay in Boulder and study with Chogyam Trungpa, the Tibetan Buddhist teacher. Mai-Ting and Tall Paul Mushen decided to stay in the valley and make it their home. The Bergs planned to travel East and winter in Maine. Jeff and Carla decided to return to California. Jeff traded his truck for a red MG and confessed to me how much he missed the city and the fun of getting high. His confession made me cringe, remembering how many times I had been high with him and other young people with whom I should have been a role model rather than a codependent. Just before he departed, he searched his gear and retrieved a photo of me he called "Coyote Crash." In the photo, I am stoned on heroin and pasty gray; my eyelids seem to have andirons dragging them down, and my lower jaw is moronically slack. Jeff gave it to me conspiratorially, as a bond between us, teasing me by saying, "I'll be there again before you will." Then he piled Carla and Owl Pickens, who was going west to see his older sisters, into his new MG and roared off down the road in a cloud of dust.

That was the last I saw of Jeff. Several years later, the picture of his coffin, a fifty-gallon drum weighted with chains, appeared on the front page of the *San Francisco Chronicle.* He had been murdered after having confessed to Carla that he had witnessed something that scared him witless, making the rounds one day with Hell's Angel Moose. When he left the house the following day for an appointment at a local chop shop where he had been fabricating false compartments in pickup trucks for smuggling drugs, he never returned.

The ceremonial punctuation mark of our stay in Colorado was a big peyote meeting, held with the Red Rockers and some Cato Indians from Oklahoma. Originally intended to be our welcome to the Huerfano, by the time it was organized it served as our farewell. The first task in preparation was to cut the trees for the tepee. A slow-talking, chunky blond Red Rocker named Tush picked me up one day and we drove into the mountains toward Rainbow Lake, climbing past stands of aspen, scrub oak, and blue spruce until we arrived at a shadowed lodgepole pine grove, where the slender trees stood erect as porcupine bristles. We apologized to each and stated our purpose before cutting them. Others had left for Texas to gather "buttons" in the peyote fields, and we kept them in mind as we worked, wishing them luck and a safe journey.

It was dark by the time we finished. The combination of high altitude and a debilitating case of diarrhea had made me disoriented. My feet were blistered from not wearing socks, and the task of pulling the spiny, twenty-five-foot trunks up the steep hillside in the dark was exhausting. Branches poked and tore me, snagging my clothes and scraping my skin. I recalled reading somewhere how peyote always grows amid thorns.

We tied the poles to the truck rack and stopped in Westcliffe at a coffee-shop whose "Western" decor announced its owners' hope that an Aspen-type boom was about to transform the homely Huerfano Valley into moneymaking real estate. Drinking our coffee, we overheard that people were planning to build a ski resort and that Bob Hudson, one of the local hippie haters, was going to run for county supervisor. He had promised to tar all the roads to increase property values. It was a disheartening vision, but it clarified the tensions in the valley. Like black people and Mexicans, hippies were considered bad for real estate.

On the drive home, a fat, happy coyote danced down the center of the road in front of Tush's truck. He spun in a double circle, winking at us in the headlights. Tush looked at me oddly, and I nodded. A good sign.

It required another two days to skin the poles with a drawknife. It was nice work, straddling a pole and watching the long tendrils of bark curl over the blade, leaving long trails of white moist skin shiny behind it. The pine pitch crusted on my fingers, and my muscles were sore from stooping and working the knife, but I felt as if these labors were preparing me for the meeting.

Mai-Ting squatted next to me while I worked one day. She described an underlying panic in camp, as people prepared for the impending breakup and wondered anxiously if they were prepared for living without the support of the group. The peyote meeting could not be coming at a better time.

Not far away, Ben Eagle and his wife Chipita had built a camp. They had arrived on horseback from southern New Mexico. Ben and Chipita were true edge dwellers. They had wintered again in the bitter cold Sangre de Cristos in their little canvas tents, spending their days hiding from the "tree police," as they referred to the Forest Service. This was where Sam had found them on her trip earlier in the year.

Ben was completely immersed in the peyote path and had taken to preparing elk hides for the ceremonial water drums. He became so purely dedicated to the process that one conservative Indian elder, after meeting Ben and reviewing his drum, confided to a friend that he had not known that "the Spirit spoke English."

The way life braids experience, strands disappear and then surface unexpectedly. In 1993, I was walking on the Rue Princesse in Paris when two strangers in 1940s retro Western garb approached from the opposite direction, saying, "Hey, Peter" as they passed. Assuming it was someone recognizing me from films, I acknowledged the greeting but did not stop until they both began laughing, and the man said, "You don't know me, do you?" Ben was beardless now, in his midforties; Chipita, still petite and attractive. They manufacture earrings in the Huerfano Valley, employ six hundred people, and sell them all over the world. They no longer live in a wikiup but in a modern, high-tech house they'd built and showed me in photographs. Both are still on the peyote road. Both are still grand and fearless. We spent the evening in Paris eating Mexican food and reminiscing about the life we had shared thousands of miles and many years ago.

As I worked on the poles for the second day, I meditated on the social tensions in the Huerfano Valley. I could see that despite their poverty, the hippies were aristocrats in the valley and deeply resented. Their real wealth, aside from access to cash, consisted of their education, their social and political skills, and their mobility. They were not sharing these with the local shopkeepers and farmers and consequently not creating a common economy. Instead, they organized their own cooperatives and drove into Pueblo and Denver to buy food more cheaply than valley merchants could afford to sell it to them. They might have placed their orders through the local stores, allowing local merchants a commission that would have linked their economic fates. They might have been teaching local families how to cooperatize their purchasing as well. Even at Ortiviz Farm, land was lying fallow that might have been leased to local farmers, creating community and shared interests.

Only a common consciousness of place based on the Huerfano as a shared home could save the valley. Failing such an agreement, the hippies would eventually tire of the struggle to live there and move away, and the valley would be colonized by a new migration. A dialogue needed to be initiated. Did the inhabitants want wealth or stability, neighborliness or tourism? It occurred to me, as I peeled poles, that the worship of different gods in the same locale usually leads to war.

I was disturbed by these thoughts. They reminded me of an earlier campfire conversation with Ben Eagle. He had been railing against the Red Rockers, demeaning their collective efforts as a "white comfort trip," berating them for possessions that came directly from the earth's skin. He demanded to know in what way they reciprocated. From the minimalist perspective of his horseback mode of life, he was correct, but compared to most people in the United States, the Red Rocker per-capita use of energy and resources was minimal. I told Ben I thought he was being harsh but could appreciate that he'd set a standard for himself and was determined to take no more from the planet than he absolutely needed. We probed this point a long while, trying to determine the degree to which one's personal ethical decisions are applicable to others and what, if anything, a universal ethical principle might be.

As I considered relationships in the valley from the perspective of this conversation, I became confused by an edgeless moral relativism, an inability to create a system of thought that might demonstrate "the good" self-evidently. On impulse, I put down my drawknife, placed the tanned coyote skin on my head, wrapping the front legs around my neck, and walked off. My shadow on the sandy ground had ears, and the thick fur disguised the outline of my human neck. I trotted around for more than an hour, breathing like a dog, clearing my head of all thoughts: *I am something else, between animal and human.*

I returned tired but unconflicted. The only solid ethical position I could determine, as true for dogs as for humans, is that place itself must be the determinant of how we live. Moving to Nevada and expecting to eat strawberries in January is indulgent, contrary to natural processes there, and thus unethical. The concept of a "national lifestyle" appeared ridiculous from this perspective, and I had a nightmarish mechanistic vision of people trying to transform topsoil, water, timber, and minerals in diverse environments into identical pickup trucks, snowmobiles, and gas ovens.

In the midst of these thoughts, Gristle sat down beside me and announced that he intended to stay in the valley and open a free store. He felt that a presence dedicated solely to the valley's interests might serve as a first-line defense against predators from Denver and New York. Remembering Gristle's dominant role in prior troubles at Bryceland, California, that culminated in the town's being sacked and burned by people associated with our family, I listened skeptically, suddenly enervated. Common vision appeared to have evaporated from our camp, and I felt as solitary and self-contained as a stray dog.

Skinning the poles was finally completed, and the next several days were dedicated to clearing a tepee site and waiting for the peyote gatherers to return. I spent much time considering the prayer that I would offer at the meeting, how I would ask for vision, for common purpose, so that our various "sleeps" (my term for unconscious behavior) might end.

Finally the day arrived, yet not even a celebration could occur in our camp without some conflict. Lars from Triple A and Red Rocker Little Richard stopped Owl and me just outside the ceremonial tepee to warn us that the Cato Indians didn't like owls *or* coyotes. According to Cato Indian lore, the owl was a backstabber (I don't know what they thought about the eagle's thieving and carrion eating), and Lars and Richard didn't want to offend their guests. They were not too damn sure about me either, but I was dressed simply and rather formally out of respect, and carried only a striped blanket and one eagle feather. Owl amicably left his owl-wing fan outside, but our revenge lay in the fact that owls and coyotes virtually surrounded the tent, hooting and howling from a nearby grove throughout the meeting.

Inside the tepee, the floor had been swept clean. On the far side was a large, knitted U.S. flag without stars. I was told that someone's wife had made it in jail. It hung over the officers: Lars, Little Richard, and Binjo, who were joined by a blond man I hadn't met who would serve as the fireman. The flag made the tepee look like a kid's fort; it embarrassed me.

The Indians were serene and physically strong. There were three of them: an old man, his grandson, and the grandson's friend, a Vietnam vet who never removed his dark glasses.

A raised altar in the shape of a crescent moon had been fashioned from the soil on the floor in the center of the tepee. The tips of the moon pointed East toward the door, through which the morning light would eventually enter. A line bisected from tip to tip, and in the center of that line was the roadman's "chief," his largest, oldest peyote button. This button represented the sun, and the line was the sun's path. The roadman, the official who runs the meeting, studies his chief button throughout the meeting, and old-timers claim that sometimes the cotton tufts on the cactus will glow, illuminating the world inside and outside the tepee. The fireman had cut and stacked enough wood to keep the fire going throughout the night.

The ceremony began with people being blessed with cedar smoke. A pigtailed Red Rocker, acting as the cedar chief, was fanning the smoke over our bodies with extremely balletic movements, which made it appear he was more interested in the ritual and paraphernalia than the essence of the ceremony. He spoke officiously, explaining the ceremony's complicated rules and obligations interminably. The Indians tried to hurry him along, at first helpfully, then ironically, and finally scornfully. It was obvious that the white officers were not yet up to the task of running a meeting; though well intentioned, they were too inexperienced.

Like the native people, the caravan family members were restive but for different reasons. Our shibboleth and guiding principle was *absolute freedom*, and we tended to be competitive and a bit superior about our disregard for discipline of any kind. Superficial readings of ancient "crazy-wisdom" literature and stories about eccentric Zen adepts all supported illusions of a freedom supposed to exist independently of limits.

The peyote was passed around, and the drumming, rattling, and singing commenced. I had never heard anything quite like it before. One man beat the drum at about double the speed of a human heartbeat. The rhythm was absolutely regular and without accents or syncopation. Another man at his shoulder flicked a small rattle made from a polished gourd with a tuft of hair sticking up from the top; the handle was elaborately beaded with tiny cut-glass beads. The gourd peyote rattles have seven "stars" in them, little glass beads or pebbles of just the right size to make the sound that peyote people favor. He also held a fan made from the tail feathers of a bird, perhaps a magpie, set into another elaborately beaded handle. I had never seen such beautifully crafted objects before; it was obvious that they had been constructed with devotion and unwavering dedication. Each feather was held in a little buckskin socket, and the rim of each tiny socket was dressed with multicolored down. The firelight glimmered on the facets of the beaded handle.

As the "medicine" took effect, the singing drew my attention. Two men harmonized the curious peyote songs, with intricate rhythms and subtle, unexpected shifts of emphasis. Peyote language comes from the cactus itself, and a song is a gift from *Mescalito,* the peyote spirit. It is neither Spanish nor Indian but a language of its own; I had the feeling that if I were one notch higher it would have made perfect sense. Each singer followed the other a millisecond of a beat behind, as close as a dog chasing a dodging rabbit. To heighten the mysterious effect, they employed a kind of ventriloquism, rolling the song around the interior walls of the tepee over and behind the heads of the participants.

The throbbing from the water drum filled every available space; you could feel it in your ribs, pressing on your heart, blotting superficial thoughts from the mind. The coals from the fire glowed, filling the worshipers with amber light as if they were *luminaria.* The combination of sound and light, the scents of cedar and sage, together with the absolute concentration of the participants were mesmerizing: an optimal environment for transcendence.

People offered prayers for loved ones or requested aid. There was no grandstanding or false piety, and deviations from correct behavior were marked publicly in a curious fashion. Others besides myself were disturbed by the pomposity of the meeting's officers, but they were our hosts so it was improper to be critical. However, when Gristle made a sly sideways comment about the cedar chief, the words "wise guy" materialized suddenly as a disembodied whisper that circumambulated the tepee like a ghostly bird, marking Gristle's behavior for all to apprehend and consider.

Though he was in error for speaking out rudely, Gristle was not the only one affected by the officers' posturing. When the hippie fireman faltered, one of the Indians assumed his duties, stoking the fire with expert care. Watching him, I was struck by the difference between *doing* something and *pretending* to do it (a critical distinction for an actor). The native man dropped his self-conciousness completely to dedicate himself to the task at hand. He had no attention left over to consider what he might look like.

At a certain point in the proceedings, when the officers were muddling over some arcane procedure, the native man in the sunglasses addressed the meeting in frustration. In a tearful and passionate voice, he explained that the peyote ritual was the "last chance for native people," that its rituals and rules had been set by the Creator himself, and it was not appropriate to take any liberties with them. The man was genuinely upset. He said he was a Vietnam vet and had seen and done things in Vietnam that made him want to change his life and follow the peyote road. In his face and body were great strength of purpose. I was chastened by his speech and reconsidered my own readiness to throw away forms and conventions without considering how my behavior might affect people who held them dear. For the second time (my hepatitis-enforced vacation at Olema being the first), I took the value of limits into serious consideration.

As the night passed, the Red Rocker "officials" became progressively more pinched and wizened. They appeared prematurely aged and anxious while the Indians, sitting ramrod straight, seemed increasingly confident and relaxed. It was a stunning and unavoidable comparison.

Peyote is a teacher, and the manner in which it teaches is always unfathomable and mysterious. Smiling Mike from Black Bear, the man who had insisted on leaving with us in our overfull truck, sat opposite me in the circle. Throughout the trip, an edginess had divided us. Every time I caught his eye during the meeting he was staring at me fixedly, sending hostile vibrations in my direction. I have always had a good relationship with peyote, so I felt protected and did not take Smiling Mike's intentions too seriously.

Late in the evening, I glanced over at him. For the first time, I *saw* him: *him* and not the projection of weakness, prideful arrogance, or compensating aggression he usually manifested. He was sitting quietly, proud and calm, completely himself. His eyes were fixed on the middle distance, and his face was suffused with wonder. He gazed about the tepee, studying everything as if it were all new and splendid to him. In the course of his survey, his eyes caught mine. Spontaneously, I pointed at him directly, grinned, as if to say, *"That's* the guy I've been waiting for!" He smiled broadly, understanding me perfectly, and a wave of good feeling flowed between us, resolving the chafing that had haunted our relationship.

I spent the rest of the night clarifying fallacies in my thinking and investigating areas where I found myself wanting. High ideals and visionary brilliance were no substitute for daily practice grounded in spiritual insight. I was filled with respect for the perseverance of native people and for the ceremony itself. In the light of their self-effacing behavior and dedication, their conservative Western clothing and "squareness" took on a new significance to me.

In the morning, the fireman raked the night's glowing coals into the shape of a phoenix, and the luminous, wavering hues emanating from them complemented a similar light apparently glowing from within each person and article in the tepee. Every time I looked at Sam, stars streamed from her eyes; she looked so beautiful that my heart fluttered with pride to know her, and to have a child with her. The glowing phoenix symbolized the rebirth of our collective and personal spirit, and when the morning sun streamed through the open tepee door and onto the altar, I thought it the holiest, most beautiful moment of my life, a direct communication from the Creator.

The meeting ended with a ritual feast of blue corn, fruit salad, and venison. The day was chilled by the first real premonition of autumn. People sat on the grass smoking and talking quietly. I lay down with Sam, Ariel, and Josephine, content, and napped most of the morning.

The Native American man in the sunglasses who had made the impassioned speech the night before came up to say good-bye, even though we had not been introduced. "You got a taste of it tonight," he said to me. "I saw that. I hope you pay attention to what you learned." I did pay attention, and practiced paying attention, but it took many more years before the insights of that evening even approached the consistency of habit.

I had accomplished everything I had come to Colorado to do, and it was time to leave for the East. I had postponed my return home indecently. I loaded the Meat and Bone Wagon with my family, my dog, and Chloe Bear's teenaged daughter, Colleen, whom Sam at the last instant had decided to bring East as an au pair. Bill Caidell from Libré was taking a lift to the East Coast with us as well. A thickly built bartender from New York City, Bill claimed to have been a mercenary in South Africa, a specialist in explosives. Perhaps it was true, because one night en route while I slept, Bill, high on speed, blew the hell out of a piston, stranding us at 3:00 A.M. on a two-lane road in Wanatah, Indiana.

We were towed to a local wrecking yard. Bill called his brother to wire us money. The junk man allowed us to camp in his junkyard while we repaired the truck. He was fascinated with our truck, our homey campfires, and our skills at living rough. Every night after his own dinner, he joined us to smoke his pipe and listen to our music. He told stories about the glory days of his own youth, during the depression, when he'd hopped freight trains and wandered around the country much as we were wandering today. It was clear that those adventures and the sense of freedom the memories resurrected meant a great deal to him and colored the way in which he regarded us.

It was pleasant camping in the canyons of wrecked vehicles, propped on discarded truck tires, eating fry bread before a fire contained by a semitrailer's wheel rim. Light glinted off the twisted chrome and glass, and eerie shadows poked and probed through the smashed car carcasses. This was the heart of the Midwest, real redneck country, but we never found the malignant spirits imagined in *Easy Rider*. This man adopted us warmly and shared his tools with easy generosity. The wind has whipped his name from my memory, but I am forever grateful.

Three days later we drove off, and two days after that, I pulled the Meat and Bone Wagon up the maple-shaded street of my boyhood town, into the driveway of the stately old house where I'd been raised.

21

roman candle

At number 90 Booth Avenue, in Englewood, New Jersey, is a dark-brown-shingled, three-story house with forest-green trim and a prominent porch that faces the street and continues around one side. The porch roof, like a skirt around the waist of the house, is supported by solid, tapered columns resting on generous sills. Colloquially known as "the hill," my neighborhood was the prosperous ward of this well-to-do Manhattan suburb. The granite slab sidewalks were tipped by upthrust roots of stately maples, and the sunlight on the blacktop street was dappled and shaded by their green leaves. This house, where I spent much of my childhood and early teens, was the locus of as much complexity and countermanding signals as I could ever bear at any moment. Simultaneously a sanctuary and a source of menace, it proffered with bewildering irregularity both orderly calm and the roiling intensity of corrosive emotional turmoil.

During my early childhood, I often thought of the Booth Avenue house as an omnipotent and caring friend. The ancient, polished maple, walnut, and cherry of the bureaus, breakfronts, secretaries, and Queen Anne and Hepplewhite chairs emitted a glowing amber warmth. The silver salvers and tea services flecked the room with puffballs of reflected light and offered distorted views of the heavy drapes and valances embroidered with bucolic scenes, and the delicate white curtains that reduced outside views to impressionistic shimmers. The air was always fresh and scented with hints of starch and ironed linen. Floor-to-ceiling shelves packed with books made the walls seem solid and fortified. I learned early that books could be an escape from the pressures building within those walls, allowing me to pass effortlessly through the their pages into the free zone of imagination.

I loved this house. I associated its beauty with a feeling of "specialness" that hovered, palpably but unexpressed, beneath the surface of adult conversations. The concept of "taste" came to emblemize a host of qualities pertaining to education and sophistication, and, though unknown to me at the time, social status. The house felt invulnerable and indestructible; I could hardly know then how naive such feelings were or that in the not-too-distant future, this bastion of security would, along with virtually every other relic of my family's quotidian existence, be whisked away in the debacle attending Morris's death. I had thought of the house as the foundation of our family, but in the larger reality to which children are not privy, the actual foundation of the house was *money*, and the bedrock of that money was the national economy, which was about to teach my mother, my sister, and me an exceptionally strict definition of the term *interdependence*.

My grandfather had made himself wealthy, lost everything, and made himself wealthy again. So did his son. My father's investment brokerage firm, Morris Cohon and Company, produced the capital for personal investments in antiques, cattle, oil, and land. He was, for a time, president of both the Hudson-Manhattan Railroad and the Phoenix-Campbell Oil Company. He was the invisible banker and partner of John Walton and Company, a famous Manhattan dealer in museum-quality English and American colonial furniture. Morris and a partner in Harlingen, Texas, were among the first to import white Charolais cattle into the United States, painting black spots on them and running them across the Rio Grande as Holsteins to defy strict import quotas, then raising them on a series of ranches they owned. They assiduously bought up extraneous bloodlines to give themselves dominance in the rapidly growing market, and this dominance secured Morris the chair of the National Association of Charolais Breeders for some years.

Morris never created a corporate shell for these affairs, because regulations would have made it cumbersome to move money among his various

interests, and he was a man who did not like to wait. While this arrangement gave him the flexibility he wanted, it also left his sole partner in *all* his
ventures exposed and vulnerable to creditors at his death. That partner was
my mother.

Growing up wealthy has its downsides as well as its advantages. As a
child, I was continually abashed by the sense of exclusion that accompanied
my status as "rich." Though my father was not among the five percent privileged to live without working, we were definitely flush. I remember the embarrassment of being delivered to school in a chauffeur-driven limousine.
The gift of an expensive miniature football uniform with shoulder pads,
numbered jersey, regulation pants, helmet, and spikes was a humiliation
when I tried to play football against far more expert and fearless peers in
jeans and T-shirts. Wealth, to a child, is something that sets you apart, something other children tease you about. It makes you look different and feel
different and does you no service in your own milieu. I possessed no personal money, authority, or autonomy whatsoever. I owned only a surfeit of
unspecified confusions about why all my "wonderful" advantages made me
feel powerless and lonely.

Early memories place me in the front seat of a leather-roofed Cadillac
limo beside a succession of uniformed chauffeurs: Chris, who had refused to
dig a foxhole on Iwo Jima because he believed he was going to die anyway
and did not want to go to the trouble; Percy, who quit in a huff one day because my mother asked him to carry something out to the garage, and he
"didn't carry"; rascally Melvin, who'd once killed a man in Arkansas but
was now a deacon in his church; and Jim, the only white chauffeur, a surly
Irishman who drank surreptitiously while he drove. Riding in the limo, staring out the window at other kids playing on the street, I was envious of their
ease and autonomy. No one seemed to care about them, and they didn't
seem sad about it at all. They had no money, no responsibilities, and didn't
seem "special" in any way. They seemed happy, they dressed as they liked,
and they had friends they knew how to play with. I understood that I was
supposed to feel sorry for them, but I would have rather *been* them. They
might have felt the same way, watching *me* drive by, but I remember being
aware, even then, that one day I would demand of myself that I stand alone
on the streets as well, to pass or fail its cold tests and judgments on my own

merits and thus discover the extent of my true limits and abilities. All that prevented me, at the time, was too much anxious parental attention and too much money.

The money problem resolved itself. I remember the beginning of my father's financial tumble very clearly because it was the day the U.S. government invaded Cuba at the Bay of Pigs. I was home when he walked into the living room of our summerhouse near Gay Head on Martha's Vineyard, poured a water glass half full of scotch, and knocked it back. He was standing at the big salt-specked windows, staring over the expanse of scrubby blueberry and salt brush that grew thick and wild between our house and the ocean. His hands were on his hips, and his legs were spread as if facing an adversary. He stood absolutely immobile, and there was something unnerving about his stillness. I was afraid to approach him. I learned later that this day marked the beginning of the end of the life he had imagined and built for himself.

He had secured all his save-your-life money as well as the savings of other relatives in American government bonds, bought on margin for a small percentage of their worth, freeing dollars to pursue more profitable investment opportunities elsewhere. If the value of the bonds ever dropped, he would have to pony up, but that almost never happened with government bonds.

War is never normal, however, and with its attack the United States had effectively (if not officially) declared war on Cuba. One repercussion of the international humiliation that followed our defeat there was that the bottom fell out of the American bond market. At the time that I returned home from the caravan, my father's firm was paying close to four hundred thousand dollars a year in interest on outstanding debt incurred to cover those margin losses.

To add insult to the injury, the invasion coincidentally marked the beginning of an unusual ten-year "flat spot" for Wall Street, which lasted through the sixties and into the seventies. Entrepreneurial brokers responded with practices that Morris considered shabby or dangerous, so while his colleagues managed to stay afloat through "creative" financial arrangements, he refused to forsake his principles of sound business practice and dug in, mortgaging here and borrowing there, anticipating an eventual upswing, the cyclical return of prosperity.

The cornucopia stocked with plenty metamorphosed into a water spiral disappearing down a drain. Without my mother's knowledge, more money was borrowed and farms were mortgaged or sold off to deter the inevitable. Morris's inner life became intolerable; illnesses chipped away at his strength and, sad to say, his character. He sought relief from kidney stone attacks with Demerol and became addicted for the rest of his life, tired, and despondent. His behavior grew more erratic.

One night when I was visiting from California, I found him standing unconscious at the refrigerator, propping himself up on the open door. He had taken too much Demerol and Seconal trying to sleep and come downstairs to eat, hoping to diminish the effects. I threw his arm over my shoulder and led him up the stairs to his room. At the end of the hall, he suddenly threw a totally committed punch into the wall, smashing the plaster. The hall light had projected our shadows onto the wall; in his stupor, he had mistaken them for assailants and attacked without hesitation.

His life was haunted by phantoms, and he stayed stoned more and more often. One night, he passed out over a lit stove, burning himself badly. Just before he went into the hospital for the last time, he had my mother take his picture and then, very uncharacteristically, told her to make six copies. In the hospital, he lost his grip and tumbled into that dark, dollar-shaped rectangle awaiting each of us. His last words were "Oh, boy," repeated over and over in escalating intensity, until the silence indicated to my mother, pacing the hallway, that he had died.

Coincidentally, the week after he died so did his lifelong accountant, the only person who understood all the byzantine intricacies concerning his money. Another week later, Mother received a million-dollar check from the sale of one of Morris's farms. The business chewed through it in eight days. "In his hands it would have been worth five million," Ruth said numbly. It might have staved off the final disaster had he lived, but she had already been crushed by serial ironies and reversals, and this last was simply one more.

When I drove the Meat and Bone Wagon into the driveway, the principals and creditors of Morris Cohon and Company were entreating Ruth for her husband's minuscule personal insurance in order "to keep the firm going." It was a chaotic time for her, and I was not much help. She had been simultaneously widowed and bankrupted, humiliated to learn that she had been living on borrowed money for years, money that she felt personally (and ignorantly) responsible for, as if she were depriving these poor bankers and investors (many of whom had been friends) of food. Complicating matters was the fact that as Morris's legal partner, who had signed unread papers at his instructions, she was personally liable for his mountain of debt.

Sam, Ariel, Colleen Bear, Josephine, and I—along with Sam's stupid black Great Dane, Crow, a gigantic, clumsy dog I loathed—invaded this precarious environment. Our arrival would have been a nightmare in the best of times, and the fact that my mother did not kill each and every one of us *and* the dogs should certify her without question as the first Jewish saint. Sam is an impulsive woman. She has moved more often than most people redecorate, and she treats impulses like commands. She had invited Colleen to join us on a whim, but the two began to quarrel. Furthermore, Colleen became infested with scabies, and her skin became encrusted with itching red papules and eruptions. Before it was diagnosed by a horrified Park Avenue doctor, she had infected everyone in the house except my mother.

Once Colleen was cured, Sam sent her home and began quarreling with my mother, who assumed that her own household did not require a second mistress and resented being rudely and thoughtlessly colonized by wild people. Sam, in turn, took umbrage at Ruth's authority, and things became very tense.

The Martha's Vineyard house was sold, as were all the farms but Turkey Ridge, and even that one, Morris's first and favorite, was finally put on the block. Estate specialists pored over the Englewood house, tagging the rugs, silver, and crockery, the drop-leaf tables and Chippendale chairs. Drapes and gilt-edged mirrors were examined and carefully appraised. Even the hand-carved mantel had a price tag taped to it. Ruth stayed mildly drunk for two days, watching people amble casually through the detritus of her life, fingering and critiquing her personal treasures in front of her as if she were invisible. Business partners and acquaintances who might have helped her took advantage of her distress and made yard-sale offers for the book collections, the silver, and the rugs. Gawkers treasure-hunted through the rooms, commenting to companions how they "loved" this or "hated" that and describing how they would alter things if the house were theirs. My mother reeled from room to room, offer to offer, unprotected and completely alone.

God knows what prospective buyers made of the stoned, longhaired, and exceedingly cranky cadaver with bones in his ears, rolling cigarettes at the kitchen table and regarding them with undisguised disdain. I didn't understand how to help. To me, these people were already wealthy so that paying them back at Ruth's expense for investments that were gambling losses, not bread-and-butter money, seemed like an injustice to my mother. I treated them like ambulance chasers and pimps. I knew that I should have been doing *something* for Ruth, but my efforts to comfort her were pitifully ineffectual because I was part of the problem. The least I could do to help, I decided, was to move my menagerie from under her roof. Therefore, we migrated eighty miles west to the Delaware Water Gap and settled in at Turkey Ridge.

As we departed, my mother gave me unequivocal admonitions to take good care of the farm. She wanted it to remain impeccable for a top-dollar sale. My personal though unexpressed hope was to arrange for my father to be reburied there. This task assumed a symbolic importance in my imagination as an act that might compensate both Morris and Ruth for a host of disappointments and transgressions that they'd suffered from my behavior. It would be an act of contrition and a demonstration to her of my power to make things happen in the world. To make a reburial possible, however, the farm first had to be secured from creditors.

Turkey Ridge was Morris's pride and joy. Beginning with an original homestead and 150 acres bought forty years earlier, he had assiduously collected almost three thousand acres of farms, forest, pasture, and cropland only two hours from New York City. A brochure my mother designed to facilitate the sale reminded prospective buyers that the land was "within a five-hour drive of sixty million people." The centerpiece was the eighteenth-century house with a whitewashed stone foundation and wooden siding capped by a slate roof. It had been modernized well, with a good kitchen and central heating to augment the three original fireplaces. The house was surrounded by over an acre of perfectly groomed lawn bisected by a dramatically curving long driveway of sparkling white gravel. The original barn and outbuildings had been repaired and repainted classic red with green trim. They were still in use, and Morris had added a heated garage, bull barns, open hay sheds, and sturdy oak corrals, all constructed of lumber milled from our own trees. He had spent many nights laboring over blueprints he'd drawn himself, meticulously refining his plans for these structures.

The fields grew thick with his personally prescribed mixture of grasses and clover, and when they were dotted with white Charolais, the grass was so abundant, rising above their knees, that the cattle resembled tufted clouds that had settled to earth. It was his heaven, a picture of bucolic splendor matted by charming stone fences and framed by the shadowy second-growth hardwood forest surrounding it all.

Besides being his refuge, Turkey Ridge was Morris's justification for his time in thrall to Wall Street. It was the Wall Street money that bought the cattle, built the physical plant, and employed the men who kept the fences taut and trim, the buildings painted, and the grounds lovingly cared for.

Morris's intimacy and identification with the place was touching. Whenever the weather even hinted rain or snow, he called the chauffeur of the moment to drive him there to spend the night. Somehow the buffeting of inclement weather increased the sense of shelter and protection he received from the house. It was not unusual to walk outside on snowy mornings and find him under the snow in a sleeping bag, as if he could not get intimate enough with that earth.

This was the most appropriate place to bury him, and I resolved to do it if I could.

It was difficult living alone with just Sam and Ariel after the rough-and-tumble intimacy and mutual support of commune life. The stresses and strains between Sam and me, never easy in the best of times, were now unbuffered by others. The house was large, cold, and utterly quiet, without distractions. There was firewood to cut and poultry to tend, the beautiful yellow pine floors to care for, and the inevitable truck repairs, but despite the good work, it was lonely, and the loneliness frayed both of us. Even Josephine began snarling at strangers.

My father's old business associate and crony, Joe Konwiser, arrived unexpectedly one day. Joe was a droopy-eyed, gravel-voiced Wall Street hipster in his late sixties. He had once done some minor jail time, taking the fall for the principals in a soured stock deal, and was undyingly grateful to my father for having given him a chance to work again. Gratitude did not diminish the accuracy of his appraisals, however. He considered my mother "a class act who deserved better" and my father "the most self-destructive son of a bitch I've ever known."

Joe loved them both and intended to help. I had known Joe all my life. He and his glamorous wife Jean, a smoky blonde who existed in her own personal film noir, had always been fixtures in our lives. I trusted him as an intimate family friend and counselor. Working a Pall Mall cigarette pensively, he suggested pointedly that I could be of more service to my mother. I listened attentively, eager for the opportunity, but the plan he described seemed preposterous. He told me that if I came into the brokerage firm and told the creditors that I wanted to run it for my family, there was a chance that they might suspend interest payments on the debt and give us time to get the business in good order. Our leverage was the threat that we would declare immediate bankruptcy and settle with them for a nickel on every dollar of debt. We still had many good salespeople left, he argued, as well as a top-flight research division, all the old clients, and a great reputation.

"Your father invented the over-the-counter business," Joe said. "He brought out [the public offering] Mallinckrodt Chemical and found Xerox when they were making cafeteria trays." I wasn't sure what all this signified but gathered that it was impressive to the cognoscenti. "The business made a fucking fortune once," Joe declared emphatically. "Why not again?"

Joe was a lifelong salesman and nothing if not persuasive. His eyes appeared ancient and sage, and his raspy voice detailed his plan with hypnotic certainty. He was blunt about utilizing my guilt over having delayed my return so long, and dismissed all my excuses for that delay as "bullshit."

What Joe skillfully *avoided* mentioning was that the indispensable asset possessed by Morris Cohon and Company was Morris Cohon. He was the man who could multiply six-digit numbers in his head, who played chess every week with master player Edward Lasker, who debated economics with Paul Swayze and Leo Huberman, editors of the *Monthly Review*. Morris was the genius. I was the one who couldn't figure out when Train A would intersect Train B.

I was stunned by Joe's proposal. I knew absolutely nothing about money or business. In fact, my father had always discouraged any curiosity about financial affairs. Both my parents were cultured people who had nurtured me with plays and movies, museums and concerts. Morris romanticized my imagination and protected and nurtured it, exaggerating my impracticality as a subtle justification for his own rapaciousness in business. He imagined that I would be an English professor at some fine Ivy League university, dressed in elegantly rumpled tweeds, while he sent stipends wrested from his daily wars on Wall Street to ensure that my life would not be deprived of amenities. It would be a kind of partnership, he assured me—he was a salesman too, remember. His pitch sounded elevated, worthy, and carefree, offering abundant time to write and travel.

Since I had no glimmers of my own concerning what adult life might be like, his version seemed viable enough, and without either accepting or rejecting it, I moved toward my majority under its dominion. I realize today how many people might cherish such an offer, and lest I appear ungrateful, there *was* fine print in the contract. Implicit in the bargain, since he was the producer, was the right to cast the drama according to his predilections. He would get to play Odysseus, the cunning, resourceful, sexually potent adventurer pillaging the world for treasure and adventure, and I would play the faithful dog waiting at home to wag its tail when the master returned. He never actually said, "Sign here and check your balls at the door," but that was definitely implied in the fine print.

To prepare me for my role as an exemplar of the life of the mind, he inculcated in me a princely disregard for all things mundane, practical, and vital to autonomy, such as earning a living. He refused to discuss how he made his money or even what the simplest things cost, rebuffing my curiosity with the reproach that such concerns were vulgar. The Diggers and Free Family obviated my fiscal ignorance by offering a mode of life without money. Now, Joe Konwiser was asking me to be the titular head of a complicated finance business that had bankrupted my father. That was one problem.

The second problem was that my community had very definite ideas about accruing wealth and the nature of worthwhile work in the world. How would they accept my debenture to Wall Street? What could I say to them, and how could I explain to myself such an about-face of every premise

I had held sacred for the last ten years? Would I be excommunicated from the only community I had ever known? It was disorienting to consider; an astronaut returning to the stresses of gravity after prolonged weightlessness must feel as I did.

My mother was floundering, though, and I had only three options: I could stand on her shoulders and accelerate her drowning, I could step aside and watch her sink, or I could offer her my shoulders to stand on to keep her head above the rising tide.

I agreed to go to Wall Street.

22

a moment's float

When I moved out to Turkey Ridge, my mother had been quite firm that I was not to overrun the place with friends. "None" was her negotiating floor, I believe. On the other hand, I could not leave Turkey Ridge for Wall Street and allow Sam and Ariel to remain isolated all week. They knew no one, and Ariel was too young for school, so she would be without other children and Sam would be a single parent without respite. Being a single mother is difficult enough; being an isolated single mother, more difficult still; but an isolated single mother with a quixotic nervous system, who read ominous portents into the shadows of birds, simply could not be left alone.

While I was pondering my options one afternoon, a battered, eggplant-colored moving van turned into the long driveway and stopped at the house. It carried Samurai Bob, his current lover "Sigh" (Peggy Darm), and Owl, whose father, J. P. Pickens, had recently been killed jumping from a window escaping a police raid. He died not from the second-story leap but from his fleeing partners landing on top of him. If it had been a movie, it would have been funny.

They had spent ten months crossing the country without money, trading labor for gas and food and spreading the gospel of "free" wherever they went. They arrived with the assumption that they would be allowed to stay. We were, after all, the Free Family.

Samurai Bob was an infamous denizen of Haight Street, a taciturn, acerbic ex-marine, easy to recognize because of his Japanese fireman's coat, bamboo flute, and nunchakus (fighting sticks) stuck in his belt. He possessed unlimited reservoirs of anger toward all forms of authority and lived an apparently random life, moving from place to place with his small bundle of gear as peripatetically as a gypsy.

He had visited Olema once to deliver *Kaliflower,* a multicolored intercommunal free newspaper printed by Irving Rosenthal and the commune on Sutter, then Scott, and finally Shotwell Street. It was delivered by hand and placed in bamboo tube receptacles mounted in far-flung communes and group houses—tubes that served the same function as the plastic cylinders for newspapers that line country roads. *Kaliflower's* artwork was impeccable, the information useful, and the subscription list a utilitarian way of networking like-minded folk. Bob began appearing at Olema regularly, stayed for a while, then drifted to the Red House in Forest Knolls, where he moved in with Judi Quick. They became a couple and had a child named Alli.

Samurai Bob was a stubborn, difficult man who drank a lot and had a pronounced judgmental streak. I liked him, but the Red House women were not fond of his macho manner and shirking of cooperative work. He appointed himself arbiter of revolutionary purity and his severe judgments often made people uncomfortable, Judi among them. One Sunday morning at Forest Knolls, she came downstairs and handed Bob a quarter, saying, "Get me a paper." When he inquired which paper, she said the *Cleveland Register.* Bob took the hint and left.

His arrival at Turkey Ridge was a mixed blessing. I enjoyed his company and radical propensities on political issues. He was a good companion for the long philosophical inquiries that occupied about 30 percent of every waking day, but he could be insensitive, even pitiless. It was Bob, for instance, who suggested that we sue my mother to win the farm from her and "free" the land. It was Bob who unilaterally removed the doors from all the kitchen cabinets so that it would be "easier" to store and retrieve their contents. The fact that this marred the beauty of the kitchen was dismissed as a bourgeois concern.

We were free people, and he felt free to act. There was no way for me to insist on more respectful behavior without asserting the prerogatives of ownership which would have violated the principles of community, so I remained silent, and in this manner abetted the transformation of Turkey Ridge from the crown jewel of Morris's possessions into another tawdry Digger way station.

Bob's companion, Sigh, was many years younger than he, a tawny cream puff of a girl with extremely poor eyesight, which made her squint distractingly as if she were examining your face for zits. Her shyness veiled an anger that matched his. Recently departed from a women's cooperative in the Pacific Northwest, she unnerved Sam by telling her assertively shortly after they met that she had just emerged from a long affair with a woman. Her primary, and apparently only, garment was a pair of overlarge Levi coveralls that offered tantalizing glimpses of her extremely ample breasts. She was one good-looking blonde too many for Sam, and tension developed between them immediately.

Not long after the arrival of Bob's van, Kent Minault and Nina Blasenheim arrived with their daughter Angeline, six months younger than Ariel. Kent's house-truck, the Big Fucker, was a two-and-a-half-ton GMC with a six-foot Plexiglas bubble mounted on the face of the cargo vault that cantilevered over the cab. Kent and Nina, close friends from Mime Troupe days, were a welcome and sane addition to the claustrophobic atmosphere developing between Sam and me (and Sam and Sigh). Now Ariel had Angeline to play with; Kent was a willing worker undaunted by the scale of any project; and Nina, as one of the triumvirate of women who had run the Red House, was extremely competent and expert at maintaining harmony in collective life. They were lovely, grounded people.

It's a mark of the impression that Peter Berg's friendship and ideas had on me that I felt it necessary to discuss my pending Wall Street adventure with him. His indefatigable revolutionary analysis served as an ideological plumb line, and it was important for me to know what he might have to say about my decision, even though it had already been made.

Peter, of course, could not have known the status he held in my imagination, and he seemed puzzled by my call. He understood the problem immediately and the necessity behind Joe's request. He urged me to go and marveled with me at the bizarre turn my life was taking. His approbation and support strengthened my resolve, so I went next to visit my mother in Englewood and attend to the practicalities of going to Wall Street.

I cut my hair short and bought two suits of the sort that passed for stylish in 1971. My only concession to Free Family style was that I left one of my six earrings in place.

For the next ten days, I pored over the official examination book, preparing myself for the test required to become a registered representative, legally entitled to sell stocks. The simplest ideas about mortgages, interest rates, types of bonds, and classes of stocks were impenetrable to me, and I no more than opened the book each day when I felt an overwhelming impulse to sleep. I solved the problem by memorizing everything in the book with elaborate mnemonics and cartoons. I studied hard, passed the test, and was legally entitled to buy and sell bits and pieces of the American dream. There was a temporary glitch when some old arrests I had forgotten to declare surfaced during my vetting by the Securities and Exchange Commission, but since they were not felonies and since any number of criminals seem to function quite well on Wall Street, I was granted a license.

That was the easy part. The more difficult part involved living at Turkey Ridge from Thursday evenings until Monday mornings, rising at 5:00 A.M. and dressing for the two-hour bus ride into Manhattan. At the George Washington Bridge I switched to the subway downtown, traversed the entire length of Manhattan, and then walked to the Morris Cohon and Company offices at 19 Rector Street.

Monday through Wednesday nights, I stayed with my mother, who was now, at fifty-six, working at her first job since she'd married thirty-four years earlier, as a secretary for a vitamin company, shoring up an inept young employer who overworked and underpaid her. It would not have been fun in the best of times but now she labored under a cloud of anxieties about her bills, her future, and pending old age.

She had sold 90 Booth Avenue after it had been gutted of everything but memory, and moved into a small apartment in a quiet lower-middle-class neighborhood across the street from the public high school where I had graduated after being dismissed from the town's only private high school for grades that a student with Down's syndrome could have bettered handily. I spent my nights in her small spare room. Joe had kept his part of the bargain and used the occasion of my arrival at the firm to win a year's concession on interest payments from the creditors. All I had to do now was—make big money!

This period of shuttling between Wall Street and Turkey Ridge was one of the darkest and most confusing times of my life. I was completely beyond my abilities in the world of commerce. I did not possess the most rudimentary understanding of how business was conducted; what's more, my inclinations and political principles were diametrically opposed to the premises and values of the Wall Street milieu.

Compounding these obstacles were difficulties within the business itself. After my father's death, the salesmen had divided his prize clients among themselves. They had liberated hundreds of boxes of his aged Cuban cigars from storage and dispensed them as favors and lubricants for sales. The client list had been chewed over and picked clean, and the fundamental asset bestowed on me, the titular owner, was a book about four inches thick, listing the names, addresses, phone numbers, and officers of every corporation in the state of New York that employed two or more people. My job was to go through that book telephoning people and pitching stock to them cold, which in the parlance of sales means without introduction or preparation.

Imagine how *you* would respond if your phone rang and a stranger said, "Hello, my name is Peter Cohon from Morris Cohon and Company on Wall Street, and I have a very interesting investment opportunity I'd like to discuss with you." Everyone I called did what you would do: they hung up.

Making fifty telephone calls a day is a time-consuming proposition. Making this many calls a day without a single success is demoralizing. After several depressing weeks of this, I began refining my technique, employing my actor's skills. When the receiver was lifted at the other end, I shouted to an imaginary secretary, "No, I told you he *can't* buy more. Fifty thousand is what he gets, period."

Cut to the phone: "Oh, excuse me, I'm sorry." Introduce myself. Cut back to the imaginary secretary: "Absolutely *not*, Claire. I *told* you, I'm saving that block for *new* customers."

Cut back to the mark, apologizing profusely about the "action" in our office and begin my pitch. The other salesmen in the big room outside my office (I *was* the new owner, after all) might not have been able to decipher my incomprehensible ranting, but since all transactions were posted publicly, they knew as well as I did that whatever I was doing I was not making any sales.

When several weeks of this theatrical idiocy produced no success, I began experimenting with outlandish claims. As soon as my call was answered, I would say, "If you listen to me for sixty seconds, I *guarantee* that I will make you a million dollars." This strategy was no more successful than probity. I did not have a knack for selling.

In the year that I labored on Wall Street, I made *one* sale. The day it was announced, all $1,200 of it, the salesmen applauded "Morris's boy" in a sentimental frenzy, praised me extravagantly, and assured me (and by implication themselves) that *now* things were starting to roll. Considering the bizarre cries emanating from my office, they must have wondered how I had made even that sale.

Times were tough; these men too were hanging on by their fingernails. Many of them had worked with my father for years and loved and respected him. Customers had deserted the firm after his death, and the point was being revealed to them with brutal clarity daily that without "Moishe's" brilliance and charisma, the firm was not going to survive. Dad's lifelong friend, his cashier Eddie Mulligan, was dying of bleeding ulcers trying to untangle the knot of promises, deals, mortgages, and markers that my dad had filed in his head and carried with him to the grave.

I walked around Wall Street by day cast as the rising star of a respected firm, but in actuality I was a salaried extra paid sixty dollars a week. I exuded failure that repelled people as if I had burned a swastika into my forehead. I visited watering holes where the bright young brokers (and their women) congregated, hoping to meet some companions for these city sojourns. After my close friendships in college, the camaraderie of the Mime Troupe, and the intense society of communes, it was devastating to be so isolated from the simple pleasures of human society. I craved the company and balm of women, but every conversational overture I made fizzled like a match dropped into a wet ashtray.

I developed a sulky resentment for the trim, laughing girls with good clothes and tasteful appointments, the Muffies and Buffies with boarding school accents and casual glamour, the carefree sexuality they passed out like a gold coin to the boys deemed most promising. Nothing in my life heretofore had prepared me for such consistent failure. No personal charm, no skills as a raconteur or an empathetic listener provoked the slightest interest. The truth was, I was an interloper, an impostor, and they recognized it.

I had lived without electricity for the past five years, was not conversant with the television sit-coms to which they referred, and rarely read a newspaper (why bother, when my friends and I felt we *were* the news?). I had scorned their values and aspirations and mocked them from the stage, but now was trying to pass as one of them, and they were too smart to be seduced. I was on "the Street" only to buy my mother a little breathing space and secure my dad's pittance of insurance money for her old age. Fate had cast me in a poor role in a rotten play, and I can hardly blame the other actors for not wanting to perform with me.

Aside from a brief liaison, there was one bright hiatus from my enforced solitude. For a short period near the end of my year-long indenture, I developed a relationship with an elegant, "uptown" woman named Barbara, a handsome brunette with a deep cultured voice, a ready sense of humor, and an illuminated smile. I have not seen her since and eliminate her last name because I have no way of knowing whether or not publication of her identity might cause her pain or embarrassment and I am too much her debtor to chance such a risk. Her tiny apartment became an oasis from my unremitting disappointments, and I cannot forget (or thank her enough for) the balm of resting in her candlelit tub while she bathed me with scented water as devotedly as if I were a private savior, tendering me every imaginable physical and spiritual comfort.

Unfortunately, I was emotionally useless to her, preoccupied as I was with the affairs of my mother and the Digger family and still living, though tenuously and tempestuously, with Sam. After the business closed its doors for the last time, I was liberated from Wall Street and the necessity of traveling to New York each week. It was the end of our relationship, sealed in a wrenching, tear-stained good-bye. She was generous to a fault, a grand woman, and I gorged on the feast she provided and then cut and ran like a man fleeing the bill in a restaurant. I hope that life has rewarded her as she deserves. I hope she has forgiven me.

Occasionally my two lives, past and present, Digger and broker, would collide, strewing bizarre wreckage. After several months of slogging through my cold-call phone book, I learned of a realm of business called "venture capital"—the raising of money for new enterprises. Hoping that this might provide a more interesting and appropriate milieu for my creativity, I began researching the possibilities. After meeting eager inventors hawking lotions that prevented the windshields of planes from misting, revolutionary energy modules that ran on water, and geothermal speculators, I fell in with a joker who had invented an automatic record-keeping seal for freight cars and semitrailers. It would record the number of times and the times of day that the doors were opened and closed, theoretically preventing employee theft and thereby (theoretically) reducing insurance premiums. He convinced me, and I decided to raise the money to bring this unwanted product to market.

Pursuing this goal, I met a handsome young speculator I will call Angus. My old pal Cadillac Ron, business manager for the Grateful Dead, introduced us and told me that Angus had, that very year, made more money speculating in oil than anyone else in the world, and he wanted to "do things" with it. Angus had some interesting theories. He believed that the Scots and the Jews were the two most successful "races" on the planet. (I didn't remind him that Judaism was a *religion*, since even I was bright enough to understand that it might be better not to argue with someone you hoped to separate from some money.) He had done a great deal of "original anthropological research" to prove that the Scots were actually the lost tribe of the Jews and could speak for hours, quoting arcane authorities, tracing, if I understood it correctly, the hegira of "your people" from Judea to Glasgow.

Because he was a Scot, he explained, he had quite consciously taken a Jewish wife to mingle their genes, and he expected superchildren from the union.

I winced inwardly for the children as Angus and I strolled around Battery Park "creating a relationship," which primarily consisted of me listening patiently to his theories, under the impression that if he was crazy enough to believe in a Scottish-Jewish superrace, he might believe in automated truck locks.

As we walked one day and as I, by my grave demeanor and judicious questions, tried to convince Angus of my intelligence and substance, we passed three derelicts clustered around a Sabrett's hot-dog cart. Suddenly the most scrofulous of the three peeled himself away from his comrades and approached, calling, "Pierre! Oh, Pierre. Coyote-man!" My blood chilled when I realized that it was Gregory Corso, Beat poet, old friend, and drug comrade, toothless, filthy, and bug-eyed, lurching toward us with his fore-finger raised.

Angus recoiled as if someone had passed a skunk's ass under his nose, but to his credit, he stood his ground. Thinking quickly, I made a rather formal introduction of "Mr. Corso, one of America's *foremost* poets," to "Mr. ———, one of the nation's foremost financiers and developers," implying to Angus by my exaggerated civility toward Gregory that I was a patron of the arts, *hardly* an intimate, who might have met this eccentric *artiste* at a charity fund-raiser. I tried to walk on, figuring I'd square it with Gregory later, but he followed me, rambling on piteously about having been stoned on bad her-oin the night before, then mugged, and now how sick he was. Angus looked as if he were afraid Corso might puke on his shoes and began to manifest an exaggerated interest in the Hudson River, while I, with a combination of head jerks and glares, tried to wise Gregory to my now-endangered hustle.

Corso, who kept referring to me as "Coyote-man," needed a bus ticket to Buffalo so he could perform at a contracted poetry reading. "It's *only* fifty bucks," he said, eyeing my suit pointedly. What could I say? I was dressed to impress and couldn't confide that I only made sixty dollars a *week* without blowing my cover—so I gave him the money with what I hope passed for sangfroid.

Angus and I continued our walk, only now *I* was doing all the talking, ex-plaining Gregory's importance to American letters much too enthusiasti-cally. Angus's manners were perfect, but the spell had been broken. Maybe it was the "Coyote-man." I never heard from him again.

On Thursday afternoons I reversed Monday's migration and caught the bus for Portland, Pennsylvania. Arriving around 4:30 in the afternoon, I would change into my work clothes and "Coyote" consciousness and be laboring at farm chores before my psyche had a moment to shift gears. This switching occurred so seamlessly that one day I was driving to the fields in the farm Jeep when, observing myself in coveralls and work boots, I became severely disoriented. I had no idea where I was or what I was doing—the classic ac-tor's nightmare of being onstage as the curtain rises on a full house and having no idea what the play is or how you arrived there. Only this was not a dream. It was my life. I pulled over and sat in stunned confusion until my interior reality caught up with my location. I was going crazy.

My two worlds were becoming increasingly divergent and incomprehensibly difficult. Sometime in the summer of 1972, Sam invited a favorite girlfriend of mine, Nichole Wills, to join us. Most women would not arrive at the conclusion that integrating a nubile, sexually guiltless young woman into a troubled marriage would be an efficacious way to preserve it. But Sam's personal power rests on her absolute fidelity to impulse; in this regard, she behaves like a fine actress, moving from moment to moment with total commitment. There was, however, no playwright behind the scenes, integrating these moments into coherent form and governing their consequences.

Sam had been corresponding secretly with Nichole, entreating her to come because "it would make Peter happy." From her correspondence, Sam was aware that Nichole had become addicted to heroin and was anxious to leave the temptations of the West Coast. She did not share this information with anyone else, however. Sam was flighty but far from stupid; I suspect that the disintegration of our relationship panicked her, and her panic provoked a momentary vision of relief—an image in which I would be doled out maintenance doses of sanctioned sex and would consequently be grateful to and less critical of her. Sam explains her reasoning in this way: "I just said to myself, 'Look, Peter's been wanting another wife for a long time. Let's just get this over with.' I thought, 'Well, if I have a hand in this, maybe it can be done . . . in some kind of way that I can handle.' "

So one sunny day Nichole appeared with her curly-haired, wise-eyed two-and-a-half-year-old son Jeremiah. Nichole was as radiant and charming as ever, and we established them in the attic room. There was no word about addiction nor mention of any problems at all. Even years later, with the claws of a ravaging, full-blown addiction sunk in the back of her neck, Nichole's voice over the phone was invariably cheerful and upbeat, her good humor glib and bullet-proof. For Nichole, withholdings like this are not precisely lying. Years later, her sister revealed the psychosexual nightmare of Nichole's childhood, and it became apparent to me that she existed in a world of absolute denial.

Up to now, my relationship with Nichole had consisted of little more than chance encounters that blossomed into amorous interludes with affectionate partings, without demands or expectations. After fantasy-like frolics with Nichole, the real-life demands of lovers and mothers felt like returning to gravity after a year on the moon.

With hindsight, it's easy to see that what appeared to be free offerings of her body were *never* really free for Nichole. The desire in a man's eyes and his attentions implied that she was worth something—at least his attention. This was the flimsy prophylactic that protected her from too-naked contact with her virulent psyche. When circumstances breached these pitiful defenses, her inner life felt like being skinless in a sandstorm. Stronger medicines were called for, prayed for, and found. I don't blame myself unduly for failing to see past the illusion of her charming surface. Beauty is its own amoral compulsion, and Nichole's sincerity and charm made calculation and suspicion heretical.

But her grim future was not even superficially evident the day she arrived at Turkey Ridge. Nichole's personal problems, like everyone else's, ticked away like naval mines in deep seas, awaiting opportune targets.

More of the Free Family appeared. Shortly after Nichole arrived, Joanna and Vinnie Rinaldi, their two children, Nicky and Malcolm, and Everett Hill's son Jagger—a whimsical little carrot-top everyone called Froggy—arrived in their converted school bus. They had been East visiting Vinnie's parents and were looking after Jagger while Everett was finishing up a jail term in San Quentin for a legal misunderstanding involving money and methedrine.

Vinnie was devoid of personal affectations, the best imaginable companion for our life of adventure and uncertainty. He was the kind of man who would (and did) hitchhike from New Mexico to Boston one midwinter in order to pick up a free truck and drive it back to New Mexico because his friends there needed one. He and I had shared women, laughter, and music; we had partied till we passed out. He was a trusted brother, always high-spirited, a natural comedian and a skilled musician. His arrival was a blessing.

His wife Joanna was part of the triumval center of gravity (with Marsha and Nina) that ensured the maintenance of the Red House. Unsentimentally practical, acerbic, and possessed of boundless energy for the details of daily living, she and Vinnie are nuts-and-bolts, get-the-job-done people. With Nina, Joanna, Vinnie, and Kent present, a sizable component of the Red House population had been reinstated at Turkey Ridge, and I was optimistic and enthusiastic about our future. I always envied the easy bonhomie of the Red House, enhanced no doubt by the fact that three of the women there were blood sisters but due in large measure, too, to the harmony between Joanna and Nina. I now had reason to believe that Turkey Ridge might be a marked improvement over Olema.

On the physical plane, Turkey Ridge looked good to Joanna. She reviewed the heated workshop large enough for six vehicles where Kent labored contentedly; the three-story house with only eight people in it instead of thirty (their arrival would swell the population to fifteen); the generous grounds, tight and dry outbuildings, room for gardens, and best of all, old friends. When the invitation to stay was tendered, she and Vinnie accepted readily.

All the ingredients were now assembled for another Free Family stew, but somehow the safety valve on the pressure cooker had jammed without anyone being aware of it and there was no mechanism to release the escalating pressures momentarily obscured by our initial elation at being together again.

Walt Poliscewicz (colloquially shortened to Poliski) had worked for my father for more than twenty years. He and coworker Bill Jelinek were a Mutt-and-Jeff team under the authority of the farm's manager, my childhood mentor in the "laws of nature," Jim Clancy, the man who had taught me to hunt, fish, and trap. Walt and Bill were responsible for the day-to-day operations of the physical plant, or at least they had been while Morris was alive.

Bill was a handsome, gregarious, square-jawed Czech with a provocative wit, who must have hidden considerable stress in his life somewhere because his lunches usually consisted of bottled baby food to salve an ulcer. He had been a Seabee during World War II and loved to recount how he hit the beaches in his bulldozer, shielded by the raised blade, and "just drove the hell over everyone and everything." He also loved teasing Walt, who labored under the lash of Bill's tongue like a patient ox.

Walt came from a big family. His brothers Pete and Johnny ran the family farm along with "Pop," whose banty posture, collarless shirts, and huge soup-strainer mustache made him appear as if he'd just stepped out of a turn-of-the-century daguerreotype. I imagined the family as the evolutionary climax of centuries of Polish dirt farmers, since they appeared to be constructed of natural elements: turned hickory bodies, ham-thick thighs, ore-colored skin. Walt was red-cheeked, shy, slow, and watchful. He pursued every task—feeding the animals, pitching hay, or resting to drink a beer—in the same measured manner. He had a finely calibrated internal clock that kept him true to an unflagging beat.

In the summer of 1972, Walt's brother Johnny broke his back. Besides having sixty head of cows to milk twice a day, Johnny had crops to plant and the winter's hay to cut, rake, bale, and put up in the barns, or he would lose his farm. Since fostering local culture and sustainable economies was one of our primary organizing principles, helping Johnny seemed like a heaven-sent opportunity for us to introduce ourselves and our intentions to the local community. Furthermore, we genuinely liked the Poliskis, so we agreed to take over John's farmwork. In return, the Poliski clan gave us nine baby pigs, a ton (literally) of potatoes, and all the milk we could drink or turn into yogurt, ice cream, and butter. They also plowed our large kitchen gardens and gave us generous advice, as good neighbors everywhere in the world do for one another.

Nothing could be more of a reality check to fantasies, even durable fantasies like our own, than farming. In the Delaware Water Gap area of northeastern Pennsylvania, every spring thaw pushes tons of rock up through the topsoil like bubbles surfacing in ginger ale. I came to believe that these natural impediments to plowing, harrowing, and planting were sent by Mother Earth to punish anyone who would slice her breast with iron.

The fields had to be cleared of stones every spring. Johnny's fields were actually at Turkey Ridge, now leased from Morris's estate. The main field was about sixty acres, roughly the size of sixty football fields. It was bordered by stone fences constructed from the annual drawdown on nature's rock account. The thick woods, primarily second-growth oak, maple, hickory, and occasional cedars, were crisscrossed with abandoned stone rows, evidence that human relationships with this geologic munificence had strong historic roots and, furthermore, did not always triumph.

Walt would arrive in our kitchen early each morning and doff his grease-stained hat. The bald spot on his head shone unnaturally white against the baked red of his face and neck. He'd sit in the ladder-backed chair in the corner near the door and sip his coffee in a preoccupied but attentive manner as we finished breakfast and divided up our own responsibilities: children, cooking, gardens, repairs . . . and a contingent to clear the fields with him.

Nina remembers, with some incredulity, the ease with which Walt was able to get us organized. "Nobody put up any resistance. Everybody jumped into the truck and split and went to work. When we tried to do something like that ourselves, everybody was like, 'Oh, no, do you think this is a good idea?' But when Walt came, we just went."

Day after day both men and women toiled beside him, huffing and panting equally, lugging and rolling boulders onto a tractor-drawn sledge, dragging the sledge to the edge of the fields, and then relugging and rolling the rocks onto the stone walls.

The work was grueling, but our bodies responded quickly, becoming strong and hard, and we surprised ourselves with our endurance. Furthermore, the common work enhanced group cohesion and made us increasingly tuned to one another. The women in particular thrived on their growing competence and the revelation that they were equal to such hard labor. Freedom from household chores was an added dividend.

Walt's no-nonsense approach made the time pass quickly. Our smoke breaks, beer breaks, and lunch breaks were regulated by Walt's sense of appropriate timing. We played silly games and practical jokes and refueled on satisfying meals delivered by Pete's or Walt's wife: succulent Polish sausage dripping with fat, hot, crusty bread, cold beer, and (particularly coveted) rich chocolate cupcakes with creamy centers. We ingested enormous amounts of calories and burned them off with no residue of body fat. I hesitate to use the word, but there was a purity to our lives at this moment. It was deeply satisfying to sit in the stubbly grass, feeling the burn of hard labor cooling from the small of your back and thighs, the sweat suddenly chilled on your shirt. Skin glowed with ruddy vigor. Humor was pointed and coarse. Breughel would have been comfortable here. We had a common intention, common aches, a common humility before daunting tasks (we cut, raked, baled, stacked, hauled, and restacked twenty-three thousand bales of hay), and common pride in the monument of full barns we created. By our respect for Walt's mastery, we were made equal and homogeneous as his pupils. Happy pupils, for this interregnum, I might add.

This was what we had come to do. These labors were the clear and concrete steps by which we would fashion a new world from the old, by which we would take our place in continuity with archaic, self-evidently worthwhile labors and values. Each transplanted rock was another unit of currency banked in our accounts with this value-rich, cash-poor farming community. Each pulled ligament, smashed finger, and day dedicated to work until flattened by exhaustion were tithes to our vision. After years of playing roam-where-you-will, invent-it-as-you-go, we were finally, and blissfully, yoked to a fine, clear task. Such focus is its own reward.

Day by day, the fields were cleared and prepared for plowing. The blade of the wind lost its keen edge and the occasional warm breeze prophesied the coming of spring. Frost evaporated off the grasses earlier each day, and the sun burned with renewed vigor. The grazing deer were fat with foals, and traces of new leaves appeared as a green wash on the gray forest. The stalls had been emptied and the winter's accumulation of hay and manure spread over the fields as pungent nourishment for the next season's grass. The world was right in its orbit.

For those taking their turn at house duties, there was much to be done as well: five children to be tended, the house and gardens to be cared for. Fifteen people had to be fed three times a day, which involved planning menus, shopping (gleaning or harvesting), ensuring that everything was ready at the right time, and cleaning up. It was difficult, stressful work, and people working as hard as we were in the fields were unsparing of the cook who stinted on effort.

Joanna remembers: "Even though the women may have embraced and enjoyed their tasks, they were not tasks that were coveted." She is right, of course. All of our "appreciation" of the women and their work did not extend to valuing that work as dearly as our own. With hindsight, our division of labor seems archaic, particularly for a visionary community. The Digger scene was quite conventional in terms of men's and women's roles, until the labors at Turkey Ridge demanded radical changes. Sam remembers very clearly the creak of my inner wheels adjusting the first time I had to cover the house while the others went to the fields: "So Coyote finally gets his day in the kitchen and as we're pulling out, he comes running out of the house going, 'Hey, look, you can't leave all the *kids* here. I've gotta *cook!*' The women all looked at each other and said, 'Right!'"

It was a wrenching awakening, to say the least, and for the first time, the men experienced the never-ending, distracting, and maddening demands of simultaneous children and housework, the fragmenting of every thought and task into small, child-ruled increments. A chastening experience.

On off days, we attended to collective necessities of our own—primarily firewood, it seemed. We'd fell trees and buck them into eight-foot lengths, manhandle the logs to a tractor-mounted rotary saw and cut them to fireplace length. We split and piled wood until the porch was stacked five feet high. Firewood was ubiquitous, fragrant, and pregnant with future comfort.

We gleaned corn from neighbors' fields for our pigs, gathering fallen ears dropped by the mechanical harvesters and transferring them by the bucketful into the back of our Jeep. We filled a corncrib this way and were able to feed our pigs for free. When they reached two hundred pounds each, we shipped them to a local butcher, who in return for two, turned the other seven into hams, bacon, chops, lard, sausages, and everybody's local favorite, scrapple.

Apples and pears littered the frost-stiff autumn lawns, and we collected sack after sack and brought them to the local press and filled three fifty-gallon wooden barrels with apple and pear juice, which we fermented carefully into potent cider. The town's plumber, an old family friend, bequeathed me a kitchen-sized copper still from his depression income-enhancing days. It could "cook" five gallons of cider or wine at a time. Cooking that distillate again, giving it a "double twist" in brewer's parlance, produced a 90 percent pure alcohol that could be mixed back into fruit wines or cider to produce a potent energizer for music and storytelling that we called "rocket fuel."

The larders were full, our bodies were healthy and hard, and at night, after our boisterous communal meals, we made music until the house vibrated. Vinnie, Kent, Nichole, Sam, and I played guitars, piano, tambourines, and drums. The songs were free form, sometimes country-and-western or rock-and-roll classics, more often than not homegrown meanders that grew in intensity and power until finally the music overwhelmed language and directly expressed the joys and ills, bounties and strains of our collective life. Fires glowed and crackled in the stone hearths, children played, quarreled, and raced among the players, and snatches of conversation penetrated the instrumental solos until the whole complex polyphony became the song of our existence.

Years have passed and I continue to play music, often with professional and remarkably able players, but I have never again experienced that same intense mélange of shared experience, commitment, and risk expressed in those musical Free Family fetes. It was transcendental . . .

Sometimes.

23

gravity wins

Two of the unfortunate by-products of heroic visions are heroic expectations and the inordinate cost such expectations exact on psychic life. How
could "heroes" be troubled by greasy sinks, disorderly workshops, envy,
spite, anarchic sexual passions, jealousy, and depression? We associated such
petty feelings with civilians and the workaday world. If we recognized them
at all, we identified them as the psychological by-products of capitalism and
private property. We were forging a new nation and believed that the old
would reduce itself to ashes.

While we developed refined vocabularies to discuss free economies, bioregional borders, subsistence economy, intercommune trade, media manipulation, political subversion, and drug-related mental states, we possessed
almost no tools for discussing interpersonal conflicts and personal problems
or resolving the sometimes claustrophobic stresses and strains of communal existence.

Nichole's visit, conceived as a simple gift from Sam to me, developed into
something more byzantine. Sam decided that the fact that Nichole and I
were sleeping together was no reason for her to abandon the field. She suggested that the three of us create a new unit, sleep together, and get it over
with.

It was a stimulating experience to be regularly attended by two comely women, intent on and even competitive about giving me pleasure, and it was eye-opening to hear them compare notes: "Oh, I never thought of moving that way," or "Hey, that looks like fun. I want some of that." This was precisely my idea of a good-humored, openhearted, and cooperative future.

Several weeks into this brave new world, Sam sat bolt upright one morning and said, "What is that woman doing in my bed?" Startled, embarrassed, and with no ready answer, I pointed out lamely that we had already "been through all this"—but to no avail. Sam was adamant; she wanted her own bed back.

I discerned an advantage to acquiescing, reasoning that if each woman had her own bed, then I would have two. I concluded Sam just needed some private space. But the following day, Sam delivered an ultimatum: either Nichole left or she did. As far as I was concerned, Nichole was now a part of the family. By invitation, she and her child had traveled three thousand miles to live and work among the rest of us, and the decision about her residency at Turkey Ridge was not Sam's to make unilaterally. When I said as much, Sam announced that she was leaving.

Nichole and I moved into a downstairs room, while Sam began making her plans in our room over the kitchen, haunting it like a mad ghost. If she was deranged, she had reason. I remember this period as "the time of carrying my mattress" and have an enduring image of myself as Kokop'ele, the humpbacked, pack-carrying flute player from Anasazi petroglyphs, laboring up and down stairs carrying mattresses from room to room, exchanging singles for doubles and vice versa. Nichole and I then moved from the main house into a little cabin by the barn that had once belonged to the caretaker and later became the ranch office. It was in that cabin, twenty years earlier, that Arthur Donovan, the farm's dour Scot manager, had killed himself one lonely winter night with my dad's pistol. The smell of wood smoke and lamp oil that I remembered from childhood visits still lingered. It was double walled and well-built, with a lovely slate roof. Nichole and I removed the old office equipment and files and swept and washed the floors, walls, and windows. I spent several days constructing a bunk bed from pungent cedar logs for Ariel and Nichole's son Jeremiah. We installed it in one corner, opposite a large pot-bellied stove with the word ABENDROTH cast into the top and

MONICA cast into the bottom. I built a trampoline-sized platform bed for Nichole and myself with space beneath it to stow our gear. Besides being charming and cozy, the cabin was *quiet,* blessedly removed from the chaos of the main house.

Sam decided she couldn't take Ariel with her. She didn't know where she was going or how she would live and felt that Ariel would be better served by staying in her current environment with familiar adults and children. Sam chilled the house and grounds like a bitter wind, her pale skin parchment tight, her hair fastened in a severe knot on top of her head like a samurai warrior. While Sam's usual relationship to people was tangential, her isolation was now absolute, sharing no contact whatsoever. She moved among us in a parallel reality, visible but beyond communication. Life swirled around her—farmwork, convivial chatter, gossip, communal plans—while she appeared and disappeared wordlessly, a specter floating terrified through the house, pinched off from the mother group like a dandelion seed, waiting for a gust of wind to deliver it to an uncertain fate.

I drove her to the bus the day she left. She said she'd write for Ariel when she was settled, but could not meet my eyes. She was traveling in "straight" clothes, a plain blouse and skirt. The tiny black star beauty mark that I had tattooed on her cheekbone with a needle and thread winked at me accusingly. The door of the bus opened and closed around her like the shell of a giant clam, and then the bus, roaring and groaning, disappeared around the corner.

Sam's absence calmed things temporarily. At night after singing the children to sleep, Nichole and I lay in the quiet, cheery cabin, spinning fanciful stories about the mythological gods of our stove, the love of Abendroth for his paramour Monica. Nichole was warm and fragrant. The kids were snug in their beds. Everything was right with the world—unless I thought of Sam, wandering alone without the comfort and support of her tribe, or considered the anxieties that might be roiling in Ariel's mind concerning her mother's abrupt and corrosive departure. If those thoughts didn't unhinge my equilibrium, I could ponder the humiliations of the pending week on Wall Street or the fundamental uncertainty of the future of Turkey Ridge.

But I had a cure for *all* these blues. A local doctor loved to fish our well-stocked lake. During one of his visits, I confessed to him (in an earnest and responsible manner, of course) how I "used to" abuse heroin but had given it up now that I was a parent. Still, from time to time, I told him convivially, I did like to get a buzz, just as he might from a couple of martinis. But responsibility to my health and family had made me vow never to use street dope again. How would he feel, I wondered aloud, implying by my manner that it was merely an exploratory question of no consequence, about prescribing me something like, "oh, say, Demerol or Dilaudid so that from time to time, I could get off the hook—recreationally, that is, of course?" He had no principled objections to this—or to much else I suspected, having previously explained to me that he had arrived at his decision to become a proctologist only after researching the Medicaid reimbursement schedules. He confided that he did have some anxiety about his reputation and the law, and I assured him I was experienced in such matters and would cause him no problem.

The day after our conversation, I appeared at the back door to his office, swathed in stained bandages that obscured my head and right arm and, not incidentally, my identity. He opened the door, saw me, said, "Oh, my God," and closed the door without another word. Rather than resembling the accident victim I'd intended (justifying powerful painkillers), he later told me that I looked like the failing final exam of a mummy maker. While I stood there wondering what to do, he opened the door again and thrust a brown paper bag into my hands, then disappeared. Inside the bag were several syringes and a brand-new bottle of Demerol—synthetic morphine.

After that, the ice was broken, and whenever the "doc" came to fish, he'd chat a while in the living room. After his departure, I'd search the couch and find another brown paper bag under the pillows. It made country life so convenient and certainly helped mask the twisted reflection of Morris's life I had made of my own. Here I was, back on the family homestead, working in the family firm, and I'd already replicated the most sophisticated of my father's support systems.

Despite the good doctor's generosity, other problems stressed group solidarity—little things supposedly beneath the notice of heroes: social fault lines as anxiety-producing as small tremblers in earthquake country. As a "free" family, we had neither patriarchal authority nor claims of ownership available to us to resolve conflicts. Furthermore, our commitment to exhaustive reexamination of cultural premises demanded that nothing be taken for granted, since the most innocent personal predilection might represent decadent conditioning.

Nina remembers this period with clarity: "I think we had expectations of one another that were kind of heroic. And sometimes it was very hard to live up to them. When we saw them falling apart, it was difficult because how do you talk about this stuff and stay heroic?"

Freeman House defined the Free Family malaise accurately: "We were creating a culture instead of creating a life."

It's difficult to convey to outsiders how far removed from the majority culture we had become. We did not have a TV and never listened to the radio or bought newspapers and magazines. We did not have the money to buy records or tapes so we made our own music. Nothing in the major media reflected our interests or concerns. *We had no money*—and so were forced to *create* the culture that most other people buy. While we were political and understood current events, our concerns, like most people's, were specific and provincial.

We operated under the assumption that America's leaders would continue to support their class interests and shortchange the people, refusing to invest in education and infrastructure repairs, and that no major media would seriously question or propose altering the dominant cultural paradigm. We reasoned that as more people became impoverished, disenfranchised, and betrayed by the corporate state, our numbers would swell; then we would be prepared with the operative alternatives produced by our social research. Reviewing the past twenty-five years, I am saddened to observe that even though we were perhaps wrong about our swelling numbers, we were certainly correct in our assumptions about our leaders and the fate of American workers.

Yet this stringent political focus was part of the problem, since world events did not offer islands in time on which to experiment endlessly. Current events demanded participation, exacerbating our overextension and stress.

Metropolitan Edison Company (MECO), the local utility company, planned to build a nuclear power plant in our community. Ironically, before he died, my father had already arranged the sale of several farms and rights-of-way to MECO. As dates for community hearings approached, we began to consider the ramifications of such a plant on our future and on the area.

I knew nothing about nuclear power but did understand how to use a library, so I volunteered to do basic research for the family. One book, *Poisoned Power*, by nuclear physicists John W. Gofman and Arthur R. Tamplin, impressed me greatly. It pointed out plutonium's impossibly long radioactive half-life (twenty-five thousand years to diminish its potency by *half*—two and a half times the number of years since the invention of agriculture!) and argued the impossibility of guaranteeing social stability long enough to keep it out of the biosphere. Furthermore, the book argued that once nuclear power was ubiquitous, the dangers critics now cited would become the justification for political repression to ensure the necessary public stability to prevent possible disaster. The authors went on to explain that the Price-Anderson Act passed by Congress to encourage the new industry relieved utility companies from financial responsibility for a major calamity, making it impossible for citizens to get sufficient insurance. By the time I was through with my research, it was evident that the power generated in this tiny rural community was intended for New York City and that the plant was being located in Portland, Pennsylvania, because it was considered expendable. I decided to attend the board of supervisors meeting, where the issue was to be discussed, and to make a case for the opposition.

The Northampton County Board of Supervisors met in a utilitarian, undecorated chamber with church buffet tables at the front and several rows of folding metal chairs for the audience. Four or five elected officials shuffled papers and saluted people from their seats behind the row of tables. A motley assortment of civilian petitioners seeking easements and permits coagulated in small clusters around the room. My presence created a stir because our group was locally infamous, and I was no longer the "li'l Petie Cohon" some of the locals remembered.

When the issue of nuclear power was raised, I asked to be recognized and spoke uninterrupted for nearly fifteen minutes. Though the subject was new to me, I'd studied it intensively for several weeks. The information was fresh, and I was able to reel off facts and statistics with assurance. When I finished, there was a stunned silence. The audience was, in Lenny Bruce's words, "an oil painting." After a few uncomfortable moments in which the loudest sound in the room was the squeaking of metal chairs, the chairman turned to two men sitting beside him, dressed in starched white coveralls. They were engineers from the power plant, sent by MECO management to dispel public anxiety, and he asked them if they'd like to respond. They were disoriented, like witnesses to a disaster. One of the two, a pleasant-looking man with a red mustache, declined for them both, saying, "Gee, I'm sorry, but we were just not prepared for something like this." Their abdication galvanized the audience. Two supervisors and several members of the audience expressed interest in learning more about the subject, and the Atomic Energy Information Group (AEIG) was formed then and there to study and disseminate information about nuclear power. It exists to this day, a grass-roots citizens' group that has successfully blocked the building of any nuclear facility in the Delaware Water Gap region.

There were additional repercussions from the nuclear power issue. Nuclear power plants demand uninterrupted access to vast quantities of water cooling the reactors, and this in turn requires the construction of dams. Near Turkey Ridge, where aeons ago the Delaware River cut through the Kittatinny Mountains to form the Delaware Water Gap, a bucolic farming community called Shawnee-on-the-Delaware nestled on the river's floodplain. The required dams would flood the area permanently, so the power companies seized the land under the quaintly named but brutal process called eminent domain and evicted the farmers who had worked the land for generations.

When construction of the dams was delayed due to the uncooperative ignorance of locals like myself, selfishly advancing our own interests over the concerns of strangers in a distant metropolis, the power companies decided to rent the now-vacant properties until matters could be resolved. They did *not* rent the farms back to the original inhabitants but advertised for tenants in the Manhattan newspapers, perhaps hoping the displaced owners would not notice. The lovely farms were soon inhabited by Puerto Ricans from the lower East Side, hippies of every color, back-to-the-landers, welfare mothers, and anyone else who fancied rural life at bargain-basement government foreclosure prices.

Local bitterness (and xenophobia) caused the power companies to pirouette again and compound their maladroit decision by evicting the new tenants. However, the immigrant rabble did not mimic the acquiescent behavior of the original farmers. They dug in their heels, invited more friends to join them, and the "Squatter Community," an anarchic, free-for-all aggregation of tents, shacks, farms, and buses sprouted on the floodplain like mushrooms after a rain.

Like the Haight-Ashbury, Wheeler's Ranch, Olema, or the Huerfano Valley, Shawnee became a magnet for "the best and worst of men," as Stewart Brand has aptly characterized the dominant contradiction of outlaw communities. There were druggies and welfare deadbeats, subsistence farmers, hunters and gatherers, psychedelic pilgrims, dope growers, wanna-be shamans, craftspeople, even an Amish carriage maker—all manner of souls seeking new lives and space in which to invent them. Colorful, multiracial, and undeniably "other," the newcomers strained social services that the self-reliant farmers had never deigned to use. Understandably, these new settlers were a bitter pill for the displaced owners to swallow, and public sentiment rallied against them.

To us at Turkey Ridge they were a cousin family, and Samurai Bob would eventually gravitate there, linking our two communities. Dented and dirty vehicles and unkempt folk migrated up the road to Turkey Ridge in increasing numbers, seeking the use of our shop or carrying goods for barter. Their influx strained our resources and alienated many of our neighbors. One such was my mentor, Jim Clancy, who after my father's death had left his position as farm manager and gone to work for the Park Service. As a federal employee, he was now on "the other side," and due to the growing polarization between the straight and hip communities, we became personally estranged, with unfortunate consequences.

We could not turn the squatters away. Whether we approved or disapproved of their behavior, they were under attack by the Army Corp of Engineers and the Forest Service, and as political bedfellows we were forced into an alliance.

Compared to the squatters, we were rich, even if our life was a daily regimen of hard farm labor (or Wall Street cold calls). At day's end, we returned to spacious lawns, solid houses, and a well-equipped shop, free from harassment by the authorities. We were no longer the most extreme, self-sacrificing purists on the set. In the eyes of the Shawnee folk, *we* were the "upper class," and they turned on us the same subtle, manipulative guilt trips that we had used so effectively on wealthy Hollywood hippies and Haight-Ashbury merchants.

This perception of an inverse relationship between wealth and righteousness held true even among our own people. Gristle, sporting his foxy grin and rubbery ethics, appeared one day driving his patched-up school bus. He was followed up the drive by a partner in another bus whom he'd met on the road, red-bearded Texas Bobbie, a quiet hipster from Austin, Texas. The "school-bus people" represented a new subclass in the Turkey Ridge community, dividing us subtly into "farmers" and "gypsies." Gristle used his relative disenfranchisement masterfully to justify constant pilfering. Every "game" has its form, even the "formless" game we played, and as long as selflessness was measured by poverty or lack of attachment to material goods, those who had the least could use their situation to lever advantages from those who had even marginally more. It did not matter if the "more" was a tool or a clean shirt; having surplus proved that you were a revolutionary backslider.

There were limits, though, and despite the fact that Gristle was family and Texas Bobby a nice fellow, the day that Griz ostentatiously drained his filthy crankcase oil all over the pristine white gravel driveway, we kicked their asses out.

After the high and heady spring and summer work had ended, and after harvest time, and after the cider, firewood, and foodstuffs had been laid away and winter closed in, the collective claustrophobia intensified. Winter winds funnel through the Delaware Water Gap relentlessly, and with the temperature hovering between zero and ten degrees, it was punishing to be outside. With no farmwork to be done, more and more time was spent in the main house—together.

Tensions between Samurai Bob and the rest of the house continued to rise, and one night the women convened a meeting to discuss his continued residency. My loyalties were divided. I realized that Bob was a difficult man to live with and that he had alienated people in the house, but driving him away appeared to me to be bullying by the majority. If we were seeking new cultural alternatives, I argued that we had to test our ideas in the world, which included Bob and others with whom coexistence was, well, difficult.

Hindsight offers some clarity, and now I realize that our fixation with total freedom condemned us to marginality. While we believed that we were creating "alternatives" that the majority culture could take advantage of at a later date, we were actually scoring a line in the sand between our way of life and everyone else's.

Internal pressures produced a fault line at Turkey Ridge between those who clung to countercultural alternatives and those who felt that assimilating into the community and working invisibly in place would spark a transfer of revolutionary ideas and energy.

The problem for Bob was that his vision did not fit into either of these frameworks—or into any other. For those of us who accepted the responsibilities and limits of maintaining home and hearth, his laissez-faire attitude was destructive deadweight. From his point of view, we were selling out his revolution for creature comforts, but he was not raising children and had little understanding of their requirements. He somehow exempted me from his rigorous judgments, perhaps because I was never severe with him or perhaps because, when all was said and done, I owned the farm.

The afternoon before the scheduled meeting, I was troubled over what I knew would be an ugly confrontation. I went for a walk by myself along the lake. The leafless trees were black against a lowering sky, and the gray water lapping the saw-toothed ice around the lake's edges made it resemble the mouth of a nightmarish shark. At one moment, a single wild duck landed on the water and reminded me of Ibsen's play. In *The Wild Duck*, an eccentric family, bonded by innocent rituals and fictions (the life lie), is destroyed by an idealistic young visitor who insists on telling the "absolute truth" and destroying all illusions. The play perfectly embodied the conflicting intentions of Bob and the group, and I regarded the duck as a heaven-sent sign that understanding might lead to a resolution.

But it was not meant to be. The meeting, held on a freezing night before a roaring fire in my former bedroom, was the nightmare I had anticipated. Bob had decided to weather it on LSD, which only made communications more problematical. I attempted to mediate between the "commonsensers" and Bob, who by this time had transcended or descended into obscure realms of para-sense. At one point in the evening, after I mentioned the day's omen and explained the story of *The Wild Duck* to him, he served neither of us with a Freudian slip, replying, "Of *course* I understand you. I side with the *absolute truth* . . . I mean the life lie." His slip was seized by the others as evidence of his deepest intentions, and my sign from the heavens became the agency of his undoing. Bob left permanently and moved into Shawnee the next day.

As the meeting reached its ragged conclusion, the downstairs door slammed, and Ariel and Jeremiah appeared at the bottom of the stairs, shivering in their blankets and crying with fear and cold. They had awakened in the cabin and, finding no one there, had walked the fifty snowy, windy yards barefoot to the main house. Their howling was accusatory, and in that synchronistic way that physical acts sometimes mimic emotional states —a glass falling and breaking into sharp edges during an argument, for instance—the children forcefully expressed the forlorn feelings inside the house.

The federal assault on Shawnee was brutal and effective. Early on the drizzly morning of February 27, 1974, the Army Corps of Engineers, accompanied by U.S. marshals (many of the same marshals used against the Native American occupation of Alcatraz), arrived at Shawnee-on-Delaware with bulldozers. They gave the squatters fifteen minutes to gather what they could, then fired up the mammoth D-9 cats. Lovingly tended gardens were scraped away, and domestic animals cut loose to forage untended. Ramshackle houses filled with homemade furniture, beaded charms, stained glass, and children's drawings, were ground into rubble under the clanking steel treads. The pitiless metal blades sliced through the walls in a cacophony of snapping timbers, tinkling glass, dull implosions of hot water heaters, the bleating of goats, curses of the dispossessed, and the inconsolable keening of children and infants. Afghanistan? Lebanon? Israel? No, this was the United States of America in 1974, disciplining its citizens for trying to slip through the nets that held them in thrall.

For those previously aware of the lengths to which some would go to protect the interests of the "owning class," this should not have been surprising. Miners had been machine-gunned by John D. Rockefeller for trying to organize, students had already been gunned down at Kent State by their own National Guard, and Native Americans had recently been truncheoned off abandoned Alcatraz Island to render it safe as a valuable tourist concession. Now it was the hippies' turn. The Shawnee squatters were not the first to feel the full force of America's rapaciousness, but like today's aging, bewildered middle managers, sacrificed to the "imperatives" of the global economy just before their pensions were fully vested, the cut was not made kinder by knowledge of that shared heritage.

Kent remembers this period as a time when people at Turkey Ridge began singling out people, trying to locate the growing malaise in an easily identifiable (and removable) source, like a latter-day Salem witch trial. One day during lunch, Nichole blurted out, "It's you, Kent. You're just fucked up and you make everyone miserable. Everything would be *so* much better if you just left."

Kent was mystified and said nothing. Later that afternoon Nichole came to him in the field and apologized, throwing her arms around him, and reported that she had simply been expressing the distillation of gossip she had heard at different times around the farm. There *was* gossip, of course—not necessarily malicious, but the small complaints and gripes that occur when people cannot or will not confront one another directly. Emotional geysers like these erupted unexpectedly, small panics, like steam escaping from fissures in the earth, indicating pressure building below the surface. It was time for me to take a trip.

After struggling with our own economy so diligently, we had often wondered how other alternative communities addressed the problem. The idea of fulfilling the original caravan dream of linking other groups into a conscious, mutually supportive network seemed attractive and became the genesis of the "Trade Route."

Nichole and I planned a midwinter trip, taking the children in Kent's truck, the Big Fucker, through New York, Rhode Island, Massachusetts, Vermont, and New Hampshire. We would visit other communes and communities and take a census of what they produced that might be sold or bartered. At journey's end, we would print that information and mail it back to everyone we visited so that all could share in the information. At each commune, we would leave a square of material to be embroidered, and at next year's harvest, we planned to rendezvous and join the patches together in a quilt symbolizing the new network.

We piled the kids and Josephine into the truck and took a January test run to Woodstock, New York, where we stayed with friends of Freeman House Martin and Susan Carey. Martin is a small man with tiny hands, feverish energy, a large nose, and an infectious giggle; he created many of the complex graphics for free events in the 1960s, including several Digger posters. His wife Susan, a distractingly beautiful earth mother and equally consummate artisan (a jeweler), embodied for me boundless tolerance and an endless faith in the ultimate trustworthiness of the universe. We stayed with them and their collective family, the True-Light Beavers, for several days, laughing while designing an absurd TV sitcom about life on a commune, peopling it with the freeloaders, fuck-ups, religious cranks, and revolutionaries we had all encountered. In the process, we became lifelong friends.

Nichole and I drove tirelessly from town to town, group to group, promoting the Trade Route gospel while the kids rode in the large plastic bubble overhead. Once, noticing stranger than usual reactions to our truck, we pulled over and found the children stark naked in the bubble, screaming with laughter, emulating the thrashing movements of copulating adults for the locals we passed on the road.

Each commune had its idiosyncrasies. One place in Phoenicia, New York, had lost five members in a car crash just before we arrived. They were in deep mourning but chose to tell us nothing about it, so we lingered for several days describing our plans with the oddest feeling that something was wrong. As we were about to leave, I told them how we felt, and the story emerged.

At a place called the Wooden Shoe in New Hampshire, when we headed for the outhouse in the subzero weather, they gave each of us a bowl of iodine-water to "rinse with" in lieu of toilet paper. We didn't spend a second night, which might have been the point, the iodine being their equivalent of Olema's three-meals-a-day black-bean cuisine for guests who overstayed their welcome.

The trip was generally successful. We met weavers raising their own sheep and farmers plowing with horses, organic produce growers and potters. New England was dotted with small groups who had ducked below the surface of the mega-economy, building lives based on belief systems they could support without reservation. Almost everywhere we stopped, people loved our idea, contributed to our list of needs and surpluses, took a square, and promised to meet us at the harvest celebration.

We were received well everywhere but at one of our own houses, which, given the general level of crankiness of Free Family people, shouldn't have surprised me. One frigid, blustery night, after having been lost for hours in a remote corner of Maine, we stumbled through a hundred yards of waist-deep snow to carry the children into a farmhouse. Carol Baleen lived there, the widow of Alan Hoffman, who had been killed several years earlier when a semi truck smashed into the back of a pickup he was riding in en route to Black Bear, catapulting him sixty feet.

The residents immediately set us to work cleaning food for the evening's dinner, snow still clinging to our clothing. No one offered a cheerful greeting, a cup of hot tea, or comfort for the children. The aggressively unstated subtext was "*Here* we work and are all equal." When Nichole rose to get herself a cup of coffee and asked if I'd like one as well, she was targeted by hostile women who read her simple civility as subservience.

Later that night, during a discussion about sexuality and children—what they should see or know and how to tell them—Carol suddenly demanded, "What's *wrong* with incest?" She spat the question at me as if my predilection to exempt my daughter (or any child) from my sexual attention was proof of fatal bourgeois conditioning. I was stunned and, I must admit, speechless. The issue was so intuitively repugnant that I had never even considered it. I must admit to an impulse to slap her face, but the ghost of Mary Corey, the Red Rocker I'd almost struck years earlier, interceded. I collected myself and managed to respond that as a woman, my daughter might have a number of sexual encounters in her life, and I thought that she might appreciate having at least one male relationship that would be a refuge from such attention. It still seems like a suitable response to me—almost as good as the one I thought to myself but did not utter: "That's the creepiest fucking question I've ever heard, Carol."

By the time we returned to Turkey Ridge, several months had passed, and Nichole and I were barely speaking. She had stormed out of one household, shouting that she could not bear the sound of my voice any longer. I was hurt, but I could understand why. At every place we stopped, I offered some evangelical variant of the same speech, exhorting others to participate in "the evolving, countercultural nation that will support regionally organized, self-sufficient communities."

I'm certain that I painted overly rosy pictures of the scene at Turkey Ridge, glossing over problematic details and allowing my optimism to transform rough sketches of the new world into finished oils. I'm also certain that while I was creating an enchanting self-sufficient future, the feeding, care of the children, and our laundry was left to Nichole. Tonto was pissed.

Nichole's son Jeremiah was also acting out. He was angry with his mother for repeated absences, manipulation, and the kind of irresponsible behavior associated with drug use. This increased Nichole's general level of irritation and impatience. When I pointed out that she often lied to him opportunistically and sometimes neglected his needs, she turned on me and declared that his behavior was my fault for not loving him as much as I did my own daughter. Perhaps I didn't love him as much as Ariel, but I did take care of him equally well, and loved him for who he was. I felt badly for him because I knew his anger was justified. Nichole's abundant charm could finesse numerous adults, but her son knew what he needed and, failing to receive it legitimately, was determined to get it any way he could.

I was so distracted by my relationship with Nichole and the growing tensions at the farm that when we returned I never cleaned and repaired Kent's truck. After three months on the road, it was filthy and in need of much mechanical tweaking. Not to express my gratitude and respect by taking care of it was an affront to common decency, let alone our evolved trucker etiquette. It also created an extra burden on Kent, who, like the rest of us, was overworked. True to his nonjudgmental nature and impeccable manners, Kent said nothing and dived into the catastrophe we had made of his beloved truck's innards, patiently sorting and repairing, degreasing and soaping while I argued bitterly with Nichole, flushed with shame and trying to repress the conclusion that I had replicated with her the same dynamics of my relationship with Sam.

While Nichole and I were away, Nina had become ill and no one knew precisely what was wrong with her. She went to consult my father's doctors in Manhattan. They intimated that she might have liver cancer but stressed that they could not be sure. Nina absorbed this information and sat in front of the fireplace in her bathrobe day after day, musing and smoking cigarettes in silent depression. By her own admission she was "gone." Her daughter Angeline was taken over by the group, and life washed over Nina as if she were a rock in the center of a turbulent stream. She became a piece of living sculpture, her unbreachable isolation a mockery of group hopes.

Her life with Kent deteriorated at the same time. The qualities that made Kent a fabulous companion—his abundant energy and unflappable rationality—made him of no use to Nina; his compulsive detachment from emotional "messiness" was like a brush scrubbing the raw wound of her depression. Unable to get the succor she needed from their relationship, Nina fell into a despair so fixed as to resemble catatonia. Kent decided to leave, and Nina refused to go with him, feeling that her support system was the women at Turkey Ridge. He drove off into the cold, and she stayed by the fire.

Perhaps, before the rest of us could or would acknowledge it, she intuited that our "tribe" was not going to be a workable option for much longer. The demands of growing children, their educational needs and varying requirements, were already stressing group coherence. She knew for sure that her own nuclear family was disintegrating and that no one on the face of the earth could help her. Day by day she slipped deeper and deeper into her psyche, surrendering like a swan diver to wherever gravity was dragging her down.

Nina is grateful today for the respite from responsibility that communal life afforded her. Had there been no support system, had her daughter not been looked after, had food and laundry not been attended to, she would have been forced to repress whatever she was dealing with then or seek the consoling refuge of madness. Her reemergence the following summer catalyzed events dramatically, but that story must await its proper place in the narrative.

The hard work continued for the rest of us: six children to be looked after, meals to be prepared and cleared, vehicles to be repaired; split knuckles, dirty hands, staph sores, and, nagging away like an insistent toothache, the inevitable struggles for money. Meals reached the table every day, laundry was managed, fires laid, cows milked, yogurt cultured—but people were not happy. We still made music but more rarely, and for Nichole and I going down together, there were hard drugs.

Occasionally, the fates dictated diversion, and for that we occasionally had the FBI, searching for Joanna's sister Kathleen. Kathleen was a fugitive radical, and the fact that it was she and not Joanna was a curious turn of events, because of the two girls, Joanna had always been the political one. She went to Goucher College, got involved in the SDS and political demonstrations, was arrested on Saturday nights the way other students went to the drive-in. Kathleen wanted to be like the other kids and belong, while Joanna reveled in her differences.

Consequently, it surprised Joanna when Kathleen began seeing Don, a very political guy who decided that his contribution to world revolution would be demolishing symbols of imperialism. When their fingerprints were found on remnants of a bomb that exploded at a Bank of America in Berkeley, Kathleen fled the country and stayed underground for seventeen years, raising two children in a succession of countries, under a succession of identities.

During their fruitless searches for Kathleen, the FBI appeared at Turkey Ridge from time to time. As our domestic Doberman, Joanna dogged the suited representatives of "lawn order" on their forays around the place, critiquing their abilities and strategies. Once, at the foot of a large empty silo whose only access was a ladder that disappeared into a long, dark cover of corrugated tin, the duo stopped and peered inside as Joanna watched and offered a wry, running commentary: "So who gets the Efrem Zimbalist Jr. award? Which big brave agent gets to crawl into the dark, scary tunnel alone, eh?"

The agents finally concluded that we were harboring nothing more lethal than bizarre yeast cultures—or else they grew tired of the chickens pecking at their shiny brown shoes, and eventually their visits stopped.

Eventually the bare Pennsylvania trees began to sprout fuzzy buds. The soil pushed up more rocks, and the cycle of plowing, hauling, raking, and planting began again. The weather became balmy and then hot. The air buzzed

and pulsed with the songs of cicadas and crickets; frog choirs chorused in
the lake.

The Wall Street business collapsed for good in 1973 and I was freed from
my imprisonment. Turkey Ridge was advertised for sale, and I began court-
ing purchasers for luxury fifty-acre lots. This was my plan to keep the population down and the ecology of the ridge intact and, not incidentally, to preserve the original 150-acre homestead as a final resting place for my father.

One fine summer day, Nina awoke from her spell. She left her seat by the
fireplace, dressed, mounted a bicycle, and rode hard. When she returned,
drenched in sweat, she dived into the frigid, springwater pool and surfaced
from that ersatz baptism shimmering as if covered with new skin. She was
cured. Life ("the force that through the green fuse drives the flower") was
again flowing through her body like sap. Her eyes sparkled with mischief.
She was sultry. She was languorous. She was a hot single woman in the midst
of a commune of couples.

She came to me one day soon afterward and announced that she had
picked me to be her lover. I couldn't deal with it. I had barely survived two
wives at once the prior autumn, and the prospect of resurrecting a similar
tension-riddled triangulation filled me with dread. I muttered something
about Nichole, about my confusion, about—who knows. Nina listened
calmly, smiling sardonically, knowing me better than I knew myself. She announced her plans to Nichole as well, who responded by leaving to spend the
summer in Woodstock. With my characteristic iron will and steadfast sense
of purpose, I abandoned all prior declarations and embarked on an affair
with Nina that had disastrous consequences for everyone.

That is how *I* remembered the beginning of our affair. After reviewing a
draft of this chapter, Nina smiled at me and purred, "*I* never hit on anyone
that directly in my life. I seem to remember *you* appearing at my door one
night wrapped in a towel." I was stunned. My memory had been so clear! I
looked at Nina, who today still causes teenage boys to stammer when she
saunters past, and know that she is a woman who has never had to *ask* for attention from men. I have absolutely no memory of that door or towel, but
Nina is one of the most honest people I know and I may have misremem-
bered my part. Whichever version is true is immaterial; what matters is
what followed.

It's a psychological truism that when one member of a dysfunctional family changes their behavior, the other actors in the drama scramble to recreate the familiar equilibrium by maneuvering the miscreant back into their customary role. In this instance, however, one of the roles was invisible to the rest of us because it was secret.

Unbeknownst to everyone, Vinnie had for a long time nursed a deep and abiding love for Nina. They had been mates on the food runs, driving to and from the farmers' markets early in the morning. They had lived at the Red House for years, where Vinnie's constant flirtatious banter with Nina had been dismissed as generic lust. It had been such a fixture of our group dynamic that Vinnie's wife Joanna could even comment on it blandly: "There's always been a thing with Nina and Vinnie. She understood him when other people didn't. She knew how to manage him when he was being weird. It wasn't threatening to me, and in fact it was almost an honor. . . . I always thought it was transitory."

But it wasn't. When Nina and I became lovers, Vinnie was devastated. The depth of his attachment became visible, frightening Joanna, who confronted Nina, "*You* opened this up, you close it down so that it's okay." But there was no way to make it okay. Joanna had always allowed Vinnie a very long leash for what she called his "chuckle-fucks," trusting that good sense and the strength of their personal relationship would always call him home. This was different. Vinnie was grievously wounded, and his despair was piercing Joanna's certainty about their relationship and sundering the community.

One night at dusk we heard a loud splash. Joanna had thrown herself into the old swimming pool in a suicide attempt so hapless (the water was only five feet deep) that it was transparent as a cry of pain.

Vinnie was furious with me and embittered, convinced that I had seduced Nina to bolster my own ego. He shadowed me around Turkey Ridge scowling, unnervingly close on my heels. When people arrived with whom I had to speak, he would squat behind me spitting, interrupting the conversations, calling me "Mr. Bullshit," and laughing scornfully if those conversations happened to touch on a common purpose or our family's future. I had lost the benefit of the doubt, one of those intangible precious currencies in a relationship you never value until it disappears.

Group life was fractured, and we possessed no tools or skills to remedy the situation. I had received boundless emotional support and unconditional love from this family. They had seen me at my worst, knew my secrets, and loved and accepted me anyway. When that love became conditional, the loss was horrific; it was like standing in the center of your house as it is being decimated by a tornado, watching treasures that were there moments before whisked into the void.

A group meeting was assembled in the workshop to try and staunch the hemorrhage of goodwill. In the grip of heightened emotion, trying to demonstrate the seriousness of my intentions to Vinnie, I became carried away and blurted out that I was in love with Nina. Nina's eyebrows shot skyward skeptically, and she snorted, "Love?" with an ironic laugh, indicating that love had nothing to do with it. She was being candid, but her detachment twisted the dagger in Vinnie's heart; he spat disgustedly and looked away, refusing to participate. Joanna appeared deflated and wretched. The four of us stood there estranged, all looking in separate directions, in a room full of tools that could repair anything made of wood or metal. We were members of an organism riddled with cancer that no tool or surgeon, no shaman or therapist could cure.

That day, we were reborn from our undifferentiated bondedness into singularity, separated from our comfortable illusions with the same contractions and pains, terror and disorientation that accompany a rudely delivered infant. Though it was a birth into a new, perhaps more mature reality, it was mournful as a death. It *was* a death—of a fond and cherished dream. With the dream gone, what remained were four adults who knew too much about one another, standing emotionally naked in the midst of a desolate cinderblock chamber stinking of grease, gasoline, and cold concrete. The only reason to fix the trucks now was to escape from one another.

24

s p l a t t e r

> *Only one ship is seeking us, a black-*
> *Sailed unfamiliar, towing at her back*
> *A huge and birdless silence. In her wake*
> *No waters breed or break.*
> PHILIP LARKIN, ''NEXT, PLEASE''

Life continues after something dies, it simply does not continue in the same way. We maintained our chores and responsibilities, but the activity was pro forma, the purpose eviscerated. Everyone knew that the Free Family as a source of future security was a fiction.

My personal future arrived with Danny Rifkin one evening. Danny had taken another of his habitual hiatuses as manager of the Grateful Dead and traveled to Guatemala. There he met a lovely young girl with a freckled Irish face, sexy overbite, and quiet watchful intensity named Marilyn McCann, who had left a teaching job in her native Ohio to travel down the Amazon by herself. She had abandoned that journey in Guatemala when she met Reina Ícu, a native weaver who took her home and gave her a small house of her own, and she spent the next year in the Guatemalan mountain village of Comalapa learning the intricate native weaving of the indigenous people.

While there, she met Danny, and they began traveling together as a couple. Hitchhiking in Guatemala one day, she was given a ride by a serene, totally bald American man. After talking with him for a while, Marilyn thought, with her characteristic intuitive precision, "This guy knows something." She was right. The driver was Zen master Philip Kapleau, and after their meeting Marilyn resolved to study Zen Buddhism when she returned to the United States.

Danny was living at an old homestead on the rugged Marin County coast called Slide Ranch, next door to Green Gulch Zen Center, and he invited her to join him there. They were en route West when they stopped in to visit.

The night they arrived at Turkey Ridge, we were preparing a group sauna, and I could see that Marilyn was uneasy about joining us. I told her there was no need to sauna if she didn't want to and that it would be a real service if she would mind the phone while the rest of us sweated. Shy and very private, she was relieved by this easy out, and the smile she flashed was more than sufficient reward for my intuition.

The next day, I drove the two of them to the bus to begin their journey back to San Francisco, Danny to rejoin the Dead and Marilyn to investigate Zen practice. While Danny went into the drugstore to buy gum, I made what was, to me, a casually complimentary remark to Marilyn. I told her I appreciated the way that she came into a room, kept her mouth shut and her eyes open, and didn't seem to worry about creating an impression. I told her that I got the feeling from watching her that she didn't miss a trick and perceived things on a deep level. Consequently, I was curious to know her thoughts about Turkey Ridge.

There was no time to pursue the conversation because Danny and the bus arrived simultaneously. I said good-bye to them, unaware of the degree to which my remarks had affected her. She said later to a mutual friend that she felt that she had been "seen" by someone, and that she knew at that moment that I would figure importantly in her life. Again, she was right.

Turkey Ridge was under a dark enchantment, and in this new and poisonous environment, demons manifested spontaneously. Tommy Lavigne, for instance. Tommy was a window dresser from Manhattan, a slight, dapper Italian with a miserably spoiled teenage daughter. Tommy was not at all "country" and would never have stayed or been tolerated at Turkey Ridge had it not been for his ability to procure drugs. Nichole returned from her summer in Woodstock, and she, Tommy, and I formed our own little doper's ghetto within Turkey Ridge.

After months of travel, seeking shelter from the cyclones whirling in her skull, Sam had resettled in the Bay Area. Ariel asked about her often, and it had not helped her anxiety that Sam had neither written nor called since leaving. I felt that Ariel needed to be reunited with her mother, at least for a while.

I no longer owned a vehicle capable of driving cross-country. The Meat and Bone Wagon was on its last legs; a weeklong bus trip seemed too arduous for a young girl and would have cost me an extra week coming back by myself. The solution was to fly, but I had no money.

I thought of the Grateful Dead, who could sometimes be counted on for aid. It was a dodgy issue because of the low-level status competition between our families, but I needed help for Ariel now, so I went to petition Jonathan Reister, the Dead's road manager, about springing for round-trip airline tickets to the West Coast. Jonathan was a hickory-tough cowboy-doper with equal amounts of dash and megalomaniacal self-regard. His job was to oversee the on-time delivery, loading, and unloading of tons of amplifiers and loudspeakers for Dead concerts, and he drove his crews like mule trains.

Jonathan had lived at Olema, we had partied together, and I assumed we were friends, a word with much elasticity in its definition. Once in the midst of friendly banter, he had called me a "Jew bastard." He'd said it again a little later. I had marked it both times and dismissed it as a tasteless liberty: he was a pal, and I *was* some kind of Hopi-Jew-Buddhist mongrel anyway. Shortly after the second incident, he said cheerfully, "Hey, I just called you a Jew bastard . . . twice," playing it as a perverse game point, curious to see what I would do. Had I cared enough, I might have punched him or, if the stakes had been higher, really surprised him and shot his toe away. I regarded him flatly and said, "Yeah, you did. Now I know your hole card." He laughed it off. Morris once advised me, "People always tell you who they are. If someone laughs and says, 'Boy, am I a shit!,' believe them!" I should have remembered.

The Dead were performing in Manhattan, so I tracked Jonathan down. I told him of my plight, and he assured me it was no problem. The Dead would issue me one round-trip and one one-way ticket through their travel agency. Piece of cake, done deal. A little later, he gave me a number to call and check but declared he had already arranged things. We spent the evening together partying hard, and my sense of relief made me light and happy for the first time in months.

At the night's end, as we were separating in the elevator, he reassured me again that everything was taken care of. He took down my number at Turkey Ridge and my travel dates, "just to check." Some gesture to Jonathan was appropriate at this point. I didn't have money, but what I did have was a beautiful coral and turquoise Navajo ring my father had given my mother and she had passed on to me. The ring was forty years old and finely made. I gave it to Jonathan impulsively, as a token of gratitude, and he slipped it on his finger just as the elevator doors opened. When he saluted me good night, the ring sparkled on his hand. It was twenty-four years before I saw him again. I never saw the tickets.

I borrowed the money for two one-way tickets and flew Ariel to the coast for a joyful reunion with her mother, who took her north to Humboldt County where she had made a camp near Gypsy Trucker Jed Sherman.

While in California, I encountered my old pal James Koller, a poet and the editor of *Coyote's Journal*, a well-respected literary magazine, and we decided to drive back to Pennsylvania together. Jim was en route to Maine, where he'd built a small cabin and eked out a living as a landscaper and woodcutter while he wrote poems. He and I were both fascinated by the beauty and totemic power of animal parts—skull, bone, tooth, and pelt. A coyote and a grizzled lone wolf, we traveled east together, competing with each other to be the first to spot gifts from the "highway god"—roadkill that might offer us talismans.

Just outside Santa Fe, we came upon a cluster of six freshly killed ravens, smacked dead while eating some previous sacrifice to the god of the automotive age. We smoked tobacco, prayed over their bodies, and then buried them after taking the wings, talons, and heads for ourselves. We pinned the wings on the backseat of Jim's Ford to dry and added the talons to the pile of skins, cedar boughs, feathers, and gris-gris we'd collected on the dashboard. The heads posed a problem, until we thought to put them in a nylon stocking and hang them out the rear window to air dry as we drove. One of those heads, still shiny and iridescent, with a lump of turquoise as an eye, watches me from my desktop altar as I write today.

Pit stops provided interesting theater. The raven heads were an inexplicable and creepy bundle hanging from the window, and every square inch of the car's interior was covered with drying animal parts. When Jim and I emerged, unshaven, longhaired, wearing crusty boots, belt knives, and earrings, attendants backed away from the pumps and civilians gathered their children back into their cars.

We drove and talked our way across country, punctuating emotional moments by firing Jim's Ruger .357 magnum dog-leg six-shooter out the window. We reached Pennsylvania from Santa Fe in sixty hours of hard driving—good time, though hardly a personal record, considering that after the final Mime Troupe performance in New York, Charlie Degelman and I (on a modest amount of methedrine) drove back to California in fifty-four hours, which included a four-hour layover to visit a girlfriend in Des Moines.

Not long after this return to Turkey Ridge, my mother delivered a stunning announcement. She was being sued by creditors for fraud, a serious charge that could not be avoided by bankruptcy. The creditors were pressing her for an immediate sale of the farm for whatever it could bring as the only alternative to being taken to court.

Elly Clancy, the disaffected manager's wife, had, we were told, informed one of the creditors in a phone call that my mother had signed the farm over to me and that I was planning to take the money and run to South America. The farm *had* been signed over to me years before by my father, then signed back to him when he needed to mortgage it. My mother *had* put it back into my name, hoping to save it at best or at least delay the inevitable. But she would not have picked a nickel off the sidewalk that wasn't hers, much less defraud people to whom she was in debt. Elly's story was a fiction with just enough truth to give it credibility.

I was dumbfounded. I had adored Elly like a grandmother since I was an infant. Among my first experiences of childhood autonomy was the half-mile walk to her tiny storybook cabin for a piece of pie and milk. She was an effervescent, cheerful woman, "a cunnerman" as she referred to herself, meaning of Pennsylvania-Dutch mountain stock. She kept chickens, dogs, raccoons, and birds around her charming little home and painted oils of the region's natural beauty in a gifted naïf style. Before Morris died, he had given Jim and Elly their cabin and seventy acres of land surrounding it as a reward for their constant and loyal labor. They *had* their house and home, and if this suit was successful, I would have nothing. I could not believe Elly would begrudge me my share.

In retrospect, it is not difficult to understand, and I must accept some blame for what transpired. After Morris's death, Jim had worn the uniform of the Forest Service. To him, we represented the forces of anarchy, and to us he had sided with law and repressive order. He had only to drive by Turkey Ridge to see the accumulating clutter of old vehicles, the large kitchen garden plowed into the once-pristine lawn, and the general deterioration of the house and grounds he had dedicated a third of his life to maintaining. No matter how hard we labored, no matter how many good deeds we offered the community, we were indisputably *different* from the local people and in many ways a threat to their values.

Part of the problem was duration. We had not lived there long enough. In other communities, like Black Bear, where Free Family people organized a tree-planting cooperative, worked for the Forest Service, and took roles teaching in the local schools, familiarity led to integration and acceptance, direct results of long-term residence. At Turkey Ridge we'd had time to extend feelers but no time to sink roots.

We were shocked and hurt one night when a local childhood friend, Raymond Van Wuys, told us that Walt often recounted satirical stories about us to amuse his friends at the local bar. Raymond knew we assumed that our labors for the Poliski family had won us a measure of friendship and respect; now he cautioned us against making unfounded assumptions about the depth of those feelings.

People in that area were hardworking, thrifty, resourceful, generally clean and sober. They eschewed welfare rigorously and harbored little if any antigovernment sentiments. The day another childhood friend, Bruce Kessler, lost his license as a tractor-trailer driver, I asked him if he was going on welfare. He looked at me as if I were deranged—and had a new job the next day. As members of a counterculture, we defined ourselves by our opposition to the majority. The local people *were* the majority culture. We could not have it both ways at once.

We had behaved with both arrogance and naïveté, assuming that we were leading the way to a future of our own design. We had assumed the task of creating a culture from whole cloth, certain that our example would shine brilliantly enough and that more traditional people would join us. I can't blame Elly or Walt for rejecting our example. There were aspects of our life that did not compel me: the chaos, the impossibility of refined group expression, the moral self-righteousness, and the personal failings and indulgences that undermined some of our best efforts. I viewed such problems as part of the process, but to outsiders, our problems represented *what we were,* and they found us offensive.

The pending sale made relocating a necessity, and I wanted to return to California to be near Ariel. Nichole and I discovered a beautifully constructed but rundown handmade house trailer in a neighbor's ancient barn. It had been lovingly fashioned of wood in the late thirties and was eighteen feet long, with smooth curves to the roof over a somewhat boxy body, like a modern Airstream. However functional and prosaic it appeared from the outside, the inside was carefully crafted, varnished wood like a sailboat. The tires were flat and the roof was shredded, but the structure was sound, so we bought it for a hundred dollars and hauled it back to Turkey Ridge.

We insulated the delicate rafters with mattress pads, and cut and stitched a new roof of canvas, which we stretched and tacked down tight as a drum head, sealing it with aluminum-asbestos paint of a high silver sheen. We painted the body a deep forest green and the window and door trim barn red. I located a varnished plank door that I cut to size and trimmed with found brass Victorian hardware. The primitive two-burner gas stove, sink, and counter were still in good order, and I added propane lights and a small cylindrical woodstove. I constructed a double bed across the back for Nichole and me and fold-down bunks for Jeremiah and Ariel, whom I planned to pick up in California.

Since the Meat and Bone Wagon could no longer survive a cross-country trip, I traded a friend my worn Mannlicher deer rifle and the farm's antiquated Land Rover for a clean 1964 Dodge Town Wagon, a beautiful panel truck with side windows and two rear doors. It was the newest vehicle I had ever owned, originally ordered by the Florida State Survey Department and set up for them with one-ton suspension, oversized brakes, and seventeen-and-a-half-inch wheels. Its 225 slant-six engine was a paragon of reliability that could propel it at seventy miles an hour all day long.

One of our squatter friends from Shawnee, a Chicano from Compton, California, whose name I've misplaced, painted the truck electric blue and stenciled crescent moons with the morning star in silver on each door. For some reason I christened this blue truck "Sadie Green." I still have it today. It has accumulated more than 380,000 miles and in the interim has been converted to four-wheel drive (a task of monumental proportions), and painted forest green to match its name. Presently powered by a 318 V-8 engine, it has been rebuilt from end to end and, as my alter ego in some wise, reaffirms to me that, despite scars and wear, old machinery (like my body) can still be of value and service.

Nichole and I and the others left for our various destinations, and Tommy Lavigne was left to sit the house (although "plunder" would have been a more appropriate verb to describe his residency). The spring after we had returned to California, my mother received an alarmed call from my cousin Arthur who lived nearby in a home he constructed single-handedly, informing her that he'd noticed an announcement in the paper of a yard sale at Turkey Ridge. With true junkie resourcefulness, Tommy auctioned off the contents of the house and outbuildings to raise personal spending money. When he was finally pried out, it was discovered that he had also sidestepped the inconvenience of carrying his garbage to the dump by throwing it down the cellar stairs to molder there all winter. That was the Free Family legacy at Turkey Ridge Farm: a festering garbage pile in the center of my father's heaven-on-earth. Not a pretty thing to remember, or admit.

Nichole, Jeremiah, Josephine, and I began our cross-country trek with seventy dollars in cash. On our first day, the highway god delivered a pheasant to us, which I skinned. We stopped at a shop in Port Jervis, New York, bought a gross of ear wires, some bails to hold the feathers, and corkboard on which to mount finished earrings. I drew a catchy little logo of a snake eating its own tail and trademarked our intended product "Eternal Circle

Earrings." A paragraph under the title described the origin of the feathers (poetically, to be sure, avoiding the word *roadkill*) and assured customers that by "recycling" these feathers as jewelry, they would be participating in an eternal circle (not to mention supporting my family). It was a thin premise on which to base an economy, but it worked out well enough, so that by the time we reached the West Coast three and a half months later, we had a bankroll of slightly over four hundred dollars.

It was a nice trip. It was winter and freezing cold, but we stopped at lumberyards along the way and got "short ends" of milled lumber for free. They burned fast and hot and made the trailer toasty. We were already skilled at raiding supermarket dumps for slightly overripe produce, and we had enough friends or contacts along the route to keep us showered and in clean laundry.

In areas without friends, we'd park by the road, and while the winter winds of Illinois or Nebraska rocked the trailer on its suspension, we stayed warm and dry inside. Jeremiah and Josephine slept, and Nichole and I arranged feathers into pleasing designs and sang in harmony for hours. I remember it as a long, easy crossing. I never wore a watch in those days, and today, pressured by a relentless schedule and myriad obligations, I look back at life on the road as a relatively carefree period. It couldn't have been as rosy as I remember, though, because shortly after we reached San Francisco, Nichole and I decided to live apart.

We spent our first night back in San Francisco at Peter and Judy (Goldhaft) Berg's Victorian house that Judy's father had bought for them. When Peter awoke the following morning, he stumbled into the bathroom where Nichole and I were washing and muttered something disparaging about "life on the commune." There was no mistaking the chill of that crack. Nichole and I looked at each other knowingly and moved out that day. Solidarity has its limits, and Berg had never been enthusiastic about communal life.

I moved into a two-room basement apartment on Holly Park Circle, a small hilltop in the outer reaches of the Mission. I parked my trailer in the street and used it as an additional room. I had no idea how I was going to survive in the city, but Danny Rifkin solved the problem for me by offering me his unemployment benefits. He had made it a practice to learn to live on half of his current earnings. In that way he was guaranteed a future week off for each week he had worked. He was about to take a year off from his duties with the Grateful Dead, didn't need his benefits, and knew that I did.

With an income assured and something left over for Sam and Ariel, I could afford to rebuild the engine on Sadie Green. To do that I needed a car. There was a wheeless VW bug abandoned in front of my apartment that the neighborhood children had used as scratch paper. I appropriated it. To me it had some charm, but it must have been pretty rank. About two years later, Phil Esparza, a friend from El Teatro Campesino (Luis Valdez's brilliant theater company in San Juan Bautista), regarded it one day and asked me in all seriousness, "Man, aren't you *ashamed* to be seen driving that thing?" To tell the truth, I never thought about it. It was free.

I registered the car in the name of Amanda B. Reckonwith, figuring that I had little money to spare for parking tickets. I had never voted for the presence of parking meters anywhere I had ever lived and considered their presence an insult to my inalienable right to lounge around. When the police stopped me from time to time and informed me that "Miss Reckonwith" had "lots of warrants," I told them dutifully that Amanda was out of the country but that I would tell her to take care of them the minute she got back. The system is not calibrated to work with people who do not want to own property; this made things much simpler for me.

When the VW stopped dead with an expensive-sounding grinding noise and "thunk" on Market Street during rush hour one day years later, I felt I had received my $150 investment from it and abandoned it where it stopped. The vehicle had numerous outstanding warrants, and I thought it was time for the car to turn itself in and take its punishment.

Holly Park was an unlucky neighborhood for me. My apartment was plundered shortly after I moved in and then my guitar was stolen out of my VW while I ran in to use my bathroom one afternoon. It was a large, blond maple Guild F-50 given to me by a writer friend, with my initials "RPC" inlaid at the fourteenth fret and a little Barcus-Berry electric pickup under the bridge. It would resonate against my chest as I played, and I imagined that if you could play a cathedral, it would feel something like that. I mourn its loss to this day, reflexively scan pawnshops and newspaper ads for it, and it's a measure of my love for it that even as I now write nearly thirty years later, I fantasize some reader revealing its whereabouts.

A few years before, in Woodstock, I had convinced a friend of Martin Carey's to give Nichole an extra guitar he owned. We played together often, and she needed something to do with her hands. It was another Guild, a D-50, smaller than mine, but with a lovely voice. Now that mine was gone, I asked to borrow hers. She almost never used it, and music was a daily preoccupation for me. Nichole told me that she had loaned it to someone and couldn't get it back at the moment. Several nights later I woke from a dream inflamed by the certainty that Nichole had pawned it for drug money. I was indignant. "She would not even *have* a guitar had it not been for my efforts," I told myself, en route to her house at 3:00 A.M. By the time I reached her apartment I had worked myself into a self-righteous fury. I broke down the door and demanded the pawn ticket. She denied any knowledge of it at first, telling me I was crazy to believe a dream, but then she recanted and turned the pawn ticket over to me. I left, and still have that guitar. I was pleased as punch with myself and never considered that I had been prepared to hurt someone for a material object.

The random disorders in my physical life mirrored my emotional life. Nichole and I were living apart but seeing each other occasionally, getting high together, sleeping together, codependent as sociopathic Siamese twins. I took my truck and trailer to visit Freeman House in La Conner, Washington. At the time of my flight from Nichole, Freeman had just written a beautiful piece called "Totem Salmon," published in Peter Berg's new magazine, *Planet Drum.* Among other things, this prescient piece calculated the calories required to catch one calorie of fish with current industrial methods, demonstrating that the modus operandi of the fishing industry was insupportable for the long term.

Planet Drum was a forum for bioregionalism, a cutting edge of deep-ecological thought. A bioregion is a distinct plant-animal-climate community (including humans) marked by the presence or absence of certain species. A bioregion's inhabitants have more in common with one another than they do simply as citizens of a state or county, which are abstract lines often including several bioregions. Los Angelenos and northern Californians inhabit the same state but radically different bioregions. Many cultural differences between the two areas can be traced to that distinction. Bioregions are the way the earth actually organizes itself.

Our evolving thought held that if humans wanted to avoid destroying our life-support systems—water, soil, air, and plant and animal species— both urban and rural people would have to learn to live according to the dictates and processes of their bioregion. If it takes seventy-five years to grow a usable tree, you have to incorporate that fact in any planning. If that tree is necessary to prevent topsoil slipping into the streams and killing the salmon spawn or silting up downstream estuaries, employment may have to be adjusted to that objective reality. If the annual rainfall can support X number of people, that too must be factored in to planning commissions and real-estate permits. Human industries and lifestyles that murder their biological supports are patently untenable, and no amount of "reasonable compromise" will change that fact. Learning how and what to change and creating cultures that embodied such changes as conventional wisdom were the tasks at hand. *Planet Drum* was created to be the mouthpiece and the messenger.

The ostensible purpose of my visit to Freeman was to sound out his thinking on this subject. The secondary purpose was to get away from the city, drugs, and Nichole. One of my self-conscious functions in the family was as a messenger and catalyst. I have an ability to translate and transmit ideas clearly, and since conversations at many Free Family houses and kindred groups were concerned with the same subjects, it was often my task as a traveler to be the cross-pollinator of ideas and institutions, one of the time-honored contributions of nomads. Information was a currency in which I was wealthy.

I consoled myself for my difficulties with Nichole by keeping company with an Indian woman from the reservation in nearby Yakima. I met her playing pool in La Conner, and although she was pretty drunk, she was deadly at the table. She was exciting and unpredictable, not above winging a pool ball at an idiot who offended her. She looked about thirty-five, and confessed to having a "clutter" of children back in Yakima. Had she drunk less and her teeth not been cracked and chipped, she would have been stunning, but none of the ravages she inflicted on herself could obliterate the residual wisdom of her culture.

One morning she dropped by as I was cooking, I asked her if she was hungry and she said nothing. When I asked a third time, she said, "Don't make people *say* that they're hungry. Put food in front of them. If they're hungry, they'll eat."

This protocol attending the offering of food interested me. It highlighted our culture's carelessness about food (which has resulted in an obsession with obesity). Living on the road, I'd noticed that you could visit a white person's home and wait for hours before being offered food or water. This was equally true in many counterculture homes. White people assumed that people ate or drank when they *wanted* to; they were not being deliberately rude, they just never had to think about hunger. Travelers in need learn to search out people of color—black people, Chicanos, and Indians—who rarely let you sit long without putting something to eat or drink in front of you.

Nichole and I patched things up temporarily when I returned to the city, but I was ready to move on, in a number of ways. The sixties had turned into the seventies, and the hard life had changed a lot of things. A lot of friends were dead: Richard Brautigan by suicide; Kirby Doyle's lover Tracy the midwife, of an overdose; Marcus, Bill Lyndon, Billy Batman from gunshot wounds; Pete Knell of cancer; Paula McCoy thrown off the roof of a hotel in Terra Linda during a soured drug deal; J. P. Pickens; Janis Joplin from an overdose. The list is longer than I have the heart to type. Brooks Butcher, boyfriend of Pam Parker who bought the Diggers a truck, wound up in a state hospital after blinding himself on an acid trip from which he never returned; he drowned trying to escape. Moose was lost somewhere in the FBI witness protection program.

Faced with these cautionary episodes, a lot of people got well. In the late seventies Phyllis went to school and became a nurse and a college professor; Natural Suzanne became a public defender who litigates for her indigent clients with the passion of one who feels that except for luck, she might be in their place. Nina, Freeman, David Simpson, and Jane Lapiner moved upstate to the Mattole River and today defend their watershed while they labor at the slow, careful work of creating the cultural détentes among ranchers, loggers, hippies, and New Agers required for a sustainable existence.

Somewhere in these transformations, Emmett got lost. I went to see him once, in 1973 or 1974 shortly after the publication of his autobiography, *Ringolevio,* in which we all figured prominently. He was riding high, married to a beautiful French-Canadian actress and living in a luxurious apartment in Brooklyn Heights. He was proud of having returned home wealthy and famous—"so near and yet so far" was how he put it.

I admit to feeling envious of him then. I was completely without money, living at Turkey Ridge, still using street drugs and the occasional bottle of Demerol. Most of my energy was absorbed by the splintering relationship with Sam, the simmering tensions of communal life, and group survival.

I couldn't help feeling that it was our collective life that had paid for Emmett's laundered sheets, elegant rooms, and well-stocked refrigerator and bar. Proud as I was of his success, I was sore about the egocentric tone of his book and agreed with Kent Minault's sardonic assessment of it: "Oh, yeah, Emmett *sauntered* while we all *walked!*"

Consequently, on this visit, when I saw that Emmett's eyes were "pinned" and knew that he was using heroin again, I allowed myself to blow up. Louise smiled beside him in bed—pleased, I think, that someone was telling him what she could not. I told him that I didn't care if he wanted to die, but if he did, why did he want to die such a boring, useless death? If he wanted to go out, why didn't he die for *something* and take on the system? I called him "a boring motherfucker" and left, too cloaked in self-righteousness to admit the degree to which jealousy had informed my anger.

From that time on, our relationship changed, and Emmett related to me as if I were another audience for him to win over. He was proud to tell me he had begun writing songs (the Band even recorded two) and that Etta James might record one. He had been spending a lot of time with Robbie Robertson and the Band and consequently was going with them to "The Last Waltz," the Band's farewell concert at San Francisco's Winterland auditorium on Thanksgiving Day, 1976. I declined his invitation to join them because, as I told him, I was bored with rock and roll's self-congratulatory pretensions. This was a high-status cheap shot on my part, suggesting that while *he* may have been seduced by the glitz of rock and roll, I was not. But after Emmett arranged for a number of San Francisco poets to read there I relented, attended the event, and had a fine time.

Despite these activities and interests, nothing was sustaining Emmett.

The "play" had changed with the decade, and the perfect role he'd crafted for himself had become anachronistic. His inability to produce something new and grand was diminishing his confidence. Trapped by the glamour of his persona, he needed time to disappear, to take beginner's steps in new directions, free of his old role and beyond the glare of public attention. But he seemed preoccupied with maintaining his old identity and status. He developed curious mannerisms, particularly a knowing wink he overused to suggest that his last remark had a deeper, hipper side easily missed without this alert. It was as if he sensed his act growing threadbare, and instead of reformulating it, resorted to tricks that suggested that it was the audience's perceptions that were faulty, not his performance.

The last time I saw him, in the winter of 1978, our situations had reversed. I was then the chairman of the California State Arts Council, pressing an exciting and radical agenda through the state legislature, and Emmett was adrift, looking for a new game. I kept a rendezvous with him at a Malibu beach house. When no one answered repeated knocks and yells, I peered through a window and spied Emmett passed out in bed. I broke in, checked the pulse at his throat, and satisfied that he was living, shook the place down as only a druggie can, checking the light wells and behind the toilet ball, the heat vents and the undersides of drawers, and found enough drugs to open a small pharmacy. I woke him and we had a corrosive fight about it. As a strategy for getting me off his back, Emmett confessed to a suicide attempt the previous day. I didn't believe it (despite the fact that heroin use *is* suicide on an extended-payment plan), but I was stunned nonetheless. Even as a ploy, Emmett was asking me to feel sorry for him, and that was so uncharacteristic that it frightened me.

Because I lived four hundred miles away, I called a friend who lived close enough to monitor him. Duvall Lewis was a brilliant young black man who had served as staff on the arts council with me. A tall and charming hipster with a devilish sense of humor, Duvall was fearless and never missed the joke. I thought he and Emmett would like each other; they did and began hanging out together.

It was Duvall who called with the news of Emmett's death, his call just one in a series that crisscrossed the country, stitching old friends into a new sorrow. Not many years later, Duvall himself died by his own hand. Their two lives and two deaths haunt me as unnervingly similar, and I can never think of either of them without understanding what Allen Ginsberg meant when he opened his epic poem *Howl* with the line, "I have seen the best minds of my generation destroyed by madness."

Emmett told you what he thought. He was stand-up. He was extreme and contradictory, quarrelsome and kind, charismatic and self-destructive. He willed himself to be a hero and died trying to honor that self-imposed responsibility.

It might be enough for most people to have been a living legend, to have Bob Dylan dedicate an album to you (*Street Legal*), to be an icon of freedom and known to Puerto Rican gang leaders, presidents of recording companies, professional thieves, movie stars, Black Panthers, and Hell's Angels, but Emmett was chasing his own self-perfection, and each achievement raised the standard for the next.

Emmett was a guidon, the emblem carried into battle behind which people rallied their imaginations. He proved with his existence that each of us could act out the life of our highest fantasies. This was his goal and his compassionate legacy, which I will not minimize, despite his inconsistencies and flaws. When that example was still untarnished, its luster summoned me and many others from safe havens and comfortable futures into the chaotic, unpredictable hard-rock moment of life in the streets. Without his example I might have remained domesticated.

25

stepping out of the wind

*Only he who has eaten poppies with the
dead will not lose ever again the gentle cord.*
RILKE, *Sonnets to Orpheus*, IX

When I returned from Washington, I inherited Michael Tierra's tiny apartment over a garage behind the house where Efrem and Harriet Korngold lived and practiced acupuncture. The neighborhood was Bernal Heights, a working-class, multiracial clutter with the kind of sleepy anonymity that made it a perfect place to disappear. It was here that the FBI captured Patricia Hearst after incinerating her fellow Symbionese Liberation Front soldiers in Los Angeles the year before. I had no space there for my trailer, so I loaned it to a friend and unfortunately lost track of it.

I was at loose ends, trying to earn a living neither on the street nor off, performing in a lusterless production of Paul Sill's *Story Theater*, working with several old cronies from the Mime Troupe and the Mime Troupe's main competitor, an improvisatory comedy group called The Committee. *Story Theater* was an unthreatening improvisatory confection, and there was much conflict in the company about its lack of political focus between the Mime Troupers and Paul Sills, who was accustomed to being regarded as a genius and resented our critiques. I performed several numbers as a guitarist-singer. Other than that and being cheated out of my salary by Mr. Sills, I remember little of the event.

I needed something to do, and fate dealt me three good cards. The first came from Judy Goldhaft and Peter Berg, who were searching for an artistic expression of the "reinhabitation" concepts. Judy assembled a group of former Mime Troupers and Firesign Theater folk from Minneapolis who had moved to San Francisco after meeting the troupe on tour, and we began exploratory rehearsals at a community center called the Farm.

Bonny Sherk and Jack Wickert had taken over a mammoth abandoned sportswear factory built of incongruous white clapboard and shadowed by an elevated freeway in a bleak intersection of the Hunter's Point and Mission Districts. Bonny was a fulsome woman with unruly chocolate-colored hair, a dazzling smile, unshakable enthusiasm, and extremely persuasive energy. She lived with Jack, a rail-thin, psychologically vague, sardonic English musician who gave the impression of being unshaven and hastily dressed even when he wasn't. The two were intent on transforming the old wooden buildings into an urban farm and community center. They begged and borrowed animals, grass, plants, and cages and created a unique indoor barnyard that they offered to local schools as an educational opportunity and to community groups for fund-raising benefits and concerts. They wheedled funding shamelessly and, by hook, crook, and enormous expenditures of energy, kept the institution alive.

Our company met upstairs every morning at the Farm in a large open room, and after warm-up exercises began the arduous process of inventing a new theater piece. Our organizing principle was to use "stories" from our bioregion, both ancient and new. Our perspective would be "multispecies"—telling the tales from the points of view of all local species, not just humans. We researched indigenous legends and creation myths and found several that we felt were suitable for translation into the comedic, commentary-a-second Mime Troupe style.

Judy is a dancer and keenly discriminating about movement. Though nonauthoritarian, she managed to keep our group focused and on schedule. We spent hours at the zoo, studying the movements and gestures of animals and then returning to try our imitations on our friends. Results were often comical and embarrassing, but after countless failures, we refined dominant characteristics, detail by detail, for Bear, Coyote, Fox, Lizard, Bobcat, and a host of other featured players. By improvising and retaining what made our friends laugh, we learned to present our subject in an amusing and interesting way.

As contemporary history, we dramatized a story from Gary Snyder's homesteading experience: his killing a bobcat that had decimated his chicken flock. Our human characters were Branch and Crystal, New Age hippies played to perfection by Marlow Hotchkiss and Muniera Christianson. The sinuous and lethal Bobcat was played by Judy herself, feasting on methedrine-manic chickens liberated from factory farms to run wild "in nature." In what I hope was not too deliberate an irony, I was cast as one of the drug-fuddled chickens.

The show became locally popular, and we began booking small runs out of town, performing in fields, barns, movie houses, and wherever else we could develop a venue. It was fun to act again, working with skilled friends, expressing political ideas we cared about. I had not realized how much I missed the stage, and something in me began to quicken.

My second good card was dealt by the federal government. A local political visionary named John Kreidler convinced a federal agency to use funds from an employment program called the Comprehensive Education and Training Act (CETA) to create a pilot program for the employment of artists. Word of the program filtered through the streets, and since I had no other conceivable trade, I hastened downtown with my longtime pal, fellow Mime Trouper and musician Charlie Degelman, and we joined three thousand others queuing to audition for one hundred job slots.

After hours of waiting on line, I was led before a table of well-dressed people who represented the selection committee. Of the group, I remember only two: one was a handsome woman with a proud demeanor whose prematurely gray hair was pulled back severely behind her ears. She had the scrutinizing air of a suspicious French intellectual, which in fact she was. Her name was Anne-Marie Theilen, a decent woman soon to be driven to distraction attempting to supervise my activities. The other was a rumpled, professorial-looking man in a bow tie who changed the course of my life and subsequently became a good friend. His name was Stephen Goldstine.

If such a thing as a selfless patron of the arts has ever existed, Stephen is it. An amateur in the best and most classical sense, he has spent his life studying under various masters for pure pleasure. His childhood photography teacher was Imogen Cunningham, and he pursued the piano under a succession of gifted teachers. He could recite the curriculum vitae and personal history of symphony orchestra musicians the way other people recite sports statistics. Devoted to all forms of excellence, he later became the director of San Francisco's Art Institute. That morning he looked at me as kindly as Anne-Marie regarded me skeptically, and asked what I had prepared as an audition piece. I was dumbfounded. I told him I had assumed this would be an exploratory session (true!) and that I had brought neither a guitar nor any prepared performance piece. "Well," he said, "do *something!*"

I began drumming a polyrhythmic figure on the table, beneath the startled nose of Ms. Theilin, and improvised a song about coming to the meeting and needing the work. I felt like a shoe-shine boy dancing for pennies, but I'd had lots of practice entertaining around campfires and woodstoves, and I surprised them with some clever lyrics. Anne-Marie appeared perplexed and underwhelmed, but Stephen spoke up for me, and I was given my first real job since bartending twelve years earlier, hired as an artist to do something to be invented later. I was to be paid six hundred dollars a month, three times what I'd survived on for the last ten years. I was euphoric.

The CETA artists were a lively group, featuring, among others, future MacArthur "Genius" Award–winner and metaphysical clown Bill Irwin; a brilliant English vaudeville performer named Geoff Hoyle, who later mesmerized Manhattan's theater critics with a one-man show; Larry Pisoni, founder of the Pickle Family Circus; and ex-chef Peter Frankham, an honest-to-god English gypsy who started Make-a-Circus, a community arts organization designed to create festive local events and teach circus skills. All except Peter, who died prematurely, continue performing today. I mention my closest friends first, but in fact, every one of the CETA grantees—poets, actors, writers, musicians, and artists of every stripe, representing a broad range of cultures—expended extraordinary energy to raise the general aesthetic sophistication of San Francisco. If the arts are, as I believe, society's research and development division, exploring the contradictions, common visions, and potential in the culture, the minuscule amount of public money used for this program was well spent and has probably been repaid several times over from the taxes of the initial recipients.

If my public life was perking up, my private life was tepid at best. Nichole and I had broken up for good, so I looked up Marilyn McCann, the shy girl who had visited Turkey Ridge with Danny Rifkin. True to her word, Marilyn was practicing Zen Buddhism at San Francisco's Zen Center. There was something compelling about her depth and quietness and a wholesome quality to her beauty that I found intriguing. It was obvious that she was not a woman to be trifled with, and after considerable hemming and hawing, backsliding and panics on my part, we became lovers. Her small, tidy apartment next door to the Zen Center felt like an oasis of calm. My daughter was growing older and needed stability, and so did I. A year after we began dating, I asked Marilyn to marry me.

For me, *karma,* a Sanskrit word sometimes translated as "fate," is often clearest in the interval between a decision to change and the first rewards from new behavior, a period of time usually much longer than anticipated. Most of us have had the experience of intending to change and being deterred by residue from our past. That momentum carrying past actions into the present is how I understand karma. No sooner had I married Marilyn than Sam dropped Ariel off to live with us. She had chosen to move to Colorado for some reason and wanted Ariel to finish the school year in San Francisco. Although we'd been married less than two months, Marilyn threw herself into being a stepmother with her characteristic dedication. She researched schools for Ariel, enrolled her in ballet lessons, painted and decorated a lovely room with handmade curtains, took her shopping for new clothes (for perhaps the first time in Ariel's life), and began to teach her the rudiments of civilized behavior.

Ariel blossomed, and I was thrilled to see my once-feral child thriving with the advantages of a normal home life. Unfortunately, Sam became disenchanted with Colorado and moved back to San Francisco about six weeks later. Ariel was supposed to remain with us for the duration of the school year. One day, five or six months into that year, Sam decided arbitrarily that the experiment was over: Ariel was to return to her house immediately. Marilyn burst into tears, weeping for the opportunity that Ariel would miss. I was bewildered and did not see how to refuse, but Marilyn was crystal clear: "That child will never stand a chance if she's raised by her mother. She'll have no education, no training, and the options for her future will be reduced to nothing. I don't care if she chooses to be a hippie when she's grown, but I'd like her to know how to eat at a formal dinner, or study for college, or get a straight job if she wants to. You know that no one will see to that if she goes back."

This was classic Marilyn. Raised in a tiny southern Ohio community, she had pored through fashion magazines as a child, determined to experience the wider, more sophisticated world she knew existed beyond the borders of her town. When her father, a well-respected country lawyer, agreed to pay for any "educational" summer camp, she found one in Vogue's back pages that taught French. The camp, on the East Coast, catered to the daughters of New York's elite. Marilyn charmed them, absorbed what they could teach her, and never looked back. She understood the value of training and made her case passionately. I concurred, and we began the grueling and cruel process of a custody battle, which even an eventual victory could not sweeten.

The court dictated that Ariel live primarily with Marilyn and me, but the stress of the hearings and the bad blood between the households caused rents in the fabric of our relationships, extending even to the grandparents. Ariel's behavior began to change; she seemed confused and unhappy. While her mother was away, she had not had to feel torn in her loyalties or guilty about her new good fortune. Sam's authority as Ariel's biological mother added to the normal strains of stepmothering, and her intrusions into our life became intolerable to Marilyn. Ariel reacted to the tension as a child will, and Marilyn began to regard her not as a confused nine-year-old but as a competitor with the power of a peer. My guilt and attempts to please everyone exacerbated the problems between them. I can think of nothing crueler than trying to arbitrate a duel between people you love equally. The relationship between Marilyn and Ariel deteriorated to the point that I was forced to send Ariel away to school, and the day I explained to Ariel that she would have to go away is unequivocally the worst memory of my life.

I had one more lucky card coming. This one was dealt by Gary Snyder, and it landed on the table shortly after I became a CETA artist. In 1975, Snyder's book *Turtle Island* won the Pulitzer Prize for poetry, and then-governor

Edmund G. "Jerry" Brown appointed him chairman of a newly constituted state arts council. Before Brown, the state arts "commission" had been a high-status afterthought composed primarily of wives of the governor's friends, distributing a niggardly one million dollars to California's cultural institutions. At the time of Brown's inauguration, California ranked forty-eighth among the states in per-capita arts spending.

The governor's idea was to create a council of working artists to revitalize the state's culture. Gary asked me if I would consider joining the council and baited his hook with an offer no visionary could refuse: "You'll have an opportunity to define the state," he promised. I shrugged "why not" and forgot about the conversation—until several months later, when I found myself sitting with the governor and his éminence grise, the enigmatic Jacques Barzhagi, once a cinema hustler from the Côte d'Azur and now the governor's most trusted personal adviser.

Ours was an improbable job interview. My hair had grown back to shoulder length after Wall Street and I arrived in jeans and boots, intent, I suppose, on communicating that none of this was a very big deal to me. Barzhagi's head was shaved so close that his hair seemed to be a fine coating of dust. Rimless glasses magnified his bright eyes, and his unblinking stare hinted at a penetrating intelligence melded with a disquieting unpredictability.

He had an edge on me at the meeting, because en route to Sacramento, my scrofulous VW had been stopped by the highway patrol, and I couldn't resist flaunting the fact that I was en route to a meeting at the governor's office. The trooper must have checked out this apparent absurdity, since Jacques asked immediately, "What did the cop want with you?"

The governor was relaxed, and we talked casually for about twenty minutes, while several advisers mutely witnessed our exchange. I don't remember the details of the conversation, but I do remember disagreeing with many of the governor's perspectives. The last ten years had given me plenty of time to ponder cultural questions, and I was certain that neither the governor nor his advisers had been as close to the underbelly of American life as I had been. I reasoned that if I had anything to offer, it would be by remaining true to my own experience. Furthermore, though it might be fun to have a job, I was not about to sell myself to get it. I had much to say and must have struck a resonant chord, because the next thing I knew, I was a member of the California Arts Council.

From the farthest edge of the outside, I had, after one conversation, been invited to the inside of the inside. The irony of my appointment was sharpened by the contrast in status between my lowly CETA employment and my now-elevated status as a council member. My CETA supervisors, who had gamely attempted to track my peripatetic whereabouts and comprehend the elusive nature of my project-to-be, would soon be applying to the arts council for their own funds, and this new wrinkle in our relationship was not lost on them—or me. I was magnanimous in victory, however, and turned the situation to my advantage by declaring my long-awaited project to be: the counseling of San Francisco Bay Area groups in applying for state funding! (I was so successful at this that several years later there was a political hullabaloo over the fact that the Bay Area, with a population of only one million people, was receiving 40 percent of all state arts funding, which immeasurably peeved the artists of Los Angeles, with its population of twelve million.)

In my early days on the council, my revolutionary sentiments were raw and heightened by years of living without money. I identified more closely with the underclasses and, despite my love of the art forms, was antagonistic to the political proponents of "Western European High Art," as I was fond of calling opera, symphony, and ballet. I wasted no time in announcing that it was "payback time," that there was scant money available for the arts, and I was damned if it was all going to go to "aristocratic watering holes." This kind of rhetoric made me poor friends and rich enemies.

It is easy to understand how proponents of the "high arts" might have been fearful of our new regime. Governor Brown's council was a racial and ethnic fruit salad, composed primarily of working artists, many of whom were unknown to the general public. Besides myself, the members included Alexander Mackendrick, the rumpled and angular Scottish film director (*The Ladykillers, The Man in the White Suit, The Sweet Smell of Success*) drier than a Vermouth-less martini, who spent a large portion of each council meeting drawing satirical cartoons of his peers. (Mine was a headbanded hippie, his arm raised as if still knocking on a nonexistent door, while tuxedoed swells are waltzing about. A liveried butler with a champagne glass on a tray is standing besides him saying, "But, sir, you *are* inside.") Then there were Allaudin Mathieu, music professor and choir director from Mills College, a passionate eclectic who loved novel cultural rearrangements like pairing the Sufi choir and the Grateful Dead; Ruth Asawa, a Japanese-American sculptor, equally famous for her "origami" bronzes in San Francisco's Japantown and for her large fountains made of baker's dough tiles designed by schoolchildren; Suzanne Jackson, a prominent African-American printmaker from Los Angeles, quiet but deep and, unlike me, less interested in political wrangling than in production of good work; and Luis Valdez, an old comrade from the Mime Troupe, now the artistic director and spiritual leader of a theater company called El Teatro Campesino.

Born the son of migrant workers, Luis had left the Mime Troupe to form El Teatro after an acid trip in which, according to him, "all the grasses were pointing toward Delano." His theatrical brilliance, coupled with a rigorous intellect and deep political convictions, had made him a force to be reckoned with in the emergent Latino movement. Luis went on to write and direct *Zoot Suit*, the hit musical that catapulted Edward James Olmos into stardom, and the film *La Bamba* about rock star Richie Valens.

Luis is a complicated man, quick to laugh, and with a pointed sense of the ridiculous. Stocky and barrel-chested, with a dark Zapata mustache, he speaks English with the impeccable syntax and vocabulary of the cultural elite yet can pivot on a syllable into Caló, the English-Spanish argot of California. His political and personal ambitions are densely braided, and it was not always possible for me to determine the dividing line between them. During his tenure as a council member, he was always chauffeured and personally attended by someone from El Teatro, and his regal personal style sometimes contrasted starkly with his proletarian convictions. Although we were friends and political allies of long standing, we differed increasingly over what I perceived to be his attempts to include Native American issues under his hegemony, insisting on the authority to speak for Native concerns and to supervise programs (and funds) intended for them. My resistance was based on personal knowledge that most native people did not speak Spanish or consider themselves Chicanos (the term Mexicans used to distinguish themselves from the larger population of Latinos or Hispanics). They had concerns that were specifically their own and did not want them co-opted by another culture.

Further exacerbating differences between us, Luis sought increasing control over staff appointments, at one point going directly to the governor to subvert a council decision about personnel. These quarrels eventually ruptured our relationship when, as chairman of the council, I refused to support his candidate for executive director, an able young woman named Gloriamalia Flores who had been one of our deputy directors. Gloria was extremely diligent and competent, but young and only recently out of school. Her appointment, at Luis's behest, to deputy director of a state agency was already a major coup for an unseasoned beginner. Art politics were hotly contested and bitter internecine struggles often erupted. I told Gloria I felt she would be crushed by the competing social forces and suggested she spend another several years as deputy director under the new executive and that when that new person left (as arts bureaucrats seemed to do every several years), I promised her my backing for the job. My lack of support infuriated Luis, however, and he accused me of being a racist in a public meeting. Some years later, word came back to me through an intermediary that Gloriamalia herself agreed with my analysis of the situation.

Gary Snyder's contributions to the council were unique. He explored this political territory the same way he explored a new ridge with a pack on his back—by keeping his eyes open, practicing mindfulness, and determining carefully where to place his foot next. His method sometimes appeared stodgy (as his mountain walk did when I first noticed the way his feet splayed out flat, as if they would "splat" when they landed), but his pace never faltered and he never stumbled. Despite the fact that he rarely chose paths of obvious political expediency, he never seemed to create antipathy or enemies among those with different philosophies or opinions. It was fun to watch Gary chair meetings in the state capitol, appearing before the legislators with a red bandanna around his forehead, his hair tied Navajo style, wearing either his Amish suit bought from a mail-order catalogue (of which he was uncommonly proud) or his natty fishing vest with a hand-embroidered turtle on the breast, representing Turtle Island—the symbol of a reimagined America known by its ancient native name. Speaking from the dais under the state flag, he would cheerfully explain to the representatives of High European culture why scarce arts dollars should be shared with Asian, Latin, Micronesian, rural white, and black cultures. He would disarm community arts people with minitreatises on excellence as a form of radical practice and the necessity of being truly inclusive when speaking of cultural diversity. Restive as partisans might be with his premises and conclusions, Snyder's explanations were so interesting, informative, and articulate and his goodwill so evenhanded and genuine that I know of no one who ever took exception to the manner in which Gary considered their brief.

The two remaining members of the council played decisive roles in my further education and deserve mention. Noah Purifoy is a short, muscular African-American man then in his sixties with gnarly hands, a pugnacious thrust to his posture, and a deliberate and somewhat querulous voice. A Los Angeles sculptor of found art, he is a deep thinker about creativity and culture. According to Noah, all artists work in fundamentally the same manner, no matter what their medium is. Following a hunch, an impulse, or a hypothesis, they make a move, a line, a sentence. They step back and regard what they have done, then they act again and review again, discovering where they are going incrementally. This antipodal shifting between the realms of logic and intuition is the core of the creative process. It is, according to Noah, a problem-solving mechanism of the highest order because it utilizes and integrates both the right and left hemispheres of the brain. Noah's "hunch" was that the council itself should operate according to the same creative process, using as its starting position the policy and program intuitions of the members. Since most of us were working artists, we were comfortable leaping into the unknown in this manner. Purifoy asserted further that just as the creative process was a problem-solving mechanism for the artist, the community of artists could serve as a reservoir of creative problem solvers for the state. Artists could even save the state money if they succeeded in cracking some of the obdurate problems plaguing it.

When the council began to design programs, we used Noah's ideas as our template and discovered how readily they expedited our ideas of service. If we want to have art in the state, we reasoned, we should create opportunities for artists to serve the state's needs. If we paid a subsistence wage for twenty hours of weekly work, the artists would create art on their own nickel in the remaining time. There was no need to pay them for making art, and doing so has been one of the major controversies and political problems of arts funding. Even the densest legislator could understand the equation of payment for service.

It was fascinating to track the reactions as the council began to explore and articulate this idea. A contrary philosophy known as art-for-art's-sake was articulated among the representatives of the state's "High Art" institutions. They argued that art had no statement to make nor any practical significance (which I always considered a dangerous argument to advance when asking taxpayers for their money). They contended that to attach a work of art to any purpose outside of its own organic evolution was to debase the work, and I can certainly agree with the latter part of the statement. But such arguments could not (or would not) address that *all* choices—especially by a government agency—are inherently political and reflect the interests or worldview of one group or another. Art-for-art's-sake is the philosophy about art of a group accustomed to dominance, which mistakes its political power for revealed truth. They did not accept that their worldview was only one among many, some of which were far older and at least as well developed.

The new council was in charge now, however; this was *our* philosophy, and we were damn well going to run with it. Legislators found it easy to support our program, at least in the beginning. Once they understood that they were being asked to vote for services rendered and not grants, they were greatly relieved, and this distinction saved us a lot of political flak (a lesson that has not been learned to date by either the National Endowment for the Arts or any other state arts council of which I am aware). The major cultural institutions learned that it made no practical difference whether they received their money for community service and outreach or as a grant, but that there were tangible political benefits to the former option—such as the opera being funded to teach singing in the public schools. A father who might never go to the opera would not begrudge state funding to an institution that was giving his children tangible benefits. In this way the council sidestepped much of the class antagonism that often invisibly undermines adequate arts funding.

The remaining member of the council, my polar opposite politically, temperamentally, and stylistically, became in due course my ablest teacher in the realm of politics. Karney Hodge was president of the American Symphony Orchestra League, one of the bastions of wealth and privilege in America's upper-echelon arts community. He is a solid man with the square face and tightly curled hair of a Roman pugilist who has aged well. It was obvious that Karney was on the council to represent the art interests of those who generally do best in our society. As their representative, he was a minority of one: impeccably groomed, shirts crisp and fresh, tasteful gold accessories winking against subdued, classically tailored suits. Karney made no apologies for his style or agenda, but he was patient and extremely skillful, biding his time and reminding us consistently that the "establishment arts" (as I was fond of calling them) were also "a part of the big picture."

Karney laughed easily and expressed an upbeat bonhomie that never rang false yet never obligated him either. I began to admire his skill in addressing issues without rancor, spinning our vocabulary of "fairness" and "inclusion" on its edge to include his constituency as well. He could be stubborn when necessary, though, lowering his head and presenting an adamant forehead to his adversary like a bull. He was a keenly competitive tennis player, and through his Fresno pal George Zenovich, a jazz-playing state senator, he had easy access to the legislature. His wife Marilyn Jean was charming and ebullient, and his children seemed fit, happy, and successful. There was much to admire and emulate about Karney, and I did both.

Unlike my peers, I had no career that conflicted with my council work, so I dedicated all my time to it and became a spokesman for the majority (formerly the "minority") opinion. Because we operated at antipodal ends of the political spectrum, any compromise that suited both Karney and me was practically guaranteed to pass a council vote.

The next year, in 1976, I was elected chairman. My watch continued for more than three years and might have continued indefinitely had the legislature not passed a law prohibiting my continuance—such was my popularity with the powers-that-were. One might have thought from the press coverage dedicated to the council and its programs and from the scorn and furor that we aroused that we were the largest and most important agency in the state of California, rather than a puny afterthought to the business of making money, like public radio and television.

My tenure as chairman was a crash course in political awareness. I learned the hard way to speak to the press in concise, uninterruptible sentences. I saw firsthand the way legislators heeled to commands from important contributors, and despite my cynicism, I admit to being shocked the first time a powerful assemblyman blatantly informed me that the only way I could get his critical budget vote was to include one of his important constituents in the current round of grants. After about twelve seconds of deliberation, I did as he demanded—much to the consternation of my staff, who would have been unemployed had I refused.

Most important, I learned what I was doing wrong. My Maoist notions of "heightening the contradictions" between the haves and have-nots was not only *not* producing results but had frozen the state's arts community in gridlock. I had alienated the major cultural institutions and administrative staffs, and while they may not have been powerful enough to force their own agenda through the council, they were powerful enough to bring our political progress to a halt. Furthermore, honest reflection forced me to acknowledge that *all* the citizens of California were taxpayers and that our mandate was to serve them all. Fairness and equity and good public policy did not mean simply punishing the previously dominant class and rewarding the previously disenfranchised. This revelation created problems with several old comrades who behaved as if my tenure as chairman was a guarantee of an annuity for whatever future projects they chose to pursue. When I asked them to abide by the same rules as everyone else, they accused me of selling out and in one instance ruptured a valuable friendship. Finally, it seemed that the furor we were stirring up over a million dollars in a state the size of California was not worth the trouble. I felt that if the stakes were raised considerably and if I apologized and ate some well-deserved crow, it might be possible to build a constituency powerful enough to win sufficient money from the legislature to make positive changes.

At this critical juncture, fate delivered me an angel in the form of Arthur Bolton, the man who created the Office of the Legislative Analyst for the California legislature. Art is an owlish man with tightly wavy hair and an implacable calm, whose accent betrays his youth as a labor organizer in New York City. His work here had created the first full-time professional state legislature in the nation, and respect for him in Sacramento was universal. I don't remember who introduced us, but we met for coffee in a small, neon-lit fast-food place constructed primarily of Formica. I was on fire with ideas, plans, and optimism, and running at a hundred miles an hour. Arthur must have been amused or felt some resonance with his own youthful passion, for he agreed to sign on as a consultant to help the council formulate strategy, and from that day our fortunes changed for the better.

We determined that the sum of twenty million dollars was needed to adequately serve the state's needs. We devised a series of programs that would not only serve the various constituencies in the arts community but were designed to integrate artists and their programs into the budgets of "bulletproof" agencies like Education, Health, and Welfare (separate departments in California), and Corrections, to protect the arts from being the first to be cut in hard times.

The first step in the process was to secure a request for the funds in the governor's annual budget proposal. With Gary Snyder beside me providing moral support, I sketched out a no-lose situation for Governor Brown, assuring him that if he requested twenty million dollars for the arts from the legislature, he would not have to spend a penny of political capital fighting for it. If the council failed to organize sufficient support to win the day, the arts community could not complain about the governor and he could claim credit for trying. If we did triumph, he would get all the credit for a bold and innovative move. He concurred.

The next step required winning the support of the cultural "establishment." I scheduled endless meetings with the major opera, ballet, theater, and symphonic companies, which I always opened by apologizing for my divisive and rancorous behavior until then. It is amazing how readily an honest apology can defuse a hostile situation, and I am surprised that professional politicians do not utilize the apology more often, even as a ploy. When I introduced the twenty-million-dollar pie and the governor's support for it into our newly cordial discussions, the result was electrifying. In the proposed council budget, the major institutions were guaranteed 10 percent of the funds (a triumph in my eyes, since most state arts councils award them about 50 percent of available money, more a recognition of their political power than policy-driven need), a windfall to them. The year before, the Los Angeles Philharmonic had received two thousand dollars from the arts council; if we were successful in acquiring our new budget, their next council grant would be more than two hundred thousand dollars.

It is not too difficult to forge alliances when you come to the table with a big bag of money. (If you question this, study American foreign policy.) Sums of this magnitude afforded us the opportunity of crafting programs of sufficient size to actually effect social change. Since we were paying for *service* (à la Noah Purifoy) rather than buying art or indulging artists as a unique population, we had a reasonable chance to win the legislative support to pass the budget.

Giving money to artists and institutions to make art is a precarious undertaking politically. From a conservative perspective, it appears that the state is taking money from lots of people who may not like what they do for a living and giving it to a few who love what they do, who would probably do it for free, and whose products are often at odds with "community standards" and consequently would be punished in the marketplace. Our perspective was that artists were cultural workers and should be paid for their services like anyone else, not treated as an elite caste. Other government agencies paid consultants and contracted for services; why should the arts be an exception? This was a radical idea to which conservatives might relate— we hoped. To begin the process of winning them over, Karney Hodge and Art Bolton arranged for me to visit every important legislator on both sides of the aisle. I wanted them to get to know me without the intervening filter of the press—and it worked. Once they determined that I was not an ideologue bent on demonizing them, they relaxed. After a few minutes of apparently obligatory conversation about the length of my hair or the earring I continued to wear, we found we had much in common as we discussed hunting and fishing, land use, wilderness issues, personal responsibility, and the appropriate role of the state.

My success at bridge building and fence mending became apparent during the formal committee reviews, the rubber-hits-the-road moment when the votes are cast and counted. Several conservative committee chairs, previously extremely vocal opponents of the council, overruled their own budget analyst to ensure that our budget got to the floor for a vote. Having assured us passage, they then voted against us on the record to protect their flanks from zealots at home.

I am not so naive as to believe that all our successes were a result of my efforts. It was widely known that the arts council was one of Governor Brown's pet projects, and I'm sure that for those votes many favors were extracted from him of which I am ignorant. Still, these legislative visits were a significant help and taught me a lesson I have never forgotten concerning the efficacy of truthfulness, common decency, and respect for one's opponents.

We didn't get our twenty million. Proposition 13's tax-cutting fever, soon to ruin California's infrastructure and public school system, was just gaining momentum, and legislators were under extraordinary pressure to cut all agency budgets, across the board, by 10 percent. Fistfights were breaking out during the back room negotiations, which were sometimes corrosive and ugly. With serious money at stake, however, the state's arts communities coalesced into a potent force which pressured the legislature sufficiently so that the council budget rose from one to eight million that year and to fourteen million dollars the next, remaining there throughout our tenure, the highest it has ever been and about six million dollars more than it is today.

There is one arts program I helped create of which I am inordinately proud. Largely crafted by Luis Valdez and myself, our able executive director Bill Cook, appointed by the governor at my behest, and Paul Minacucci, a Joyce scholar who was the council-appointed deputy director. It was called the State-Local Partnership, and it broke new political ground. Several council members, myself among them, felt uneasy about designing programs that forced all interested Californians to jump to our commands in order to receive money. We felt that the diversity of California was not being served by the concentration of power fixed in Sacramento and decided that the regions should determine their wants and needs for themselves and then petition the arts council for funds to implement them.

We began by establishing one paid position in each of California's fifty-four counties. The role of that person was to organize meetings so that each county could one day produce a cultural plan. There were real issues at stake. Should each and every county have a symphony hall, or might that money be better spent sending the most excellent orchestras on tour? Should Lassen County create an imitation of San Francisco County or find its own indigenous culture and seek the means to express it? The California Arts Council would create the rules of the debate and supervise it to ensure fairness and representation of the state's varied races, cultures, and population with special concerns like seniors or the disabled. As the centralized information bank, we would make options available to cultural committees to be assembled locally to explore options. We built in rewards for attracting private and local funds and demanded that the local political structures be consulted and signed on. We gave this part of the process a five-year deadline.

From the furor following the announcement of this plan, you might have thought we had lined California's artists up against the wall to be shot. "What do you want us to do?" was the plaintive lament from all quarters, and when we responded, "Hell, *we* don't know; *you* tell us what you want," pandemonium ensued. Angry protests were organized, but the council held firm, even over the resistance of many staff members. We insisted on local initiative and local control, in *partnership* with the central government. Eventually, every county began holding hearings and organizing cultural policy. The arts were hot news across the state. Despite high resistance, we knew we were on to something when the next year, the National Endowment for the Arts created their own State-Local Partnership program, and so did the New York State Council on the Arts, after Kitty Carlisle Hart, its president, grilled me on our plan over lunch in New York one day.

My tenure as chairman ended in 1983 after Republican George Deukmejian unseated Jerry Brown as governor, and I did not get to see this plan come to fruition. However, sometime in 1989 or 1990, I received a letter from a council staff person who admitted she had been one of the staff members most resistant to the program in its early years. She had just finished calculating the new moneys attributed to the arts in California as a result of the State-Local Partnership and felt honor bound to inform me that the total was then over fifty million dollars annually.

Of course I felt pleased and vindicated by this information, but what seemed clearest to me were two things : (a) that creative resolutions of complex public problems are indeed possible but that (b) they require committed and diligent leadership that is not afraid to stand firm against public opinion when it is appropriate. I am still waiting to see evidence of such leadership in national politics.

At my last hearing before the State Senate Finance Committee, eight years after I was sworn in as a member, the crusty senators who had tried to abolish the arts council multiple times during its early years—several of whom had gone on record condemning me personally—donned hippie headbands and applauded me. The gesture moved me, and I accepted it as my passing grade in civilian life, an indication that my years in the wind had been put to good use.

The time had come to choose the milieu in which I would pursue my livelihood. The skills and insights I had gleaned from the last dozen years of free life had proved remarkably utilitarian. I could talk to anyone without judgment and rancor and usually discover some common ground between us. My political visions were communicable and often had more support than I would have predicted. I realized that I did not need to remain isolated in a remote kingdom of my own devising—which at one point had shrunk to the dimensions of my truck.

Jerry Brown had been pleased with my performance and asked me whether I would be interested in running the State Department of Education—a two-billion-dollar agency. This was a high compliment and tempting, but I had already determined that if you inspire people, they will govern themselves. The legislative landscape is reconfigured each election, and while I admire the men and women who make the necessary concessions to hang in for the long haul, chipping away at obdurate problems, this was not my temperament. I would rather *be* the pressure than *under* the pressure. The arts would be the realm in which I would henceforth work.

I began to act again, at the Magic Theater in San Francisco, rehearsing and performing continually for two solid years, shaking out the rust of a long hiatus. I was a better actor now than when I left. I had seen more of life, and experience had stretched me in new and unpredictable ways. The acceptance of the gift that I had once spurned and the relative stability and order of domestic life had had a healing effect on my life. I discovered that while acting might not be revolutionary, or even terribly important, it was not oppressing anyone (except myself sometimes) and that I enjoyed it: human behavior was the means by which I made my view of the world comprehensible to others. This epiphany, honoring the facets of my personality that I had once "needled" and "kept asleep," allowed some internal integration that finally rendered drugs not only unnecessary but an impediment to my freely chosen work.

Some combination of success in theater, including the world premiere of Sam Shepard's *True West,* and the new confidence that I felt from my work with the arts council, allowed me to admit to myself that I had always nursed a secret desire to play on the biggest of all actors' stages, the screen. From a Digger perspective this would have been unthinkable: movies are corporate culture, fueled by money and fame. But the rush of free fall had burnished my sharp edges, and the buffeting winds and tumbling had made me supple and smoother. Now the world appeared wide and boundless, curving away in all directions under a collar of fluffy cloud.

I was almost forty, an impossible age to begin a film career, but I resolved to give it a try. I gave myself five years to either succeed or pack it in, after having given it my best shot. That was eighteen years ago—but that's another story.

time to take a break

It is a bright, sunny Sunday in 1992, and I am taking Nick, my eight-year-old son, and his chum out to visit the Olema ranch, almost twenty-five years after I left to begin the caravan. I want to show them where I lived and to see it myself once more.

As we slip under the fence and begin the walk up to the house, the boys run ahead to the watering ponds to search for frogs and turtles. Their joyful cries are swept away by the brisk winds scudding in from Tomales Bay. Half a moon, pale and nearly transparent, hangs in a dusty blue sky.

The red clay road is alive for me, every square foot of ground drenched in memories. The Coast Range is still fog-capped, and I can almost see the deer and certainly remember the lairs where I hunted them for food. The small town of Point Reyes Station looks unchanged, though on closer inspection it has evolved from the sleepy town it was in the sixties into a place that now offers imported delicacies in the food shops, sophisticated crafts, and cappuccinos in the restaurants.

We descend into the gullies, wind through the Live and Chinquapin oaks draped with Spanish moss, and climb to the large field leading directly to the house where we once played football against the Red House. But there is nothing there to stop the eye: no house, no barn, no outbuildings—nothing but whispering grass. I cannot contain my amazement, and the boys and I walk forward to investigate. They ask me if I could have made a mistake; are we in the right place?

We walk the grounds, among the apple trees and past the lilac bushes that once flanked the house. There are no splintered boards, no ashes, no foundation stones, abandoned hot water heaters, or broken glass. The barn is gone, so is the shed where Bryden and J. P. hunted one another with pistols. The yard where we once dug a sweat lodge for sixty people has lost its perimeters and is patchy with coarse weeds. Only the corral fence still stands, open at the rear where it once abutted the barn. We walk past it to the site of my old cabin, but it too has turned to grass.

All that remains is a lump in my throat. The sunlight is painfully bright and I can feel myself wincing. The wind flutters against my cheek. I am thirsty and sick with disappointment. I march the boys up the steep hill behind the house where I once set a statue of Buddha on a little thumb of rock protruding from the crest. From that vantage point we can view the whole countryside, and it is exactly as I remember. The only thing that has disappeared completely is every physical trace of my history with this place. I look at the moon and realize that my past here is like its invisible other half. I know it's there but cannot see it or show it to anyone. The boys play obliviously, and I sit down and gaze over the twinkling bay. I feel that I am part of this geology; I feel responsible to it. Ghosts rustle the grasses, and if memory is to have a mouth, it must be mine. I don't know what relationship the invisible half of the moon has to the visible. I don't know what relationship my years in free fall have to the present, but I am in and of the conventional world now. My daughter is a doctoral candidate. I have made more than fifty films for the movies and television. I deal with money, have been scarred by a broken marriage, and tempered by the joys and anxieties of parenthood. I still struggle to speak for other species and defend their necessities. I had hoped to share some of the continuity between my past and the present with these blithe boys, now growing impatient with my distracted mood, but I am unable. How can I explain to them what we tried to do, what was won, and what was lost?

The establishment would like to pretend that nothing has changed, that the hippies have all cut their hair and "grown up" into chic consumers. This is the same propagandistic impulse to reduce the complex politics of the sixties into tasteless jewelry, peace symbols, and bell-bottom pants. In fact, a great deal has changed and my generation can tally a significant number of victories.

However, our victories occurred in the deep waters of culture and not the frothy white water of current events, so they rarely surface in the media, which is such a dominant factor in establishing public reality. The way people view health issues, the environment, human rights, spirituality, agriculture, women, and consciousness itself has been redefined by my generation. These changes are as ubiquitous and invisible as the atmosphere these boys breathe; they can have little idea of either the accomplishments or costs.

At the same time, much has been lost, at least for now. Conservative zealots have labeled selflessness and compassion as social afflictions to be stamped out and substituted in their stead selective, vindictive punishment of the poor. Black people, once the moral center of the civil rights movements (and the nation), have become, with the exception of a modest middle class and more minuscule celebrity class, fodder for the criminal justice industry, abandoned in decrepit inner cities. America is now the sole superpower, and her exploitation of Third World countries via the World Bank and the International Monetary Fund continues virtually unchecked. While the economy grows vigorously, and rewards the capital-owning class, American labor has been driven backward, sold out by the political class and forced into competition with the world's poorest folk. On the global scale, the downsizing of America is probably overdue, but the fact that the readjustments are being borne only by labor and the poor is unfair, disloyal, and overdue for condemnation.

With hindsight, our idea of a counterculture appears an isolating, romantic confection. The Diggers understood fundamentals about the relationship between culture and imagination, and culture and politics, but our spurning of more traditional political alliances was, I believe, somewhat snobbish and counterproductive, since it deprived us of analytical skills and traditional organizing techniques. In retrospect, the Diggers might be criticized as a decade-long performance art piece. We were, I believe, first and foremost artists, and while we were addressing real fundamentals, we allowed our commitment to "authenticity" to blunt our sensitivity to the needs and aspirations of many who were not interested in being artists, or special, or anything other than out from under the heel of an oppressive system.

The failure to curb personal indulgence was a major collective error. Our journeys down the path along which Verlaine and Rimbaud disordered their senses wasted young lives and often sabotaged what we labored so diligently to construct. Verlaine and Rimbaud were reacting to the oppressive correctness of the bourgeoisie of their time and were perhaps its necessary antidote. In our time, the bourgeoisie borders on the sociopathic, and it is the artist's responsibility to manifest sanity and health—something we did not fully understand. Neither we nor the people who supported our endeavors were fools. Many were successful hustlers in their own right, legitimate or otherwise, who believed or wanted to believe in higher ideals and a better future. Others simply wanted an interesting diversion. They saw in us what they chose to see and were never wrong because so many contradictory qualities inhabited any given moment of Digger reality. Those who saw altruism were no more mistaken than those who saw cynicism and personal opportunism. Our contradictory behavior was like Penelope, holding her suitors at bay by unweaving at night what she constructed by day. The difference between her and us was that we were not aware of our own double-handedness.

Having confessed this, however, I want to state unequivocally that hippies did not kill three million Vietnamese (and fifty thousand Americans) and defoliate a nation with toxic chemicals in a pointless war. Hippies did not open the henhouse and allow the savings-and-loan foxes to wipe out the bank accounts of millions of trusting citizens. Hippies did not pay for and orchestrate and condone, as our government did, the murder of hundreds of thousands of innocent Guatemalan and Nicaraguan civilians—men, women, and children living in inconceivable poverty, and struggling for food. Nor did they allow cocktails of lethal chemistry to poison the nation's air, water, and soft tissues of fellow Americans, creating an epidemic of cancer.

It was not hippies but financiers and their political lackeys who ruined one American industry after another, freezing American wages at 1973 levels, forcing both parents to work in order to support one household and transforming the nation's children into unsupervised and angry phantoms.

While we may have *taken* drugs excessively, we did not allow tons of heroin and cocaine to flood the nation's inner cities so that profits from their sale might fund secret wars the voters had publicly rejected. The true cost of this chicanery was an epidemic of murder and toxicity. The true cost was a generation of inner-city youth.

Our relative innocence and the impending century of struggle I envision as the heritage for these boys and their children is cold comfort as I gaze out over the Olema hills. The world is not as I once imagined it or hoped it would be, but then neither am I. Neither revelation is a total disappointment. We are, finally, our intention, and we will be known by the footprints those intentions leave. In this moment, what I *can* attend to is these boys.

I hustle them up with a promise of hot chocolate in town, and we start our sideways scuttle down the steep hill and back to the car. Looking back as we leave, I can see that what is left at Olema is what was always there. I found no trace of our presence save for an old truck carburetor. I cannot conceive how such a flamboyant people—Emmett, Elsa, Sweet William, Moose, Gristle, Carla, J. P. Bryden, Billy Batman, and Sam—people so visible in the moment, can be invisible to history, can have left no indelible mark. This book, if it is anything, is my attempt at carving a petroglyph, at creating some record of the tribes of free people who passed through here, along with the now unseen sides of myself, into that invisible half of the smoky moon.

Mill Valley, California/Gordes, France
February 1997

postscript—2009

When *Sleeping Where I Fall* was published in 1998, I was three years shy of sixty. Sixty is the watershed birthday which forces even the most stubborn denier-of-death to acknowledge that, not being able to identify any 120-year-old people, "middle age" is pretty definitely *over*. At sixty, one is approaching, *at best*, the last third of one's life; the cards have been dealt, and the future, in all likelihood, will mean playing the hand one holds. There will be no more draws or infusions of capital to back new plays. A man down to his last cards observes the game with intense concentration.

Long ago, I had a dream concerning my future. I was traveling (in reality and the dream) with a group of fellows, in a truck caravan, in the hardscrabble country of New Mexico. We were living rough, visiting communes, attempting to stitch together an alternate economy based on trade. In the dream, we were bound together by beams of light connecting our navels. One of the group, a hyper-aggressive macho guy, was constantly challenging me to fight, getting in my face, smacking his fist into his open palm, demanding, "You ready to get it on? You ready to fight me?"

In the illogical manner of dreams, I was suddenly standing at the edge of a basketball court inside a large gymnasium. Instead of the normal wooden surface, the floor was a pale, grey-green, ground glass. (Identical to the "black-boards" in my fourth grade classroom, where my beautiful Asian teacher, Mrs. Cella, wrote in charcoal). The glass floor was surrounded on all four sides by a narrow border of traditional blond flooring. The ground glass was incised with black lines forming two-by-two-inch squares, so that it resembled the board used in the Japanese game of GO, or a checkerboard where all the squares were the same color.

Lying before me at the join of glass and wood were two small, differently shaped objects made of heavy black slate that I understood were to be used as playing pieces in a pending "game." One was rectangular with rounded corners, about two inches by one inch, tapering from a thick center to thin edges. It resembled the leathery packets of stingray eggs one finds washed ashore on Atlantic beaches. The other was a traditional round Japanese GO stone, plump as a hard candy, but also with a sharp outer edge. Both were made of flawless black slate.

Next to the stones was a pair of curious slippers, constructed of white cotton flannel. A stitched pocket enclosed the toes, but instead of a cupped area to enclose the heels, the flat cloth sole divided into two white cords. I understood that I was to fold up "the sole" around my heel and fasten the cords around the ankles. Standing beside me on the board were two mute assistants dressed entirely in tight-fitting black clothing. They communicated with me by gesture, and they indicated that the slippers were to be worn on the glass surface during play.

At the far left-hand corner of the room, a pale and lovely Asian woman (resembling my former teacher) was kneeling in *seiza* (the traditional Japanese posture where the buttocks rest on the backs of the heels). She sat in perfect repose at the edge of the board and her meditative absorption was unbending. Her chasuble, sash, and *mozzetta* (a short cape worn in some Catholic ceremonies), were constructed of bright red silk. She wore a peaked mitre, the double-pointed hat worn on occasion by bishops and popes, but on hers, small, ivory skulls were attached to both sides ascending to the pointed peak. Severe bangs and black hair squared at her jawline, framing and highlighting her powdered white skin. I understood immediately that this concentrated, unapproachable woman could never be defeated. She was my death.

Contrasted with her power, my noisy adversary (who I referred to as "The Hassler") diminished in significance and disappeared from the dream. Though I had no idea how the board game was to be played, and though my eventual loss was preordained, I understood that the silent assistants were allies and that they were committed to helping me. Furthermore, I could see that it was a huge field of play and that patterns would take some time to become apparent. I intuited that if I were cautious and alert, I might extend my play for a long time. The dream ended as I placed one of my feet in a cotton slipper and dropped to one knee to fasten the ties around my ankle.

Years later, I have by now played across sizable sections of the board, making my choices and mistakes and devising strategic gambits as best I could. Patterns and potential threats have clarified alongside my victories. My opponent remains unruffled, undiminished, and unmarked by time, while I am now lined and seamed. My eyebrows, if unattended, grow long and gnarly. I have liver spots on the backs of my hands, and if I'm not attentive, stray hairs will tuft in my ears, as they did in my grandfather's. Women who once obliterated all thoughts save winning their favor, smile at me today, eyes twinkling through crow's feet and, like me, they carry more heft in their mid-regions. My gay and fearless companions, those still alive, remind me of gnarled trees flaunting scars and age with equal dignity. It is my hope that my life has made me worthy to stand as tall in their estimation as they stand in mine. These are the observations and concerns of a man considering mortality. The signs of my diminution are unmistakable, but though the territory I command on the board is shrinking, I am, after many struggles, temporary victories, and defeats—and this is the point—still "in play."

It has been my custom for a long time to honor dead friends and family by placing their names on my altar on the anniversary of their passing—"bowing in" before meditating, and offering full sticks of the incense used in the Zen monastery where I began my Buddhist practice, thirty-three years ago. As I begin writing this postscript, in the first week of April, paradoxically a small, black-edged card rests on my altar, bearing the inscription:

> **Emmett Grogan**
> **1942–1978**

Emmett died on April Fool's Day and his presence is still so vivid, I am shocked to realize that I have not seen his chiseled, freckled face in thirty years. Without him, there would have been no book, for there would have been no life-altering playing-for-keeps with the Diggers and Free Family. There would probably have been no heroin or cocaine, less reckless testing of manhood, less stud-peacock swagger and jaunty bravado. Certainly there would have been less hilarity, magic, and surprise in my life had our trajectories not intersected in the rehearsal studio of the San Francisco Mime Troupe one memorable day in 1966. Our first encounter evolved into a four-mile walk-and-talk, culminating in a friendship that lasted until the end of his life, and memories of which continue in mine.

Because he died twenty years before *Sleeping Where I Fall* was published, I never learned what Emmett thought of it. If ancient literature is to be believed, the pursuit of enduring honor and renown are eternal preoccupations of young men, and despite the Digger dedication to anonymity, we were not exempt from such concerns. I like to think he would have been gratified that his brief, luminous arc had been recorded by a witness who understood and loved him. Re-reading Emmett's chapter, I'm satisfied that it catches something of his power and marks the tensions and contradictions of his personality. It feels true to me. However, there are a few other places in the book that do not.

I labored diligently to ensure that what I attested was correct and not overly bound to my own ego. I conducted interviews with friends and family to clarify what I could remember and cross-indexed them with old journals and assiduously unraveled memories. Nonetheless, errors did intrude. I misidentified Marty Linhart as the subject of a story about a friend being sent to San Francisco for a vasectomy by a clique of feminists who had taken over Black Bear Commune one winter. Perhaps dreaming of pregnancy-free sex, they collected money and sent him south to get his tubes tied. I described "Marty" appearing "in a dress," dazed after months in the remote woods, and how his urban brothers convinced him to use the money for his operation to get his teeth fixed. Twenty years later, revisiting the environs for an annual summer reunion, my son, about ten, was enchanted (so the story goes) by the beauty of Marty's daughter of the same age.

I used the story, still vivid in my memory, as a cautionary tale. I hoped that it might be charming and help people to pause and consider before making decisions with far-reaching consequences, and thought it made the point perfectly. It may have, but unfortunately, its real protagonist was not Marty. He wrote to me after the book appeared, deeply offended and denying he was the person I had identified. I believe him, and apologize to his heirs in perpetuity for making him an exemplar of wisdom and forbearance. Another actor played the part, and alas, I can no longer retrieve his rightful identity from the overfilled bin my brain has become.

I make light of this unintentional error, but not of truthfulness. In every memoir, the facts are filtered through memory, and consequently I second the assertion of the person who observed that all biography contains elements of fiction.

There were a few other mildly discomfiting responses from friends. Usually they did not involve disputes about *what* was true as much as embarrassment about its being revealed. The ex-junkie friend who plundered my daughter's piggy bank and left an IOU was more mortified to read the story sober than I was indignant when it occurred. If you have friends who are drug addicts, such things happen. I was embarrassed to hear from my beloved cousin Arthur, a man I am as close to as a brother, that he could not finish the book. I asked him why, and he told me that when he arrived at the tale about my father forcing a driver off the road for cutting him off and then standing beside the man's car, laying twenty-dollar bills, one after another, on his hood, and offering them to him if he would just get out of the car and take his beating, Arthur had closed the book in disgust. I asked him why again, and was shocked to learn that the story I had recounted from my own point of view *had actually happened to him!* He had been driving with my father that day, not me. I was disoriented. My cousin does not lie, will not exaggerate even to make a story more dramatic. This tale was such a part of family lore, I had heard it with mingled horror and relish so often, imagined it so deeply, that the details had become resident in my mind as my own memories. I had simply appropriated my cousin's experience without realizing it and owe both readers and him an apology.

There was, however, one other blowback from the book, more deeply embarrassing and more life-altering. It shocked me, and much higher stakes were involved. After the book appeared, I received a letter of censure from two sisters correctly taking exception to the casual, one-line mention of their father, a close and intimate friend, as a drug buddy. The scale of our true relationship and his value to my life had been unintentionally whittled away as the book was cut from its original 800-page first draft to its current length. The women were deeply offended by the diminution of his identity. He was in fact a fine musician and deeply involved in the Beat and Counter-culture and he should not have been characterized solely by his addiction to Methedrine. In their hurt and anger, they pointedly criticized my behavior with them during the years we lived together communally, when they were teenagers.

Though the events in question occurred thirty years earlier, their resurrection and reexamination of the facts, reviewed according to the standards of a responsible adult today, required an intense, embarrassing, and diligent year of confession and self-examination to heal our relationship and their personal hurts—the *smallest* part of which was revising their father's description for subsequent editions. There is no way to reveal the details of this story without violating their privacy, and there is also a risk that the story's harmonious resolution might appear as a self-serving gloss of my behavior toward them, which was irresponsible, exploitative, and hurtful.

I learned from this incident—later in life than I ever anticipated having to learn something of this magnitude—that unacknowledged wounds do not heal. Their letters, sharp as paper cuts, scarred me as unequivocally and painfully as a brand. Whatever hurt they may have transferred to me, they had carried worse within themselves for thirty years until they had been heard and acknowledged. I have no wish to be coy, but that's all the detail this postcript requires to make the point of how dangerous we, each of us, can be when we are not alert to our shadowy and unexamined impulses. Not even the storyteller is exempt from consequences in the universe he creates.

It is a reflexive impulse to *assume* that we are "good," and from there everything runs downhill to the logical inference that what we *do* is good. It is something of a national habit. We have yet to fully acknowledge, and make adequate recompense for, our genocide of Native Americans or the two-and-a-half *centuries* during which we bought and sold Africans to create our national wealth, repressing every trace of their original languages and religion, destroying their family structures, and denying them education. Acknowledging that each of us contains all the positive and negative potentialities of every human who has ever lived should alert us to our own, indwelling potential to cause harm when we are careless. Danger is rarely "out there." Sleepwalking through our negative propensities is a guarantee that we will harm others.

Both praise and censure from others paled before the experience of opening the first shipment of books from my publisher and extracting the beautifully jacketed hardbound volumes. My friend and publisher, Jack Shoemaker, had warned me (trying to be kind) after I had submitted the final manuscript that publishing a book "would not change my life." He meant, I think, that after the flush of enthusiasm, book tours, and reviews have passed, one returns to one's daily rounds, usually neither famous nor wealthy. He was cautioning me against unrealistic expectations, but in my case, he was wrong.

What he could not understand was that by holding my first published book, an early glimpsed and often denied identity as a *writer* had materialized as an undeniable part of myself. The fact that I *was* a writer was now indisputable: I was holding a book with my name on it. I might not be a *great* writer, but I was among the fraternity. It was a life-altering observation that did change me. I had undertaken work as an actor to win a livelihood, but also, on some level, so that I might protect what is most precious to me and not have to write "for money." Writing is where the purest part of me touches the world. If possible, I did not want it to be tainted by the requirements of commerce, preferring, in some sense, to remain an amateur. There is an equally valid argument to make on the other shore of this decision, and I would never suggest that the work of writers who earn their keep by their craft are in any way diminished by that decision. The evidence of history would overwhelm that assertion. I am speaking to my own feelings and choices. (This is a memoir, after all.)

In 1998, when the book was released, I had not yet met and married the woman for whom I willingly ended a lifetime of compulsive womanizing, a decision I have never revisited or regretted. My daughter had not yet received her doctorate in psychology, nor had she married her brilliant, good-humored, and talented husband. They had not yet produced my granddaughter, thereby ratcheting me up into the ranks of "those-who-are-next-to-go" by slipping a new generation underneath me. The recompense for this dizzying acceleration toward my end is, of course, the delight of being a grandfather. (As I write, my toenails are still a brilliant orange where she painted them during our last visit.) My son had not yet graduated from college and moved to make his way in New York, morphing *en route* from a handsome, somewhat puzzling young boy into a shrewd, mordantly funny, culturally acute young man.

I wrote this book as much as a gift to my wife and children as I did to make sense of my own past. My son was born sixteen years after my daughter in a more stable, affluent environment. Consequently, his life has been less stamped by forces related to the times chronicled in this book. I mention my daughter and her happy family not to take personal credit for her successes, but as a positive postscript to the collective parenting she received as a Digger child.

Memories of my own childhood are not particularly happy. Life in my household (as readers will have learned) was often tense or explosive and issues of dominance and power loomed front and center in relations with my father. I didn't have the sort of patient, unthreatening family life which produces happy, confident children. (Though for eleven years, I was happily raised by a brilliant young black woman, her boyfriend-then-husband, and community—the subject of my next book.) My adolescence was tumultuous, and my 1960s and '70s given over to social and political experiments where "balance" was eventually achieved only after caroming off every limit before surrendering to gravity in a Buddhist monastery.

While many of our early experiments failed due to inexperience and excess, the country was indelibly changed by the effort and commitment of my restless peers: the planet and our reciprocal relationship with it has begun to receive recognition; more inclusive alternatives to conventional religion, therapy, medicine, spiritual practices, sexual orientation, and production of food are now widely accepted. The rights of women and people of color have been extended and expanded and have achieved enough recognition that they must be publicly acknowledged, if not always fairly applied.

While the Diggers and Free Family no longer live communally, the extended family we created continues to thrive. My daughter remains bonded to her communal sisters; she is an "aunt" to their children and remains inextricably a member of our large tribe. We no longer wake, sleep, and work together every day, a situation I continue to experience as a deep loss, but which is lightened by a palpable sense of remaining tuned to an exclusive network which transmits knowledge about how the family is faring. Like the "beams of light" connecting us in my early dream, information and news travels over a filigree of nerves in our collective body, keeping the parts linked and mutually aware.

Like many of her communal brothers and sisters, my daughter has consciously chosen work dedicated to health and healing. When queried about this, her answer was deeply satisfying to me:

> Our choice in careers—at least my own—is part of your legacy. We were raised to believe that it is a moral duty to try to make the world better than we found it.

Having been poached in the broth of ideas their parents savored and debated (and sometimes talked to death), my daughter and friends developed an early comfort with them. These sharp, self-confident young folk are as fearless about expressing their political and economic beliefs as they are unabashed about pursuing fun. (Candor demands I acknowledge that some of our children did not weather our constant experimentation so well.) They are not doctrinaire, and are more graceful than their parents, having assimilated and resolved since birth the contradictions we pulled ligaments learning to straddle. My daughter's response to this assertion was less romantic than mine:

> Many of us struggle with the same conflicts you did, but perhaps in our generation we have refined the expression [of them] . . . We hope to pass on the ability to inhabit seemingly disparate realities to our children . . . to take the middle road, eat the bowl of rice . . . try to balance material comforts [with] . . . working to ensure that compassion is reflected in our every day . . . But it *is* a conflict and we are constantly—as you do—balancing our desires with the needs of the collective. We hope our children will be even more facile than we are.

They will need these skills. It is a more seriously threatened and afflicted world than it was forty years ago or even ten years ago when the book was first published. Global warming, whose effects might have been ameliorated had they been seriously addressed ten years earlier (when Al Gore was in the White House, for instance), may now be a runaway train. Social, financial, and environmental problems are multiplying virally at the same time that we are curtailing our investment in the education of the nation's young people, and the neglect shows. National stupidity is epidemic, irony has replaced analysis, and one wonders fervently how, from this degraded environment, wise leaders and constituencies to support them will evolve. If this sounds harsh, consider the following.

In a series of polls over the last several years:

Only **41%** of Americans could name our three branches of government. **26%** could not *identify* the Vice President.[1]

50% of seventeen-year-olds could not express 9/100s as a percent. Only **4%** could use a bus schedule. Only **12%** could arrange six common fractions in order of size.[2] **63%** thought humans lived at the same time period as dinosaurs—an error of 60 million years. **53%** thought the earth revolved around the sun in a day or a month. In other words, only **47%** knew it required a year. **91%** could not state what a molecule was.[3] **21%** believed the sun revolves around the earth and another **7%** weren't sure.

Of 158 countries in the United Nations, the U.S. is 49th in literacy. **60%** of the adult population has never read a book. **6%** reads *one* a year (and it's necessary to include Harlequin romances and self-help books to reach that figure). **120 Million** adults are illiterate or read at no better than fifth-grade level.

In 1998—The Massachusetts (not Mississippi or Alabama) Board of Education gave a literacy test for teachers *pegged at the level of a high school equivalency exam.* Of 1800 teachers, *59% failed.*[4] As a result, the Commissioner of Education announced that require-ments for a passing grade would be lowered.

1. National Constitutional Center Survey, 1998.
2. National Assessment of Education Foundation, 1990s.
3. National Science Foundation Survey, 1995.
4. Shipler, David K., *The Working Poor*. New York: Alfred A. Knopf, 2004.

Referring to such data, Morris Berman, in his book *Twilight of American Culture*, addressed the costs of this intellectual poverty:

> A nation in which 87% of 18-24 year olds cannot locate Iran or Iraq on a world map . . . is not merely 'intellectually sluggish.' It would be more accurate to call it moronic, capable of being fooled into anything.

This diminution of critical skills occurs in the shadow of mass cultural and species extinction. Jim Hansen, Director of the NASA Goddard Institute for Space Studies, observed in a recent article in *The New York Review of Books*:

> If human beings follow a business-as-usual course, continuing to exploit fossil fuel resources without reducing carbon emissions . . . the eventual effects on climate and life may be comparable to those at the time of mass extinctions. Life will survive, but it will do so on a transformed planet. For all foreseeable human generations, it will be a far more desolate world than the one in which civilization developed and flourished.

Hansen predicts that unless we succeed in cutting carbon emissions by 50% *within* ten years, global warming will extinct 50% of the species on earth and raise water levels up to eighty feet, with inconceivably catastrophic results for hundreds of millions of people. Salt water will intrude on many drinking water supplies and the planet's newest wars may be over the most basic of resources. Of course, he *might* be wrong. But he also might *not* be, and would it not be precautionary to play it safe?

In the *San Francisco Chronicle* (April 24, 2008), I learn that the glacier on which *800,000* Bolivians depend for their water, has dwindled from a massive 150-foot thick, rock-scouring behemoth to a "patch" nine feet high. When such folk mass at our borders searching for water, will we create a "fence" of our SUVs to keep them out? Given such facts, the quibbling, "gotcha" politics of Democrats and Republicans is to public policy as pornography is to sex. Our Congress and its paymasters are shooting craps on the deck of the Titanic.

My generation's counter-cultural efforts to reduce the human footprint on the planet were a critically important, correct intuition. The "poverty" of the "hippies" was actually an act of generosity towards other humans and species, the first large-scale American attempts to cut the calories of energy and quanta of "stuff" required for a fulfilling life. In his concise and chilling book, *The Limits of Power*, Andrew Bacevich observes that "Americans never cease to expect more" and that there is a direct connection between these expectations, the rise of the Imperial Presidency, the loss of domestic liberties, and the increased use of our professional military as an agent of Empire. "As members of a community," he writes, "especially as members of a national community, [citizens] choose to contribute less." The importance of our counter-cultural collective experiments outweighs whatever personal damage immaturity and excess wreaked on ourselves by substantial factors.

Zen master Sunryu Suzuki-Roshi once said, "Everything is perfect until you compare." I confess to difficulty achieving such repose. Compared to the culture of sleepwalkers downloading porn on their iPhones, and newspapers debating critical differences between carjack video games, while connoisseurs dress up to drink fine wines and devour the last remnants of fish plundered from the coasts of impoverished African nations, the clumsiest excesses of "the Sixties" appear enlightened.

I don't believe my feelings are simply geriatric mental road rage. My granddaughter is three. She has asthma that morphs frequently into pneumonia. She's been hospitalized several times, immobilized to have needles poked into veins barely larger than my hairs so that doctors can determine why her lungs are filling with mucus. When she was last hospitalized in Oakland, California, I visited her bed, set out in a hallway and separated from other struggling, coughing children by a hanging sheet. There were no rooms left and when I inquired why, I was informed that they were suffering "an epidemic of asthma."

My daughter and her husband have spent weeks deprived of sleep and the shadows under their eyes track their exhaustion. *They* are reasonably affluent caucasians whose baby is in a bed in the hall of a well-run hospital in the San Francisco Bay Area. What do you imagine might be happening to children in the "cancer belt" of Louisiana, Texas, and Mississippi, or in Hunter's Point and Richmond, California, where the lungs of the poor are being cauterized by the smoke, ash, and chemicals crapped into their neighborhoods to spare the wealthy.

Overfed television pundits cluck sympathetically about "the senseless violence" as ghetto murders escalate. Genteel society wonders querulously why "they" (polite-speak for "black" and "Latino") evince so little "reverence for life," and never intuit that people generally behave as they are treated. While we gossip about Britney's snatch and watch the routine humiliations of reality shows, hundreds of thousands of tons of untested chemicals and unregulated emissions are being pumped into our water, soil, and air (and my granddaughter's lungs) as if we were all inmates of a slow-motion death camp.

If *I* lived in a politically neglected, toxic hot zone and all available evidence demonstrated that the system was killing me and my community, where analyses reinforced the conclusion that my people had been abandoned, you can be damned sure that I would be struggling, by any means necessary, to amass the capital to clear out. As it is, I live in a genteel suburb outside one of the richest cities in North America and still find myself in a tumultuous hospital corridor, daydreaming about blowing up the nearby Chevron refinery.

Outside my daughter's house, the diesel trucks, buses, and ships, the oil refinery at Port Richmond, and the coal-fired electrical generator at Hunter's Point are force-feeding sulfides, mercury, and microscopic ash into the atmosphere as if it were a septic pit. It was for just such an expropriation of the commons that the original Diggers marched against Cromwell's troops on St. George's Hill in 1649.

If the wholesale despoliation of the world and my granddaughter's condition makes me, a moderately wealthy and successful man, homicidal, imagine, if you dare, the quality of rage simmering among the disenfranchised, underestimated, and overlooked. Imagine in what directions *their* fantasies might lead and you won't need TV thrillers to jack up your pulse. What coefficients of greed put public health on a debate-worthy par with corporate profits? What ignorant lunacy transforms water, air, soil, and human tissue into filters for toxic effluents? In the face of ignorance like this, anger is the *positive* pole of my emotional state.

An entire generation predicted this historical moment and placed their lives on the line to prevent it. Whether we were called Hippies, Weathermen, Diggers, SDS, Motherfuckers, Flower Children, or runaways, we saw the future with a clarity that otherwise evaded virtually the entire political class. Now, as the markets and banks melt down and implode and Congress does its best to disguise their complicity in the deregulatory mess they've created, the Sixties shine brightly as an example of an alternative path we might have taken.

Our early idea of a "counter-culture"—a sheltered place within the ribs of the dying beast of America, a refuge for those who would abandon the sinking mother ship of State—has disappeared from the contemporary landscape. You might think that I consider this a negative event, but I don't.

Friend and fellow Digger Freeman House once observed that "a counter-culture condemns you to marginality." I argued with him at the time, but understand now that he was correct, that the idea of a "separate reality" was a comforting confection. There were many change-oriented people in the 1960s and '70s who may have been dissatisfied with the political and/or economic paradigms they struggled with, but had no desire to grow long hair, smoke dope, or live communally. By cleaving to an alternative culture where membership was identified by variance from the majority, we missed the opportunity to create broad social and political alliances with many who might otherwise have cooperated with us. As the Weathermen placed African Americans so in the "revolutionary vanguard" that they missed the opportunity of organizing many in the white community, and in the way that Democrats today are missing the opportunity of finding commonality with liberal Republicans and many "conservatives," narrow, ideological provincialism blinded us to making common cause with those who differed from us. From this perspective, the dissolution of the counter-culture offers some advantages.

Since there is only one culture now and we are *all* in it, each of us has the opportunity to press for positive change at every point where we live, eat, work, play, and shop. Each of these portals offers a *jiujitsu*-like leverage point where consciousness and political power can be leveraged to create more wholesome, fair, and environmentally sustainable alternatives to free-market nonsense. I call it *Ceremonial Exchange*—the effort to make each life choice reflect the deep knowledge of interdependence and reciprocity we now understand to be the fundamental universal truth. We can invent options, if they do not exist, so that our social institutions and collaborations begin to aggregate and achieve power. Such work is often invisible, *attitudinal*, and cultural rather than directly political, but it cuts deeply and its effects, once embedded in the society, are more enduring than the political fashions of the moment.

Change is always slower than the imagining of it. Knowledge of that simple fact is the immutable watershed between youth and older age. Young men and women move in a different time scale than their elders and their impatience fuels accelerated change. What they lack is the breadth of experience to anticipate where some of those changes might lead, and the length of time it may take to produce results. Changes from within the culture will not appear as radical and dramatic as alternate lifestyles once did; however, they will be more enduring.

Paul Hawken's fine book, *Blessed Unrest*, suggests that if the world is considered a single body, the global aggregation of small efforts to save the environment and insure social justice is a gigantic force mimicking the body's immune system's response to threat. The millions of souls pressing for positive change may collectively recalibrate the planet towards a condition of more dynamic, healthy equilibrium.

Personally, I strive to be less angry at the indulgence which has created this perilous moment. My Buddhist practice informs me that greed, anger, and delusion arrive along with each human being and that I must remember that I am as much the problem as the corporate executive I fantasize throttling. Meditation offers me the tools to keep society safe from me on the street, and there is always more that we can do on a personal level to root indulgences out of our own lives.

I would like to see counter-cultural grit and entrepreneurial dedication to new thinking and paradigms reemerge, integrated with the social-networking models and the potential of the internet. I would like to see again people pouring into the streets, expressing outrage at the deceptions perpetrated on them and the horrors perpetrated in their names. Impoverished Zapatistas are doing it in Mexico. Bolivian Indians are being shot attempting to eject the corporations stealing their water. Nigerians, Ecuadorian Indians, Tamils, Nepalese peasants, Tibetan Monks, *people without shoes and food* are standing up to corporate oppression and asserting the primacy of their humanity and their right to exist without being exploited.

What I do *not* see often are the children of the richest, most entitled, indulged, entertained, diverted, and distracted culture on earth abandoning their toys long enough to band together and *demand* that the political system be cleansed and passed on in wholesome good order.

I am partial to the colorful, highly visible style of my *compañeros* from the Sixties, but finally I see no essential contradictions or discontinuities between their values and those of many of today's young people. The best are trying to wrest normalcy, social justice, livelihood, and a clean environment from corporate control and the culture's lunatic impulse to transform the entire biosphere into money. I am happy to pass on to my children this record of a time when their parents gambled much for them. Despite our errors I hope they will be proud of their lineage. When I finally disintegrate into the ethers and drop my tattered banner, I hope that one of them might be moved to snatch it up and wave it defiantly. After all, what is a life but the acting out of an example, making it available as a model for others to inhabit? In the end, we did what we did not because we thought we would win, but because it was the only way we could conceive of being fully *human*, fully interdependent and reciprocal with our fellows and the rest of Creation. I hope our examples will not be overlooked, or unfairly impugned, as today's young people press forward to claim their power and protect the earth for the quick, the green, and the living.

Mill Valley, California
April 2009

Index